Conservative Party Politicians at the Turn of the 20th/21st Centuries

Their Attitudes, Behaviour and Background

Conservative Party Politicians at the Turn of the 20th/21st Centuries

Their Attitudes, Behaviour and Background

Nigel Gervas Meek

With a Foreword

By

Dr Syed Kamall MEP

Civic Education and Research Trust
London
2012

First edition, August 2012

The right of Nigel G. Meek to be identified as the author of this work
has been asserted hereby in accordance with the *Copyright, Designs and
Patents Act 1988*.

Published by
Civic Education and Research Trust
(Registered charity 264353)
21c Lindfield Gardens
London
NW3 6PX

ISBN 978-1-4717-0080-4

British Library Cataloguing in Publication Data: A catalogue record for
this book is available from the British Library

Contents

Foreword by Dr Syed Kamall MEP...1

About the Author 3

The *CPRS 2002* Datafile and this Book 4

Abstract...5

Acknowledgements and Comments 7

    Acknowledgements 7

    Involvement in the Conservative Party 8

        Background..8

        How this relates to the approach to this study 8

        The role of Eric Forth...10

    Coining a Term: *Rhetormetrics* 11

1:   **Introduction**...**13**

    What is Conservatism? 13

        The purpose of the study..13

        From the literature 13

        From the Party as an institution..15

        From individual Conservatives...16

        Attenuating the noise 16

        A note of caution..17

    A Qualification about the Wider Context....................................17

    Existing Work about the Conservative Party 18

    The Conservative Party in 2002 19

        A nadir in the Party's fortunes 19

        The "nasty party"?...20

        But was it so bad?...21

    Britain and the World in 2002 22

        Britain..22

The world *23*
An Overview of the Following Chapters 24

2: **Methodology** **29**

Types of Study Considered 29
A Small-Scale Pilot Study 30
Issues with Developing the Questionnaire 31
Topics Covered 32
  Aims of the research *32*
  Topic ordering *33*
The Respondents 33
  The intended targets *33*
  Identifying the targets, and sampling *34*
  Who and where were excluded *35*
Ethical Issues 36
The Multi-Item Scales 36
  Types of scales *36*
  Purpose and derivation of the scales *37*
  Subject ordering *40*
Presentation of Items in the Questionnaire 41
  Types of item *41*
  Response options *42*
Physical Design of the Questionnaire 43
  Design overview *43*
  Creating the questionnaire *44*
  The introductory letter from Eric Forth *44*
  A note about questionnaire length *44*
Deploying the Questionnaire 45
  Possible methods *45*
  Despatch *46*
Data Capture 46
Responses 47
  Response rates *47*
  Responses and the multi-item scales *48*
  Statistical robustness of the multi-Item scales *50*
Were Scales from within the Data Missed? 50
Choice of Multivariate Analysis 51
Presentation of Data 52

Level of data *52*

Base size and reported analysis *52*

Unexplained variance and the danger of Scientism *53*

3: Beyond "Left & Right": The Political Map **55**

The Nature of the Problem 55

"And", not "but" *55*

Same words, different meanings *56*

Why is it Still Used? 58

Proposed Solutions 59

Another Solution: The Political Map 61

The Political Map Used in this Analysis 63

The design, layout and naming of the PoliMap *63*

A finite world *67*

Arguments Against the Model and Responses 68

Objections raised *68*

There is only one dimension *68*

An insufficiency of dimensions *68*

Poor questionnaire sets and evidence for multi-

dimensionality *71*

Unacceptable creation of internal sectors *73*

The PoliMap and the Conservative Party 74

The Dimensions Considered Separately 75

Conservative Politicians on the PoliMap 75

All respondents on the PoliMap *75*

The PoliMap and socio-demographics *79*

The PoliMap and the "Actually Existing Conservative

Party" 79

Not Perfect, But Better 80

4: Local Councillors in England **81**

Background and the Use of Secondary Data 81

What was Omitted and Why 82

Basic issues *82*

Representativeness *83*

Researcher choice and sensitivity *84*

Initial Socio-Demographic Analysis 85

Gender, age and ethnicity *85*

Education 88
Marital status 90
Geographical location of ward 91
Tenure of accommodation 94
Employment 95
Parental background in the Conservative Party 97
Service in the Conservative Party 99
Social class 102
Socio-Demographic Predictors of Attitudes 106
Rationale and methodology 106
Results and analysis 108
The Internet 109
Use of email and the Internet 109
The Internet as a refuge? 111
Other respondents 112
Idealism, Pragmatism and Time 112
Conclusion to Chapter 4 114

5:    **Attitudes about the Conservative Party 117**

Looking Inwards 117
Elitism, Inclusivity and Optimism 118
Unwarranted optimism 118
Running and changing the Party 119
A Desire for Change? 119
Was change needed? 119
Why was change needed? 120
The Conservative Party: What is it good for? 123
A perceived lack of clarity 123
Inconsistent attitudes? 125
Party Leaders 126
A first look 126
Multivariate analysis 128
Youth Organisations 132
Membership 132
Whatever happened to the "Conservative
Radicals"? 132
Conclusion to Chapter 5 133

6: Attitudes about Other UK Parties...................................**137**

One Amongst Many...137
Overview of Attitudes Towards Other Parties 137
   Questionnaire items about the other parties *137*
   Self-reported insufficient knowledge *138*
   Respondents who reported sufficient knowledge........*140*
   Differences between the groups of respondents *144*
Party-Politics and Attitudes...................................144
   Analysis..*144*
   The major UK-wide parties....................................*145*
   The smaller UK-wide parties: Splittists or ginger
   group?...*146*
   The Scottish and Welsh parties.................................*149*
   The Northern Irish parties.......................................*149*
Conclusion to Chapter 6 151

7: The Wider World...**153**

A Research Question and Beyond.............................153
Associated Attitudes about the Wider World? 153
   The research question..*153*
   Analysing the observation with CPRS 2002 data.......*155*
   The foreign affairs items..*155*
Relating Foreign and Domestic Issues 158
The Commonwealth 160
The Western and Islamic Worlds 163
Conclusion to Chapter 7 165

8: National Identity **167**

Aspects of National Identity 167
Self-Identification...168
   How respondents thought of themselves....................*168*
Other Issues Concerning the UK 170
The Legitimacy of the EU 173
A Revised Typology of National Identity 174
Conclusion to Chapter 8 175

9: The Free Market: "Necessary Evil" or "Good Thing"? 177

Pro-Free-Market, But Why? 177
Private and Public: Efficiency and Worthiness................. 178
Associations with Employment 179
Conclusion to Chapter 9... 180

10: Religion.. 183

Meanings of Religion... 183
Religion in the UK 184
    Politico-religious cleavages in the UK *184*
    Christianity and the UK... *185*
    Christianity and the Conservative Party................... *186*
Religiosity and Theocratism 187
    Considered separately... *187*
    Considered together.. *189*
Confessional and Religious Background 190
The Established Church 192
Religion and Socio-Demographics 193
Religion as Predictors of Other Attitudes 193
    A note about temporal causality *193*
    Multivariate analysis... *194*
    Religiosity and environmentalism............................ *197*
Conclusion to Chapter 10... 198

11: The Party-Political Institutions 201

The "Where" of Politics... 201
The Locus of Power 201
    Power and responsibilities....................................... *201*
    The institutions compared....................................... *203*
    Whatever happened to "Rolling back the frontiers of
    the state"? *204*
Representation at Westminster 204
Why become a Politician? 206
    Types of reason *206*
    Ideological versus representational........................... *208*
    The socio-demographics of ELCs and "idealism" *208*
Elections, Parties and Constitutional Power 209
Trust in Public Life 214

A Foray into Scale Building 215
Conclusion to Chapter 11 216

12:   The 2001 Leadership Contest..219

A Short-Lived Victory..219
The 2001 Leadership Election..220
Issues during the Contest..222
Respondents' Behaviour and Attitudes 225
Supporters of Excluded Candidates.....................................227
The Last Three Candidates 228
    All three candidates *228*
    Michael Portillo's exceptionalism..............................*231*
The Final Ballot...232
    All respondents *232*
    Local councillors in England *235*
Commentary 236
"A Word in Your Ear…"..238
"Europe", but not only "Europe".......................................239
Changing Saliency 241

13:   The Public and Electoral Politics.....................................245

Outside of the Political Bubble..245
Main Concerns Facing Britain...246
    Concerns across a range of issues...............................*246*
    Saliency and the multi-item scales..............................*247*
The Real and Imagined Views of the Public 248
    Main comparisons *248*
    The general public's own views...................................*250*
The Experience of Electoral Politics 251
    Fighting for their seat..*251*
    More on attitudes towards Labour and the Liberal
    Democrats..*256*
    Attitudes and electoral experience together *258*
The General Public and the PoliMap...................................259
    Using the PoliMap..*259*
    Identifying comparators amongst the public..............*259*
    Mapping the public...*260*
    Tribalism and party realignment.................................*262*

Conclusion to Chapter 13 263

14: Future Conservative Parliamentarians? 267

Generational Replacement 267
Identifying Potential Replacements 267
Socio-Demographics of Replacements 270
Differences between Future and Sitting MPs 272
2010 General election update 273
Attitudinal Differences 273
Conclusion to Chapter 14 277

15: Bringing the Findings Together 279

The Purpose of the Study Restated 279
The "Typical" Conservative Politician in 2002 279
Drawing a picture 279
The Conservative politician in 2002 280
The Attitude of the Party as an Institution 282
The Study as a Picture at a Point in Time 283

16: Beyond the *CPRS 2002* 287

Further Analysis of the *CPRS 2002* Data 287
Re-Running the Study 287

Bibliography 291

Appendix 1: September 2000 Pilot Study 333

Appendix 2: Letter from Eric Forth 337

Appendix 3: Content of Scales 339

Appendix 4: Responses to Scales 347

Appendix 5: The CPRS 2002 Questionnaire 353

Index 375

Foreword by
Dr Syed Kamall MEP

This study of Conservative politicians at the turn of the century is an important contribution to the study of British politics that will undoubtedly prove valuable to future historians of the period. It is a unique and wide-ranging analysis of the attitudes, behaviour and background of Conservative politicians.

In assisting Nigel Meek with the circulation of the survey to potential respondents in 2002, the late Eric Forth MP identified two important aspects of the project. First, simply that it was so wide-ranging. It did not deal merely with a small number of hot topics which, as the book notes, can quickly become old news. Instead, the aim was to capture and present a panorama of Conservative politicians, who they were and what they thought.

Second, that the project did not content itself with the big beasts and politicians-cum-personalities of the Westminster – or Brussels – "village". The study went to real villages – and towns and cities – where local councillors work with little recognition or reward. Their views are also worthy of study.

Some of the findings are fascinating. One that interests me as a Conservative MEP is that, even by 2002, a quarter of Conservative politicians who responded to the survey were neutral or even sympathetic towards UKIP. It serves as a reminder of the contested nature of political support. As the son of immigrant parents who was elected to the European Parliament on merit in 2005 before any "A" list was introduced, it is interesting to see that back in 2002 only a small minority of Conservative politicians at all levels were opposed to the affirmative promotion within the Party of women and those from an ethnic minority background.

Who in 2002 imagined that eight years later there would be a Conservative/Liberal Democrat coalition government? By the look of their then attitudes towards their current coalition partners, not the respondents to the original study!

Dr Syed Kamall MEP, March 2012

Rue Wiertz 60 (05M73)
1047 Brussels
Belgium
syed.kamall@europarl.europa.eu

Dr Syed Kamall has been a Conservative member of the European Parliament for the London constituency since May 2005. He is a member of the European Parliament's Economic and Monetary Affairs, Legal Affairs and International Trade committees. He has also contested local council, Greater London Assembly and Westminster elections. Before entering the European Parliament, he worked as a consultant to companies on marketing, strategy and public affairs, as well as running a recruitment business. He has a PhD from City University London and is a Visiting Fellow at Leeds University Business School. Amongst his numerous publications are Telecommunications Policy *(1996) that served as an EU briefing paper and* For a Free Market Europe *(2009).*

About the Author

Dr Nigel Gervas Meek was born in 1965 and attended Trinity School of John Whitgift until leaving at the age of 16 to work in the electronics industry and then the civil service. Returning to education later on, he gained a BSc Psychology (1996) and an MA Applied Social & Market Research (1998) at the University of Westminster, and then a PhD in Political Science (2010) at London Metropolitan University.

Since the 1990s, he has worked in the market research industry and in the Further and Higher education sectors and other academic fields. He has also been a full-time carer.

He is a Research Fellow at the Centre for Comparative European Survey Data, and a Member of the British Psychological Society and the Political Studies Association. He is also the editor of a number of journals and other publications.

He lives in London.

The *CPRS 2002* Datafile and this Book

This book is based upon data collected for a one-time field study originally called the *Conservative Party Representatives Study 2002* (*CPRS 2002*) conducted in that year by the author at London Metropolitan University – formally London Guildhall University – as part of a PhD.

The datafile[1] of over 125,000 cells of original and derived data is lodged as SN 6552 with the Economic and Social Data Service (ESDS),[2] a collaborative service based upon four centres located at the University of Essex and the University of Manchester. The datafile is available via registration to academic researchers and others with a legitimate interest. The web address of the ESDS is: http://www.esds.ac.uk. Researchers should then search the ESDS datasets for 6552.

In addition, the *CPRS 2002* has a dedicated section on the website of the Centre for Comparative European Survey Data. Registered users can perform analysis of both the original and derived (by the researcher) data. Users can also perform a range of recoding allowing custom analysis. Data output is available in both tabular and graphical form. The web address is http://www.ccesd.ac.uk/CPRS.

In terms of the data collected and the breadth and depth of analysis in this book, the only approximately comparable work on the Conservative Party – since its focus was on ordinary members rather than politicians – is *True Blues*[3] by Paul Whiteley, Patrick Seyd and Jeremy Richardson, published in 1994 using data from fieldwork carried out in 1992.

---

[1] Meek, 27th August 2010.
[2] ESDS, 19th June 2006.
[3] Whiteley, Seyd & Richardson, 1994.

Abstract

This study, originally conducted as the *Conservative Party Representatives Survey 2002,* was a multi-focus analysis using quantitative methods of the institutional and political culture of Conservative politicians in 2002.

A 20-page questionnaire was sent in April 2002 to all Conservative MPs, Peers, MEPs, Scottish MPs, Welsh and Greater London Assembly members, and local councillors in Scotland and Wales. A somewhat longer questionnaire was sent to a 10% random sample of local councillors in England.

The closed format items covered a range of topics under the headings: the United Kingdom; the environment; business, labour relations, welfare and the economy; Britain, Europe and the wider world; ethnicity, citizenship and national image; society and culture; the conduct of politics; the political parties; religion; and the 2001 Conservative Party leadership contest. There were a small number of experiential items for all respondents and a larger battery of socio-demographic items for local councillors in England. A large proportion of attitudinal items were not intended as stand-alone items but as part of statistically robust multi-item scales.

Also used in this book is a range of secondary data allowing relevant comparisons between respondents and politicians from other parties and/or the general public.

Statistical analysis using a range of methods was conducted, mainly using *SPSS*. These techniques were used to determine differences, associations and/or predictors of attitudes, behaviour and socio-demographic background in a range of subject areas covered by a series of thematic chapters. This affords four outcomes. First, a systematic portrayal of the attitudes, background and behaviour of Conservative politicians at the turn of the $20^{th}/21^{st}$ centuries. Second, predictions about the impact of generational replacement as lower-level politicians progress to higher positions. Third, the investigation of a number of specific research questions. Fourth, the creation and lodging of a dataset with the relevant academic authorities both to allow for further analysis of the captured data and to serve as the basis of a potential time series dataset.

Acknowledgements and Comments

Acknowledgements

Thanks are particularly owed to my mother Erna Meek and my father William Meek (1925-1993); Professor Richard Topf of London Metropolitan University; the Right Honourable Eric Forth MP (1944-2006); Dr Syed Kamall MEP; Professor Sam Whimster of LMU; and Professor Paul Whiteley of the University of Essex.

Thanks are also due to Denise Panattoni, Peter Naylor, Lorna Williams, Dr Julie Withey, Dr Wendy Stokes, Lord Maurice Glasman, Professor Shah Hashemi and all other staff at LMU who helped with aspects of the original research; Keystroke Knowledge in Northumberland; members of staff at local authorities and other organisations who responded to enquiries; Deirdre Hinwood of Orpington College of Further Education; Alison and Martin Bowman; Howard Edgar; Professor Antony Flew (1923-2010); Lucy Ryder and the Civic and Education Research Trust; the Society for Individual Freedom; Dr Sean Gabb; and Anne Clements, Edward Goodman and Michael Turner.

Also to the members of Bromley and Chislehurst Conservative Association's Plaistow branch and members of the London Borough of Bromley's Conservative group who responded to a pilot study; and my erstwhile fellow party members who tolerated my eccentricities with probably more patience than they deserved.

And, of course, to those Conservative politicians at every level who took the time to complete such a lengthy questionnaire.

Involvement in the Conservative Party

Background

I became a volunteer activist for the Conservative Party in the mid-1980s, formally joining what would become Bromley and Chislehurst Conservative Association in 1987 just before that year's general election.

During a membership lasting two decades, I sat on the committee of my ward branch and was for much of the time an elected member of the Association's executive and political committees. I was also a member of the London South-East European constituency committee.

I sat on the candidate selection boards for local council elections that took place in 1990, 1994, 1998 and 2002. Following the retirement of Sir John Hunt MP and Sir Roger Sims MP[4] and the creation of a merged constituency, I was a member of the candidate selection board for the 1997 general election which saw the selection and then election of Eric Forth MP. Following Mr Forth's sudden death in 2006, I sat on the candidate selection board that selected Bob Neill who narrowly won the subsequent by-election after a fractious campaign.[5]

I was always a dissident member of the Party,[6] being more of a classical liberal or libertarian. For this and other reasons, not least the death of Eric Forth and subsequent events, I let my membership lapse in 2007.

It is to be hoped that this does not show in either the original study or the analyses in the remainder of this book. However, it is true that on a number of occasions it and other personally held views influenced the topics chosen and/or the extent to which they were analysed.[7]

How this relates to the approach to this study

This is no "confessional". This association with the Conservative Party was an important factor in determining the nature of the research and analysis. This is why a glance at the references used

---

[4] They were among a large number of sitting Conservative MPs who retired in the run-up to the 1997 general election: Wynn Davies, 5th February 1996.

[5] UK Polling Report, 2010.

[6] Meek, July 1999.

[7] Chapter 3 on the "Political Map" is the most obvious example.

throughout this book will note that whilst many come from traditional academic sources there are also a large number from the mainstream mass media, online media such as blogs, etc.

During my time as an activist it became apparent to me that, other than opposition to the Soviet Union and radical examples of domestic socialism, the attitudes of those that I associated with on a very regular basis such as other activists and local councillors appeared "all over the place" when examined on an individual level. This became more evident after, in the space of not many years, the collapse of the Soviet Union and the rise of New Labour. For me, as someone with a background in social research, this came to a head after the Labour landslide victory in 1997. Most of my fellows seemed obsessed with New Labour, Tony Blair, Peter Mandelson and "spin".[8] The discussion was frequently some variant of how best to emulate Labour's success and so to win the next election, i.e. the "how" of politics. It seemed that only a very few of us were asking what we wanted to do with this power should we acquire it, i.e. the "why" of politics.

To look at things from another direction as an example of what this research was *not* about, in the process of writing this book, by way of regular subscription, I received a copy of the Political Studies Association's journal *Political Studies*. In it there is an article by Efraim Podoksik[9] titled 'Overcoming the Conservative Disposition: Oakeshott vs. Tönnies'. Ferdinand Tönnies is most famous for his distinction between two types of social groups: *Gemeinschaft* (community) and *Gesellschaft* (association).[10] Michael Oakeshott is often spoken of as one of the most significant British conservative intellectuals of the 20th century.[11] It is a fascinating article. However, when one reads passages such as Podoksik (p. 875) quoting Oakeshott arguing that…

> *"Rules, duties, and their like … are to be recognised as densities obtruded by the tensions of a spoken language of moral intercourse, nodal points at which a practice turns*

---

[8] By a coincidence, in 1997 I was working in a modest capacity at MORI, the well-known market research company. Some of MORI's most senior members played an important role in the rise of New Labour: Mercer, 1994: 301; Sackman, 1994: 471.
[9] Podoksik, December 2008.
[10] Jary & Jary, 1991: 663.
[11] Hickson, 2005.

*upon itself in a vertiginous movement and becomes steadier
in ceasing to be adventurous"*

… then I am *very* sure that is not the form of "discourse" of any local councillor of my acquaintance!

This is not a trivial point. I spent two decades associating with such people as a colleague – and a friend – within the Party and at the time of writing still do on an occasional and informal basis. The aim of the study was to gain an objective and quantitative measure of their views as they might be discussed between themselves and at least senior activists such as I had been, but always through using appropriate academic methods of data collection and analysis.

In this respect this book is much like the earlier *True Blues* in that it is "written with a diverse audience in mind"[12] of Conservative Party politicians and members, journalists, pollsters and academic social scientists. A local councillor might not have knowledge of some of the *methods* used but he or she should be able to perceive the *results* so acquired as being meaningful.

In short, this study is not about conservatism *qua* philosophy – although brief mention will be made below – but rather it is about the beliefs of Conservative Party politicians.[13]

The role of Eric Forth

Eric Forth had been my MP since 1997. However, he was more than that. As a somewhat libertarian-inclined Conservative[14] he was of help in some of my own political activities outside of the Conservative Party. For example, on a number of occasions he hosted luncheons at the House of Commons for the Society for Individual Freedom, a classical liberal organisation[15] partly run by me. He went so far as to formally join the SIF shortly before his death.

Mr Forth was more than willing to help me by signing an introductory letter drafted by me but approved by him. The text of this letter can be found in Appendix 2. He was also provided with a copy of the draft questionnaire prior to signing this letter. He in no

---

[12] Whiteley, Seyd & Richardson: 1994: 8.
[13] Norton, July-September 2008: 324.
[14] Roth & White, 19th May 2006; *The Times*, 19th May 2006.
[15] Society for Individual Freedom, 27th October 2004.

way contributed to the content of the questionnaire. His sole comment concerned how long the questionnaire was.

At the time of the fieldwork Eric Forth was not merely a sitting Conservative MP. A charismatic individual, he had been the chairman of the influential Conservative Way Forward campaign group[16] and was the Shadow Leader of the House of Commons under Iain Duncan Smith and so a frequent guest on radio and television. He was also well-known as previously having been, and latterly would become again,[17] a leading member of the "awkward squad". It has been argued that some of Iain Duncan Smith's initial success in curbing overt Conservative backbench dissent was due in part to co-opting Eric Forth and his like-minded colleague David Maclean into the Shadow Cabinet.[18]

I have no objective proof that his introductory letter boosted response rate. However, compared to the alternative of *only* having the letter from me on the front page of the questionnaire it seems incredible to suggest that it did *not*.

Coining a Term: *Rhetormetrics*

Many will recognise terms such as "psychographics"[19] in marketing and "psychometrics"[20] in personality testing. Both deal within their disciplines with objective measurement. There does not seem to be a similar term within political science for the sort of attitude measurement featured in this book.

Possessing long-forgotten schoolboy Latin and no Greek at all, I asked a friend and associate, the now-departed philosopher Antony Flew,[21] if he had any ideas. In brief, his response[22] was that, given that the classical Greeks did not have organised political parties with beliefs and policies about everything, the term *rhetoricmetrics* as a

---

[16] *Telegraph*, 19th May 2006.
[17] Brown, 20th May 2006.
[18] Cowley & Stuart, October 2004: 356.
[19] Gunter & Furnham, 1992.
[20] Rust & Golombok, 1999.
[21] *Telegraph*, 13th April 2010. It regrettable that, at the time of Antony's death in April 2010, the media seemed more concerned with sensationalist claims about the religious views that he allegedly acquired towards the end of his life.
[22] Personal correspondence, 7th August 1999.

measurement of what public speakers say might suffice. However, this is unappealing as a word in English. Instead, he suggested the shorter *rhetormetrics*. Strictly speaking, this is a measurement of the public speakers themselves, but it's easier on the eye and tongue. I offer it to the reader.

1

Introduction

What is Conservatism?

The purpose of the study

The survey was an empirical analysis of the attitudes, background and behaviour of individual Conservative politicians in 2002. In turn, the findings from individual respondents are aggregated to provide a picture of the Conservative elected political class – if such a singular thing exists – as a whole. In other words, to provide an overall picture of the Conservative Party.

However, before getting to the heart of the survey, brief and far from exhaustive mention should be made of some other approaches that can be and have been utilised when addressing this question.

From the literature

When looking at the literature an array of sources can be consulted in an attempt to answer this question. They can be academic or popular. They can be historical or contemporary. They can be specific with the subject matter being primarily conservatism and/or the Conservative Party – and the distinction is discussed below – or they can be general in scope. They can be works listed under many disciplines including politics, philosophy, history, sociology, economics and even humour. Throughout this, whilst it would not be true to say that all sources agree on all things, and some studies that might be considered outliers[23] notwithstanding, certain reoccurring themes can be discerned.

---

[23] Evans, 1996.

Little detail will be gone into here since it is the purpose of the study to provide *an* answer to this question in its own way. However, by way of example, three classic texts can be consulted, two decidedly historical and one a history but of more contemporary authorship. Individually, these works are held to examine the nature of Conservatism as a doctrine – Mannheim's *Ideology and Utopia*;[24] as an ideology – Marquand's *Britain Since 1918*;[25] and as a class related practice – McKenzie and Silver's *Angels in Marble*.[26] The following is a brief synthesis of relevant and compatible elements from these three texts.

For these authorities, conservatism is as much a state of mind or temperament as ideology. It accepts the existence of the irrational in the social world and denies the perfectibility of man with his limited stock of reason. It seeks a knowledge of practical control of the here and now – and so often attracts supporters of classless managerialism – and concerns itself with the "is" rather than the normative "should" that inspires liberals and socialists. It emphasizes a known past and rejects utopian dreams of the future.

Conservatism holds that men are inherently unequal and that where there is variety of quality and ability there will be differentiation into classes. But this does not mean that there should be no fluidity of movement in both directions. Conservatives liken society to a tree, accepting growth and change and, to some extent, necessary pruning.

It discovers itself after the event and is defined as much by what it opposes. In the British context this was first the 19th century laissez-faire individualism of the Liberals and so Conservatives did not hesitate to use the power of state and society to redress perceived wrongs. Then it was the 20th century socialist exultation of the collective by Labour and so Conservatives emphasised the importance of the individual. (For those raised in the last few decades and knowing only of the latter tendency, the former can come as a shock. This applies to many Conservatives as well as to the political laity.)

Conservatives believe that security of property – initially of land ownership but eventually of property as such – is perhaps the main purpose of government and that without property civilisation cannot

---

[24] Mannheim, 1936: 120, 229-238.
[25] Marquand, 2009: 57-58, 137-138, 324.
[26] McKenzie & Silver, 1968: 18-59.

endure. However, conservative principles are entirely compatible with the idea of state responsibility for such matters as social welfare and other forms of interventionism.

Conservatism makes appeals to a sense of community – including the minimisation of both individual desires and group demands wherever they threaten the stability of society – and nationalism and this sometimes veers into outright xenophobia. Part of this belief in the British context can be seen in the historical support for an established church as a national act of religious devotion although such religiosity is not taken to theological extremes and ultimately each man must hold himself responsible only to God

Conservatives tend to look back to an idealised pre-industrial society where social order was guaranteed and legitimised by a system of norms and values which were to be swept away by industrialization. Ironically – and here the problem becomes apparent when consulting such undoubtedly interesting and useful sources and trying to extrapolate them to an analysis of the late 20th and early 21st century Conservative Party – the Conservatives in the years before the fieldwork had themselves stimulated populist rage against and amongst the very institutions that it had once defended: the older universities, the liberal professions, the senior civil service and the Church of England.

From the Party as an institution

Much of this above is interesting and useful and indeed seems right in terms of their analysis. But in truth it is somewhat woolly when considering real-world politics. So, coming at matters from the other direction, one might consult formal documents and statements such as election manifestos.[27]

But the problem is that – even assuming that they are written in good faith at the time – whilst there are certainly reoccurring themes of interest – often not dissenting from the ideas rehearsed in the previous sub-section – much of the content is context-specific and ephemeral. No doubt it is a cherry-picked example, but how many Britons these days have even heard of the Colombo Plan[28] for economic and social development in the Asia-Pacific region which

---

[27] Kimber, 17th April 2010; Pogorelis et al, November 2005; Topf, 1994.
[28] Colombo Plan, 2005.

was apparently important enough to feature in the Conservative Party's 1959 general election manifesto?[29]

From individual Conservatives

Moreover, as suggested in the personal comments above, confusion reigns once individual Conservatives are consulted on a person-by-person basis. Looking ahead to Chapter 12 on the Party's 2001 leadership contest, the noise and confusion generated by internal debate within the Party was encapsulated in just two days when the *Daily Telegraph* invited and received comments from ordinary Conservative members and senior Party figures alike.[30]

Almost every conceivable view – if not the relative prevalence of such views within the Party – was mooted. Examples include pro-EU and anti-EU; for and against social liberalism; for and against increased spending on the State sector; some for more and others for less taxation; the need to replace William Hague with a more charismatic leader against having someone who appeared quiet and decent; those who thought that the party had lost due to being seen as too extreme and right-wing against those who thought that it had failed to defend traditional Conservative values; whether Hague and the Conservatives had lost the 2001 general election or Tony Blair and New Labour had won it; those who thought that the Conservatives needed to embrace inclusivity and multiculturalism against those who thought that this was a gimmick; policy failures against strategy failures; the implications of successes at a local level against failure at the national level.

Attenuating the noise

A survey and resultant book such as this cannot hope to achieve a definitive answer to the question posed at the start of this chapter when considered from all possible approaches. In Chapter 2 there is more detail on the purposes of the study, why its target was the publically elected (or appointed or inherited in the case of Peers)

---

[29] Conservative Party, 1959.
[30] *Telegraph*, 15th and 16th June 2001.

politicians of the Conservative Party rather than ordinary members and how the research was conducted. The main purpose of the study – along with some specific research questions – is to determine the nature of British Conservatism at least as it can be determined by an analysis of what Conservative politicians thought, believed and so on at the time.

A note of caution

Before proceeding it should be noted that is easy to allow some confusion and perhaps even arrogance to creep into such a study. It assumes, at least within the British context, that the Conservative Party has a near-monopoly on any discussions about the similarly-named "ism". Some have gone so far as to argue that for many years the Conservative Party as an institution has been positively damaging to conservatism as an ideology in the UK.[31] Perhaps. Perhaps not. But the milder point is well made and should always be kept in mind. (Of course, this is hardly a new phenomenon. In the late 19th century, Herbert Spencer famously made much the same point about the Liberals and liberalism.[32])

But this is indeed a study of the Conservative Party and the beliefs and background and so on of its politicians.

A Qualification about the Wider Context

On a number of occasions in the thematic chapters below comparisons are made between the data captured by the fieldwork and that captured by other studies. As will be noted where appropriate, this was done for a variety of reasons. Sometimes this might be done to explore a specific research theme. At other times it might be done to provide additional validation of the robustness of the *CPRS 2002's* data. At other times it might be done simply to highlight the obvious point that in a multi-party democracy the Conservative Party does not operate in a vacuum. Nevertheless, the main focus is the Conservative Party and not the wider British political culture.

---

[31] Gabb, 16th February 2005.
[32] Spencer, 1884/1969: 63-81.

Existing Work about the Conservative Party

As indicated above, as one of the major political institutions of Britain the "centre-right" Conservative Party has been an enduring subject of scrutiny of every sort. Some of this has been journalistic: every day the Conservative Party features in national, local and international newspapers, radio, television and latterly on the internet, and many instances are referenced in this book. Some of this has been academic: peer-reviewed politics and history journals regularly feature articles on the Party and there are many books written by acknowledged scholars, and numerous instances are referenced in this book. Market research companies also study the Party and attitudes towards it from the most basic items about voting intention to attitudes about leaders and policy as well as the general social and political environment, and again such work is referred to. There is also ongoing research on the Party at a number of universities at various levels.[33]

However, studies that are both thematically wide-ranging and quantitative are much rarer. No more will be said here since this is discussed in more detail in the next chapter.

A traditional, all-embracing literature review is also not found in this chapter. Because of the thematic nature of the report it makes for better comprehension to deal with the literature in appropriate depth in each chapter. However, whilst many of the thematic chapters can be read on their own, it is only in combination that they fulfil the main purpose of the original study which was to provide an objective measure of the attitudes, behaviour and background of Conservative politicians.

It is this mixture of thematic breadth, the type of respondent, the quantitative and replicable methodology and the rigorous way in which it was conducted that assures this study's contribution to political science.

The rest of this chapter is taken up with a number of matters. First, there is some scene-setting about the Conservative Party in 2002 and which reiterates a key element of the motivation behind this study. Following this, there are a few words of more general scene-setting about Britain and the world in 2002, particularly as it was most relevant to the thematic chapters. This chapter ends with an overview of each of

---

[33] E.g. Hayton, 2012; Heppell, 2009, 2012; Hickson, 2012.

the thematic chapters including, by way of a taster, some of the main findings in each.

The Conservative Party in 2002

A nadir in the Party's fortunes

Having been in power since 1979 under first Margaret Thatcher and then John Major, for various reasons the Party's national support collapsed from 1992 and it was finally crushed under the Tony Blair-led New Labour landslide of 1997. The Conservative Party was reduced to just 165 seats at Westminster including none outside of England. The 2001 general election produced an almost identical result. It was not until years after the fieldwork that the Conservative Party began to recapture lost national support and it took until after another narrower general election loss in 2005 for the Party to consistently lead Labour in the polls. In the meantime the Conservatives failed to win a single Parliamentary by-election between 1997 and 2005.

Mention should also be made of the relative success of the Liberal Democrats which during this period returned its largest number of MPs since the 1920s. During the period around the fieldwork any occasional apparent increase in support for the Conservatives was often due to a decline in support for Labour which moved instead to the Liberal Democrats. Support for the Conservatives remained static and often unable to break out of a 30%-35% voting intention "ghetto".

Turning briefly to the then newer Scottish Parliament and Welsh Assembly, in 1999 the Conservatives came a distant third behind Labour (in both cases) and the SNP and Plaid Cymru respectively. That said, on both occasions they edged out the Liberal Democrats for third place, largely thanks to the use of proportional representation. Brief mention will also be made of the Greater London Assembly elsewhere in this book.

On an institutional level the Conservative Party was suffering a long-term decline in membership. However, it was not alone in this with at least the larger political parties and also some major pressure groups suffering a similar decline. This is also looked at further on.

Talk of Conservative members leads to mention of another event directly affecting the Party and which forms an important chapter in this book. The fieldwork came at an historic time for the Party in that only the year before it had conducted its first all-members leadership contest where, at least in the final ballot, all members and hence all respondents to this survey had an equal vote.[34]

The "nasty party"?

It was common currency amongst many both inside and outside of the Party to claim that it had become and continued to be unelectable on a national level after 1992 largely because of its attitudes and policy prescriptions.[35] The description of the Conservatives as "the nasty party" was (in)famously made by the Conservative MP and then Party chairman Theresa May at the 2002 Conservative Party Conference. The "nasty party" thesis was that the Party was overtly sexist, racist and homophobic and generally "bigoted", as well as being mean-spirited and uncaring about the poor witnessed by a perceived opposition to state welfare and the NHS. Not only were these were bad own their own, the thesis continued, but they were also electorally damaging.[36]

Whether or not the Conservative Party and its politicians were "nasty" or "nice" depends in part on a normative – ought/ought not – and subjective assessment. It is not the purpose of this study to prove or refute such views. That is a matter of one's own political beliefs. But before that, if the task is to be undertaken with any seriousness, it requires more positive – is/is not – and objective evidence of what was actually being thought and said. This was the main task of the study.

---

[34] See, for example, the following for more detail on the facts and figures of the preceding: *BBC News*, May 1999; Broughton, October 2004: 350-351; Croucher, 8th June 2002; Davies, 6th January 2006; Dorey, 2003: 131; Landale, 13th March 2001; Leake, 30th July 2000; Leeke, 1st July 2003: 9; Mellows-Facer, 17th May 2005: 14; Morgan, 29th March 2001: 5; MORI, March 2009; Norton, 1997: 80; Norton, 2002: 68; Oborne, 23rd September 2000; Rallings & Thrasher, April 2003: 271; Raedwald, 14th May 2012; Riddell, 1997: 19; Sanders & Brynin, 1999: 219; Travis, 27th April 2002; UK Polling Report, March 2009, May 2009; Young, 11th May 2005: 7.

[35] Kent, 5th December 2001.

[36] E.g. Carr, 11th October 2002; O'Sullivan, 9th March 2009; Wegg-Prosser, 12th October 2001; Williams, 18th September 2002.

But was it so bad?

All of that said, there have been "revisionist" analyses of the period around 2002.[37] These have argued, for example, that opinion polls under-reported the level of support for the Conservatives. Also that by some measures, particularly in local elections in England,[38] the electoral performance of the Party was not wholly disastrous which suggests that the "feel on the doorstep" might be different for some respondents than it was for others. Moreover, it was argued that the first-past-the-post voting system, tactical voting, the distribution of the population within constituency boundaries and other aspects of the UK's electoral system were particularly damaging to the Conservatives when compared to the other main parties.

Others argued that the Party's long-term electoral problems were not so much because of being perceived to be unpleasant towards homosexuals, women and racial minorities but due to a failure to engage in issues such as education and crime. Conversely, others argued that the Conservative Party's adherence to supposedly unpopular "traditional" polices was often illusory. Instead, it has been claimed, the Party leadership adopted a "progressive" agenda after each general election defeat only to switch to more traditional policies when this tactic failed to gain support. In turn, this was too late to win elections but just in time to save the modernizers from blame for defeat.

Commentators have also argued that between 1997 and 2001 the Conservatives became more professional in their presentational

---

[37] Found in whole or part in, for example: Berrington, October 2001: 213-214; Broughton, 2003: 204 and 211; Broughton, October 2004: 352; Burns & Cowell, 7th May 2010 Evans, Curtice & Norris, 1998: 76-77; Glover, 9th February 2002; Heffer 6th July 2002 and 12th October 2002; Hetherington, 9th June 2001; Kimber, 3rd November 2008; McAllister & Studlar, 2000: 368; MORI, March 2009; Oborne, 2nd November 2011; O'Sullivan, 9th March 2009; Rallings & Thrasher, April 2004: 394; UK Polling Report, March 2009.

[38] In May 2010, the opposite phenomenon occurred. On the same day that the Conservatives made net gains and Labour made net losses at the general election, in local elections held in much of England the Conservatives made net losses of both seats and councils – as did the Liberal Democrats – whilst Labour made net gains: *BBC News*, 8th May 2010. This might merely be a "one of those things" coincidence or a phenomenon due to differential turnout even down to a ward level. Or it might be due to conscious and quite sophisticated behaviour such as compensatory split-ticket voting.

approach, utilising modern marketing concepts and techniques.[39] These met with little electoral success in 2001, the results confirming political marketing analysis that the Conservatives did not offer a viable product voters wanted to buy. However, it has been argued that there were long-term benefits. William Hague's marketing background and skills had attracted more young people, women and ethnic minorities to the Party as well as winning more local council seats and bequeathed to Iain Duncan Smith and in turn his successors a more professional organisation, if one that was still imperfectly so.[40]

Britain and the World in 2002

Britain

It is worth a few words placing the survey within a place in time. On a national level there were a number of issues affecting the UK such as the Good Friday Agreement as part of the Northern Ireland peace process which was signed in April 1998[41] and the devolution of powers to various extents in Scotland, Wales and London. These are matters that are explored one way or another in the following thematic chapters.

One or two of the headline economic and social conditions of 2002 should also be mentioned, not least because such issues feature prominently in the thematic chapters. By some measures the UK remained the world's fourth largest economy in terms of GDP[42] although economic growth in the UK had fallen in the preceding two years[43] but would rise again until the economic problems that came to the fore in 2008. Unemployment appeared to be at a low level.[44] In other words, the general perception was probably that things were "ticking along" reasonably well.

---

[39] Lees-Marshment, November 2001: 929, 938-939.
[40] Ashcroft, 2005.
[41] Northern Ireland Office, 2007.
[42] Nation Master, 2009.
[43] Trading Economics, 2009.
[44] National Statistics, 11th December 2008.

It is not the place here to go into the vexed question of the accuracy of crime statistics.[45] However, according to the *British Crime Survey* actual as opposed to reported crime had been falling since 1995.[46] This must be set against a huge rise in, for example, violent crime in absolute terms since the 1940s and 1950s, something that occurred within the lifetimes of many respondents and which by 2002 made the UK one of the most crime-ridden countries within the developed world.[47]

The world

Internationally, this was now a "post-9/11" world and the "War on Terror" was underway. US-led military forces including those of the UK had invaded Afghanistan. However, the fieldwork for the study was taken a year before the invasion of Iraq in which British forces would also participate to dubious effect[48] and three years before the 7/7 attacks in London. This was, perhaps, early days in a process[49] the final outcome of which – if there can be such a thing – is still uncertain. Again, some of these are matters that feature below.

The *Maastricht Treaty*, which had been particularly painful for the Conservatives,[50] was history. However, one of the first acts of the incoming Labour government was to sign the *Amsterdam Treaty* in 1997, something which for good or ill furthered the process of European integration. No comprehensive study of the Conservative Party conducted in the last few decades can possibly avoid this topic. Indeed, some might take issue with this paragraph being in a sub-section titled "The World" rather than the preceding one titled "Britain".[51]

---

[45] Ford, 23rd April 2010.

[46] Jansson, 2007: 8.

[47] Bartholomew, 2004: 15-16.

[48] North, 2009

[49] Meek, 17th February 2003.

[50] Baker, Gamble & Ludlum, 1994; Ludlum, 1996.

[51] North, 28th May 2009; 22nd April 2010; 9th February 2012; Szamuely, 16th March 2010; Waterfield, 8th February 2012.

An Overview of the Following Chapters

Chapter 2: The *Methodology* of the *CPRS 2002*. Following this there are a number of thematic chapters.

Chapter 3: *Beyond "Left & Right": The Political Map:* This chapter explores the failings of the traditional one-dimensional "left and right" model of ideology, looking instead at a two-dimensional model combining socio-economic relationships on the one hand and civil liberties and morality on the other. This model is refined and operationalised using statistically robust values dimensions into a device termed the Political Map (PoliMap). This is used to measure and plot respondents and when used in this manner they are seen to inhabit a constrained area of the PoliMap.

Chapter 4: *Local Councillors in England:* Using an additional battery of items – asked only of this largest group of respondents due to the potentially identifying nature of the items – concerning matters such as age, sex, race, education, political experience and employment, a picture is drawn of Conservative Party local councillors in England at the time. They are compared in a number of ways to councillors from the other major parties and also the general public. The "typical" Conservative local councillor was a middle-class, middle-aged, white male; but so too were those from the other main parties. The association between socio-demographic differences and attitudinal differences is also studied, with the perhaps surprising finding that there was very little.

Chapter 5: *Attitudes About the Conservative Party:* Issues such as the Party's beliefs, prospects, public image and leadership are studied here. The evidence suggests that many respondents were out-of-touch and overly optimistic about the state of the Party in 2002. However, there was a perceived need to change the Party's public image if not actual beliefs inasmuch as respondents believed that they knew what these were. Regarding attitudes towards present and past leaders of the Party, there were striking results for Edward Heath, who was somewhat disliked, and Margaret Thatcher, who was the object of something approaching worship.

Chapter 6: *Attitudes About Other UK Parties:* To those versed in Conservative local politics in particular there was the unsurprising finding that the Liberal Democrats were more disliked than Labour[52] although it was not *objectively* clear why from the data. When looking at attitudes towards some of those that were generally perceived to be smaller, single-issue parties, attitudes towards them were significantly associated with their signature issue and in the direction of these parties' perceived inclinations.

Chapter 7: *The Wider World:* Of particular interest was to see if a general observation that attitudes towards the EU, the USA and Israel were associated was also true amongst Conservative politicians. They were. Euro-sceptic, pro-USA and pro-Israeli views tended to be associated with each other and some explanations are tentatively offered. Other issues explored include the Commonwealth, where there was support for stronger ties to both the Old and (albeit less so) New Commonwealths, and the Islamic world where there mixed views about the prospects for long-term peace between the Western and Islamic worlds.

Chapter 8: *National Identity:* This chapter looks at attitudes about England, Scotland and Wales vis-à-vis the UK and also the EU and how respondents perceived themselves. Whilst there was evidence for a mixed British and English/Scottish/Welsh identity there was much less support for European as a component of self-identity. Also studied were issues such as devolution and an English parliament. Whilst there was little appetite for Scottish or Welsh independence or an English parliament let alone English regional assemblies, there was acceptance from respondents from what was the most anti-devolution of the major political parties of the constitutional changes that had actually happened by 2002. There was also an attempt to develop and deploy a typology of national identity in a more general sense. However, this suffered due the extreme directional loading of responses although there were some interesting results when this same typology was used to analyse the general public by way of comparison.

Chapter 9: *The Free-Market: "Necessary Evil" or "Good Thing"?:* This short chapter examines whether a demonstrable tendency amongst respondents to support free-market economics and the private sector was likely based upon utilitarian or ideological grounds. It was clear that whilst respondents believed that the private

---

[52] Hence Dr Syed Kamall's comments in his Foreword to this book.

sector was more efficient than the public sector this tendency was less evident when considering its worthiness. Drawing upon data from local councillors in England, there was some evidence that experience of employment was associated with differing attitudes towards the private and public sectors with those employed in the latter less likely to believe in the superior worthiness of the former.

Chapter 10: *Religion:* Looking briefly at confessional background, more space is given to looking at both private religious views and attitudes towards the role of religion in society and what impact religious views might have on more secular attitudes. Whilst respondents tended to be personally somewhat religious they could hardly be described as zealots when it came to the role of religion in public life. "Religion" in either sense seemed to have little impact on more earthly values. The possible exception was attitudes towards the environment, where stronger personal religious beliefs were positively correlated with holding "green" views and the "stewardship versus dominion" debate about religion and the environment is noted.

Chapter 11: *The Party-Political Institutions:* Issues such as where respondents believed political power should lie at an institutional level are analysed, as is why people become politicians. There was a perhaps conservative and/or nationalist attitude towards the various legislative bodies, with noticeably more hostility to the newer bodies such as those in Scotland, Wales, London and Europe compared to Westminster or elected local authorities. This was mediated by an unsurprising tendency of respondents to be more favourable to the legislative body on which they sat than were others and this was irrespective of whether they were in power in those bodies. With the exception of Peers, there was a noticeable divide between parliamentarians of all sorts who tended to cite ideological reasons for going into politics and local councillors who were more likely to regard themselves as representatives of the electorate.

Chapter 12: *The 2001 Leadership Contest:* All stages are analysed, from the MPs-only initial contest with five candidates through to the final contest between Ken Clarke and Iain Duncan Smith where all members had a vote. Along the way matters such as informal input into the contest by non-MPs at the earlier stages are also studied. Attitudes associated with support for the various candidates are identified. It is clear that, based upon the response from politicians, the final choice between Clarke and Duncan Smith was to a substantial degree an internal Party referendum on the UK's relationship with or even membership of the EU, with a secondary issue being perceptions of the condition and general popularity of the Party. The more Euro-sceptic and the more optimistic respondents were then the more likely they were to have backed Ian Duncan Smith.

Chapter 13: *The Public and Electoral Politics:* Drawing in part on material from some of the preceding chapters and making considerable use of secondary data, this chapter opens up the study to the beliefs and voting behaviour of the general public. First, the views of respondents and the public about the main concerns facing Britain are compared and whilst in ordinal terms these were similar there were clear differences in that the public was more concerned about bread and butter issues than were our respondents. The next section looks at the experiences of respondents in fighting elections, particularly against Labour and the Liberal Democrats. The antipathy towards the latter is again noted. However, it is also clear that electoral considerations were not as important as ideological ones when looking at attitudes towards the Party's two main rivals. Finally, the chapter returns to the PoliMap and it is used to plot and compare both our respondents and the public. It is shown that both inhabit constrained areas of the PoliMap and that whilst these overlap there are considerable differences. The implications of this on gathering electoral support are discussed.

Chapter 14: *Future Conservative Parliamentarians?:* By identifying a subset of Conservative local councillors most likely to become MPs or MEPs at subsequent elections and comparing these to sitting MPs, an impression is formed of whether the ideological and socio-demographic profile of senior Conservative politicians might shift in some manner. In fact, absent of socio-demographic positive discrimination and/or attitudinal litmus testing, based solely on generational replacement it seemed unlikely that there would be many dramatic changes in the intakes of the two or three general elections after 2002. This is a finding – or a prediction – that is now open to testing.

Chapter 15: *Bringing the Findings Together:* This chapter offers some concluding remarks including the drawing of a word picture of the "average" Conservative politician of the time but also discussing differences between the average views expressed by our respondents and the views of the Party as an entity as expressed, for example, in manifestos. The chapter concludes by arguing that the fieldwork came at a time that was a notable juncture in the history of the Party.

Chapter 16: *Beyond the CPRS 2002:* The brief final chapter notes the possibilities of further research, both additional analysis of the data captured by the fieldwork and as using this data as the starting point for a time-series dataset. In doing so, and by treating the *CPRS 2002* as a pilot study and candidly acknowledging some of its weaknesses, some advice is offered about how subsequent studies might improve upon it.

2

Methodology

Types of Study Considered

In deciding how to conduct the fieldwork, issues of practicality were of great importance. What might have been possible for a large and well-funded team was not for a lone researcher. Similarly, although qualitative research might be able to produce richer data, the nature of the main study with aims including providing a wide-ranging thematic picture of the attitudes, behaviour and background of Conservative Party politicians made quantitative research a more appropriate tool for a number of reasons. At the simplest, it is more straightforward to analyse.[53] The use of statistically validated, multi-item scales – the chosen method to obtain a wide-ranging but objective picture – directed the use of quantitative techniques. Flavour could have been added with the use of some open questions,[54] but given how time-consuming coding even these can be[55] it was decided against it mindful of how lengthy was even the purely closed-item questionnaire.

A review of studies of the Conservative Party indicates a variety of aims and methodologies, for example quantitative or qualitative, general histories or analysing specific themes. Of course, a work that broadly falls into one type will often contain elements of another and the borders can be fuzzy. To reiterate, there is nothing wrong with qualitative research and in-depth interviews. However, such things would not be the

---

[53] Bryman, 2008: 238.
[54] Moser & Kalton, 1971: 341-342.
[55] Bryman, 2008: 232.

right tools commensurate with the aims and resources of the study however desirable it might have been to be able to capture the "essence and ambience" of an issue via qualitative as opposed to quantitative research which deals in "counts and measures".[56]

In short, this study is quantitative and general. The only comparable study is that by Paul Whiteley, Patrick Seyd and Jeremy Richardson published in 1994 as *True Blues: The Politics of Conservative Party Membership.*[57] However, there are important differences between it and this present one. The main difference is the respondents within the Party. *True Blues* was a study of Conservative Party *members*, whereas this one focuses on Conservative Party *politicians*. In addition, although not a difference in kind, there is the passage of time. The fieldwork for the *True Blues* study was conducted in January to April 1992[58] when the Conservative Party formed the government whereas that for this study was conducted a decade later in April 2002 when it assuredly did not.[59]

A Small-Scale Pilot Study

Before proceeding, mention should be made that nearly two years before the fieldwork for the *CPRS 2002* proper a small-scale pilot study looking at just two issues was conducted. One was an attempt to create an alternative operationalisation of the PoliMap that will be discussed in Chapter 3. This used a question set along the lines of a semantic differential format.[60]

The other was an attempt to create a new multi-item scale, provisionally called the "Judeo-Christian Concerns" scale, based upon a speech given by the then leader of the Conservative Party, William Hague, to the Black Majority Churches' joint millennium "Faith in the Future" celebration in July 2000.[61] In his speech Hague focused on a number of alleged threats to society such as Third-world debt, drug use, family breakdown, crime, the easy availability of

---

[56] Berg, 1995: 3.
[57] Whiteley, Seyd & Richardson: 1994.
[58] Whiteley, Seyd & Richardson: 1994: 240.
[59] This book came out a decade later still. A further study is now due.
[60] De Vaus, 1996: 88.
[61] Hague, 7ᵗʰ July 2000; Buchanan, 6ᵗʰ July 2000.

violent and sexually explicit material, and the promotion in schools of homosexuality.

The two-page questionnaire, covering letter and pre-paid reply envelope were despatched in September 2000. Further details can be found in Appendix 1. The recipients of the questionnaire were elected members of the Conservative group on the council of the London Borough of Bromley and also all members of the committee and all ordinary members of Plaistow Branch, Bromley & Chislehurst Conservative Association. From the 70 questionnaires despatched the response rate was 69%.

Neither of these devices were included in the final questionnaire. In the case of the PoliMap, however innovative the operationalisation used in the pilot study might have been with further development, it was superseded by the more conventional and tried-and-tested Left-Right and Authoritarianism scales.

That said, according to the measures used in the pilot study respondents – including local councillors – tended to have mildly free-market economic views coupled with mildly socially authoritarian views. These findings do not go against what is described throughout this book.

The Judeo-Christian Concerns scale looked more promising. However, it too was superseded by existing scales that dealt with similar issues. In what was an increasingly lengthy questionnaire, it was decided to omit this potential new scale.

Issues with Developing the Questionnaire

Unfortunately it was not possible to pilot the main questionnaire, responses to which form the basis of the following thematic chapters. This was for two reasons, both time-related. First, the mailing lists for most groups of potential respondents were easy to compile. Even local councillors in Scotland and Wales were not too difficult given how few of them there were. However, local councillors in England, who numbered in their thousands, were another matter. A database of local councillors in England was purchased from a commercial supplier and then kept up-to-date each week by following local by-elections on both specialist politics and local authority websites – which at the time were often slow and hard to navigate – and where necessary email and hardcopy enquiries to local councils. However, in May 2002 local elections were scheduled throughout England and this would have undone a great deal of work.

Second, the Party's leadership contest of 2001 was a major component of the questionnaire and time was slipping away when it came to accurate recall of the events and participation in them.

Topics Covered

Aims of the research

The study is an analysis of attitudes and beliefs along with a smaller number of behavioural and socio-demographic items. It is a multi-focus study centred on an analysis of the attitudinal culture of Conservative politicians in 2002. Within this there are a number of main objectives. First, to provide a wide-ranging snapshot of the values, attitudes, beliefs,[62] socio-demographic background and to a lesser extent behaviour of Conservative Party politicians. In other words, what has been referred to as "value and ideological orientations", "cultural/national orientations" and "underlying social structure".[63]

Second, to identity the sort of existing lower-level Conservative politicians most likely to "move up the ladder" and then to examine their attitudinal and socio-demographic profile both by themselves and against those they are most likely to replace in the years after the fieldwork.

Third, to analyse a number of more specific issues such as work on a two-dimensional mapping of ideology, predictors of support during the Party's 2001 leadership contest and other topics that are covered below.

Fourth, and looking beyond the survey itself, to construct and lodge a dataset with relevant academic bodies to allow analysis and comparison by other researchers of the data itself and also the possibility of using it to form the start of a time-series dataset.

To allow all of this, the questionnaire covered a variety of topics ranging from questions about abstract political, economic, social, religious and moral beliefs to more concrete issues of the day.

---

[62] Schwartz, 2007: 169-170.
[63] *European Social Survey*, 2007[a]: 4.

Topic ordering

The questions or items were grouped in subject blocks under distinct headings.[64] Some of these contained only one battery of items, others rather more. In order, these headings were (with page numbering referring to the original questionnaire):

- The United Kingdom (page 3)
- The Environment (page 4)
- Business, Labour Relations, Welfare and the Economy (pages 4 to 5)
- Britain, Europe and the Wider World (pages 5 to 7)
- Ethnicity, Citizenship and National Image (pages 7 to 8)
- Society and Culture (pages 8 to 9)
- The Conduct of Politics (pages 9 to 11)
- The Political Parties (pages 11 to 14)
- The 2001 Conservative Party Leadership Contest (page 15)
- Religion (page 16)
- A Few Questions About Yourself (pages 17 to 18)[65]
- Additional Questions for Local Councillors in England (pages 19 to 20)[66]

Although is it impossible to ask about everything, it can be seen from this list that a very wide range of topics was covered in the questionnaire.

The Respondents

The intended targets

With a view towards obtaining as wide-ranging as possible picture of Conservative politicians, the fieldwork targeted all main groups of the

---

[64] Bryman, 2008: 204.
[65] Mainly but not wholly about their experiences as an activist and politician.
[66] Mainly consisting of a battery of socio-demographic items.

Party's publically elected – or appointed or inherited in the case of Peers – politicians. These groups were the Party's members of/of the:

- House of Commons (**MPs**)
- House of Lords (**Peers**)
- European Parliament (**MEPs**)
- Scottish Parliament (**MSPs**)
- Welsh Assembly (**AMs**)
- Greater London Assembly (**GLAs**)
- Local authorities in England (**ELCs**)
- Local authorities Scotland (**SLCs**)
- Local authorities in Wales (**WLCs**)

Identifying the targets, and sampling

Questionnaires were sent out to all members of all groups with the exception of ELCs where, because of the numbers involved, a 10% random sample was used. Except again for ELCs, mailing lists for all of the groups of respondents, whose names and some form of contact address were a matter of public record, were constructed from various online or hardcopy sources and any changes such as those due to by-elections were also easily dealt with in the same manner.[67]

There were two duplicates between the groups. One member of the House of Lords was also an MEP, and one local councillor in Scotland was also a member of the Scottish parliament. These individuals were assigned solely to the MEP and MSP groups respectively because these two groups were better served by the boost in increased size than the alternatives.

In short, for these groups the fieldwork was an attempted census.[68]

For ELCs a census was impractical. With approximately 6550 Conservative local councillors in England at the time of the fieldwork, a comprehensive database would have been difficult to construct from scratch. Moreover, it would have been prohibitively expensive to print and despatch this number of questionnaires. Instead, a ready-made mailing list of all Conservative ELCs was

---

[67] Edkins, 2005
[68] De Vaus, 1996: 60.

purchased at a reduced cost from Keystroke Knowledge[69] in Northumbria, England, and then kept up-to-date until just before despatch using online and hardcopy sources and where necessary direct enquiries to the local councils involved.

When it was time to despatch the questionnaires a number of operations were involved in obtaining the 10% random sample of ELCs. First, there were rather more Conservative local council positions (6818) than there were individual councillors (6549). This was because a number of ELCs were members of both district and county councils. These duplicates were identified and removed mainly using various permutations of Microsoft *Access's* "find duplicates" query function. This two-tier system of local government was only found in the English shire regions, with most urban local authorities in England and all local authorities in Scotland and Wales being unitary in nature.[70] No distinction was made between these two tiers since, in combination they were, in effect, what unitary local authorities were elsewhere.

The 6549 ELCs were each then assigned a unique number from 1 to 6549. An online random number generator[71] was then used to generate the required 10% sample, i.e. 655 numbers ranging from 1 to 6549. Where necessary, duplicate random numbers were identified and removed and more random numbers generated until 655 unique numbers had been generated. These were then matched against the full list of 6549 local councillors and the final 10% sample identified.

The numbers despatched of each type and in total can be found in Table 2.3 below.

Who and where were excluded

All the respondents represented wards, regions or constituencies in mainland Britain (although one could argue that Peers represented the whole of the UK). Around the time of the fieldwork there were some local councillors sitting in Northern Ireland who had been elected as Conservatives,[72] but too few to study.

---

[69] Keystroke Knowledge, c. 2008.
[70] Fenney, 2000: 15-16, 231.
[71] Haahr, 1999.
[72] Taylor, 2000: 1418.

Members of parish or town councils[73] were also excluded for a number of reasons. At the time of the study members of such bodies were often difficult to locate, and there was still a strong ethos of ostensibly non-partisan representation with candidates standing as "Ratepayers" or similar.

As for the other British Isles – the Isle of Man, the Isles of Scilly and the Channel Islands – at the time of the study none of the mainland political parties were represented on locally elected governing bodies[74] and/or these places were not constitutionally part of the UK.

Ethical Issues

There are a number of ethical issues of which researchers need to be aware. These include "lack of informed consent", "deception", "invasion of privacy" and "harm to participants".[75] Given the use of a voluntary, self-completion questionnaire, the first of these falls.

There was no deception involved. The items in the questionnaire were just that, no more and no less. Given the use of a postal questionnaire, there was no meaningful invasion of privacy as there might have been with real-time techniques such as telephone interviewing or face-to-face interviewing.

This leaves harm to participants. It is possible that some respondents might have feared for their standing with the Party, press and/or electorate if they "said the wrong thing". This is why the survey was conducted under the cloak of anonymity and not just assurances of confidentiality. It was also why few potentially identifying questions were asked about sex, age and so on except in the case of ELCs where the sheer number made identification of individual respondents unlikely.

The Multi-Item Scales

Types of scales

With a view to obtaining a wide-ranging and systematic picture of attitudes many of the individual items in the questionnaire were

---

[73] Fenney, 2000: 14-16.
[74] Taylor, 2000: 1437-1446.
[75] Bryman, 2008: 118.

always intended to serve as components of multi-item scales designed to provide "a useable measure of a theoretical construct".[76]

In many cases these were values-dimensions used with a view to identifying "underlying 'deep-rooted' value orientations"[77] and as such they transcended specific actions and situations.[78] Examples include Authoritarianism and Left-Right. It has been argued that there are ten basic types of values, identifiable in terms of their goals.[79] If this is the case, then it is clear that the dimensions featured throughout this study represented some of these more than others. The most prominent were those identifying attitudes towards "power" ("social status and prestige, control or dominance over people and resources"), "conformity" ("restraint of actions, inclinations, and impulses likely to upset or harm others and violate social expectations or norms"), "tradition" ("respect, commitment and acceptance of the customs and ideas that traditional culture or religion provide the self"), "universalism" ("understanding, appreciation, tolerance and protection for the welfare of all people and for nature") and "security" ("safety, harmony and stability of society, of relationships, and of self"). Less present were the more personal ones found under the concepts of "achievement", "hedonism", "stimulation" "self-direction" and "benevolence".

Other scales were more concerned with the here and now of politics as it was relevant to the respondents. Examples include the Optimism and Intra-Party Elitism scales.

Purpose and derivation of the scales

The full wording of the items that make up each scale can be found in Appendix 3 and their purpose can be discerned from this. However, since they play such an important role in the analyses in the following chapters the name of each and a word or two about their purpose – what construct or issue they seek to illustrate – is set out in alphabetical order:

- *Authoritarianism:* Law and order; morality.

---

[76] Judd, Smith & Kidder, 1991: 147
[77] *European Social Survey*, 2007[e]: 235.
[78] *European Social Survey*, 2007[f]: 262.
[79] *European Social Survey*, 2007[f]: 267-268, 294-296.

- *Environmentalism:* State of the earth and the environment; individual/government responsibilities.

- *Europeanism:* UK's relationship with the European Union

- *Feminism:* Role of women in society at large.

- *Intra-Party Elitism*: Control or running of the Conservative Party

- *Intra-Party Inclusivity:* Promoting women and minorities within the Conservative Party.

- *Left-Right:* Economic relations; egalitarianism versus inegalitarianism

- *Optimism:* Present state and future fortunes of the Conservative Party

- *Political Elitism:* Control or running of the government and country

- *Postmaterialism:* Physical security versus self-expression.

- *Pride in Heritage and Culture*: Of the UK

- *Pride in the Way the Nation Functions*: Of the UK

- *Protectionism:* Towards foreign goods/services.

- *Religiosity:* Personal religious beliefs.

- *Theocratism:* Role of religion in public life.

- *Traditional British Liberties*: ID cards, jury trials etc.

- *Welfarism:* State versus personal responsibility

- *Xenophobia:* Towards foreign people

Table 2.1 provides more information about these scales, specifically the number of individual items within each and its derivation. The derivation refers to any direct connection between other studies and the *CPRS 2002*. However, many of the non-original scales are frequently encountered elsewhere in at least somewhat similar forms.[80]

---

[80] *European Social Survey*, 2007[e]: 236.

TABLE 2.1: MULTI-ITEM SCALES: NUMBER OF ITEMS AND DERIVATION		
Scale	Items	Derived from…
Authoritarianism	7	*British Social Attitudes* series[81]
Environmentalism	5	*British Social Attitudes* series[82]
Europeanism	7	Baker *et al*[83]
Feminism	5	*British Representation Study 1997*[84]
Intra-Party Elitism	3	Lees-Marshment & Quayle[85]
Intra-Party Inclusivity	3	*British Election Panel Study 1997-1998*[86]
Left-Right	5	*British Social Attitudes* series[87]
Optimism	10	Original to the *CPRS 2002*
Political Elitism	4	Copus[88]
Postmaterialism	4	Ronald Inglehart[89]
Pride in Heritage and Culture	5	*British Social Attitudes Survey 1995*[90]
Pride in Way the Nation Functions	4	*British Social Attitudes Survey 1995*[91]
Protectionism	5	*British Social Attitudes Survey 1995*[92]
Religiosity	3	*International Social Survey Programme's* survey *Religion I*[93]
Theocratism	3	*International Social Survey Programme's* survey *Religion I*[94]
Traditional British Liberties	4	Original to the *CPRS 2002*
Welfarism	8	*British Social Attitudes* series[95]
Xenophobia	8	*British Social Attitudes Survey 1995*[96]

[81] NCSR, 29th October 2008[d].
[82] NCSR, 29th October 2008[a].
[83] Baker *et al*, 1998.
[84] Norris, 1997.
[85] Lees-Marshment & Quayle, April 2000.
[86] Heath, Jowell & Curtice, 1999.
[87] NCSR, 29th October 2008[d].
[88] Copus, April 2000.
[89] Inglehart, 1990: 74-75.
[90] Dowds & Young, 1996.
[91] Dowds & Young, 1996.
[92] Dowds & Young, 1996.
[93] *ISSP*, 1991.
[94] *ISSP*, 1991.
[95] NCSR, 29th October 2008[c].
[96] Dowds & Young, 1996.

The two scales noted as being original to the *CPRS 2002*, Optimism and Traditional British Liberties, were not piloted as they were relatively late inclusions. Whilst statistically robust, the latter made little impact on the analyses below. However, as will be seen in particular in the chapter on the Party's 2001 leadership contest, Optimism, which looked at attitudes towards the present state and likely fortunes of the Party, was a more successful development. It was largely a product of what were originally intended to be a range of stand-alone items about the Party but which provably amounted to something more.

Subject ordering

The ordering of blocks of topics, and hence multi-item scales, was not haphazard. In particular, relatively personal questions were deliberately left to the end for fear of putting off some respondents.[97] Other than that, there was no need to order the blocks in the sense that there was a logical requirement either to have answered one before another or not to have done so.[98]

There is evidence that there can be a fall-off of response rate for batteries placed near the end of a lengthy questionnaire.[99] However, it is hard to calculate whether this was the case with the *CPRS 2002* questionnaire since, looking at the multi-item scales, it is difficult to untangle presentation order, the number of component items, the position of items on the page and the nature of the subject of the items. However, an informed opinion can be arrived at. Response rates were analysed for the first *item* at the top of each page where these all used the same five-level Likert-type response sets. Little detail is required. Based upon the whole dataset of 505 respondents, response rates for these items were remarkably consistent at between 97% and 100%. In other words, there is little evidence of any fall-off in response rate based upon how far along the questionnaire was the item.

The influence of the ordering of individual items within subject blocks is equivocal.[100] It was accepted as something about which little could be done within the constraints of our study. For example,

---

[97] Bryman, 2008: 204.

[98] Bryman, 2008: 202-203; Moser & Kalton, 1971: 346.

[99] Moser & Kalton, 1971: 347.

[100] Duffy, 2004; Siminski, 2008.

it was impractical to create and despatch multiple versions of the questionnaire even if this was methodologically acceptable.[101]

The direction of the wording of individual items is another matter. The potential problems of a response set and "the tendency to answer all questions in a specific direction regardless of their content"[102] caused by wording all questions in the same direction – such as all "agree" responses indicating Euro-sceptic views – are well known. Wherever possible the use of such unbalanced sets[103] was avoided. However, often it could not be. In particular, some of the more important multi-item dimensions such as the Authoritarianism scale are often encountered in an unbalanced format despite there being evidence for some effects on responses because of this.[104] However, in practice the effects may often be small[105] particularly amongst the better-educated[106] which, certainly relative to the general public, includes the majority of our respondents as demonstrated in Chapter 4.

Whatever the effects of unbalanced sets of items, since a direct comparison between our respondents and the British general public of approximately the same period formed a part of some of the analyses this problem had to be accepted. Again, this meant that potential solutions such as multiple versions of a questionnaire with different item ordering could not be used.

Presentation of Items in the Questionnaire

Types of item

Most of the items were about attitudes, beliefs or normative standards and values.[107] These terms are used in this book somewhat interchangeably and in an everyday sense. A psychologist might argue that, for example, "attitudes" are themselves an enduring system of

---

[101] Bryman, 2008: 204.
[102] Frankfort-Nachmias & Nachmias, 1996: 263.
[103] Evans & Heath, 1995: 192.
[104] Heath *et al*, 1991: 9-17.
[105] Evans & Heath, 1995: 191.
[106] Evans & Heath, 1995: 192 & 202; Heath et al, 1991: 22.
[107] Bryman, 2008: 239.

associated "beliefs".[108] However, this is a work of political science and not political psychology.

There was a much smaller range of behavioural and experiential items. These included respondents' experiences of fighting elections, behaviour and attitudes during the Party's 2001 leadership contest, background in the Party and use of the Internet.

Local councillors in England were also presented with a range of socio-demographic items such as sex, age, occupation and duration of Party membership. These were deliberately not asked of the other respondents. Many of the other groups consisted of small numbers of individuals and it was believed that asking such people these types of questions would lead to identifying individual respondents, thus going against the promise of anonymity and not just confidentially made in the introductory letter printed on page 1 of the questionnaire reproduced in Appendix 5. In turn, it was feared that this would lower the response rate. Of course, anonymity meant that sending out reminders and duplicate questionnaires – even if practical, which it was not – was impossible.[109]

Response options

The majority of attitudinal items within the questionnaire used a Likert-type response set.[110] The majority of *these* used a five-point, "Agree strongly" to "Disagree strongly" response set including a "neither/nor mid-point option. Where this was not the case this was often because the items concerned factual issues such as socio-demographic indicators or else the source of the items and scales used a different set of response options. Where appropriate this will be made clear in the thematic chapters.

In almost all cases respondents were not offered a "Don't know" option.

The use or not of mid-points and/or "Don't know" options continues to divide opinion concerning issues such as forcing responses, obtaining a stronger sense of the intensity of feeling or mitigating social desirability bias.[111]

---

[108] Cottam *et al*, 2010: 59-61, 131-132.

[109] Oppenheim, 1992: 105.

[110] Bryman, 2008: 146-147.

[111] Bryman, 2008: 244; Converse & Presser, 1986: 35-37; Garland, 1991: 70.

The choices offered within the questionnaire were for two reasons. First was the desire to maximise response rates from an often small number of potential respondents. It is likely that any forced responses would even out over the course of the whole dataset. Second, it was anticipated that some comparisons were to be made between data from the *CPRS 2002* questionnaire and that other from other studies. In those instances most *did* provide a mid-point option and did *not* provide a "Don't know" option.

Physical Design of the Questionnaire

Design overview

The questionnaire consisted of 20 pages or sides. There were two different versions of the questionnaire: one for local councillors in England and one for all others. In every case the front cover of page 1 carried an introductory letter from the researcher along with a set of instructions for respondents. In every case page 2 was left deliberately blank. In every case pages 3 to 18 consisted of a number of items dealing with the topics discussed above.

Most items were universal but there were a small number that only applied to some of the groups of respondents. For example, the unelected Peers were not asked about the nature of their constituency or ward. Where this was the case, there were clear instructions such as "For all except Peers" although any invalid responses would have been weeded out either at the data input or analysis stages.

Allowing for this and the very small number of questions that had a filter, there were approximately 215 questions in total on pages 3 to 18. For all respondents except ELCs, pages 19 and 20 were left deliberately blank. The version of the questionnaire for ELCs had two further pages, totalling 18 questions, on page 19 and the back cover, page 20. These pages contained the socio-demographic items noted above.

Since the questionnaire was to be sent to potential respondents and in turn sent back by them, it was of a paper type. Since all groups except ELCs shared exactly the same questionnaire in terms of content, the various groups were distinguished by a combination of having different coloured covers (i.e. pages 1, 2, 19, and 20) or using different sized paper as described in Table 2.2.

TABLE 2.2: TYPE, COVER COLOUR AND PAPER SIZE OF QUESTIONNAIRES			
Group	Type	Paper Size	Cover Colour
Local councillors in England (ELCs)	Full	A3	White
House of Lords (Peers)	Partial	A3	Blue
House of Commons (MPs)	Partial	A3	White
Local councillors in Scotland (SLCs)	Partial	A3	Orange
Local councillors in Wales (WLCs)	Partial	A3	Gold
European Parliament (MEPs)	Partial	A3	Pink
Scottish Parliament (MSPs)	Partial	A3	Green
Greater London Assembly (GLAs)	Partial	A4	Cream
Welsh Assembly (AMs)	Partial	A4	Red

A resized facsimile blank specimen of the questionnaire sent to ELCs can be found in Appendix 5. The other questionnaire has not been included since it was the same as the one for ELCs but with pages 19 and 20 left blank.

Creating the questionnaire

The questionnaire was created using the *SPSS Data Entry Builder*[112] software which had advantages over using a straightforward DTP package in that it automatically created both the data input mask and the *SPSS* file needed for subsequent analysis.

The introductory letter from Eric Forth

The questionnaire was accompanied by a separate introductory letter from Eric Forth, Conservative MP for Bromley and Chislehurst and the then Shadow Leader of the House of Commons. These were photocopies of an original written and signed on Mr Forth's House of Commons notepaper. The text of this can be found in Appendix 2.

A note about questionnaire length

The length of a questionnaire is likely to have some effect on response rate. Longer questionnaires will tend to have lower

---

[112] SPSS, 2006.

response rates than shorter ones because of the sheer length and/or because of the nature of any additional items not found in a hypothetical shorter version.[113] According to some authorities, questionnaires of the length of the ones used in this study in terms of both the number of pages and items[114] might be expected to experience a drop-off in response rate. However, there is no objective evidence that this was the case here and it was not possible to contact non-responders to ascertain the reasons for their non-response.

Deploying the Questionnaire

Possible methods

From the start, a self-completion postal survey was the only method of deploying the questionnaire that was seriously considered. It is true that face-to-face or telephone interviews can increase response rate by a substantial margin.[115] However, the hundreds of geographically widely distributed potential respondents made face-to-face interviewing wholly impractical. Telephone interviewing was just as impractical given the same problem plus the length of the questionnaire and, more importantly, the unlikelihood of being able to reach many of the respondents even with a notional contact number. Computer assisted personal (CAPI) or telephone (CATI) interviewing[116] were also not practical given the nature of the respondents and the resources and contact details available.

It was not plausible to use the Internet whatever the advantages are such as lower cost.[117] Email addresses were not available for many on the list of potential respondents (and general Internet access or lack thereof is discussed in Chapter 4 on the socio-demographics of ELCs). Even if they had been, it could not be guaranteed that such a large document would get through any firewall or anti-virus software even assuming that it could be

---

[113] Bryman, 2008: 221; Moser & Kalton, 1971: 263-264.
[114] Dillman, 1978: 55.
[115] Frankfort-Nachmias & Nachmias, 1996: 226.
[116] Bryman, 2008: 199.
[117] Bryman, 2008: 653.

accepted in the days before the widespread use of broadband, nor was it practical to design an online survey in the time available.[118] Moreover, as was anticipated, when asked about their use of email and the Internet in the actual questionnaire large minorities of some groups of respondents made little or no use of what was then relatively novel technology. The least "switched on", reporting use of email less often than once a week or never, were ELCs (23%), Peers (42%) and MPs (20%).

Despatch

All questionnaires were despatched from the University by normal second class post – or the appropriate EU postal rate to MEPs in the European Parliament in Brussels – in the first two weeks of April 2002. Along with the separate letter from Eric Forth all questionnaires were accompanied by a pre-paid, printed reply envelope addressed to the researcher at the University. The reply envelopes for the use of MEPs had the appropriate Belgian postage affixed.

Data Capture

It had been intended to electronically scan in the responses. However, because of the physical design of the questionnaire, the physical nature of responses and the technology available it proved impractical to do this. Instead, the data was manually entered over a deliberately prolonged six-month period to lessen the chances of error from fatigue.

As noted above, the use of *Data Entry Builder* to create the questionnaire also created a data input mask. This lessened the chances of error in manually entering the data since it prevented implausible responses being entered. For example, the number "6" cannot be entered for an item that only had five possible responses such as found in a standard "Agree strongly" to "Disagree strongly" response set.

---

[118] *BBC News*, 19th March 2003.

Responses

Response rates

The literature is equivocal about how high response rates have to be for a survey to be considered acceptable.[119] The actual response rates per group can be found in Table 2.3. Regarding the larger groups, the response rates varied by audience with that for Peers being rather low and that for MSPs very high. In general, the rates were between 35% and 45%. This was at the higher end for a postal survey without a follow-up[120] although somewhat lower than some comparable studies[121] although these often had the advantage of more resources such as seen in the use of reminders and duplicate questionnaires. In this respect the work of single researcher could not be expected to be comparable to the 70% or more that some high-end surveys obtain.[122]

Logistic constraints coupled with the promise of anonymity as well as what might be considered moral considerations meant that devices such as advance letters, reminders, duplicate questionnaires (which anyway have the problem of inviting more than one response) let alone such devices as monetary incentives were not used even though these might have an impact on response rates above that of a single-shot mailing.[123]

The true response rate is not merely the proportion of questionnaires returned but the proportion returned that are both fully completed and indicate that the respondent understood what they were doing and took the task seriously.[124] The returned questionnaires indicated little problem with the latter and, whilst not every item was completed by every respondent, most were fully and appropriately completed (the slight problem with the Postmaterialism scale is noted below). It cannot be stated objectively that respondents were taking the survey seriously. However, it is very unlikely that someone would bother to go through so many items "just for a laugh".

---

[119] Bryman, 2008: 219-220.
[120] Frankfort-Nachmias & Nachmias, 1996: 226.
[121] E.g. Denver *et al*, 1999[a]; 1999[b]; IaDA, 2001: 1; Baker *et al*, 2002)
[122] *European Social Survey*, 2007[j],; 2007[k].
[123] E.g. Boser, April 1990: 6; Frankfort-Nachmias & Nachmias, 1996: 230; Madhok *et al*, 1990; Nakash *et al*, 2006; Paul, Walsh & Tzelepis, 2005.
[124] Bryman, 2001.

TABLE 2.3: NUMBER OF QUESTIONNAIRES DESPATCHED AND RESPONSE PER GROUP			
Group	Sent	Returned	Response Rate
Local councillors in England (ELCs)	655	283	43%
House of Lords (Peers)	221	60	27%
Westminster MPs (MPs)	166	52	31%
Local councillors in Scotland (SLCs)	112	48	43%
Local councillors in Wales (WLCs)	70	28	40%
European Parliament (MEPs)	36	14	39%
Scottish Parliament (MSPs)	19	14	74%
Greater London Assembly (GLAs)	9	4	44%
Welsh Assembly (AMs)	8	2	25%
Total	1296	505	39%

Non-response is not a problem providing that "the people lost…
were themselves a random subset of the sample, but this is very unlikely
to be the case".[125] However, because of both the anonymity involved in
the study and also the deliberate omission of potentially identifying
items of a socio-demographic nature it is difficult to explore non-
response bias in most of the groups beyond the data presented in Table
2.3. For example, the response rate amongst all three groups of local
councillors was remarkably consistent. More will be said about this in
Chapter 4 about ELCs and how well the socio-demographic profile of
our respondents matched that of the statistical population.

Responses and the multi-item scales

As was noted above, the scales were not all of the same length in terms
of the number of individual items of which they were comprised. Nor
were the response rates for the scales: in other words the total number of
respondents who validly answered *all* items – no form of substitution
was employed such as using a mean figure for missing data although this
would have increased the valid response rates a little – for each scales.
Table 2.4 provides details about the response rates – based upon the 505
entered questionnaires – for the scales used.

---

[125] Sapsford, 1999: 95.

TABLE 2.4: MULTI-ITEM SCALES: RESPONSES AND RELIABILITY			
Scale	Responses	Response rate	Cronbach's alpha
Authoritarianism	492	97%	0.71
Environmentalism	484	96%	0.71
Europeanism	459	91%	0.73
Feminism	489	97%	0.62
Intra-Party Elitism	501	99%	0.69
Intra-Party Inclusivity	495	98%	0.80
Left-Right	488	97%	0.72
Optimism	484	96%	0.74
Political Elitism	493	98%	0.69
Postmaterialism	436	86%	n.a.
Pride in Heritage and Culture	489	97%	0.57
Pride in Way Nation Functions	489	97%	0.64
Protectionism	495	98%	0.61
Religiosity	482	95%	0.84
Theocratism	495	98%	0.74
Traditional British Liberties	477	94%	0.60
Welfarism	493	98%	0.72
Xenophobia	483	96%	0.84

The relatively poor response rate for Postmaterialism will be noted. A study of the returned questionnaires indicates that this was a presentational matter rather than anything to with the concept of Postmaterialism. Postmaterialism was different from the other scales in the way that the individual items were presented. Here, respondents had to make mutually exclusive first and second choices out of four options and this confused some respondents who provided invalid responses.

Except for Postmaterialism for the reason just indicated, bivariate analysis was conducted to see if there was a significant correlation between the number of items in a scale and the response rate for that scale. Although there was a negative correlation in that longer scales tended to have lower response rates it was not statistically significant: one-tailed $p = 0.13$ using the Pearson statistic.

Statistical robustness of the multi-Item scales

Before any of the multi-item scales could be used for analysis, it first had to be confirmed that they were statistically robust. This was done by using *SPSS* to calculate the Cronbach's alpha value using the entire *CPRS 2002* dataset. The alpha value is a measure of how well a set of variables measures a single construct, with the nearer to 1.0 the better. That said, there is no firm agreement as to how near to 1.0 the Cronbach's alpha value should be before a scale is considered acceptably robust.[126] However, a "liberal" level of 0.5 was treated as the minimum throughout this study. As can also be seen from Table 2.4, all of the scales displayed a value greater than this and usually much greater.

Most of the scales used in the various analyses below were constructed as intended. However, calculating the alpha value meant that in a small number of cases individual items that degraded the overall alpha value could be discarded prior to any further analysis. For example, the original version of the Intra-Party Elitism scale had five component items, but these were reduced to three items leading to a more robust scale. Similarly, testing the alpha value followed by factor analysis indicated that the initial version of the Theocratism dimension overlapped with Religiosity to a noticeable degree. Removal of two items remedied this overlap and also boosted the alpha value from 0.69 to 0.74.

Were Scales from within the Data Missed?

Even such a wide range of scales – even without taking into account stand-alone items which will be referred to in the following chapters – cannot hope to capture everything. What is not there, just is not there. However, it is possible to explore if anything was missed from *within* the data captured by the fieldwork. Specifically, whether the data suggested the presence of "underlying 'deep-rooted' value

---

[126] Bryman, 2008: 151; Bryman & Cramer, 1999: Campbell, 2004: 34; 65; Scarbrough, 2000: 410.

orientations"[127] not clearly covered by the range of named multi-item scales such as Left-Right and Authoritarianism.

This was done by taking together all of the items making up the named scales – except for Postmaterialism because of its unusual nature – plus almost all other stand-alone items presented with a comparable response set. In total, this amounted to 148 items. All of these items were loaded into a confirmatory factor analysis in *SPSS* with varimax rotation, with principal components extraction, with the maximum iterations eventually raised to 55, rotated factor solution, with only Eigenvalues over 1 extracted and with absolute values less than 0.3 suppressed. The entire dataset was used without distinction between the groups of respondents.

The analysis produced 45 factors and these were unremarkable. No hitherto undetected factors emerged that could not be explained by reference to either the named scales or clearly related items that might result in factors in a statistical sense such as items concerned with views on proportional representation at different levels of electoral representation.

From within the data there was little that suggested that anything major had been missed in the way of undiscovered and unused attitudinal scales that might have had substantial additional explanatory power in the various multivariate analyses described in the chapters below. (When the data was examined in finer, topic-related detail, there was the inkling of a scale concerned with views about the efficacy of local and/or participatory politics. This is discussed in Chapter 11.)

Choice of Multivariate Analysis

Brief mention must be made about why certain methods of inferential statistical analysis were used rather than others. In particular, why to a greater or lesser extent these were limited to analysis of variance (ANOVA), partial correlation coefficients (where a causal relationship was ambiguous), regression analysis (where a causal relationship could be justified) and factor analysis. The major reason refers back to the personal comments at the start of this report. It was always intended that the results of this study

---

[127] *European Social Survey*, 2007[e]: 235.

as presented should be comprehensible to those who formed the basis of the study. Without suggesting that there were a series of objective trials, experience with informally discussing or formally presenting the *CPRS 2002* to politicians, political activists and academics from outside the empirical social sciences indicated that the "in words" methods and results of (say) regression analysis were acceptable in this regard.

As noted elsewhere, the data captured by the fieldwork is available for further analysis by other researchers using different techniques if they so wish.

Presentation of Data

Level of data

As is often the convention within the social sciences, data produced by Likert scales was treated as interval or ratio level data rather than the ordinal level data that, strictly speaking, it is.[128] Particularly at the level of multivariate analysis, statistical analysis with such data "raw" is often the most appropriate method. Reporting it on the page, particularly with univariate or bivariate analysis, can be a different matter. In most cases in the following chapters for ease of reporting the data was collapsed into three-level categorical-level data. As such, except on occasions where responses were heavily loaded towards one pole, the "in betweens" are clearly identified.[129]

Base size and reported analysis

The sizes in absolute terms of some of the groups of respondents are very small and would have been even with a 100% response rate. This can cause problems. For example, some statistical tests have assumptions such as the minimum number of expected frequencies in any cell in chi^2.[130] Even at a basic descriptive level caution is urged when reporting in percentage terms where the base number is below

---

[128] Bryman, 2008: 322.
[129] Blastland, 5th August 2008.
[130] Clegg, 1982: 93.

50 and it is possibly an exercise in spurious accuracy when the base number is below 20.[131] From this perspective, reporting in percentage terms responses from ELCs (283 total respondents) is certainly acceptable and from Peers (60), MPs (52) and SLCs (48) probably so. A decision was made early on in the analysis that WLCs (28) and even MEPs and MSPs (14 each) would be reported, but where necessary the small numbers in absolute terms would be highlighted.

However, GLAs (4) and AMs (2) were too small to report. To save repetition, this explains the absence of these respondents in most of the tables in the following chapters where the results are analysed by group.

Unexplained variance and the danger of Scientism

What is not usually actively discussed in the following thematic chapters is unexplained variance.[132] This can arise both through normal differences amongst respondents – the fact that humans emit noisy data – and/or that there has been a systematic but unidentified omission in the independent variables used.

This is a routine problem within the social sciences. However, beyond the procedure described above that analysed whether any multi-item scales had gone undetected and unexamined nothing more can be made of this. Except, that is, to note the caution against scientism and "the belief that the methods and vocabulary of science can eventually account for the whole of reality".[133] They cannot. As one philosopher argued, "We should recognise that not all coherent questions about human nature and conduct are scientific questions, concerning the laws governing cause and effect."[134]

---

[131] Marsh, 1988: 126.
[132] Klassen, 12th September 2008.
[133] Lachman, 2003/2005: 58.
[134] Scruton, 17th March 2012.

3

Beyond "Left & Right": The Political Map

The Nature of the Problem

"And", not "but"

"Left" and "right" are amongst the most common shorthand terms used to describe the ideology – the "fundamental and enduring attitudes towards general moral and political principles"[135] – professed by an individual or group. The terminology is rooted in the French parliament of 1789-91 – when Royalists sat on the right of the room and revolutionaries on the left – although it probably did not take on its modern meaning about political parties until the late 19th or early 20th centuries.[136] The underlying assumption is that the ideology of any individual or group can be found somewhere along a bi-polar scale. So powerful is its hold that most people try to locate themselves or others within the confines of the model.[137] As one writer put it, "From Left to Right, most people would accept the following spectrum: communism → socialism → liberalism → conservatism → fascism".[138] Others have stated it straightforwardly in that the terms left and right are "fundamental to ideological debate".[139]

However, that something is in common usage does not mean that it is correct. An individual can believe in comprehensive tax-funded

---

[135] Heath *et al*, 1991: 2.
[136] Arthur, 2004: 10; Brittan, 1968: 32-33; Cossins, May 2012.
[137] Evans, Heath and Lalljee, 1996: 94; Harris, 1996.
[138] Heywood, 1992: 19.
[139] Rose & McAllister, 1990: 91.

welfare and state intervention in the economy, generally seen as a "left" position, *and* believe in the repatriation of certain immigrant groups and "traditional" gender roles, generally seen as a "right" position. Such combinations of views, combining economic and personal collectivism or traditionalism, are held by many that are sometimes described as "fascist". (It is unfortunate the terms such as "fascist" have become mere terms of abuse[140] whereas they describe potentially coherent – which does not necessarily mean correct, of course – sets of views.)[141]

On the other hand, an individual can believe in the wholesale denationalisation of the NHS and the education system, generally seen as a "right" position, *and* believe in the legalisation of narcotics and the right to engage in sado-masochism,[142] generally seen as a "left" position. Such combinations of views, combining economic and personal individualism, are held by many that are sometimes described as "libertarians".

Examples of pairs of individuals or regimes normally regarded as exemplars of left and right yet who or which share important features can be found in a number of places.[143] However, these often have another feature found in mass-media articles on the subject[144] which is that there is a sense that the problem has not been noticed before.

In short, whilst the one-dimensional left-right model may well be parsimonious it is demonstrably true that its use leads to a confusion of important political distinctions.[145]

Same words, different meanings

To describe the problem on another level, beyond just "brand name confusion",[146] it is that given words are but symbols lacking intrinsic meanings then their meanings must be agreed by mutual consent.[147] If people mean different things when using the same words then rational debate is impossible.[148] This is compounded when it is noted how

---

[140] Levitt, 2003; Wharton, 1999: 36.

[141] Paxton, 2004.

[142] Meek, 2006.

[143] E.g. Kenny, 5ᵗʰ February 2005.

[144] E.g. Delingpole, 28ᵗʰ February 2009; Riddell, 9ᵗʰ December 1997.

[145] Grendstad, 2003: 1.

[146] Finemann, in Fritz, 1988.

[147] Gabb, 2011: 49-50.

[148] Nolan, 1971: 3.

certain words have changed their meanings over time, a frequently cited example being the word "liberal" which has not only undergone a semantic change since the 19th century[149] but which is internationally inconsistent as well.[150] Of course, this is equally true of the subject matter of the *CPRS 2002*. The problem of the upper case and lower case use of "conservative" in the UK to donate variously a party, an ideology and a temperament is well known.[151]

Moreover, even when labels such as "libertarian" or "fascist" or "conservative" are understood and used – and often they are not[152] – they are in practice often only categorical-level or nominal-level data. They do not convey some sense of relationship towards other views that, for all its faults, the left-right model does. Similarly, various terms are often used for single-issue labelling with little or no attempt at coherence between issues.

Matters possibly become even worse when commentators attempt to describe foreign politics using the traditional terminology. As one writer complained when noting the BBC's description of Iran's theocratic Guardian Council as being "dominated by right-wingers", did that mean that the Council believed in "free markets, and a smaller state?"[153]

To give an academic example of this confusion, two articles in the October 2008 issue of the *European Journal of Political Research* can be cited. The first, by Timothy Hellwig, 'Explaining the salience of left–right ideology in post-industrial democracies: The role of structural economic change', cites a number of studies which generally locate "left and right" as terms donating "positions on state involvement in the economy".[154] The topic of the second, by Jens Rydgren, 'Immigration sceptics, xenophobes or racists? Radical

---

[149] Lillie & Maddox, 1981: 63.

[150] Danziger, 1998: 42. Indeed, in the case of US politics, the apparently mutually exclusive and all-encompassing terms "liberal" and "conservative" seem to possess the same iron grip as "left" and "right" along with their associations with the Democratic and Republican parties respectively: Cottam *et al*, 2010: 132-141. As suggested by Chapter 6 below, the situation in the UK is more pluralist from a party-political perspective.

[151] Garnett, 2003[b]: 109; Norton, July-September 2008: 324.

[152] Friedman, 1999.

[153] Whittles, 11th January 2003.

[154] Hellwig, October 2008: 689

right-wing voting in six West European countries',[155] is self-explanatory and, *in the same issue of the same journal*, clearly takes "right-wing" to mean something rather different.

In short, there is a profound "conceptual failure common in most forms of modern political debate".[156]

Why is it Still Used?

Yet the obviously flawed left-right model continues to be used, even by commentators who have previously acknowledged its failings.[157] A number of reasons have been suggested for this.[158] For example: its very familiarity and simplicity such as the way that it can be depicted on a piece of paper[159] ensures its continuing use by "custom and practice"; that those who cannot be readily situated along the dimension can be dismissed as "inconsistent";[160] and because the traditional model is indeed sometimes "accidentally correct", lending validity to it.[161]

It has also been argued[162] that it can be use to "smear" individuals or groups with labels that possess at the time objectionable connotations. This was seen very clearly in the treatment accorded to the eventually assassinated Dutch politician Pim Fortuyn. He was routinely associated with "fascist" or "right-wing" politics because of his views on Islam and immigration despite professing and living a life of considerable social and economic "liberalism".[163]

At a psychological level, it may also be a manifestation of a seemingly hard-wired tendency that humans have to analyse the social world in a bipolar "us or them" manner.[164] This may be an evolutionary

---

[155] Rydgren, October 2008.
[156] Evans, 1996: xiii.
[157] Riddell, 9th December 1997; 20th September 2004.
[158] Lillie & Maddox, 1981: 61 & 64.
[159] 'JK', 11th January 2000.
[160] Cottam *et al*, 2010: 135.
[161] Herrera, 1993, in Herbst, 1998: 128-129.
[162] Halcombe, 1996.
[163] Boyes, 7th May 2002; Riddell, 23rd April 2002; Browne, 1st January 2003; Meek, 9th May 2002; *The Spectator*, 7th February 2004.
[164] Baron & Byrne, 1994: 228-229; Crisp, 2002.

device to limit the amount of cognitive processing required in stressful situations.[165]

Proposed Solutions

What is to be done? Or rather, *what else can be devised and used to describe the political views of an individual or group in a manner that is both more meaningful than the left-right model and which is still reasonably comprehensible to "the intelligent layperson"?* If a measure of success in these two tasks can be achieved, then our respondents can be analysed and then compared to the general public of the time.

To tackle this long-acknowledged problem a number of solutions have been proposed.[166] From the worlds of political science, sociology, opinion polling, political philosophy and psychology they have included:

- To describe a near-circular or horseshoe scale whereby "extreme Left" and "extreme Right" almost meet up.[167] As has been acidly noted, this concept, used by serious writers[168] and bar-room philosophers alike, means that Western liberal democracy is thus defined as being halfway between Stalin and Hitler.[169] Or, as Ludwig von Mises asked,[170] "What is 'left' and what is 'right'? Why should Hitler be 'right' and Stalin, his temporary friend, be 'left'?"

- A single scale that more specifically defines its end-points as representing complete collectivism and complete anarchism.[171]

---

[165] Such rumination aside, it is worthy of a major interdisciplinary study just to look at why such an obviously flawed model as "left and right" retains its hegemonic grip on popular and academic political discourse.

[166] Bergland, 1993: 30.

[167] Lester, 1995: 1.

[168] Thompson, 2000: 103.

[169] Aaronovitch, 28th June 2005; Nolan, 1971: 4.

[170] von Mises, 1940.

[171] Burns, 1989, in Evans, 1996: 81-82.

- The sometimes *ad hoc* models of political polling organisations.[172]

- A triangular model with the major historical strands of British politics of socialism, liberalism and conservatism all pulling against each other.[173]

- Various personality scales such as "Conservatism-Radicalism", "Egalitarianism-Elitism", "Radicalism-Orthodoxy" and "Liberalism-Authoritarianism".[174]

- More sophisticated variants of the standard two-dimensional model whereby, for example, attitudes towards socio-economic egalitarianism are mediated via means to various ends[175] or by intensity of feeling towards the various possible positions on the scale[176] or the degree of "reason" in any given ideological system.[177]

- A series of one-dimensional scales which are relative to the ideological standpoint of the analyst.[178]

- The use of statistical techniques such as multidimensional scaling "to detect meaningful underlying dimensions".[179]

- The taxonomies and models developed or used by academic researchers.[180]

Others have taken a different approach. They argue that the "old" ideological cleavages and political alliances have weakened.[181] Instead, they have been superseded by or at least must now include "new" or alternative politics[182] such as environmentalism,[183]

---

[172] Evans, Heath & Lalljee, 1996: 93.

[173] Hayek, 1960: 398; Greenleaf, 1983.

[174] Brittan, 1968: 87-99; 1976: 354-373; Eysenck, 1954; Wilson, 1973: 184.

[175] Bobbio, 1996.

[176] Caplan, 1997.

[177] Pournelle, 1986.

[178] Tansey, 1995: 104.

[179] StatSoft, 2003.

[180] E.g. 6, 1998: 26-27 & 80-82; Baker, Gamble & Ludlum, 1994[b]; Cowley & Stuart, 2004; Gamble, 1974: 213-214; Grenstad, 2003; Heppell 2002 & 2005; Heppell & Hill, September 2005; Norton, 1990 & 2002; Peele, 1997: 102-107; Whiteley, Seyd & Richardson, 1994.

[181] *European Social Survey*, 2007[d]: 191; Gibbins, 1989: 23.

[182] Inglehart, 1989: 250-251.

feminism[184] and Postmaterialism.[185] In short, a shift away from values concerned with "consumption and material progress" towards values centred on "personal autonomy and identity".[186] Alternatively, others have stressed the importance of cultural, ethnic, and/or national identity.[187] Others have suggested taking a more pragmatic or case-by-case approach.[188]

However, whilst some of these provide interesting and important analyses, none are wholly acceptable. Their problems may include: being conceptually unclear; being largely descriptive or qualitative rather then quantitative; being of little use in describing ideology in a manner that is both reasonably comprehensive *and* comprehensible to the non-specialist; being overly dependant on time and/or place; or simply failing to conform to the conventions of methodological good practice in political science.[189]

Another Solution: The Political Map

It is not the intention of this chapter to start from scratch and to investigate all possible alternatives to the standard left-right model. Instead, an alternative is noted and refined which in some form can already be found in academic literature and which in a populist and often unsatisfactory form already exists as a tool for describing ideological positions.

The literature indicates that many researchers wishing to go beyond left and right have come to the same conclusion and therefore have used much the same solution.[190] This solution has two components. First, that two dimensions or axes are used to describe "core political beliefs and values"[191] rather than the single dimension of the left-right model. Whether this is for theoretical or practical reasons can only be judged on a case-by-case basis. However, a two

---

[183] Nas, 1995.
[184] Lundmark, 1995.
[185] Inglehart, 1990.
[186] Gundelach, 1995: 412.
[187] Cable, 1994.
[188] Brittan, 27th September 2002.
[189] Bryman, 2008; Gunter & Furnham, 1992: 99; Meek, 1999: 3-4.
[190] E.g. Campbell, 2004; Schofield, Miller & Martin, 2003; Topf, 1989: 69.
[191] Evans & Heath, 1995: 191.

dimensional model has the advantage that whilst it has the potential to be far more informative than a one-dimensional model it can still be depicted on the page. Three dimensions can still be presented physically, but more than three becomes a mathematical abstract.

Second, that these two dimensions measure matters connected with economics or socio-economic relationships on the one hand and civil liberties, morality or law and order on the other. Some authorities have argued for the paramount importance of these two dimensions.[192] Heath and Topf[193] argued that,

> "... we need to consider two contrasting sets of values and perceptions. The first set relates to the economic order of society, in particular economic equality and perceived conflicts... The second set of values relates to social order and covers such matters as civil liberty and respect for the law. These two sets of variables might be said to represent the two most fundamental ideological principles in contemporary society."

Fleishman[194] argued that a,

> "... two-dimensional model adequately describes the structure of social attitudes. General orientations to economic welfare, on the one hand, and individual liberties on the other, organize attitudes toward more narrowly focused issues and objects... implying a dualistic model".

Aspects of economics or socio-economic relationships, are generally regarded by political scientists as one of the most important dimensions along which political parties compete.[195] Furthermore, it "has also been widely argued that the most important value orientation to cut across the left-right (*sic*) dimension is a libertarian-authoritarian one".[196]

---

[192] Evans & Heath, 1995: 191; Sanders, July 2006: 179.
[193] Heath & Topf, 1987: 59.
[194] Fleishman, 1988, in Heath *et al*, 1991: 3.
[195] *European Social Survey*, 2007[d]: 191.
[196] *European Social Survey*, 2007[e]: 241.

For the purposes of this chapter this particular two-component solution is accepted and from now on it shall be referred to by the name "Political Map" or "PoliMap" for short. Problematic versions of it, often using the name "Political Compass", are available on the Internet and elsewhere as self-administered tests such as the one provided by the politically committed Advocates for Self-Government[197] and the one provided by the ostensibly politically neutral PoliticalCompass.org.[198] (A number of them are presented in once place by the Liberty League,[199] which itself is indicative of who is most vexed by the problem of "left and right".)

It should be noted that the PoliMap developed in this chapter does not derive from any of the other alternatives to the standard left-right model described above. Instead, it is a synthesis of two multi-item scales used in this study. It is a means of combining attitudes towards two areas of great social and economic importance to produce a more meaningful yet still comprehensible picture of an individual's or organisation's *Weltanschauung*.[200]

The Political Map Used in this Analysis

The design, layout and naming of the PoliMap

So far this alternative method has been described only in outline. The creation of the model used in this chapter has now to be described. However, to avoid repetition the method by which the PoliMap was created – such as statistical considerations – is described in greater detail in the section following this one. This section is primarily concerned with its physical design.

The PoliMap is formed by separately measuring attitudes along two scales – from now on termed "Economic" and "Personal" – useable as measures of the sorts of economic and personal beliefs noted above. Then these measures, using a standardised scale so that a like measure on one equals a like measure on the other, are joined at a right-angle at one end: the lowest possible score for both in this

---

[197] Advocates for Self-Government, c. 2003
[198] PoliticalCompass.org, 2004[a].
[199] Liberty League, n/k.
[200] Jary & Jary, 1991: 708.

case. The scores along both scales are traced perpendicular to the axes and where the scores meet this is the respondent's position within the PoliMap.

The basic model is shown in Diagram 3.1a. "0" represents the lowest possible score along either axis and "1" represents the highest possible score. It also displays the position of a hypothetical respondent who has views that are individualist or laissez-faire or a similar description along the Economic scale and who also has views that are collectivist or traditionalist or a similar description along the Personal scale. The "X" is the meeting point for the separate scores from the two scales used as measures for the PoliMap.

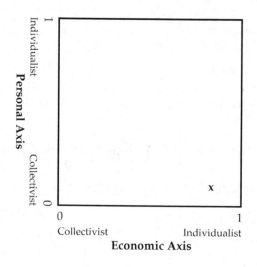

Diagram 3.1a: The basic PoliMap

As it is, particularly when used to collect date from numerous cases, this provides a scatter-plot with a wide range of possible positions within the PoliMap. Although this can elicit useful information this is hard to use as an everyday description of political attitudes.

Therefore, three-level ordinal categories of the sort used throughout this book are used by recoding each scale into three levels measured in absolute terms, i.e. the lowest, middle and highest thirds of possible scores on each scale.

Using these measures produces a PoliMap containing nine internal sectors as shown in Diagram 3.1b. Again, "X" marks the position of a hypothetical respondent who has views that are individualist or laissez-faire or a similar description along the Economic scale and who also has views that are collectivist or traditionalist or a similar description along the Personal scale.

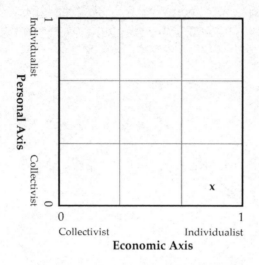

Diagram 3.1b: The Basic PoliMap with internal sectors

Certain presentational issues need to be dealt with here. It has become the convention in some of the existing (if flawed) versions of what is here called the PoliMap to rotate the model so that the sector combining individualist positions along both scales forms the top of the PoliMap and the sector combining collectivist positions along both scales forms the bottom. There is no right or wrong to this presentation. If it is thought that such a layout of the diagram implies a more positive view of the top-most sector then the model can be flipped if so desired.

The other orientation has a certain commonsense justification. The PoliMap sector that combines an individualist position on the Economic scale and a collectivist position on the Personal scale is placed on the right and the sector that combines a collectivist position on the Economic scale and an individualist position on the Personal scale is placed on the left. This is because these sectors somewhat conform to stereotypical notions of left and right of the sort noted near the start of this chapter. It surely makes sense to retain this degree of familiarity.

There is also the matter of the nomenclature of the sectors. As far as possible the names used must make sense in describing what one is physically seeing and also that they should strive to be affectively neutral. A number of methods have been used[201] including somewhat messy terminological hybrids. Instead, the version used in this study uses the conventional points of the compass. The final PoliMap can now be displayed in Diagram 3.2.

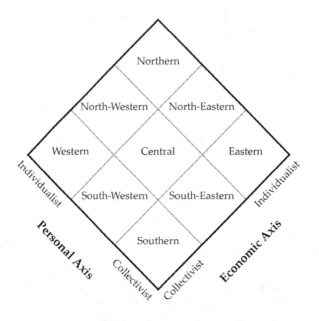

Diagram 3.2: The PoliMap

Those falling into each of the nine sectors of the PoliMap can be described as follows in terms of their political beliefs. Starting at the top-most sector and moving clockwise:

- Northern (N): an individualist position on both axes.
- North-Eastern (N-E): Economic individualism combined with a centrist position on the Personal axis.
- Eastern (E): Economic individualism combined with Personal collectivism.

---

[201] Lester, 1995; Lopez, 2002; PoliticalCompass.org, 2004[b].

- South-Eastern (S-E): a centrist position on the Economic axis combined with Personal collectivism.

- Southern (S): a collectivist position on both axes.

- South-Western (S-W): Economic collectivism combined with a centrist position on the Personal axis.

- Western (W): Economic collectivism combined with Personal individualism.

- North-Western (N-W): a centrist position on the Economic axis combined with Personal individualism.

- Central (C): a centrist position on both axes.

The hypothetical respondent located in the previous diagrams would be located in the Eastern sector: Economic individualism combined with Personal collectivism.

Something like the PoliMap used in this chapter appears to have been in existence since the late 1960s or early 1970s although the original authorship is disputed.[202]

A finite world

There is a conceptual issue that needs to be acknowledged. The PoliMap is like an ancient map of the earth in that it describes a world that is flat and finite. As for the first of these, the possibilities and problems of additional dimensions are discussed elsewhere in this chapter.

As for the second, it is certainly possible to find (say) individuals who are more extreme than would be suggested even by someone who responded in the most extreme manner to all the questions put to them to determine their score on the Personal and Economic scales and hence their position on the PoliMap.

However, whilst in theory there may be no edge of the ideological world for such individuals to sail off, in practice they represent vanishingly small tails of the distribution and they do not delegitimize the PoliMap within the context of providing a device of service to everyday debate.

---

[202] Nolan, 1971.

Arguments Against the Model and Responses

Objections raised

A number of objections have been raised against the PoliMap, all of which have at least some validity and which must be addressed. Moreover, in doing so, the creation of the PoliMap used in this chapter can be described in greater detail.

There is only one dimension

Some commentators have argued from certain philosophical positions that there *is* only one, indivisible dimension[203] such as from freedom to unfreedom or anarchy to omnarchy and that all aspects of political debate revolve around this single issue. Perhaps this is true according to some political philosophies. It certainly makes more sense than the Stalin-to-Hitler, left-right one-dimensional model.[204] However, if the aim the of this chapter is to describe the political views of an individual or group in a manner that is more meaningful than the left-right model but which is still reasonably comprehensible to the layperson, then the PoliMap does a better job. Indeed, even some of those who argue for the principle of a single dimension accept the socio-political reality of the two-dimensional model used by the PoliMap.[205] There is also a real-world and statistically demonstrated rebuttal of this objection that is examined in greater detail below.

It must be stressed again that the PoliMap is not an exercise in esoteric political philosophy. It is a device to shed light on everyday political debate that amongst other things will enable at least the more interested of the general public to visualise the political positions of individuals and parties both alone and relative to each other.[206]

An insufficiency of dimensions

The next objection is the mirror image of the first. Even amongst some who accept that the PoliMap is better than the standard left-right model

---

[203] Skousen, 2000; Roberts, 14th February 2004.
[204] Arthur, 2004: 11.
[205] Tame, 1998, in Meek, 1999: 5.
[206] Lent & Sowemimo, 1996: 137.

it is argued that it is limited in its scope and in particular that it omits issues to do with foreign and military affairs.[207] This is of particular salience when one considers the less-than-uniform Conservative response to world events since the 11th September 2001,[208] the continuing importance of the EU to internal Conservative Party debate,[209] and the debate over protectionism.[210] Others have also noted the continuing importance of religion,[211] something not directly covered by the PoliMap.

Accordingly, some have used an axis concerned with such issues as an *alternative* to one of those used in the "standard" PoliMap.[212]

Others have kept variants of the PoliMap's two dimensions but have added a third. For example, Ross[213] added one concerning the nature of political participation so that – to mix it in with the terminology of this present chapter – it is possible for an individual to be a "Anarchist-Northerner" or a "Monarchist-Northener" depending upon how one believes one's particular choices are best defended. This has echoes of a unipolar model sometimes encountered that talks of an "autocracy-democracy" continuum.[214] It is explicitly about how – if at all – power is transferred and only implicitly about what policies are followed by whoever wields political power at the time. Alternatively, the Vosem Chart retains the PoliMap's Personal and Economic axes but adds a third axis concerning "corporate issues" and whether businesses can be considered as private individuals with all their rights.[215] With specific reference to the lack of mention of military and foreign policy issues in the standard PoliMap, Quintiliani[216]

---

[207] Blundell & Gosschalk, 1997: 9-10.

[208] Duncan Smith, 1st September 2002; Nixon, 17th May 2003.

[209] Burdett-Conway & Tether, 1997: 89-90; Cowley & Norton, 1999: 90; Heppell, 2002; 2005.

[210] Congdon, 9th September 2000.

[211] Nelson, Guth & Fraser, 2001; Van Deth, 1995: 1.

[212] Baker, Gamble & Ludlum, 1993 & 1994[b]; Dunleavy, 1993; Heath, Jowell & Curtice, 1985: 116-121.

[213] Ross, 2004.

[214] Fox & Sandler, 2003: 469.

[215] 3ebnut, 15th June 2003.

[216] Quintiliani, 2004.

takes the two existing dimensions and adds a third concerned with such matters.

A variant of this objection is that it does not distinguish between different individuals or groups that end up in the same sector of the PoliMap but who profess *philosophically* distinct ideologies.[217] This is addressed below.

A similar objection is that there is no attempt to identify any differences in the saliency for respondents of the dimensions used in the model. This has an importance when one considers the clear evidence that the issues that were most important for the public around the time of the fieldwork were not necessarily the ones on which the Conservative Party focussed.[218]

All of these objections make fair points. However, firstly, it has already been noted above that this chapter accepts the opinions of acknowledged authorities concerning the particular salience of the two dimensions used in the PoliMap. Secondly, the response is the same as in the previous sub-section: that the two-dimensional PoliMap does a better job of describing political debate in a comprehensible manner: and certainly in the simplified "desert island" form sometimes used by economists.[219] A third dimension can always be added and the results can still be presented physically, albeit with difficulty. For example, both the Vosem Chart and Ross's model may be conceptually useful but are extremely hard to read. More than three dimensions and it becomes a formula of little use to anyone except the mathematician.

It should be emphasised that this model is primarily a measure of "how one should go about things in the real world". It does not distinguish between different philosophically-derived ends or justifications.[220] Equally, it does not inherently distinguish between normative and positive reasons for advocating this or that political direction. Indeed, politicians have been known to argue for normatively "awkward" policies on utilitarian grounds.[221] Hitler and Stalin may well have adhered to different philosophies and purposes

---

[217] de Havilland, 21st May 2003.
[218] Broughton, 2003: 208-209.
[219] Mankiw, 2001: 533-534.
[220] Gove, 1st January 2000.
[221] Conservative Party, 25th January 2002.

but their means had more than a passing resemblance to each other.[222] Looking at the mainstream of UK politics, previous work indicated that despite their ostensible differences *all* of the mainland UK political parties that won seats at the 1997 general election mapped into the same Centre sector of a somewhat differently configured PoliMap.[223] In short, it measures the "where" of the distribution of political beliefs rather than the "why".[224]

A study of the two dimensions actually used for this chapter's PoliMap noted in the next subsection suggests a good deal of trans-national applicability. Certainly this is true in the Anglophone world but also in much of the rest of the world following suitable translation. However, the more dimensions that are used then the greater the possibility that this trans-national applicability is lost. For example, a PoliMap analysis that added a third axis about attitudes towards the EU – and it appears that at least in a British context this is an issue that cuts across others similar to those measured by the Authoritarianism and/or Left-Right dimensions[225] – would have less relevance to a Bolivian or Ghanaian than it does to a Briton.

Poor questionnaire sets and evidence for multi-dimensionality

The next objection is methodologically the most important. It has been rightly claimed that the various questionnaire sets used in different versions of the PoliMap have often been unsound. In some manner or other they do not satisfy the conventions for the creation of acceptable multi-item dimensions.[226] For example, the World's Smallest Political Quiz (WSPQ), probably the most commonly encountered variant and the one used by many US libertarians,[227] clearly leads people into giving answers in a certain direction.[228] The

---

[222] Goldberg, 2009; Paxton, 2004: 212.

[223] Meek, 1999: 14.

[224] Ball, 1988: 227.

[225] Heath, Jowell, Taylor & Thomson, 1998: 100-101.

[226] Rupright, 1997.

[227] Advocates for Self Government, c. 2003; Taher, 24th October 2004.

[228] Huben, in Raphael, 1996.

version used by PoliticalCompass.org[229] is also somewhat biased, albeit in a different manner to that of the WSPQ,[230] and is also rather long. Others take a decidedly odd view of what one or both of the dimensions actually mean in practice.[231]

Besides being a reminder not to confuse a model in theory with its deployment in practice, there are ways around this problem. One solution is to make use of existing and proven dimensions that can be regarded as meaningfully representing the Economic and Personal dimensions.

For this study it was decided to use two dimensions with a long history[232] of use in social research. The Left-Right (*sic*) scale was used as the Economic dimension. It looks at attitudes towards issues such as business, trades unions and wealth. The Authoritarianism scale was used as the Personal dimension. It looks at attitudes towards issues such as conformism, censorship, homosexuality and the death penalty. Both of these have been used in the well-known annual *British Social Attitudes* (*BSA*) series[233] and were included in this study. The wording of the items making up these two dimensions can be found in Appendix 3.

The first objection noted above can now be returned to: the claim that there is only one dimension. Indeed, analysing responses using the entire *CPRS 2002* dataset to all 12 individual items from the Left-Right and Authoritarianism scales using the Cronbach's alpha test – a measure of how well a set of variables measures a single construct – provides a value of 0.69, suggesting a valid single dimension. However, in this instance it would be a mistake to take this result at face value. It is not the purpose here to argue for or against any *philosophical* argument that holds to the view that there is only one dimension. Instead, it can be demonstrated that *in practice* in the way that people think about these matters, if not necessarily consciously, there *is* more than one dimension.

By using factor analysis it could be determined whether the commonalties of individual items for the two scales were those of the multi-item scales used to describe the PoliMap. Again using the entire dataset, confirmatory factor analysis – using varimax rotation,

---

[229] PoliticalCompass.org, 2004[a].
[230] de Havilland, 21ˢᵗ May 2003.
[231] Rozenburg, 6ᵗʰ April 2005.
[232] Heath *et al*, 1991.
[233] E.g. NCSR, 29ᵗʰ October 2008[d].

with principal components extraction, with a maximum of 25 iterations, rotated factor solution, with only Eigenvalues over 1 extracted and with absolute values less than 0.3 suppressed – was carried out using the 12 individual items from the Left-Right and Authoritarianism scales. The result is not shown in any detail here because the finding was so clear. Factor 1 was simply Left-Right, containing all five items and none other, and Factor 2 was clearly Authoritarianism containing six of the seven items. As is sometimes the case with factor analysis there was also a weaker Factor 3 that contained some items from each. Little can be made of this and it may be no more than an artefact of the nature of the respondents.

The alpha value of 0.69 for the combined items from the Left-Right and Authoritarianism scales demonstrated that to some degree the separate items from the two dimensions are correlated with each other. At first sight this accords with those who suggest that something very like these two dimensions are not truly unrelated to each other.[234] Within the context of discussions about the Conservative Party this can also be seen in assertions that "Thatcherism" was "incoherent" since "while it preached economic freedom, it often practised social authoritarianism and the politics of intolerance".[235] However, the more detailed factor analysis clearly indicates that the actual rather than theoretical commonalties of responses to the individual items robustly fall along the two dimensions that were used for this version of the PoliMap. Attitudes towards economic and moral issues *are* correlated to each other.[236] However, for our respondents the components of objective measures of these issues are more strongly correlated *within* than *between* the two issues.

Unacceptable creation of internal sectors

As noted above, internal sectors need to be constructed in any variant of the model that wishes to do more than display the results as a two-dimensional scatter-plot. Exactly where respondents end up depends upon the geometry of the sectors.[237] However, other versions of the

---

[234] Janiskee, 15th October 2003; Nolan, 1971: 6-7.
[235] Evans, October 2004: 383; Redwood, 2005: 202.
[236] Heath *et al*, 1991: 1
[237] Lester, 1995: 3.

PoliMap have used methods of categorisation that, whilst not necessarily "wrong", can seem strange or cumbersome. For example, the five-sector WSPQ has a Centrist sector that is a different shape to the others[238] and there is in existence a nine-sector variant that uses three different sector sizes.[239]

Instead, as described above, a "pure" method of creating discrete categories or levels was used by recoding each of the dimensions into three levels measured in absolute terms – labelled "collectivist", "centrist" and "individualist" – thus providing a diagram of nine equal-sized and equal-shaped sectors.

The PoliMap and the Conservative Party

One issue that the media highlighted around the time of the fieldwork – for example in *The Times*, although that newspaper may have had its own agenda[240] – was the split in the Conservative Party between the "authoritarian Right" and the "libertarian Right"[241] that had once been the alliance at the core of "Thatcherism" towards instead a new coalition of the Conservative "Left"[242] united more on social issues than economic ones. This was sometimes picturesquely depicted as a struggle between "mods" professing social liberalism, "rockers" professing a more traditionalist view of things and the "muddled in the middle" self-evidently between the two.[243]

Taking a longer-term view, both academics and the mass media have argued for the presence of long-standing and often antagonistic factions within the Party: in particular the Left, the authoritarian Right and the libertarian Right or some variations upon the theme.[244] Within the context of the Conservative Party as mapped onto the PoliMap, these three groups could be interpreted as Centrist, Eastern/South-Eastern and Eastern/North-Eastern respectively.

---

[238] Advocates for Self-Government, 1995.
[239] Thies, 2000.
[240] Glover, 22nd June 2002.
[241] Baldwin, 2nd November 2000.
[242] Charter, 12th October 2002.
[243] Baldwin, Webster & Watson, 5th October 2000.
[244] Seyd, 1980; Pilbeam, 1998: 280-281; The Times, 3rd November 2000.

The point of this for the purposes of the present chapter is that, explicitly or implicitly, it has been noted by others that matters that are plausibly to do with the Personal scale are different from issues connected with the Economic scale let alone traditional notions of "left and right".

The Dimensions Considered Separately

The responses to the Authoritarianism and Left-Right dimensions broken down into three categories and also by group of respondent can be found in Appendix 4 and little needs to be restated here. Regarding Authoritarianism, all groups of respondents split between the "authoritarian" and "in between" categories with almost no "libertarians". Regarding Left-Right, all groups split between the "right" (*sic*) and "in between" categories with almost none on the economic "left". Greenleaf[245] was therefore largely correct to say that Conservatism has a "twin inheritance" of individualism and collectivism. Overall, Conservative representatives were inclined towards individualist views on the economy or at least not inclined towards economic collectivism, and inclined towards social and personal collectivism or at least not inclined towards social individualism.

Whilst from these findings it cannot be predicted how the Personal and Economic axes will interact, some predictions of a negative nature can be made. In particular, it can be predicted that Conservative representatives will map onto only a limited area of the PoliMap since it can be known that there will be very few or no respondents in those sectors dependent upon respondents falling into certain sectors along the Authoritarianism and Left-Right dimensions. These unpopulated sectors will be the Northern, Southern and all those with the West suffix.

Conservative Politicians on the PoliMap

All respondents on the PoliMap

At this stage the positions of our respondents can be mapped. Table 3.1 shows the positions of the respondents within the nine sectors of

---

[245] Greenleaf, 1983: 189.

the PoliMap broken down by respondent group. Diagram 3.3 shows the same analysis for ELCs transposed onto an actual PoliMap by way of (literal) illustration.

TABLE 3.1: POLIMAP SECTORS BY GROUP							
Sector	**ELCs**	**Peers**	**MPs**	**SLCs**	**WLCs**	**MEPs**	**MSPs**
Northern	2%	0%	0%	0%	0%	0%	0%
North-Eastern	19%	36%	43%	25%	23%	43%	39%
Eastern	22%	22%	18%	25%	12%	21%	15%
South-Eastern	31%	13%	12%	25%	50%	7%	23%
Southern	5%	0%	0%	0%	0%	0%	0%
South-Western	2%	0%	0%	0%	0%	0%	0%
Western	0%	0%	0%	0%	0%	0%	0%
North-Western	1%	2%	2%	0%	0%	0%	0%
Central	18%	27%	25%	25%	15%	29%	23%
Base	266	55	51	44	26	14	13

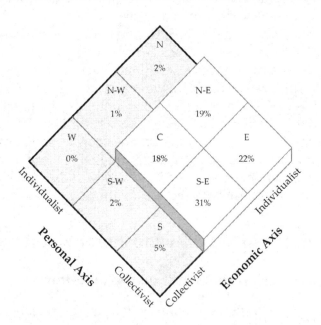

Diagram 3.3: PoliMap distribution of ELCs

Certain findings stand out. Looking at all of the groups together, and in line with the predictions made above, there were no respondents located in the Western sector, and virtually none in the Northern, North-Western, South-Western and Southern sectors. Out of the nine sectors in the PoliMap only four contain substantial numbers of respondents: Central, Eastern, North-Eastern and South-Eastern.

Significantly, these four sectors are contiguous. Within the PoliMap they form a mini-PoliMap of their own. Interestingly, when the diagram is examined, within the context of the two-dimensional PoliMap it is quite legitimate to describe the Conservative Party as "centre-right". However, this statement has a degree of meaning wholly absent when that term is used in the conventional sense. Here it describes a political party whose public representatives could be described as adhering to a set of beliefs that are generally economically individualist and personally collectivist but with a strong "moderating" influence.

Whether it was ever true that "the Conservative party acts or thinks as unrelated, *ad hoc* groups of members, groups whose members join together to contend for one specific objective, and then fall apart once the goal has been attained or has been by-passed by events",[246] it is clear that our respondents inhabited a constrained part of this ideological map. Overall, in terms of its politicians at least, the Conservative Party was not a catchall, open-forum debating society. When "allowed" to step away from here-and-now issues and focus instead on something deeper and more enduring, then the "all over the place" attitudes described at the top of this book turn into something more coherent.

This has a further implication that whilst new leaders of the Party *qua* artificial entity may change the Party's policies and/or image in search of votes they cannot so easily change the Party *qua* aggregate of attitudes.[247]

There were some differences between the groups of representatives. Looking at the four sectors containing substantial numbers of respondents, SLCs were evenly divided between them.

---

[246] Finer, Berrington & Bartholomew, 1961: 110.
[247] Goldberg, 28th January 2004. By the time that this book went to print, David Cameron was beginning to discover this.

There was a noticeable difference between the "senior" representatives of MEPs, MPs, MSPs, and Peers on the one hand and WLCs on the other. In the case of the former groups, a plurality fell into the North-Eastern sector, a fair number fell into the Central and Eastern sectors and relatively few – except in the case of MSPs – fell into the South-Eastern sector. It might be argued that overall this indicates a tendency towards that brand of conservatism noted above as "liberal conservatism", either of a more recent kind[248] or elements of an older "New Right" that questioned whether such things as sexual morality were a wholly legitimate pursuit for a cause that in general promised to "set the individual free".[249] On the other hand, WLCs, although almost a quarter (23%) fell into the North-Eastern sector, also displayed the largest proportion that fell into the South-Eastern sector (50%), and indeed no other group displayed such a large proportion in a single sector. It might be argued that overall this indicates a tendency towards "conservative conservatism", albeit one tempered with a sizeable minority of "liberal conservatives".

Turning to ELCs, somewhat like their Welsh colleagues, albeit not to the same degree, South-Eastern was the most populated sector with a plurality (31%) mapping into it. The remainder mapped relatively evenly into the other three sectors of the mini-PoliMap. However, in one sense ELCs were unique in that a small number of respondents mapped into the diametrically opposed PoliMap sectors of Northern and Southern. One group adhered to robust economic and personal individualism – the Northerners – and the other to robust economic and personal collectivism – the Southerners. In both cases it was possible that such respondents self-consciously acknowledged themselves to be on the fringes of the Conservative Party. However, perhaps meeting on occasion their mirror image from the other sector, it is to be wondered if they ever asked themselves what either they, the other or both of them were doing there or hoped to achieve. In any event, there must have been *something* to unite them – whether "for" or "against" something – as members of the Conservative Party and it was not ideology as measured by the PoliMap. Unfortunately, the numbers were too small to allow meaningful further investigation.

---

[248] Dorrell, 13th March 2002.

[249] Durham, 1989: 70.

The mini-PoliMap identified by the mapping of respondents might suggest that only part of the PoliMap is valid. However, the result of mapping members of the English public discussed in Chapter 13 below indicates otherwise. The mini-PoliMap results from the particular nature of the *CPRS 2002's* respondents.

The PoliMap and socio-demographics

Further analysis was conducted using the range of socio-demographic data collected from ELCs and which is dealt with in detail in Chapter 4. However, there were almost no statistically significant associations between such variables and position on the PoliMap. Only two analyses just satisfied the two-tailed 5% significance level: subjective view of the rural or urban nature of their ward (two-tailed $p = 0.05$), and highest level of education (two-tailed $p = 0.05$). Little can be made of this. There is always the danger when running a lengthy sequence of bivariate analyses of a Type 1 error of incorrectly rejecting the null hypothesis.[250] It is safest to say that location within the PoliMap had little association with the socio-demographic characteristics of ELCs.

The PoliMap and the "Actually Existing Conservative Party"

To summarise the mapping for the *CPRS 2002* groups – and keeping in mind the probably minor biases introduced by the use of unbalanced Authoritarianism and Left-Right scales[251] discussed above in Chapter 2 – within the context of PoliMap it is legitimate to describe the Conservative Party's politicians in 2002 as "centre-right". The Conservative MP John Hayes,[252] one of the sitting Westminster MPs targeted by the fieldwork, argued that,

> *"Conservatives are the party of freedom. We believe in giving people more control over their lives, by cutting taxes and reforming public services. But there is more to*

---

[250] Clegg, 1982: 66.
[251] Evans & Heath, 1995: 203.
[252] Hayes, 2004.

> *Conservatism than freedom. In recent times the dangerous myth has developed that the economic liberalism championed by Margaret Thatcher must now be matched by social liberalism. The myth has grown to the point where it is now widely believed that to be truly compassionate, Conservatives must be liberal. In fact, the opposite is the case. Britain today is marked not by an absence but by an excess of social licence. We must match economic liberalism not with social liberalism but with social conservatism."*

Analysed through the PoliMap, Hayes was describing a position that could be described as Eastern or Centre-Eastern and as such was describing a Conservative Party that, at least according to the views of its politicians, actually existed.

Not Perfect, But Better

Modest claims have been made in this chapter for the PoliMap and its operationalisation. For example, using the PoliMap with two different dimensions for the Economic and Personal axes – assuming that they were both clearly to do with economic and personal issues and were statistically reliable scales – may lead to a different distribution within the PoliMap for respondents so analysed.

Nevertheless, the PoliMap as a theoretical model along with the operationalisation used in this chapter has allowed the construction of a typology of ideology that is much more meaningful than the traditional left-right model whilst still being comprehensible to the intelligent layperson.

If political scientists, media commentators and politicians alike started "pushing" the PoliMap, then whatever risks there might be of initial confusion amongst the public would soon be outweighed by the benefits of much greater "exactness of expression".[253]

To sum up the PoliMap: Not perfect, but better.

---

[253] Tucker, 1897: 21.

4

Local Councillors in England

Background and the Use of Secondary Data

In this chapter, the additional battery of socio-demographic questions presented to ELCs is studied in detail. The first aim is to provide a descriptive analysis of ELCs in 2002 – and where appropriate make comparisons with local councillors from other political parties and/or the general public – accompanied by a commentary on the more noteworthy findings.

Following this, there is multivariate analysis using these socio-demographic variables as predictors of attitudes as measured by the multi-item scales described elsewhere.

Other organisations conducted socio-demographic research on local councillors in England and Wales at about the same time as our fieldwork. In particular, reference is made in this chapter to work carried out by the Employers' Organisation for Local Government and the Improvement and Development Agency.[254]

Regarding these other studies, there are three matters to note. First, where they can be identified, the response rates to them were not dramatically higher than that for the *CPRS 2002*. For example, the response rate for the IaDA study of local councillors in England and Wales was a combined 57%.[255] This compares to our response rates for local councillors in England and Wales of 43% and 40% respectively. When it is considered both that the IaDA study had greater resources available and also that it was little more than the equivalent of a few pages of the much longer *CPRS 2002* questionnaire, then our response rates compare well.

---

[254] EOfLG 2001; 2003; IaDA, 2001.
[255] IaDA, 2001: 1.

Second, where they can be compared, the results provided by the EOfLG[256] study are remarkably similar to ours. This must be counted in favour of the robustness of the present study in terms of obtaining a representative sample of local councillors in England (unless both studies are similarly inaccurate). It shows that it is as possible for a relatively small-scale survey – in terms of the resources available – to get robust results as a much larger one.

Third, it will however be noted that these other studies refer to councillors in "England and Wales" combined whereas ours separated them and this present chapter is only about those in England. Whilst unfortunate, in practice this is a relatively minor issue. Around the time of our fieldwork there were under 1000 local councillors sitting in Wales[257] whereas there were over 21,000 councillors sitting in England and Wales.[258] The difference in numbers means that data from local councillors in Wales was swamped by their colleagues in England. Nevertheless, where they could be identified from the EofLG data councillors representing Plaid Cymru were removed from the analysis. In other words, in any of the tables below where a column is headed 'Other local councillors in England & Wales', this should be taken to indicate those from the Labour Party (37% of the total and 55% of non-Conservatives), the Liberal Democrat Party (21% of the total and 31% of non-Conservatives), the Green Party (0.4% of the total and 1% of non-Conservatives), independents (8% of the total and 12% of non-Conservatives) and others (1% of the total and 2% of the non-Conservatives) with councillors from Plaid Cymru omitted. The EofLG data suggests that at the time councillors from Plaid Cymru made up approximately one fifth of local councillors in Wales, so any impact of Welsh councillors is attenuated still further.

What was Omitted and Why

Basic issues

Before proceeding, there must be a few words about why certain socio-demographic variables were used whilst others were not. For

---

[256] EOfLG, 2001.
[257] *BBC News*, 15th June 2004.
[258] EOfLG, 2001: 1.

example, the questionnaire contained items about age and sex but not about weight. There are a number of reasons why this was the case. The most obvious is a matter of practicality. There is a limit to the number of questions that respondents can be expected to answer. This could be due to fatigue on the part of respondents or because individual items require too much work on the part of respondents or because the questions become increasingly intrusive and personal. This does not answer why this or that indicator was or was not studied, but simply states the obvious that not everything can be asked.

Another reason is one of replicability, or custom and practice. Generally, in political science age and sex might be studied whereas weight usually is not. Citing "because it's what everyone else does" may seem unconvincing, but given the limits of practicality just noted there have to be very good reasons for introducing novel measures beyond an exercise in data trawling. To some extent, it might be argued that this is also a reflection of what is "fashionable" in social research.

Representativeness

There were other reasons of greater substance. Beyond a sociological analysis of "what sort of people were Conservative local councillors in 2002", there was the more political matter of "representativeness". In other words, given that our respondents exercised power over citizens of the United Kingdom to what extent were they *like* the citizens of the United Kingdom? (That said, it would be an error to claim that if it is found that in some respect deemed important they were not like them then this is in itself evidence that something is amiss.)

By itself this might not be important and it is inevitable the members of *any* profession including that of politician will never be a mirror image of the country as a whole. They will always diverge, particularly along measures such as age. However, it does assume an importance given that aspects of Conservative Party doctrine and general political debate at the time specifically addressed representativeness.

This can be summed up by quoting then Shadow Secretary of State for Foreign and Commonwealth Affairs and former Party Chairman Michael Ancram[259] in a speech that he gave to the

---

[259] Ancram, 29th November 2001.

Conservative Women's Conference a matter of months before the fieldwork. Said Ancram,

> *"One of my greatest disappointments as Chairman was my failure to see more conservative women elected to Parliament. I know that if we are to present an acceptable face to the electorate it must be a representative face, representative of the world we live in where women outnumber men... I believe that this is one of the most important challenges facing us in the next year."*

In turn, this relates to the then controversial issue of local versus central and even non-Party selection of, in particular, parliamentary candidates.[260] In short, matters such as the sex and perhaps to a lesser extent age and ethnicity of politicians were a headline issue around the time of the fieldwork and it would have been strange not to look at this area.

Researcher choice and sensitivity

In any study making claims to some originality there is the matter of the personal choice of the researcher, in particular concerning specific hypotheses and research questions. In the case of our study it is not obvious what information about weight or shoe size – to offer a frivolous example – would contribute.

The battery of socio-demographic items included ones about sex and marital status. What it did not include were items concerned with sexuality. Although by 2009 at the latest this issue amongst Conservative politicians and candidates was being analysed more openly,[261] it must be recalled that it was not until a few months *after* the fieldwork that Alan Duncan became the first openly homosexual Conservative MP.[262] It was felt that it was too sensitive an issue to include in the questionnaire even allowing for assurances of anonymity. Future research might not need to be so nervous about this topic.[263]

---

[260] Catling, 8th March 2002; Baldwin, 21st October 2002; Bennett, 26th June 2003.
[261] Isaby, 1st July 2009.
[262] Waugh, 29th July 2002.
[263] Whitworth & Baldwin, 26th February 2010.

Initial Socio-Demographic Analysis

Note that in the tables in this chapter the data for ELCs – which includes any data not stated to be otherwise – are from the *CPRS 2002*. All other data sources are as cited.

Gender, age and ethnicity

TABLE 4.1: GENDER			
Gender	ELCs	Conservative councillors in England & Wales[264]	Other councillors in England & Wales[265]
Male	75%	73%	70%
Female	25%	27%	30%
Base	**281**	**6,872**	**13,957**

TABLE 4.2: AGE				
Age	ELCs	Conservative councillors in England & Wales[266]	Other councillors in England & Wales[267]	General population in England and Wales[268]
Up to 44	15%	13%	15%	60%
45-54	17%	20%	26%	13%
55-59	17%	16%	18%	6%
60-64	20%	19%	17%	5%
65-69	17%	15%	13%	4%
70-74	9%	12%	8%	4%
75+	4%	5%	3%	8%
Mean[269]	58	59	57	39
Base	**276**	**6,632**	**13,445**	**52,041,916**

---

[264] EOfLG, 2001: 1.

[265] EOfLG, 2001: 1.

[266] EOfLG, 2001: 1.

[267] EOfLG, 2001: 1.

[268] National Statistics, 21st March 2005: Table S001; National Statistics, 22nd August 2007.

[269] The mean ages calculated from the EOfLG data are approximates.

TABLE 4.3: ETHNICITY				
Ethnicity	ELCs	Conservative councillors in England & Wales[270]	Other councillors in England & Wales[271]	General population in England[272]
White	100%	99%	96%	91%
Other	0%	1%	4%	9%
Base	279	6,870	13,913	52,041,916

The IaDA report[273] notes that local councillors in office at start of the 21st century were generally white, middle-aged males. As the EOfLG report[274] indicates, this applied to councillors irrespective of which political party they represented. Regarding age, it is inherently implausible that members of *any* occupation could mirror the population at large. (Although there is evidence that the proportion of young Conservative local councillors – i.e. under 35 – was much the same as the proportion of non-councillors of the same age range *in the Party* around the time of the fieldwork.)[275] "White, middle-aged males" also described Parliamentary candidates and actual MPs for *all* major political parties and had done so for a long time.[276]

Regarding the "100% white" finding, as is reported in Chapter 10 on religion there were a number of Jewish respondents. All that can be said is that 99% of Jewish respondents to the *2001 Home Office Citizenship Survey* considered themselves to be white.[277]

The view that seems to have taken hold around this time that the Conservative Party was *especially* at fault on such matters as the gender and ethnic composition of its sitting politicians and candidates[278] seems puzzling. Tables 4.1 and 4.3 suggest that, at least in its selection for winnable seats of local council candidates, the

---

[270] EOfLG, 2001: 2.

[271] EOfLG, 2001: 2.

[272] National Statistics, 21st March 2005: Table S101.

[273] IaDA, 2001: 2

[274] EOfLG, 2001.

[275] Travis, 18th November 2004.

[276] Watt, 16th October 2000; Brivati & Baston, 2002: 8.

[277] O'Beirne, March 2004: 9.

[278] Phillips, 1st July 2001; Kite, Baldwin & Miles, 19th January 2002; Simple, 1st February 2002; but see also Yule, 2000.

Conservative Party at the time was neither better nor worse than the other main parties. It must also be noted that on occasion the other major political parties were criticised on this issue.[279]

Nevertheless, this period saw increasing demands for the Conservative Party to reform its candidate selection process at all levels. In other words that the process should be made more appealing for, and less hostile towards, potential female, non-white and homosexual candidates.[280]

However, some within the Conservative Party strongly resisted moves to "force the pace" of increasing representation of such groups.[281] Others argued that it was not actually that important as far as voters were concerned[282] or simply that, regarding ethnicity at least, it was an empirically dubious aim.[283]

In any event, such attempts that were made met with both (alleged) success[284] – although some claimed that the Conservative Party was going out it its way to "show off" such candidates[285] – and (alleged) failure.[286]

(At the level of crude head-counting, the proportion of elected female politicians in the UK at the start of the 21st century was similar-going-on-a-bit-worse when compared to many other major Western nations.[287] In absolute terms women rarely made up more than a third of the main national legislative body with the Scandinavian parliaments tending to have the largest proportion of female members.)

---

[279] Black, 3rd February 2002; Hurst, 28th December 2002; Sieghart, 11th August 2000.
[280] E.g. Baldwin, 1st October 2002; Catling, 8th March 2002; Glover 9th April; Keswick, Pockley & Guillaume, 1999; Maude, 24th June 2002; Pierce, 23rd October 2000; Watt, 25th June 2002.
[281] Kite, 25th October 2002; Odone, 26th January 2003.
[282] Steven, 28th July 2002.
[283] Meek, 2003.
[284] Adams, 14th March 2002; Thomson, 30th October 2003; Villiers 20th December 2004.
[285] Hames, 7th October 2000.
[286] Kite, 17th January 2002; Vaizey, 9th June 2002; Sieghart, 20th December 2004.
[287] International Institute for Democracy and Electoral Assistance, 2006.

Education

To simplify matter for respondents, they were only asked about their highest level of education achieved, not their educational careers.[288] For these purposes, someone who took a conventional O-level then A-level then university progression was taken to be educated to the same level as someone who had (say) left school with no qualifications but who had later acquired an Open University degree.

TABLE 4.4: EDUCATION: HIGHEST LEVEL			
Education	ELCs	Conservative councillors in England & Wales[289]	Other local councillors in England & Wales[290]
University or professional equivalent or higher	60%	58%	57%
Lower	40%	42%	43%
Base	**277**	**6,829**	**13,829**

TABLE 4.5: EDUCATION: TYPE OF SCHOOL	
Fee-paying secondary school	35%
Non-fee-paying secondary school	65%
Base	**279**

Regarding formal education, it is unsurprising that local councillors from all parties tended to have achieved a higher level than the general public given that in 2001 only 37% of the UK population possessed a first degree.[291] However, this latter figure does not take into account university-level professional qualifications. That said, this should be offset against the fact that, given the much older age profile of local councillors compared to the general public, many of the former will have gone through the

---

[288] *European Social Survey*, 2007[b]: 28.
[289] EOfLG, 2001: 5.
[290] EOfLG, 2001: 5.
[291] National Statistics, 4th February 2004.

usual school and university age period before the more recent substantial expansion of the Higher Education sector in the UK[292] or even that of the earlier expansion in the 1960s around the time of the *Robbins Report*.

To add to the confusion a little, the 2001 *British Social Attitudes* survey[293] suggests that 28% of the general population had at least some Higher education. However, only 15% of the total had at least a full first degree. In any event, Conservative local councillors – and probably all local councillors – tended to have attained higher levels of education than those that they represented.

Table 4.5 perhaps confirms the stereotype of "public school" Conservative politicians,[294] something particularly true at the most senior ranks.[295] (Although the Party has historically been electorally popular amongst the working class and certainly in previous times enacted legislation to ameliorate the lot of the working class, that same class has been historically under-represented amongst both Conservative MPs and senior members of the voluntary side.[296]) They confirm it inasmuch as only 7% of the general population in the United Kingdom – probably a little more in England alone – attended an independent school at around the time of the fieldwork[297] whereas 35% of Conservative local councillors in England did (assuming that "independent school" and "fee-paying secondary school" are usually different labels for the same thing). That said, almost two-thirds of Conservative local councillors in England had *not* attended a fee-paying school. A substantial majority of them had attended state schools "just like everybody else".

(The proportion of ELCs attending a fee-paying school was less than Conservative MPs where nearly two-thirds (64%) had attended such schools although this had been on a generally declining trend since at least the 1970s.[298])

---

[292] Clarke, 22nd January 2003.

[293] NCSR, 29th October 2008[d].

[294] Baker & Fountain, 1996: 96.

[295] Cowley & Melhuish, March 1997: 27.

[296] McKenzie & Silver, 1968: 38-39, 45-47.

[297] Independent Schools Council, 2006.

[298] Marquand, 2009: 324; Sutton Trust, 2005: 8; 2010: 7.

The two items about the type of school that respondents attended and whether or not they subsequently acquired a university or equivalent level education allows a few words about educational progression.

TABLE 4.6: ATTENDANCE AT A FEE-PAYING SCHOOL AGAINST HIGHEST LEVEL OF EDUCATION			
		Type of school	
		Free-paying	State
Highest level of education	Secondary or equivalent	25%	49%
	University or equivalent	75%	51%
	Base	97	179

Using the chi^2 statistic, it can be seen in Table 4.6 that there is a significant association (two-tailed p = <0.001) between the two variables in the expected direction. Those who attended a fee-paying school were more likely to have later acquired a university or equivalent level education than those who had not, a finding similar to that found in the general population.[299] Nevertheless, half of those who had attended a state school later received a university level education. The proportion of ELCs educated at state schools who acquired university or equivalent qualifications was broadly in line with that of the general population (42%) around the time of the survey.[300] However, given that many of them would have achieved this before the expansion in the Higher Education sector then in practice state-educated ELCs tended to end up better qualified than most state-educated members of the public.

Marital status

Support for "the family" and "marriage" remained strong in William Hague's Conservative Party.[301] However, by then many were noting that those two terms were not always synonymous.[302] Some inside the Party were arguing that the Party's continuing stress on "traditional

---

[299] *BBC News*, 27th November 2007.
[300] Lightfoot, 21st July 2006.
[301] Gledhill, 25th September 2000.
[302] Cooper, 2001: 15.

marriage" was "politically unwise"[303] and that it had to accept the new realities of, for example, increasing co-habitation.[304]

TABLE 4.7: MARITAL STATUS	
Married	78%
Living with a partner	4%
Widowed/divorced/separated	11%
Single	7%
Base	**279**

How did ELCs live up to the Party's then ideal in these matters? At first glance, rather well. The non-married cohabitation rate of 4% amongst this group of respondents shown in Table 4.7 was much lower than that of the general population of England around the same time which was approximately 25%.[305] However, it has already been noted that the age distribution of local councillors in England was not like that of the general population, with most councillors being in their 40s to 60s. Non-married cohabitation rates for the general public in this age range in 2001 ran from approximately 10% at age 40 to approximately 2% at age 70.[306] As such, these respondents were little different to the same age range within the general population.

Geographical location of ward

TABLE 4.8A: PERCEIVED RURAL/URBAN NATURE OF ELCS LOCAL AUTHORITY WARD	
Rural villages or farms	38%
Town	39%
Suburb or outskirts of a major city	17%
City or metropolitan	6%
Base	**280**

---

[303] *BBC News*, 8th August 2000.
[304] Kite, 18th September 2002.
[305] National Statistics, 2nd March 2005.
[306] National Statistics, 7th July 2005.

TABLE 4.8B: RURAL/URBAN NATURE OF MAIN ACCOMMODATION OF GENERAL PUBLIC[307]	
Hamlet, isolated dwelling or village	10%
All others	90%
Base	**49,138,831**

Tables 4.8a and 4.8b do not allow an exact like-for-like comparison. The items in the *CPRS 2002* questionnaire and the 2001 *Census* were different: the former analysed the nature of the local authority ward represented whereas the latter analysed the population's main accommodation. Nevertheless, the finding that over a third (38%) of our respondents considered that they *represented* a mainly rural ward whereas only 10% of the population as a whole *lived* in such areas highlights the disproportionately rural or non-metropolitan nature of the Conservative Party by then.

This rural background was seen as both strength and a weakness of the Conservative Party at the time. It was seen as a strength – or at least a crumb of comfort – in that the more rural areas was where the Conservative vote held up relatively well preventing a complete electoral collapse.[308] The Party sometimes deliberately highlighted its championing of rural areas and issues.[309] This was particularly true for local elections, although Labour made gains in rural areas at the 1997 and 2001 general elections.[310]

It was seen as a weakness because, along with other demographic issues such as the age of Conservative supporters,[311] it meant that the Party's support was drawn disproportionately from those most resistant to "change" whereas it was argued that in previous times the Party had embraced it and this was a necessary and good thing to do.[312] It anyway was argued that there was little future for a party of "rural geriatrics".[313] Moreover, by 2001 there were few

---

[307] National Statistics, 30th March 2005.

[308] Berrington, 2001: 212-213; Riddell, 29th March 2001; Hetherington, 9th June 2001; Tyrie, 2001: 11.

[309] Brown, 11th September 2000; Dorey, 2003.

[310] Woods, 2002.

[311] Parris, 10th July 2001.

[312] Gove, 12th October 2002.

[313] Rees-Mogg, 18th June 2001.

areas in England in particular that were truly rural – perhaps only 10% or so of all constituencies by some measures – and so the overall impact of such rural strongholds was small.[314]

Of course, the main problem was that it meant that the Party was simply not winning enough votes and seats to gain power. It needs to be remembered what a change the by then "parlous" condition[315] of the Conservatives in urban areas represented. For example, the Conservatives controlled Liverpool in the 1950s, and into the 1960s returned a majority of MPs representing the city. By the time of the fieldwork the Party had long had no MPs representing the city and the Party's percentage of the popular vote at the 2002 local elections was down to single figures.[316] By the opening years of the 21st century, in urban local elections in England – although it would take matters too far to extrapolate this to a national level – the Conservatives were sometimes pushed into fourth or even fifth place behind not only Labour and the Liberal Democrats but sometimes even the Green Party or the British National Party.[317]

TABLE 4.9: GEOGRAPHICAL AREA OF REPRESENTATION		
Area	ELCs	General population in England[318]
South East (except London)	35%	16%
Midlands	19%	19%
North	14%	29%
East	13%	11%
South West	13%	10%
London	6%	15%
Base	**283**	**49,138,831**

The item about where in England was the ward that they represented came from the main body of the questionnaire. Table 4.9 reinforces the fact that around the time of the fieldwork – at all levels of representation – south-east England *excluding London* was the

[314] Berrington, 2001: 212-213.
[315] *The Spectator*, 21st July 2001.
[316] Jenkins, 17th May 2002.
[317] Sherman, 14th May 2003.
[318] National Statistics, 2005.

Conservative Party's stronghold.[319] Their numbers there as a proportion of all ELCs was over double that of the general population as a proportion of the whole population. (Perhaps unsurprisingly, it was also the UK's richest area and disproportionately the biggest contributor of taxation.[320]) Conservative local councillors were disproportionately under-represented in northern England, having half the representation that they would have had if their distribution matched the general population.

In short, allowing for slightly different boundaries and remembering the small number of SLCs and WLCs who also featured in the study, the vast majority of Conservative local councillors came from areas defined by some[321] as being part of the UK's "inner core" or "outer core" of London, south-east England, the Midlands, East Anglia and Wessex rather than the "inner periphery" or "outer periphery" of north England, Wales, south-west England and Scotland.

Tenure of accommodation

TABLE 4.10: TENURE OF MAIN ACCOMMODATION		
Accommodation	ELCs	General population in Great Britain[322]
Own the property outright	61%	29%
Own the property with a mortgage	37%	40%
Rent the property	2%	31%
Base	**278**	**24,418**

Differences in age, social class, geographical location and so on make a direct comparison between Conservative local councillors in England and the general population difficult. Nevertheless, looking at Table 4.10, it is safe to say that the former were much more likely to own their home, either outright or with a mortgage, rather than rent it than was true of the general population. Indeed, renting was virtually unknown amongst this group of our respondents.

---

[319] Rallings, Thrasher & Johnston, 2002: 281.
[320] Denham, 23rd November 2002.
[321] Steed, in Heath, Rothon & Jarvis, 2002: 169.
[322] National Statistics, 29th March 2005, weighted base.

Employment

In the questionnaire there was no further split in what was termed "public" into nationalised industries and the like and the NHS, state education and so on.[323]

TABLE 4.11: EMPLOYMENT SECTOR			
	ELCs	Conservative councillors in England & Wales[324]	All councillors in England & Wales[325]
Private	71%	81%	41%
Public	20%	16%	51%
Voluntary	9%	3%	8%
Base	**277**	**3434**	**7073**

TABLE 4.12: EMPLOYMENT STATUS OF ELCs	
Employed	62%
Self-employed	38%
Base	**274**

In 2001 and 2002 the proportion of the mainland UK general public employed in the public sector was between 20% and 30% depending upon the region of the country.[326] Table 4.11 suggests that Conservative local councillors more nearly matched the employment profile of the public compared to other councillors who were far more likely to work in the public sector.

Self-employment rates of respondents are not directly comparable with the data from other sources since the former took together present or most recent past employment if the respondent was unemployed or otherwise economically inactive. However, calculations based upon secondary analysis of official figures[327]

---

[323] *European Social Survey*, 2007[b]: 48.
[324] EOfLG, 2001: 4. This indicates current employment only unlike the data for ELCs which indicates current or most recent employment if no longer working.
[325] EOfLG, 2001: 4. See the preceding footnote.
[326] *British Social Attitudes Survey* 2001; National Statistics, 28th October 2005.
[327] Weir, 2003: 442.

suggest that the 2002 self-employment rate amongst economically active members of the general public was approximately 13%. Table 4.12 therefore suggests a much higher rate of self-employment amongst Conservative local councillors in England than amongst the general public. Moreover, further data[328] suggests that, however measured, the rate of self-employment amongst ELCs at the time was nearly one-and-half times greater than amongst Liberal Democrat councillors and over three times higher than amongst Labour local councillors. Coupled with the lower rate of public sector employment amongst ELCs compared to their Labour and Liberal Democrat colleagues it might be argued that this suggests a degree of "sturdy independence" amongst elected Conservatives at a local level.

The questionnaire went into a little more detail by asking respondents to fit their occupation into one of a number of broad categories. As a result, exactly half (50%) could be placed in a collapsed category of "service sector management or the professions" with nearly a fifth (18%) in that of "manufacturing or agriculture" and 9% in "retail". Although it is not a like-for-like comparison, what was noticeable if expected was the relative absence of those describing themselves as either "skilled artisan" or "other manual" (5% in total) when compared to the English public of the time where a third, 32% in total, described themselves as either "skilled manual" or "semi-skilled or unskilled manual".[329]

There was no attempt to go into detailed sociological analysis of this area,[330] but the broadly middle-class and white-collar nature of the respondents can be seen.

---

[328] EOfLG, 2001: 3.
[329] *BSA*, 2001.
[330] *European Social Survey*, 2007[b].

Parental background in the Conservative Party

TABLE 4.13: FAMILY BACKGROUND IN THE CONSERVATIVE PARTY		
	ELCs	**Conservative Party members**[331]
Both parents a member	16%	32%
Mother only a member	3%	6%
Father only a member	3%	6%
Neither parent a member	66%	44%
Not available[332]	12%	13%
Base	**259**	**c. 2446**

Table 4.13 suggests that family involvement was not an overwhelmingly important pathway into the Conservative Party for ELCs. Only a fifth (22%) of respondents were certain that at least one parent had been a member of the Party and two-thirds (66%) were sure that neither had been. That said, there is some evidence that those who *did* come from a Conservative family background came from quite a strongly Conservative background. Only 6% said that only one parent had been a member whereas 16% said that both had been.

The comparison with the results from the earlier *True Blues* study is here to flesh things out. It would appear that by 2002 local councillors were less likely to have had a parental background in the Conservative Party than had been the case with ordinary members a decade previously.

It cannot be directly claimed whether the differences in parental background observed in these two studies were due to the different types of respondents being studied or the passage of time. However, looking just at our respondents it can be seen whether there might have been a pattern of increasing or decreasing parental socialisation into the Party. It cannot be said whether there *was* parental socialisation only that that the figures suggest that there could have been.

---

[331] Whitely, Seyd & Richardson, 1994: 250.
[332] Includes all who did not respond either "Yes" or "No" for both parents.

First, the responses to the items about parental membership of the Party were recoded into a new variable with two categories: those who were sure that at least one parent had been a member in the Party (28% out of a base of 252) and those who were sure that neither had been (72%). Independent samples t-tests for age (two-tailed p = 0.471) and length of service as a local councillor (two-tailed p = 0.697) suggested no significant connection between respondents' service in the Party and that of their parents (and it is hard to see what we would make of the latter anyway as indicated below).

However, there was a significant difference (two-tailed p = <0.001) between "family" and "non-family" respondents and how long they had been members of the Party. Further analysis using cross-tabs analysis – and the chi^2 statistic indicated a significant association, two-tailed p = <0.001 – is shown in Table 4.14.

TABLE 4.14: PARENTAL BACKGROUND AND LENGTH OF MEMBERSHIP IN THE CONSERVATIVE PARTY

		Parental background in the Conservative Party		
		At least one parent a member	Neither parent a member	**Base**
Number of years as a member of the Conservative Party	0 to 9	11%	89%	53
	11 to 19	22%	78%	46
	20 to 29	25%	75%	53
	30 to 39	49%	51%	37
	40 or more	38%	62%	39
	Base	**62**	**166**	**228**

It can be seen is that there was a decline in the proportion of those with a parental background in the Party amongst who joined in the last 30 years or less compared to those who had been members for 30 or 40 years or more. Furthermore, this trend accelerated in the decade before the fieldwork. There are at least two plausible reasons for this. First, that because there had been[333] a marked decline in membership of the Party in the years before 2002[334] and so there were simply less people in the Party to be the mothers and fathers of newer

---

[333] But see Landale & Baldwin, 13ᵗʰ March 2001.
[334] Landale, 21ˢᵗ April 2000; 13ᵗʰ March 2001.

members. (In the years immediately before 2002 the Labour Party had suffered a proportionally even greater loss of membership so that by 2002 the Conservative Party again had more members. However, this was on the back of a surge in recruitment in the years leading up to Labour's landslide victory at the 1997 general election.[335])

The other is that declining parental membership might suggest the decline in the importance of the "social" aspects of Party membership and in particular youth membership.[336] This can be tentatively examined by correlating parental membership with an item from the main body of the questionnaire that invited responses to the item, "The Conservative Party is not an ideological party". It is not implausible to hypothesise that those without a parental background in the Party would be more likely to disagree with this item – because their motives for joining were more political than social – than those with a parental background in the Party. However, cross-tabs analysis using the chi^2 statistic found no significant association (one-tailed p = 0.374) between the two variables.

Service in the Conservative Party

TABLE 4.15: YEAR FIRST JOINED THE CONSERVATIVE PARTY	
1945 to 1949	4%
1950 to 1959	9%
1960 to 1969	12%
1970 to 1979	25%
1980 to 1989	18%
1990 to 1999	29%
2000 to 2002	3%
Base	**269**
Mean	**1978**
Median	**1979**
Mode	**1970**

---

[335] Baldwin, 28th January 2002[a]; *Guardian*, January 2002.
[336] Evans, 1996: 17; Holroyd-Doveton, 1996: 156-157; Billen, 5th April 2000. But see for example Cramb, 15th September 2000, for a more modern understanding of what "social" might mean.

TABLE 4.16: YEAR FIRST BECAME A CONSERVATIVE LOCAL COUNCILLOR[337]	
1950 to 1959	1%
1960 to 1969	3%
1970 to 1979	10%
1980 to 1989	19%
1990 to 1999	52%
2000 to 2002	15%
Base	**278**
Mean	**1992**
Median	**1996**
Mode	**1999**

TABLE 4.17: YEARS BETWEEN JOINING THE CONSERVATIVE PARTY AND FIRST BEING ELECTED AS A LOCAL COUNCILLOR	
0	12%
1 to 4	23%
5 to 9	16%
10 to 19	20%
20 to 29	16%
30 to 39	8%
40 and more	5%
Base	**269**
Mean	**13**
Median	**9**
Mode	**0**

Regarding Tables 4.15 and 4.16, the inherent arbitrariness ought to be noted of collapsing what is near enough the scale data of individual years into the ordinal data found in the tables. If, for example, instead of using a "traditional" or "easy on the eye" calendar decade as the main span of each category some other span

---

[337] It is possible that a small number of respondents had been elected as non-Conservative councillors beforehand.

had been used then the tables might look different and "reveal" something else.

That proviso aside, in the case of Tables 4.15 and 4.16 it is hard to relate contemporary political events with either recruitment into the Conservative Party or election as a local councillor. For example, the effects of any political events that might be expected to have had an impact on recruitment – such as "Black Wednesday" in 1992 and the Party's subsequent loss of public support[338] – are confused by the almost never-ending cycle of general, multi-level local, European and Greater London Assembly elections and by-elections. There is also the uncertain and in practice unknowable influence of particularly vigorous or slack local campaigning.[339]

Nevertheless, it would seem too much of a coincidence not to note that the most common year for joining the Party, 1970 with 8% of the total, was also a general election year. A year-by-year analysis indicates that the only other years to account for 5% – there were none greater – of all ELC respondents' initial entry into the Party were 1980 (the first full year of Margaret Thatcher's premiership), 1990 (the year of her ejection from office by the Party) and 1998 (the year after the Party's devastating general election defeat). It might be speculated that dramatic events in the Party's history, whether for good or bad, were a boost to recruitment.

The so-called flatline years of relatively low and static levels of support for the Party after 1992[340] did not seem to have had too negative an impact on recruitment into the Party regarding future ELCs. More detailed analysis indicates that nearly a quarter (23%) of ELC respondents joined the Party between 1993 and 2002 (inclusive).

With the proviso at the start of this section again in mind, what is also interesting is the finding in Table 4.15 that the most successful decades in terms of recruitment into the Party – at least as far as the respondents under analysis in this chapter are concerned – were the 1970s (25%) and the 1990s (29%), not the main era of "actually existing Thatcherism", the 1980s (18%).

---

[338] Pattie & Johnston, 1996; Norton, 2002: 68; Travis, 27th April 2002; but see Sanders & Brynin, 1999: 223; Anderson, 25th November 2000.

[339] Denver, Hands & McAlester, 2004.

[340] Tory Reform Group, 11th June 2001.

Despite the small number of respondents who had been local councillors for two or even three decades, there is evidence of quite a high replacement rate. Detailed analysis indicates that over half (56%) of ELCs had first become councillors seven years or less before 2002.

The finding in Table 4.17 that over a third (35%) of ELCs had been members of the Conservative Party for four years or less before becoming a local councillor is worth noting. Over one in ten (12%) had joined the Party and been elected as local councillors within a year *and this was the most common gap between the two events*. These respondents had, in effect, "walked in off the streets" and almost immediately become local councillors. Such people must have had little formal track record within the Conservative Party and yet almost immediately become amongst its most prominent local spokespersons.[341] Earlier in this chapter the relative lack of a *family* history within the Party for the majority of ELCs was noted. In a substantial minority of cases this could be qualified to *any* history within the Party.

On the other hand, well over a quarter (29%) of ELCs had been members of the Party for two decades or more before being elected and had grown grey in the service of the Party on the voluntary side before being elected as local councillors.

Social class

Respondents were asked to rate their social class both at the time of the survey and of their family when young. This item was not

---

[341] I noted my own involvement in the Party near the start of this book. An important rationale behind the study was to use academic methods to study my own political milieu. Whether I liked or disliked what the findings said was neither here nor there. Nevertheless, I admit that this was perhaps the single most *surprising* finding of the study. My own constituency association was in good shape: a subs-paying membership of many hundreds and a large number of enthusiastic activists at branch and association levels. Add this to the fact that the constituency and the local authority as a whole were fairly safe Conservative territory and this routinely led to *contested* intra-party elections merely to be selected as a local council candidate. The findings of the study indicate that this was not the case everywhere. They suggest that some local associations, even in "good" areas that returned Conservative councillors, were virtually moribund and pathetically grateful to anyone willing and able to put their name on a list of candidates.

calculated using indicators such as income or educational level but instead was the subjective rating of respondents.

TABLE 4.18: SUBJECTIVE SOCIAL CLASS		
	Of family when young	**Of respondent now**
Upper class	3%	2%
Middle class	49%	68%
Working class	40%	10%
No social class	8%	20%
Base	**279**	**276**

Certain features stand out from Table 4.18. First, very few respondents regarded themselves as upper class at either point in their lives. However, there was a marked sense of upward social mobility amongst respondents through their lives. Half (49%) said that they came from a middle class family background and a large minority (40%) said that they had come from a working class one. However, by 2002 two-thirds (68%) regarded their status as middle class whereas only 10% regarded it as working class. This progression has been noted in previous studies.[342]

Only 8% felt that their families had no class background, but by 2002 a fifth (20%) did not regard themselves as members of a particular social class.

TABLE 4.19: CHILDHOOD TO CURRENT SUBJECTIVE SOCIAL CLASS CHANGE				
		Of family when young		
		Middle class	Working class	None
Of respondent now	Middle class	91%	54%	10%
	Working class	2%	24%	0%
	None	7%	22%	90%
	Total	**135**	**110**	**21**

Omitting the small number of those who regarded themselves as upper class at either point in their lives, Table 4.19 displays the nature

---

[342] Whiteley, Seyd & Richardson, 1994: 47.

of the class progression. The pattern is very clear. Those who regarded themselves in childhood as either middle class or not belonging to any particular social class strongly tended to say the same about their current social class: 90% or more in both cases. However, over half (54%) of those who felt that they had come from a working class background thought that by 2002 they were now middle class and more than a fifth (22%) now regarded themselves as belonging to no social class. Only a quarter (24%) retained their working class self-image.

When subjective social class is correlated with the more objective measures found in the questionnaire such as level of education and whether respondents attended a fee-paying school, then the results are in the expected direction. (In the following analyses, the tiny number of those who responded "upper class" to the subjective social class item are omitted.)

TABLE 4.20A: CHILDHOOD SUBJECTIVE SOCIAL CLASS AGAINST HIGHEST LEVEL OF EDUCATION

		Highest level of education	
		Secondary school	University
Current subjective social class	Middle class	58%	77%
	Working class	21%	4%
	No social class	21%	19%
	Base	**110**	**157**

TABLE 4.20B: CURRENT SUBJECTIVE SOCIAL CLASS AGAINST HIGHEST LEVEL OF EDUCATION

		Highest level of education	
		Secondary school	University
Childhood subjective social class	Middle class	39%	59%
	Working class	51%	34%
	No social class	10%	7%
	Base	**110**	**157**

At either time, there was little correlation between level of education and the self-identification of not belonging to any social class.

Using the chi^2 statistic, there was, however, a significant association overall between the variables in both Table 4.20a (two-tailed p = 0.007) and Table 4.20b (two-tailed p = 0.001). In both cases those who had a university or equivalent level of education were more likely to rate themselves as middle class than those who did not.

Rather more who had a university education described themselves as middle class at the later period of their life than the earlier (77% against 59%). This is likely a result of the real or perceived upwards social mobility already noted. That those who went to university where more likely to say that they came from a middle class family background is probably a reflection of the reality that historically university was "for" the middle class.[343] It would be surprising, however, if in at least a small number of cases this was not due to a degree of retrospective analysis on the part of respondents. In other words, "I went to university, therefore I must have come from a middle class background."

Turning to whether or not respondents attended a fee-paying school, Tables 4.21a and 4.21b tell a somewhat similar story.

TABLE 4.21A: CURRENT SUBJECTIVE SOCIAL CLASS AGAINST ATTENDANCE AT A FREE-PAYING SCHOOL

		Type of school	
		Fee-paying	State
	Middle class	83%	63%
Current subjective social class	Working class	2%	15%
	None	15%	22%
	Base	**92**	**176**

TABLE 4.21B: CHILDHOOD SUBJECTIVE SOCIAL CLASS AGAINST ATTENDANCE AT A FREE-PAYING SCHOOL

		Type of school	
		Fee-paying	State
	Middle class	81%	35%
Childhood subjective social class	Working class	12%	56%
	None	7%	9%
	Base	**90**	**178**

---

[343] Babb, 2005: 9.

Using the chi^2 statistic, in both cases there was a significant association overall between the variables (two-tailed p = 0.001 in both cases), clearly as a result of the larger proportion of those who attended a fee-paying school describing themselves as middle class at either stage of their lives. The proportion of those who had attended a public school and describing themselves as middle class was nearly the same at both stages of their lives. In what was again probably the impact of perceived social mobility, a much higher proportion of those who had not attended a fee-paying school described themselves as middle class at the time of the fieldwork (63%) compared to when they had been children (35%).

Socio-Demographic Predictors of Attitudes

Rationale and methodology

Numerous works have indicated that differences along various socio-demographic attributes are associated with differences in attitudes. (Although, perhaps unsurprisingly, in certain circumstances it has been demonstrated that, against expectations, some such variables are *not* associated with attitudinal differences, e.g. social class and the views of so-called "Essex man" Conservatives.[344]) For example, age has been implicated in a range of generational or cohort (where older people are simply replaced by younger people), life-cycle (for a range of possible physiological, psychological or social reasons) and period (where something effects everyone in society) effects on various social and political attitudes and behaviour,[345] often involving complex interactions.[346] So, too, has education[347] and sex.[348] The list is almost endless.

To take just two examples. Looking specifically at Conservative Party politicians, it has been noted that there have been observable differences between different cohorts. It has been argued that those entering Parliament as the "class of 1959" had a special role in the

---

[344] Baker & Fountain, 1996: 97.
[345] Hames, 12ᵗʰ January 2004; Rothon & Heath, 2003.
[346] Tilley, 2002.
[347] Heath & Topf, 1986.
[348] Campbell, 2004; Childs & Withey, 2004.

rise of Thatcherism in that they were not haunted by the "hungry thirties" or the election defeat of 1945. As such, they were more prepared to question the post-War consensus.[349] Similarly, in research into Conservative candidates for parliament seats in the run-up to a presumed 2010 general election, it was noted that many were a product of the 1980s "Thatcher revolution" and not always in favour of some of the policies espoused by David Cameron and the leadership of the Party.[350]

Looking at it from a different direction and more generally, there is a wealth of evidence[351] from research amongst the general public that those who are better-educated and/or younger tend to be more socially tolerant, for example, of homosexual relationships.

Because the *CPRS 2002* only has one point in time available, the analysis cannot be as ambitious as some other studies. However, a range of socio-demographic variables collected from the responses of ELCs can be analysed in terms of whether they have any predictive power on attitudes described by the multi-item scales set out in Appendix 3. This was done by running a series of regression analyses in *SPSS* using the multi-item scales as the dependant variable on each occasion. The putative predictive variables were of two sorts:

- Sex, marital status, current subjective social class, childhood subjective social class, highest academic qualification, type of school attended (private versus state), location of ward (rural or city etc.), tenure of property (owned or rented), employment sector (private or state) and employment status (self-employed versus employed). Because of the nature of the data and the demands of regression analysis, in most cases dummy variables were created.
- Age, number of years a member of the Conservative Party and number of years a local councillor. These variables could be entered raw as scale variables.

It is reasonable in the instances of many of the socio-demographic variables to make assumptions about their potential

---

[349] Green, 2002: 237.
[350] Montgomerie, 30th April 2009.
[351] Evans, 2002: 218-219.

causal relationships with the multi-item scales. Clearly, such variables as age and sex precede placement on any of the scales. This is not always the case: placement on certain scales might be argued to determine (say) career choices. But it is sufficiently so to allow for the use of regression analysis.

Results and analysis

First, there were a small number of socio-demographic variables that *never* appeared as significant predictors, even at a trivial level. These were type of school attended, location of ward and employment status.

Second, there were seven multi-item scales for which socio-demographic variables were not significant predictors of variability. These were Environmentalism, Political Elitism, Intra-Party Elitism, Political Elitism, Theocratism, Pride in the Way Nation Functions and Left-Right.

Third, there was a large group of scales which did have statistically significant regression models associated with them but of a marginal sort where the final model explained less than 10 % of variability and/or no single variable accounted for more 5% by itself. These were Authoritarianism, Europeanism, Intra-Party Inclusivity, Optimism, Postmaterialism, Pride in National Heritage and Culture, Protectionism, Religiosity, Traditional British Liberties, Welfarism and Xenophobia.

This left only *one* dimension where socio-demographic variables accounted for a significant and substantial amount of that dimension's variability. This was Feminism – which looked at attitudes towards the role of women in politics and so on – where the variables in the final model accounted for 13% of its variability. All that needs to be said is that of this 13% two socio-demographic variables accounted for 5% of the total each. One was age where younger respondents were more likely to display feminist attitudes and the other was sex where female respondents were more likely to display feminist attitudes. Both of these findings were to be expected.

In the case of sex, the finding tallies with the actual voting behaviour of near-contemporaneous female Labour MPs.[352] There are indeed "women's issues" which are disproportionately supported by

---

[352] Childs & Withey, 2004.

mainstream female politicians irrespective of their party allegiance. (Of course, it is contestable what ideologically based "claims and actions" really are "for women".[353])

It is also worth noting the frequent claims around the time of the fieldwork that it was the "blue rinse brigade" of older, female Conservative activists who were most opposed to female candidates for elected, particularly Westminster, office.[354] This might have been true for *members*, but if so it is a phenomenon much attenuated (to say the least) amongst female Conservative local *politicians*.

The Internet

Use of email and the Internet

The only item in the questionnaire directly looking at media consumption concerned the "new media" of email and the Internet as opposed to the "old media" of newspapers, magazines, radio and TV.[355]

It can be hard to remember the growth of the Internet since the 1990s and certainly since 2002. Just between 2002 and 2008 the proportion of households in the UK that had Internet access increased from less than a half to two-thirds.[356]

Respondents were presented with two items, one concerning how often they used email and the other concerning how often they used the Internet for news and information.[357]

TABLE 4.22: INTERNET USAGE AMONGST ELCS	Email	Internet
At least once a day	64%	29%
At least once a week	13%	29%
Less often than once a week or never	23%	42%
Base	**274**	**275**

[353] Celis & Childs, March 2012.

[354] Watt, 8th February 2000.

[355] *European Social Survey*, 2007[c]: 124.

[356] National Statistics, c. 2003; 15th March 2007; 26th August 2008.

[357] Eric Forth famously disliked such things and said so to me on a number of occasions when I tried to persuade him of the opportunities presented by blogging. See Meek, September 2003.

It is clear from a comparison of the data columns in Table 4.22 that rates of email usage were apparently much higher than Internet usage. This could have been because some respondents understood "email" to refer to internal electronic mail systems provided by the councils of which they were members or by their other places of work.

Returning to the main theme of this chapter, the relationship between a number of socio-demographic indicators and email and Internet usage was analysed. One-tailed hypotheses were used since the literature was clear that higher rates of usage were to be expected amongst younger, male and/or better educated respondents.[358]

TABLE 4.23A: EMAIL USAGE BY AGE AMONGST ELCS					
	Up to 39	40-49	50-59	60-69	70+
At least once a day	96%	89%	64%	59%	35%
At least once a week	4%	3%	17%	16%	14%
Less often than once a week or never	0%	8%	19%	25%	51%
Base	24	36	72	100	37

TABLE 4.23B: INTERNET USAGE BY AGE AMONGST ELCS					
	Up to 39	40-49	50-59	60-69	70+
At least once a day	72%	47%	28%	18%	19%
At least once a week	24%	33%	36%	31%	13%
Less often than once a week or never	4%	20%	36%	51%	68%
Base	25	36	72	100	37

Tables 4.23a and 4.23b could hardly be clearer. Higher rates of email and Internet usage were associated with relative youth. This, of course, was similar to the pattern amongst the general public.[359]

The results for sex were interesting. There was no significant association (one-tailed $p = 0.25$ using the chi^2 statistic) amongst ELCs between sex and email usage. There was, however, between sex and using the Internet for news and information (one-tailed $p < 0.001$ using the chi^2 statistic), with male respondents much more likely to have done

---

[358] Gardner & Oswald, 2001: 162-163.
[359] National Statistics, c. 2003; 15th March 2007; 28th August 2007: 6.

this. This discrepancy might indeed indicate that by "email" respondents were referring to internal mail systems provided by their local councils or other places of employment and which might have been used more commonly. This becomes more plausible when one considers that 60% of female and 65% of male respondents said that they used email at least once a day against only 9% and 36% respectively who said that they used the Internet at least once a day. Nevertheless, the higher rates of Internet usage amongst men is again consistent with many years of data collected from the British general public.[360]

An analysis of email or Internet usage based on level of education also found results in the expected direction. At a simple binary level of university or equivalent against less than that, there was a significant association with both email (one-tailed $p = 0.046$ using the chi^2 statistic) and Internet (one-tailed $p = 0.032$ using the chi^2 statistic) usage with those educated to degree level more likely to have used both.

The Internet as a refuge?

Given that our respondents were relatively homogenous when compared to UK society as a whole, this chapter need not concern itself with the so-called "digital divide" that was being discussed around this time in terms of "social exclusion" and so on.[361] However, around the time of the fieldwork it was claimed by a number of writers and activists that the Internet would be of particular help to those with ideological views perceived by them to be under-represented and/or misrepresented by the mainstream media. This, it was claimed, was particularly true of conservatives, libertarians and Euro-sceptics.[362]

This possibility was analysed way of regression analyses with email and Internet usage as the dependant variables and the range of multi-item scales as the putative predictive variables along with age (given what was described above). Without detailing the results, the problem is that age drowned out virtually all other variables and in practice was the only meaningful significant predictive variable for both email and Internet usage.

---

[360] National Statistics, c. 2003; 28th August 2007: 6.

[361] Citizens Online, 26th July 2007.

[362] Crozier, 2000; Meek, September 2003; Micklethwait, 2002; but see also North, 12th April 2009.

Remove age from the analyses and almost none of the multi-item scales were significant predictors of the two dependant variables. The marginal exception was Protectionism which was the most important – relatively speaking – predictive variable in both cases. It explained 5% (out of a mere 7% total based upon the adjusted R^2 figure) of the variability in email usage and 4% (again out of 7%) of the variability in Internet usage. Bivariate analysis indicates that in both cases those who were less protectionist tended to be heavier users of both email and the Internet. When the items making up the Protectionism scale are studied then these results make an intuitive sense. Such respondents tended to be less afraid of new things. However, without taking age into consideration as well, nothing more can be made of this.

Other respondents

For the sake of completeness, it should be noted that all respondents were presented with these items about email and Internet usage. The most "switched on" were MEPs and the least were Peers. Little needs to be said about the average age of the latter group. 68% of MPs said that they used email at least once a day with a further 12% saying that they used it at least once a week.

Although it had been dubbed the first Internet election, analysis after the 2001 general election suggested that Internet use by both local and national parties as well as individual candidates was patchy, generated little additional interest amongst the electorate and above all had a negligible impact on election outcomes.[363] However – and the specific circumstances in which they used it were not identified – by May 2008[364] the vast majority of MPs stated that they used email (92%) to communicate with their constituents. Most (83%) had a personal website. Matters had changed in a short space of time.

Idealism, Pragmatism and Time

Measures of attitudes such as the ones used above may suggest what people think but not how important these issues – or just "ideals" at all –

---

[363] Ward & Gibson, May 2003: 189.
[364] Williamson, 2009: 8.

are to the respondent nor how this might change with the passage of time. Within the context of the Conservative Party it has been claimed that there were two mutually reinforcing factors at work: "The leaching out of idealism and the ageing of the party membership".[365]

Here a tentative analysis can be conducted using the "The Conservative Party is not an ideological party" item from the questionnaire. If this view was correct then, given the direction of the wording of the item, there ought to be a significant correlation between it and the time-related variables. In other words, older respondents should be more likely to downplay the importance of ideology within the Conservative Party than younger ones. The item can also be run against the number of years respondents had been members of the Party and the number of years that they had been local councillors. Altogether, this might offer a guide regarding maturational processes (age) as against experiential processes (length of membership in the Party and time served as a local councillor).

Looking first at the variable alone, out of the 278 valid responses 40% agreed that the Conservative Party was *not* an ideological party against 31% who disagreed (that is, they thought that the Conservative Party *was* an ideological party) and 29% who took the "Neither/nor" option. In short – and their own motivations cannot be disentangled from their views of the Party in whose name they had been elected nor whether they thought their view was "good" or "bad" – only a minority viewed the Conservative Party as substantially "ideological". Instead, a plurality seemed to have regarded the Party as being substantially pragmatic.

In fact, bivariate analysis using the Pearson statistic indicated no significant correlation between the "not an ideological party" item and either simple age or how long respondents had been local councillors. There was, however, a significant correlation (Pearson correlation – 0.127, one-tailed $p = 0.02$) in the expected direction between the "not an ideological party" item and length of membership of the Party. For example, only a third (31%) who had been members for five years or less agreed with the item whereas a half (49%) of those who had been members for 30 years or more did so.

Given that length of membership of the Party was significantly correlated with age – indeed, all three of the time-related variables were significantly correlated with each other (p = <0.001 in all cases) in the expected direction – but that age itself was not significantly correlated with the "not an ideological party" item, this seems to offer some evidence that there was an experiential processes at work.

It might be that there was a tendency that as time went by the initial ideological enthusiasms that prompted someone to join the Party – and at some point perhaps to become a local councillor – made way for an increasing focus on "procedure". This could either be the internal processes of the Party, usually at a local level, or on "getting the vote out" at election time as a political but often non-ideological process of salesmanship. In short, a focus on the "how" rather than the "why".[366] All of this is particularly true in the context of local politics where for many years local government had a decreasing independence vis-à-vis central government and there was correspondingly relatively little room for ideologically motivated activity.[367]

Conclusion to Chapter 4

Looking first at the descriptive analyses in the first part of this chapter, as might have been expected the large majority of Conservative local councillors in England were – objectively or subjectively – white, middle-aged, middle class and non-metropolitan and a majority were also male. (Much of this was not confined to Conservative local councillors.) This was contrasted with the general population in England which was less so in each aspect although in some areas this disparity, particularly in the case of ethnicity, was attenuated given the geographical areas that most of the respondents represented, i.e. non-metropolitan. They tended to work in the private sector – much more so than non-Conservative councillors – and although they tended to be employed rather than self-employed their

---

[366] Which, readers might recall, is where we came in. Near the start of this book I briefly noted my own experiences as a Conservative Party activist for two decades. Over the years I witnessed many people initially fired with strong ideals turn into "machine politicians", particularly as they gained named positions on the voluntary side of the Party or were elected as local councillors. No doubt, they would turn that accusation around and say that I had been naive.

[367] *Telegraph*, 4th September 2006.

rates of self-employment were higher than was the case amongst the general public.

As for their service as a member of the Party and as a local councillor, there was a considerable range. On the one hand a small but noticeable proportion could trace their membership back to the 1950s or earlier and their political office back to the 1970s or earlier. However, many were newer entrants with over a third having been members of the Party for very few years before being first elected as a councillor.

Turning to more complex analysis, there was little to report in the "rejecting the null hypothesis" sense about socio-demographic variables and attitudes. With relatively few exceptions – perhaps most noticeably regarding sex and age and views towards women in public life as measured by the Feminism dimension – who a respondent was socio-demographically made little difference in reported attitudes.

The section on the Internet found little that was unexpected. Younger, male and/or better-educated respondents tended to have higher rates of usage and in this respondents were the same as the contemporary British public.

The final part suggested that whilst neither age nor length of time as a local councillor were correlated with any difference in "ideological fervour", length of membership of the Party did seem correlated with a leeching away of idealism. Depending upon one's view about the "goodness" of a degree of ideological drive in British party politics,[368] this may or may not be a depressing finding.

---

[368] North, 27th October 2010.

5

Attitudes about the Conservative Party

Looking Inwards

Other than the Party's 2001 leadership contest which is analysed separately in Chapter 12, there were three batteries of questions specifically looking at attitudes towards the Conservative Party: Intra-Party Elitism (which analysed the role or not of grass-roots members in running the Party), Intra-Party Inclusivity (which analysed attitudes towards promoting women, ethnic minorities and homosexuals within the Party) and Optimism (which looked at how optimistic or pessimistic respondents were about the then current state and likely future fortunes of the Party). There were also a small number of stand-alone items of relevance to this chapter.

In addition, respondents were asked to rate on a five-point scale their attitudes towards the then most recent leaders of the Conservative Party: Edward Heath, Margaret Thatcher, John Major, William Hague and Iain Duncan Smith. The first three had all been both leaders of the Party and Prime Ministers, Hague had been leader of the Party only and Duncan Smith was at the time leader of the Party although would soon be forced out of this position.

Respondents were also asked about their membership of the Conservative Party's youth organisations.

Elitism, Inclusivity and Optimism

Unwarranted optimism

It is not the intention to look at the multi-item scales in any great detail by themselves. They can be found elsewhere as components in multivariate analysis. The results, split by type of respondent, for the Intra-Party Elitism, Intra-Party Inclusivity and Optimism scales can be found in Appendix 4. However, there were a few findings that might be noted here.

Regarding Optimism, most respondents were indeed optimistic about the then current state and likely future fortunes of the Conservative Party and ANOVA found no significant differences between the groups of respondents.

Looking at just a single item from the Optimism scale, given what happened at the 2005 general election where Labour was "merely" reduced to an overall majority of 66, it speaks of a lack of realism amongst respondents[369] that in 2002 very few thought that the Conservatives could *not* "win the next general election". For Peers the proportion was 10%, for MPs 8%, for WLCs 7%, for MEPs 14% and for MSPs 7%. ELCs were a little more cautious with the proportion at 18% and SLCs easily the most cautious of all at 29%. That said – and to turn the question around – the only ones amongst whom there was *not* a majority who thought that the Conservatives *could* win the next general election were MEPs. Only 43% thought that they could and exactly the same proportion affirmed the middle neither/nor response on the questionnaire.

In contrast, it should be noted that a year before the fieldwork a YouGov poll of Conservative activists found that no less than two-thirds (77%) of activists believed that Labour would win the general election.[370] In other words, ordinary Conservative *activists* seem to have been more realistic than Conservative *politicians*. However, it cannot be said whether this divergence was because of the respondents being different, the short passage of time or an artefact of the nature of the research. It might be the case that Conservative politicians were particularly sensitive to the perceived failings of the

---

[369] Gill, Atkinson & Davidson, 10th April 2002.
[370] Ahmed, 4th March 2001.

main pollsters during previous elections campaigns such as in 1992 and 2001 where the polls were seen by many to have been unduly "pro-Labour".[371]

Running and changing the Party

Regarding Intra-Party Elitism, Appendix 4 displays the predictable finding that local councillors tended to be more in favour of grass-roots control of the Party than parliamentarians in Westminster.[372]

Looking at just the "Women" item from the Intra-Party Inclusivity scale and taking ELCs alone for the sake of convenience, it is of note that there was no significant difference (using the chi^2 test, two-tailed p = 0.24) between male and female local councillors. Only 16% and 12% respectively disagreed with the notion of advancing women within the Party, a finding at variance with the perceived "traditionalist" views of grass-roots *activists* around that time.[373]

A Desire for Change?

Was change needed?

Some have argued that after the 1997 and 2001 elections the Party became more proficient at the use of professional marketing, but that there had been too little analysis of the product itself, in other words policy.[374] Two items looked at this area. Using a standard five-point response set, the items were each prefaced with the statement that, "The defeats at the 1997 and 2001 general elections show that the Conservative Party…" followed by "Needs to change its principles and beliefs" and "Needs to change its style and presentation".

ANOVA detected a single significant between-groups difference (p = 0.005) between ELCs and MPs (Bonferroni post-hoc test, p = 0.003) on the question of whether respondents thought that the Party needed to change its principles and beliefs. Irrespective of this, amongst all groups of respondents only a minority believed that this

---

[371] Glover, 9th February 2002; Wyn Jones in Shipton, 16th October 2008; but see Association of Professional Opinion Polling Organisations, 8th June 2001.

[372] Lees-Marshment & Quayle, April 2000.

[373] Watt, 8th February 2000.

[374] Lees-Marshment, November 2001: 929 & 938; October 2004: 396.

was the case. However, as Table 5.1 indicates, this was sometimes a sizable minority with a smaller proportion unsure. In other words, some respondents "had doubts".

TABLE 5.1: CONSERVATIVE PARTY SHOULD CHANGE ITS PRINCIPLES AND BELIEFS							
	ELCs	Peers	MPs	SLCs	WLCs	MEPs	MSPs
Agree	28%	22%	16%	21%	28%	21%	21%
Neither/nor	14%	9%	12%	12%	11%	7%	14%
Disagree	58%	69%	72%	67%	61%	71%	64%
Base	277	58	51	48	28	14	14

When it came to style and presentation, the picture was much more clear-cut. Irrespective of which group of respondents they came from – and ANOVA detected no significant between-groups differences (p = 0.141) – the overwhelming majority (88% or more) of respondents agreed that the Party needed to change. The proportion of those who actively disagreed with the idea that the Party needed to change its style and presentation never exceeded 4% irrespective of to which group of respondents they belonged.

In short, respondents tended not to be unhappy with the Party's "ideology" but they were very unhappy about the Party's "public relations".

Why was change needed?

Having established that at least a substantial minority of respondents felt that the Party needed to change its principles and beliefs and others were uncertain about this, and also that the overwhelming majority felt that the Party needed to change its style and presentation, the next question is "why?" In others words, what was associated with a desire for change?

Unfortunately, however this question is approached – using regression analysis or partial correlation analysis, for example – no more can be made of the "style and presentation" item given the very one-sided loading of responses.

However, the "principles and beliefs" item allows a more thorough exploration of the perceived need for change. Because of its specific nature, a regression analysis was run with "Needs to change its principles and beliefs" as the dependant variable and the usual range of multi-item scales and dummy variables for the types of respondent as the putative significant predictors.

The result, whilst perhaps predictable, was nevertheless still revealing. When specifically asked about the need to change the Party's then principles and beliefs, by far the strongest independent variable in the final model (not shown in full here) as to why this might be so was the Optimism scale which alone accounted for 14% out of the total predictive power of the model of 27% (based upon the R^2 figure). Bivariate analysis was equally predictable. The less optimistic respondents were about the Party's present state and likely future fortunes then the keener they were on change. In short, arguably the main determinant of a need for change amongst representatives of a party no longer in control at Westminster was a desire to regain power. Ideological considerations were decidedly secondary.[375]

There were such secondary reasons, but they were something of a jumble. Excluding the minor if still statistically significant presence of a single dummy variable for type of respondent, there were five other attitudinal predictors of the perception of a need for change to the Party's principles and beliefs. The strongest of these was Europeanism with a predictive power of 4% of the total predictive power of the model of 27%. Bivariate analysis (not shown here) is clear. The *less* Euro-sceptic respondents were then the *more* they were inclined towards wanting change. This was true for all groups of respondents if not always significantly so because of the small sizes of some of the groups. This suggests that less Euro-sceptic respondents both viewed the Conservative Party as being strongly – even excessively so in their view – Euro-sceptic and that change to a less Euro-sceptic position was desirable to bolster the Party's fortunes.

Although minor in absolute terms, other information from the questionnaire allows a detailed examination of this finding. There was an item in the questionnaire that asked respondents to rate themselves and various political parties subjectively on a 10-point, "Euro-enthusiast" to "Euro-sceptic" scale. By subtracting the item for

---

[375] Again, I remind readers of my comments near the start of this book.

themselves from the item for the Conservative Party a new variable was calculated identifying those who viewed themselves as more Euro-sceptic than the Party, those who viewed themselves as less Euro-sceptic than the Party and those who held that their views matched.

(This variable is interesting in its own right. There was considerable variation between the groups of respondents and, perhaps surprisingly, it was MSPs and not MEPs who were most likely to have viewed themselves as less Euro-sceptic than the Party.)

It might be hypothesised that those who viewed themselves as being less Euro-sceptic than the Party tended to be the ones wanting change in the Party's principles and beliefs. This can be analysed in a number of ways. One was a series of bivariate correlations, split by type of respondent, between the two, uncondensed items – perceived need for changing the Party's principles and beliefs and the difference in subjective Europeanism of respondents and the Conservative Party – along with the one-tailed hypothesis that those who viewed themselves as less Euro-sceptic than the Party were more inclined to want change.

Given the Pearson signs and the directions of the items, the results lend support to the hypothesis. None of the bivariate correlations went against it and in two cases, ELCs (correlation = 0.212, p = <0.001) and MPs (correlation 0.535, p = <0.001), the combination of correlation strength and sample size was sufficient to raise the correlation to a statistically significant one. As was predicted, those who viewed themselves as being less Euro-sceptic than the Party tended to have been the ones wanting change in the Party's principles and beliefs *generally* although attitudes towards the EU was itself the prime visible factor in this.

This is interesting. Detailed analysis following the 1997 election indicated that overall Labour and the Liberal Democrats more nearly represented the policy preferences of voters than did the Conservatives. The notable exception was on the issue of the EU where the Conservative's perceived Euro-scepticism chimed with the views of voters.[376] However, there was disagreement amongst Conservatives about what they should take from this. Some argued for a move to the "centre". Others suggested targeting the one million

---

[376] McAllister & Studlar, 2000: 368.

presumed anti-EU voters who had voted for the Referendum Party or UKIP along with waiting for disillusion with Labour to set in.[377] Paradoxically, it was those who were relatively less Euro-sceptic amongst respondents who seemed most in favour of the Party needing to change in principles and beliefs were. It can be speculated that so dominant had the theme of "Europe" become, that reigning-in Euro-scepticism was seen as a move to the "centre".

The next strongest (3% of the total of 27%) was, rather unpredictably, Theocratism. The more theocratic respondents were then the less they were inclined towards wanting change. This might suggest that there was a belief on the part of those enthused by the idea of a strong role for religion in public life both that the Conservative Party was itself generally theocratic as measured by the scale and also that this was fine within the context of the Conservative Party's future electoral fortunes. Intra-Party Inclusivity, Authoritarianism and Postmaterialism all had a marginal significant input into the model of 1% or 2% each, but they will not be considered further here.

The Conservative Party: What is it good for?

A perceived lack of clarity

Two items in the questionnaire looked at views on the overall purpose of the Conservative Party, or at least whether it was thought that there *was* any. These were, "In recent years, it has not always been clear what the Conservative Party stands *for*" and its mirror image, "In recent years, it has not always been clear what the Conservative Party stands *against*". Both were presented with a standard five-point response set.

ANOVA detected no significant between-groups differences (p = 0.536) in the case of "stands for" item. Using the entire dataset, almost exactly three-quarters (74%) of respondents agreed with this item against 20% who disagreed.

However, as Table 5.2 indicates, there were more appreciable differences (p = 0.001) in the case of the "stands against" item.

---

[377] Butler & Kavanagh, 2002[a]: 39-40.

TABLE 5.2: NOT CLEAR WHAT CONSERVATIVE PARTY STANDS AGAINST							
	ELCs	**Peers**	**MPs**	**SLCs**	**WLCs**	**MEPs**	**MSPs**
Agree	60%	57%	36%	71%	64%	64%	43%
Neither/nor	10%	7%	2%	4%	11%	0%	0%
Disagree	30%	37%	62%	25%	25%	36%	57%
Base	**280**	**60**	**52**	**48**	**28**	**14**	**14**

In short, the belief that the Party had become "woolly" in its ideological *prescriptions* was strongly and widely held. This was generally if more weakly the same view when considering the Party's ideological *proscriptions*, although MPs and MSPs seemed to have a stronger sense of who or what was "the enemy".

Assuming some degree of objective reality to these opinions, a number of reasons can be suggested for this. In the aftermath of the crushing defeat at the 1997 general election, the Party was shell-shocked and "was slow to set up the necessary machinery to conduct long-term policy development", something that did not meaningfully get underway until after another defeat at the 2001 election.[378] Put crudely, in terms of policy, it was argued that the Party had been flapping around for years.

The longer-term problem was the disappearance of major confrontational "others" against which the Conservative Party and some form of alternative grand vision could be contrasted,[379] whether domestically such as trades union militancy or abroad with the Soviet Union. The collapse of the latter and the rise of New Labour rather put paid to that contrast.

Specifically within the context of discussing the Conservative Party, it was argued[380] that one could not give a short answer to the question "what do the Conservatives stand for?" This was at least in part because one could not give a short answer to the question "what is it that they stand against?" In other words, because they were two sides of the same coin. This was often the case with respondents. Bivariate analysis (not shown here) indicated a positive correlation between responses to the two items amongst almost all groups of

---

[378] Clark & Kelly, October 2004: 379.
[379] Gamble, 1996: 35; Gray, 2001; McAnulla, 1997: 316-322; Pilbeam, 1998: 280-282.
[380] O'Sullivan, 1999: 9.

respondents large enough to measure. The sole exception were MSPs who were noted above as being one of the two groups of respondents more sure of the enemy. The SNP, perhaps?

However, when looking in more detail, regression analysis (not shown here) using the usual range of multi-item scales and dummy variables for the groups of respondents was unable to detect any substantial predictors to the responses to the two items. Once significant dummy variables for the groups of respondents were taken into consideration (particularly for the "against" item as might have been anticipated), neither model was particularly informative. The sense of "drift" was a diffuse one.

Inconsistent attitudes?

Considering all of this but thinking also about the earlier part of this chapter, there is something of a puzzle. It was noted above that a clear majority of respondents *disagreed* with the proposition that the Party needed to change its principles and beliefs. Yet it has just been seen that, generally speaking, a majority of respondents *agreed* with the propositions that it was not clear what the Party stood for or against. To simplify matters for the sake of illustration, on the face of it the findings described a group of people who were generally happy with the Party's ideology but who had little idea what it was!

This description is a little unfair, and further analysis attenuated the apparent inconsistency. Bivariate analysis using the whole dataset indicated a significant association in the predictable direction between the "change its principles and beliefs" item and "not clear what Conservative Party stands for" (one-tailed $p = 0.02$ using the chi^2 statistic) and "not clear what Conservative Party stands against" (one-tailed $p = 0.025$ using the chi^2 statistic) items. Those less inclined to think that the Party needed to change its principles and beliefs were also less inclined to think that it was unclear what the Party stood for or against.

The inconsistency might also be an example of what happens when one approaches a problem from different directions. It might also be possible that some respondents thought that whilst *they* knew what the Party stood for or against, the Party had not communicated this to the electorate.

Nevertheless, this only goes so far in attenuating the inconsistency. Using the entire dataset and looking just at the "extremes" of this inconsistency, 43% (out of 493 respondents) *disagreed* that the Party needed to change its principles and beliefs but also *agreed* that it was not clear what the Party stood for. Similarly, exactly a third (33% of 487 respondents) *disagreed* that the Party needed to change its principles and beliefs but also *agreed* that it was not clear what the Party stood against.

One further piece of information can be taken from these cross-tabulations. Since one of the variables was held the same, by using the Cramer's V measure of the strength of association it can be determined whether a desire for change of the sort discussed earlier in this chapter was more strongly held with perceived weaknesses in what the Party stood for or against. In fact, with a finding of 0.103 for "for" and 0.102 for "against", they were virtually identical. Again, this suggests that these are probably two sides of the same coin.

Party Leaders

A first look

Respondents were asked to rate the most recent leaders of the Conservative Party on a five-point, "Very positively" to "Very negatively" scale. ANOVA detected no between-groups differences in attitudes towards Edward Heath ($p = 0.196$), John Major ($p = 0.90$) or William Hague ($p = 0.509$). Using the entire dataset for these three individuals provides the results set out in Table 5.3a.

TABLE 5.3A: ATTITUDE TOWARDS LEADERS OF THE CONSERVATIVE PARTY			
	Edward Heath	**John Major**	**William Hague**
Positive	24%	58%	55%
Neutral	20%	23%	24%
Negative	56%	19%	21%
Base	**501**	**503**	**504**

There were, however, significant between-groups differences in the cases of Margaret Thatcher ($p = 0.008$) and Iain Duncan Smith (p = 0.006). The results for these two individuals are set out in more detail in Tables 5.3b & 5.3c.

TABLE 5.3B: ATTITUDE TOWARDS MARGARET THATCHER							
	ELCs	Peers	MPs	SLCs	WLCs	MEPs	MSPs
Positive	96%	98%	96%	96%	100%	93%	71%
Neutral	3%	2%	4%	0%	0%	0%	7%
Negative	1%	0%	0%	4%	0%	7%	22%
Base	283	60	51	48	28	14	14

TABLE 5.3C: ATTITUDE TOWARDS IAIN DUNCAN SMITH							
	ELCs	Peers	MPs	SLCs	WLCs	MEPs	MSPs
Positive	58%	60%	78%	73%	79%	72%	93%
Neutral	32%	32%	20%	25%	18%	7%	7%
Negative	10%	8%	2%	2%	3%	21%	0%
Base	282	60	51	48	28	14	14

Before moving on to multivariate analysis a few items stand out from these tables. Edward Heath was rather disliked with just over half of all respondents rating him negatively. This echoes earlier findings amongst Conservative Party members.[381]

Margaret Thatcher, on the other hand, was positively worshipped (with the exception of MSPs amongst whom there was some coolness). At the risk of flippancy, her ratings were those probably more associated with the sort of "polls" held by – to name just two leaders in 2002 – Kim Jong-il of North Korea and Saddam Hussein of Iraq.

The attitudes towards the three post-Thatcher leaders were broadly similar. They were generally positive[382] but with a leavening of neutrality and sometimes outright hostility. The somewhat inconsistent attitudes towards Iain Duncan Smith may, in part, stem from a mixture of such things as loyalty (or not) towards the leader of the Party at the time of the fieldwork and/or from considerations of his shaky hold on that leadership.

In different ways, then, when analysed on this level and when compared to each other, it was Edward Heath and Margaret Thatcher

---

[381] Whiteley, Seyd & Richardson, 1994: 61.
[382] Anderson, 25th November 2000.

who stood out. It was perhaps a surprising finding given the rivalry between them and their supporters[383] that when analysed on a between-groups basis there was no significant correlation at the conventional two-tailed 5% level in attitudes towards them.

Regarding attitudes towards the three who had actually been prime ministers, other polls of the public and academics alike of 20th century British prime ministers tended to rate Thatcher near the top with both Heath and Major in the bottom half.[384]

Multivariate analysis

Were there any predictors of attitudes towards party leaders? To go some way to answering this, a series of regression analyses was run with the dependant variable being attitude towards each leader in turn and the putative independent variables being the standard range of multi-item scales along with dummy variables for the various groups of respondents. Regression was used in this instance because, at least on balance, it seems plausible to suggest a causal relationship between scales measuring attitudes, values or beliefs on the one hand and individuals on the other hand who might be regarded as champions (or not) of those values.

The much simplified Tables 5.4a to 5.4e display the leaders and the predictors of variability in attitude towards each leader left in the final, significant regression model. The percentage figures are based on the adjusted R^2 figure.

TABLE 5.4A: PREDICTORS OF ATTITUDES TOWARDS EDWARD HEATH	
Variable	**Variability explained**
Europeanism	29%
Audience dummy	2%
Pride in National Heritage and Culture	2%
Optimism	1%
Total	34%
Base	**321**

---

[383] Monteith, 22nd July 2005.
[384] Theakston & Gill, May 2006.

TABLE 5.4B: PREDICTORS OF ATTITUDES TOWARDS MARGARET THATCHER

Variable	Variability explained
Optimism	9%
Europeanism	4%
Religiosity	3%
Welfarism	2%
Political Elitism	1%
Audience dummy	1%
Total	20%
Base	**321**

TABLE 5.4C: PREDICTORS OF ATTITUDES TOWARDS JOHN MAJOR

Variable	Variability explained
Europeanism	11%
Pride in Way Nation Functions	4%
Audience dummy	2%
Intra-Party Inclusivity	2%
Postmaterialism	2%
Total	19%
Base	**321**

TABLE 5.4D: PREDICTORS OF ATTITUDES TOWARDS WILLIAM HAGUE

Variable	Variability explained
Europeanism	9%
Optimism	3%
Authoritarianism	2%
Feminism	1%
Total	15%
Base	**321**

TABLE 5.4E: PREDICTORS OF ATTITUDES TOWARDS IAIN DUNCAN SMITH	
Variable	**Variability explained**
Optimism	18%
Left-Right	3%
Audience dummy	1%
Total	22%
Base	**321**

The most notable finding must be that for Edward Heath. The final model explained 34% of the total variability. Of this total, no less than 29% was explained by just one variable, Europeanism,[385] with the remainder contributing no more than 1% or 2% each. It almost goes without saying that bivariate analysis confirms that the more Euro-sceptic respondents were then the less favourable they tended to be towards Heath.[386]

The other striking finding was at the other end of the study's timescale: the finding for Iain Duncan Smith and the predictive power of 18% for the Optimism variable. The more optimistic respondents were about the then state and likely future fortunes of the Conservative Party the more favourable they were towards Duncan Smith. However, referring the Chapter 12 on the Party's leadership contest, what is perhaps surprising is the absence of the Europeanism scale in predicting attitudes towards Duncan Smith.

Looking at the three leaders in between Heath and Duncan Smith, in each case there was one variable that explained about 10% of the total variability in attitude. In the case of Thatcher, just like Duncan Smith, the more optimistic respondents were about the then present state and likely future fortunes of the Conservative Party (9% out of a total predictive model of 20%) then the more favourable they were towards her. It is hard not too see this as a belief that there needed to be "no turning back" from Thatcherism. Euro-sceptic respondents were also more favourable towards her. Other than that, however, nothing stands out. It may seem odd to have little more to say here about Margaret Thatcher but the extreme loading of attitudes towards her makes further analysis difficult. As adored as she

---

[385] Griffiths, 1996: 69.
[386] Letwin, 1996: 175-176.

generally may still have been in 2002, it is a struggle to find obviously "ideological" reasons for this beyond the predictable Europeanism scale. As such, it is probably not far off the mark to think instead about such concepts as "charisma".[387] (It was his perceived lack of this quality which was viewed by many as a reason for Iain Duncan Smith's difficulties.[388])

In the case of John Major, Europeanism was again the main predictor of attitudes at 11% out of a total of 19%. In his case the less Euro-sceptic respondents were then the more favourable they tended to be. Given the history of John Major and the *Maastricht Treaty* then this is not too surprising.[389]

For William Hague, Europeanism was also the main predictor of attitudes explaining 9% out of a total variability of 15%. However, in his case it was the opposite of Major: the more Euro-sceptic respondents were then the more favourable they tended to be. During his time as leader, rightly or wrongly, Hague was seen by friends and foes alike as staunchly Euro-sceptic.[390]

Of note was that "economics", particularly as measured by the Left-Right dimension, had almost no predictive power, only appearing as a minor indicator in the case of Iain Duncan Smith. It might be noted historically that early opposition to Heath within the Party was substantially on economic issues[391] rather than that of "Europe".

That said, this surely is the main finding from these analyses. One way or the other, attitudes towards the EU measured by the Europeanism scale was the strongest predictor of attitudes towards Edward Heath, John Major and William Hague and was the second strongest predictor for Margaret Thatcher and Iain Duncan Smith. In turn, attitudes towards the present state and likely fortunes of the Party measured by the Optimism scale was the strongest predictor of attitudes towards Margaret Thatcher and Iain Duncan Smith. It seems that what mattered to respondents was "Europe" and "power".

---

[387] Jary & Jary, 1991: 64-65; Kempley, 2009/2010: 38; Scarbrough, 1984: 47.

[388] Jenkins, 9th October 2002.

[389] Gorman, 1993; Spicer, 1992.

[390] Oborne & Weaver, 2011.

[391] Green, 2002: 234.

Youth Organisations

Membership

Regarding the Party's youth organisations,[392] the first was the Young Imperial League created in the early 20th century. The Federation of University Conservative and Unionist Associations (FUCUA) was founded in 1931 and was aimed at undergraduates. This was followed in 1967 by the Federation of Conservative Students (FCS) which in turn was followed in 1987 by the Conservative Collegiate Forum (CCF) following the disbanding of the FCS in 1986 by the then party chairman Norman Tebbit.[393] The most famous youth organisation, the Young Conservatives (YCs), was formed after the Second World War. However, there was a consolidation in 1998 of all youth organisations – for those under the age of 30 – resulting in Conservative Future.

All respondents were asked whether they had been members of these organisations. Few respondents said that they had been members of the Federation of University Conservative and Unionist Associations (4%), the Conservative Collegiate Forum (2%), the National Association of Conservative Graduates (2%), Conservative Future (2%) or the Federation of Conservative Students (7%). However, rather more said that they had been members of the Young Conservatives (33%).

Of the groups of respondents large enough to analyse, MPs were by some way the most likely to have been members of the YCs, with 52% reporting that they had against approximately a quarter to a third of all the others. MEPs were the least likely with only 21% (i.e. 3 respondents) saying that they had been members of the YCs. MPs were also easily the most likely to have been members of the FCS, with 29% saying that they had been members against very small numbers in the other groups.

Whatever happened to the "Conservative Radicals"?

Evans's study[394] of Conservative youth structures gives rise to the plausible hypothesis of a degree of radicalisation amongst Conservatives who had been members of the FCS. The problem is

---

[392] Epping Forest Conservatives, 7th March 2006; Evans, 1996: 2-3, 12 & 44 & 79.
[393] *BBC News*, 24th June 2009.
[394] Evans, 1996; and compare the very different Holroyd-Doveton, 1996.

that there were such small numbers involved with only 35 individuals spread across a number of groups of respondents. On top of this there were possibly confounding factors such as age and sex, information not held for most groups of respondents. This makes meaningful analysis very difficult. Only in the case of MPs was there a sufficiently homogenous group with large enough numbers even to attempt such an analysis. However, analysis using t-tests on the various multi-item scales with whether or not respondents had been members of the FCS as the grouping variable found only a solitary significant difference: Pride in the Way Nation Functions.

It should be acknowledged that this is not a fair analysis. It would require much more data and/or a radically different methodology to research the impact of socialisation and possible radicalisation within the FCS, particularly in the 1980s before the Party closed it down perceiving it to be excessively "radical".[395] This brief sub-section is here to note the possibility of such research.

Conclusion to Chapter 5

Perhaps the most striking finding comes from the single item within the Optimism scale, "The Conservative Party can win the next general election", the results of which suggests just how out of touch with public opinion Conservative politicians seemed to have been in 2002. This was made starker given that polling in very early 2003, only a few months after the fieldwork, indicated that Conservative politicians were less trusted than those from either the Labour or Liberal Democrat parties.[396] It is a tedious convention that when being interviewed politicians are obliged to sound upbeat about their electoral prospects even in the teeth of all the evidence. However, even within the confines of an anonymous questionnaire this was still the "form". Perhaps, despite everything, they really believed it.

Inasmuch as there was perceived to be a need for change, this was much more strongly in the area of "style and presentation" rather then "principles and beliefs". In other words, to borrow from the standard "four Ps" of the marketing mix,[397] it was not so much the

---

[395] Libertarian Alliance, 2009.
[396] Barnett, July-September 2008: 322.
[397] Lilien *et al*, 1992.

"product" as the "promotion" that was perceived to have been at fault for the disastrous general election results in 1997 and 2001. Where the product was seen as in need of an ideological overhaul much of this desire seems to have come from the Party's less Euro-sceptic politicians. As will be discussed in Chapter 12 on the 2001 leadership contest, even under Iain Duncan Smith the Party's leadership sought to "neutralise" this strongly felt issue, at least as far as the public's perception of it was concerned.

It is also clear that by 2002 many respondents were unsure what the Conservative Party either stood for or, albeit less strongly, against. Attitudes towards these two were closely linked. However, there was little explicit reasoning behind this. Instead, it seemed to speak of a strong but diffuse sense of wooliness and drift. This sense of drift was shared by the electorate. In the previous year's general election, only 9% of voters thought that that Conservatives were the most clear and united about what their policies should be.[398]

It was seen that there was an apparent inconsistency in that whilst a majority of respondents did not think that the Party needed to change its principles and beliefs they *also* tended to believe that it was not clear what the Party stood for or against. Whilst attenuating and explaining some of this, nevertheless the inconsistency stood.

There is also a paradox here concerned with changing the Party's policies and/or image. Research after 2002 indicated that when a policy with strong support amongst the general population such as controls on immigration was revealed to be a Conservative policy, it immediately lost that support.[399] As such, it could be argued that this is support for the "policy good, image bad" views noted above. Paradoxically, it was many of these more popular policies that "modernisers" within the Party aspired to change in order to appease "liberal" critics of the Party.

Attitudes towards the Party's leaders in the years leading up to the survey indicated generally positive views of John Major, William Hague and Iain Duncan Smith, but considerable coolness towards Edward Heath and something approaching worship of Margaret Thatcher. The main significant predictors of these attitudes often accorded with reasonable expectations. This was particularly true in

---

[398] Lees-Marshment, November 2001: 939.
[399] O'Sullivan, 2009.

the case of Heath (Europeanism) and to a lesser degree in the cases of Thatcher and Duncan Smith (Optimism in both cases). The salience of these two scales is a key finding of this section. All other issues – whether social or economic – were decidedly secondary.

It is fitting to conclude this chapter with attitudes towards Margaret Thatcher. Amongst almost all groups – not just the Party's middle and lower ranks[400] – attitudes towards her were both overwhelmingly positive and yet quite hard to explain objectively by way of attitudinal variables. It was suggested that it was perhaps more to do with "charisma" and hence that attitudes towards her were visceral than intellectual. Given the reverence in which she was still held – in sharp contrast to Heath[401] – some dozen years after her (as some believed) betrayal by others,[402] then the long "shadow" which she cast for so long over the Party and perhaps the country as a whole is hardly surprising.[403]

---

[400] Green, 2002: 235.
[401] Norton, 1992: 57.
[402] Marquand, 2009: 327.
[403] Anderson, 25th November 2000; Garnett, October 2004: 367; Green, 2002: 235; Groves, 26th February 2010; Hall, 19th January 2010; Lister et al, 2002; Robertson, 7th April 2008; Whitworth & Baldwin, 26th February 2010: 26.

6

Attitudes about Other UK Parties

One Amongst Many

The Conservative Party does not operate in a political vacuum. It is but one of a number of competing political parties, albeit historically one of the most important. In this chapter, attitudes of respondents towards their party-political competitors are examined.

This is done by a series of analyses. First, by obtaining a general impression of how well-disposed or ill-disposed respondents were towards the other parties. Second, by analysing if there were any significant differences between the various groups of respondents and how they viewed the other parties. Third, by analysing if there were any variables associated with attitudes towards the other parties and in particular whether there were any universal predictors (which might say more about the respondents themselves) and/or any party-specific predictors (which might say more about attitudes towards individual parties).

Chapter 13 in part returns to this theme, but with a view to looking at the impact of electoral politics and the experience "on the ground" of competing against Labour and the Liberal Democrats.

Overview of Attitudes Towards Other Parties

Questionnaire items about the other parties

The questionnaire contained two batteries of questions looking at the other political parties of note in 2002. One was prefaced by "How do you feel towards the following mainland British political parties" and the other by "How do you feel towards the following Northern Ireland political parties". There were 13 parties included – by no means *every* political party then operating somewhere in the United Kingdom – and aside from any constitutional and historical reasons the divide between mainland and Northern Ireland parties was largely a device to split this large number into more manageable groups.

The mainland British parties were: Labour Party, Liberal Democrats (Lib Dems), Plaid Cymru (PC), Scottish National Party (SNP), UK Independence Party (UKIP), British National Party (BNP), Green Party and the Socialist Alliance/Scottish Socialist Party (SA/SSP).

The Northern Ireland parties were: Ulster Unionist Party (UUP), Democratic Unionist Party (DUP), Sinn Fein, Social Democratic and Labour Party (SDLP) and the Alliance Party of Northern Ireland (APNI). Leading up to 2002, the Conservatives were the only major mainland party that campaigned under its own name in Northern Ireland,[404] the others having relationships such as that between the Labour Party and the SDLP.[405] After an initially bright start at a local level the Conservative Party's results in Northern Ireland were very poor. It was claimed that it was one of the conditions of John Major securing the support of nine UUP MPs during the passage of the *Maastricht Treaty* that the Conservative Party would allow the Northern Irish Conservatives "to wither on the vine".[406] By the time of the fieldwork this seems to have been achieved.[407]

Self-reported insufficient knowledge

Both batteries offered a five-level response set of "Strongly sympathetic to "Strongly antipathetic". In addition – a rarity for the *CPRS 2002* – they were offered a sixth option of "Don't know enough to say" and these responses are detailed in Table 6.1.

---

[404] Conservative Party, 1998: 8.
[405] Conservatives in Northern Ireland, c. 2000.
[406] Coulter, 2001: 29-41.
[407] Watt, 5th January 2001.

TABLE 6.1: DON'T KNOW ENOUGH ABOUT PARTY TO SAY[408]							
Party	**ELC**	**Peers**	**MPs**	**SLCs**	**WLCs**	**MEPs**	**MSPs**
Labour	1%	0%	0%	0%	0%	0%	<1%
Lib Dems	1%	0%	0%	2%	0%	0%	0%
PC	31%	24%	4%	39%	0%	18%	18%
SNP	26%	13%	2%	0%	12%	9%	0%
UKIP	9%	5%	0%	7%	4%	0%	0%
BNP	7%	2%	0%	7%	0%	0%	0%
Greens	9%	2%	2%	9%	0%	0%	8%
SA/SSP	23%	15%	8%	2%	16%	9%	0%
UUP	13%	2%	0%	9%	8%	0%	0%
DUP	15%	2%	0%	9%	8%	0%	0%
SF	13%	0%	0%	7%	4%	0%	0%
SDLP	23%	8%	0%	16%	20%	0%	8%
APNI	44%	31%	6%	36%	36%	18%	8%

A cynic might define a politician as someone with the ability to talk with great confidence for long periods of time on subjects about which they know very little. However, it is clear that amongst some respondents there was an honest admission of ignorance about some of the other parties, in particular those from Northern Ireland, Scotland and Wales. (Which emphasises the largely English nature of the Party by 2002.) The APNI seemed to be the most mysterious for respondents. That it was *not* the SA/SSP is interesting because in objective terms it probably *was* the most obscure at the time although less so in Scotland under the SSP banner.[409]

The differing responses of ELCs, SLCs and WLCs towards the SNP and PC is also of note if only to be expected. All SLCs and WLCs felt comfortable giving an opinion about the SNP and PC respectively whereas notable minorities of SLCs and WLCs professed ignorance about PC and the SNP respectively. A substantial minority of ELCs professed ignorance about both.

---

[408] Since these represent 91 separate calculations, for the sake of convenience no bases are presented.
[409] Baldwin, 13th July 2000; Gove, 15th January 2002; Kerevan, 5th May 2003 & 18th November 2004; Linklater, 25th April 2002.

At the other end of the scale, almost all respondents felt that they were sufficiently knowledgeable to offer a view about Labour and the Liberal Democrats.

Respondents who reported sufficient knowledge

In Tables 6.2a, 6.2b and 6.2c the figures represent the mean attitudes rounded to the nearest integer. The responses were scored 1 for "Strongly sympathetic" – although there were no such instances – to 5 for "Strongly antipathetic" with 3 representing a neutral view.

Table 6.2a: Attitudes towards the all-mainland British parties									
	Labour		Lib Dems		UKIP		BNP		Greens	
	Mean	Base	Mean	Base	Mean	Base	Mean	Base	Mean	Base
ELCs	4	275	5	276	4	248	5	256	4	249
Peers	4	59	5	59	4	55	5	58	4	58
MPs	4	49	5	49	4	49	5	48	4	48
SLCs	4	46	5	45	4	42	5	43	4	42
WLCs	4	25	5	25	5	24	5	25	4	25
MEPs	4	11	5	11	5	11	5	11	4	11
MSPs	4	12	5	12	5	12	5	12	4	11

TABLE 6.2B: ATTITUDES TOWARDS THE SCOTTISH AND WELSH PARTIES					
	PC		SNP		SA/SSP[410]	
	Mean	Base	Mean	Base	Mean	Base
ELCs	4	190	4	202	5	212
Peers	4	44	4	49	5	50
MPs	4	47	4	48	5	45
SLCs	4	28	5	46	5	45
WLCs	4	25	5	22	5	21
MEPs	4	9	4	10	5	10
MSPs	4	9	5	12	5	12

---

[410] The SA/SSP is included here because of its mainly Scottish presence as the SSP.

TABLE 6.2C: ATTITUDES TOWARDS THE NORTHERN IRELAND PARTIES									
	UUP		DUP		SF		SDLP		APNI	
	Mean	Base	Mean	Base	Mean	Base	Mean	Base	Mean	Base
ELCs	2	239	4	233	5	241	4	211	3	152
Peers	2	59	4	58	5	60	4	54	3	41
MPs	2	48	3	48	5	48	4	49	3	46
SLCs	2	41	4	41	5	42	4	38	3	29
WLCs	2	23	4	23	5	24	4	20	4	16
MEPs	2	11	3	11	5	11	4	11	3	9
MSPs	2	12	3	12	5	12	4	11	3	11

Tables 6.2a and 6.2b indicate not a single instance of anything other than antipathy towards the other mainland British parties. Table 6.2c on the other hand indicates that there was considerable warmth towards the UUP and at least some neutrality towards the DUP and the APNI. However, there was no such warmth towards the two historically Irish nationalist or Republican parties listed, the SDLP and Sinn Fein.

Looking in more detail at the mainland parties, the antipathy shown by respondents is roughly split into loathing verses mere dislike. The contrast in attitudes towards Labour and Liberal Democrats is striking. Respondents may have disliked Labour but they loathed the Liberal Democrats. The BNP – which did *not* appear to be "attractive" to respondents[411] – and the Socialist Alliance – perhaps just because of its name – also evoked such feeling. To look at it from the other direction, along with the Green Party the Labour Party was the *least* actively disliked other party campaigning in England.

The Greens and Plaid Cymru seem to have been disliked but with no particular fervour. There were mixed views about UKIP and the SNP. Ignoring for the moment the cases of WLCs and MSPs, it is probably no surprise that MEPs particularly disliked UKIP.[412] It is also probably no coincidence that both of the specifically Scottish groups – SLCs and MSPs – were particularly hostile towards the SNP although this phenomenon was not replicated concerning WLCs and Plaid Cymru despite some claims that the opposite has been true historically.[413]

---

[411] Garnett & Lynch, January 2002: 37.
[412] Batten, January/February 2005.
[413] Evans, 2002: 5.

These results contradict the findings of the *True Blues* study[414] of Conservative Party *members* conducted a decade earlier in early 1992. Most notably, this earlier study found that the Liberal Democrats were by some way the *least* disliked out of Labour, the Liberal Democrats, the SNP, Plaid Cymru and the Greens, not the *most* disliked as our data suggests.

By looking at another dataset, this time for the *British Election Panel Study 2001*,[415] it can be seen that these findings suggest an enduring difference between Conservative Party politicians on the one hand and Conservative members and supporters on the other. The *BEPS* data used here was the person-to-person survey conducted by NOP after the 2001 general election. Attitudes towards Labour, the Liberal Democrats, the SNP and Plaid Cymru as well as the Conservatives were measured on an 11-point "Dislike" to "Like" scale. In the cases of both "Very strong" and "Fairly strong" Conservative identifiers the Liberal Democrats were *less* disliked than Labour, the SNP or Plaid Cymru.

Turning to Northern Ireland, and perhaps rather predictably, Sinn Fein was one of the most disliked of all other parties, vying with the BNP for the label of "most loathed". This might have been the finding at any time, but near the time of the fieldwork there was controversy over the Labour government's alleged plans to grant an amnesty to dozens of IRA terrorists who were on the run in exchange for any soldiers implicated in the Bloody Sunday killings not being prosecuted.[416] As an example of "today's news is tomorrow's fish and chip paper", only months before the fieldwork there was a political row when the government allowed Sinn Fein to use House of Commons facilities, a move opposed by the then Conservative opposition.[417] There was even an item devoted to this in the questionnaire (with a standard five-point Agree strongly to Disagree strongly response set): "The government was right to allow Sinn Fein MPs to make use of Commons facilities". The vast majority – 87% of the 499 who responded to this item – of respondents disagreed with the government's action. Furthermore, when split by group of respondents, there was a significant correlation (using the Pearson test in *SPSS*, two-tailed $p = <0.05$ in all relevant cases)

[414] Whiteley, Seyd & Richardson, 1994: 178.
[415] *BEPS*, 4th December 2006.
[416] Revill, 6th March 2002.
[417] Glover, 18th December 2001.

between this item and attitudes towards Sinn Fein in that the more antipathetic towards Sinn Fein they tended to be then the more respondents disagreed with the item.

The largely Catholic and Irish nationalist SDLP was also disliked, but not with the same intensity. The absolute number of Catholic respondents to our study was too small to allow objective analysis although a brief examination of the data suggests that Catholic respondents were less antipathetic towards both Sinn Fein and the SDLP than their Anglican colleagues.

After that, the picture changes. The DUP evoked some negative feelings, but tended to be viewed with some equanimity by members of other groups, not least by MPs who would have had some contact with them in the House of Commons. The cross-community Alliance Party generally evoked neutral views.

The exception was the UUP. It alone evoked sympathetic responses and this was true for all groups of respondents. This is unsurprising given the historical relationship – at the time at the EU level as well as at Westminster[418] – and openly expressed continuing closeness at the most senior level between it and the Conservatives.[419] In 2009 a joint committee of the Conservative Party and the UUP approved the formation of "a new force in Northern Ireland politics", the Conservatives and Unionists.[420]

That said, in 2000 two Conservative MPs campaigned for a DUP candidate – who was eventually victorious[421] – against a UUP candidate at a by-election and were opposed by the Conservative leadership for doing so.[422] Shortly after the fieldwork, a Conservative MP quit the party to stand for the Northern Ireland assembly as a DUP candidate.[423] This might be an expression of the neutral – as opposed to antipathetic – attitudes towards the DUP shown by at least MPs amongst respondents.

Certain items in the questionnaire were particularly sensitive to the historical context of the fieldwork. This is perhaps generally true about attitudes towards Irish matters.[424]

---

[418] European Democrats, 2007; Towler, Bordes & Rotherham, 2001: 3.

[419] Duncan Smith, 19th October 2002; Kite, 10th October 2001; Monteith, 31st October 2003; Trimble, 10th October 2001.

[420] Conservatives in Northern Ireland, 26th February 2009.

[421] Deans, 23rd September 2000.

[422] Walker, 20th September 2000.

[423] *Guardian*, 3rd October 2002.

[424] Howard, 3rd February 2004.

Differences between the groups of respondents

The tables above indicate that there were differences in how some of the groups tended to view some of the other parties.

However, ANOVA with the entire dataset excluding the two micro-groups found that this was often not to a statistically significant level. There were no significant between-groups differences at the conventional 5% level in attitudes towards Labour ($p = 0.968$), the Liberal Democrats ($p = 0.828$), UKIP ($p = 0.081$), the Greens ($p = 0.254$), the BNP ($p = 0.4$), the SNP ($p = 0.373$), Sinn Fein ($p = 0.747$) and the SA/SSP ($p = 0.252$).

To turn it around, the only parties were there were significant between-groups differences were Plaid Cymru ($p = 0.014$) and the four remaining Northern Ireland parties the SDLP ($p = 0.001$), the UUP, the DUP and the Alliance Party ($p = <0.001$ in all cases). Even here, the post-hoc Bonferroni test suggests that these differences were rarely significant at the 5% level when analysed at a group-to-group level (albeit that the small sizes of some of the groups lessened the chance of significant findings even with the omission of AMs and GLAs). The only parties about which there were at least some significant differences identifiable by pairs of groups were the DUP and the Alliance Party. Looking at the DUP, MPs were significantly more sympathetic towards it than ELCs and Peers (but none of the other groups). Looking at the Alliance Party, WLCs were significantly more antipathetic than Peers and MPs. It is not clear why this might have been the case and having run so many analyses this might be an example of a Type I error of a false positive.

Party-Politics and Attitudes

Analysis

Within the context of general antipathy towards almost all other parties, were there any significant associates of such attitudes? Since it cannot be said with certainty if there is a causal relationship between attitudes towards the other political parties and the sorts of attitudes measured by this study's range of multi-item scales, partial correlation analysis was used rather than regression analysis.

Additionally, only the UK-wide parties – Labour, Liberal Democrats, UKIP, the BNP and the Greens – are studied in any detail. This is for a variety of reasons such as self-reported insufficient knowledge for some of the smaller and specifically Celtic parties; the ANOVA results noted above which detected certain between-groups differences in attitudes; the anomalous position of Northern Ireland in terms of party representation; and the small size of some the study's Scottish and in particular Welsh groups of respondents.

The major UK-wide parties

Starting first with the major UK-wide parties – Labour and the Liberal Democrats – and using the entire dataset, Table 6.3[425] displays the significant attitudinal correlations once all other multi-item scales have been accounted for.

TABLE 6.3: MAJOR UK-WIDE PARTIES AND ATTITUDINAL CORRELATES			
Party	**Scale**	**Correlation**	**Comments**
Labour	Europeanism	0.157	The more Euro-sceptic, the more antipathetic
	Left-Right	0.138	The more pro-free-market, the more antipathetic
	Pride in Way Nation Functions	-0.136	The more proud, the less antipathetic
Lib Dems	Europeanism	0.202	The more Euro-sceptic, the more antipathetic
	Left-Right	0.126	The more pro-free-market, the more antipathetic

It can be seen that the Pride in the Way the Nation Functions scale was significantly associated with attitudes towards the Labour Party. It is hard to analyse this finding at a simple bivariate descriptive level because of the one-sided loading for both variables. However, it would seem that greater pride in Britain in this respect was associated with somewhat less antipathy towards Labour. It might be suggested that this could be due to a view of

---

[425] P < 0.3 in all cases. Base for Labour = 295; for Liberal Democrats = 296.

Labour as a longstanding element of the fabric of British culture and democracy despite any ideological differences that respondents might have. But this is speculative.

Much less speculative is an explanation of the main finding that in both cases the only other significantly associated attitudinal variables were the two important scales of Europeanism and the Left-Right economics scale. Moreover, in both cases the findings were in the same, and surely expected, direction. The more Euro-sceptic and/or supportive of free-market economics respondents were then the more antipathetic they tended to be towards either party. This suggests, at least in part, a strongly ideological assessment of the Conservative Party's two main UK-wide opponents. Both of them were perceived as not merely competitors for power but "the enemy" in a more profound sense.

In a finer detail, it is of interest that in both cases there was a stronger correlation between attitudes towards the parties and placement on the Europeanism scale. As is mentioned throughout this book, this highlights the salience that "Europe" had for Conservatives in 2002.

The smaller UK-wide parties: Splittists or ginger group?

Turning to the minor UK-wide parties – UKIP, the BNP and the Greens – it can be seen from Table 6.4[426] that a very different picture emerges.

Before moving on to the major finding, it is not hard to see the connection between less antipathy for UKIP and more support for grass-roots control of the Conservative Party as measured by the Intra-Party Elitism scale as a cry of frustration from those sympathising with the Conservative Party's often Euro-sceptic membership as opposed to its more historically Euro-enthusiast leadership.

---

[426] P < 0.2 in all cases. Base for UKIP = 294; for BNP = 296; for Greens = 296.

TABLE 6.4: MINOR UK-WIDE PARTIES AND ATTITUDINAL CORRELATES			
Party	**Scale**	**Correlation**	**Comments**
UKIP	Europeanism	-0.292	The more Euro-sceptic, the less antipathetic
	Intra-Party Elitism	0.016	The greater grass-roots control of Conservative Party, the less antipathetic
	Traditional British Liberties	-0.151	The more authoritarian, the more antipathetic
BNP	Theocratism	0.172	The more theocratic, the more antipathetic
	Welfarism	0.16	Greater self-help views, the less antipathetic
	Xenophobia	-0.146	The more xenophobic, the less antipathetic
Greens	Europeanism	-0.161	The more Euro-sceptic, the more antipathetic
	Environmentalism	0.275	The more green, the less antipathetic

The finding that the more religious (in some sense) respondents were then the more antipathetic they tended to be towards the BNP may come as a surprise. In fact, this chimes with findings on religion and social attitudes from the USA. Whilst strong religious beliefs can indeed be associated with negative views about (say) sexuality, they can also act as a "brotherhood of man" inoculation against negative views on (say) race.[427] It is perhaps going too far to speculate whether the additional finding of the Welfarism scale and attitudes towards the BNP suggests a "survival of the fittest" attitude on the part of a minority of respondents.

However, the main finding was one that involved all three of these parties. It *cannot* have been a coincidence that in all three cases there was a significant association – if not necessarily the strongest one – between attitudes towards each party and the scale used in this

---

[427] Laythe, Finkel, & Kirkpatrick, March 2001.

study that is surely the one most closely associated with that party at the time: Europeanism, Xenophobia and Environmentalism.

When examined in detail the finding was even more powerful. Such analysis makes it clear that in each case respondents supportive of the views on the relevant scale most associated with the party concerned tended to be relatively less antipathetic towards the party. 25% of those respondents categorised as xenophobic were not antipathetic towards the BNP (a phenomenon suggested at the time of the 2001 leadership contest within the context of an attack on Iain Duncan Smith).[428] 39% of those categorised as Euro-sceptic were not antipathetic towards UKIP. No less than 51% of those categorised as having green or environmentalist views were not antipathetic towards the Green Party (and that there has been a strand of Conservative thinking sympathetic to green values generally is beyond doubt).[429]

Why? There are certainly two and by no means mutually exclusive possibilities. The first is straightforward: a simple match between views on an issue and the perception of a party's views on that issue. For example, that Euro-sceptics tended to be less hostile towards other Euro-sceptics. The results do not go against this.

However, the other possibility is more "political" and provides the slightly tongue-in-cheek title to this sub-section. For example, it is perfectly reasonable to hypothesise that – particularly on apparently clear-cut issues represented by parties closely associated with those issues – a relatively Euro-sceptic Conservative politician would be *more* hostile towards UKIP because they were "splittists" robbing the Conservatives of public support and votes.[430] (Something for which there was some evidence,[431] let alone that at around the time of the fieldwork some of the minor parties such as the Greens and UKIP were experiencing a growth in membership just as the major ones including the Conservatives were experiencing a long-term decline.)[432] There were certainly some who thought that this was true the other way around. It was suggested by one observer that many UKIP activists hated the Conservative Party, regarding them as "the class enemy".[433]

---

[428] Kent, 5th December 2001; Oborne, 1st February 2003.

[429] Lovibond, summer 2006; Pilbeam, October 2003.

[430] Cash, 5th January 2005; Gabb, 21st June 2004.

[431] Travis & White, 15th June 2004.

[432] Croucher, 8thJune 2002; Marquand, 2009: 154; *Guardian*, January 2002.

[433] North, 14th June 2004; UK Independence Party, 9th July 2002.

But it is equally reasonable to hypothesise that the opposite was true. For example, that a relatively pro-green Conservative politician would have been less hostile towards the Green Party because they were a courageous if usually electorally impractical "ginger group" within British party politics. (It is also possible that, regarding the Green Party, relative lack of antipathy was somehow evidence of support for "new" politics.[434] However, this hypothesis takes us beyond the capabilities of the data.)

The Scottish and Welsh parties

For the reasons cited above, only a brief mention can be made of the correlates of attitudes of respondents towards the Scottish, Welsh and Northern Irish parties. In the case of the Scottish and Welsh parties – the SNP, Plaid Cymru and the SA/SSP – when all of the other multi-item scales were taken into consideration there were very few significant associations. There were none at all with attitudes towards the SA/SSP and only one each for Plaid Cymru and the SNP as might occur when running such a lengthy series of analyses. It is safe to say that there were few ideological correlates with attitudes towards the Scottish and Welsh parties.

The Northern Irish parties

The series of analyses for the parties in Northern Ireland – the UUP, DUP, SDLP, Sinn Fein and the Alliance Party – was a little different to that of the mainland parties in that an additional item from the questionnaire was included. This was, "Who do you think has benefited most from the recent Northern Ireland peace process?" The response options were "The Unionist or Loyalist community", "Both equally" and "The Nationalist or Republican community". It is worth reporting in its own right that almost no respondents, irrespective of which group of politicians they belonged to, thought that the peace process had benefited the Unionist community. Only 5% of SLCs and 2% of ELCs thought that this had been the case, and nobody else. Whilst there were substantial minorities who thought that both communities had benefited – between a fifth and a third amongst all

---

[434] Cable, 1994: 32-33; Nas, 1995.

groups – in every case a clear majority thought that the peace process had been a victory for the Republican community.

That said, it must be noted that when the analysis was run for the Northern Irish parties this item was never significantly associated with attitudes towards any of them when all of the multi-item scales were taken into consideration.

In the case of the two mainly Protestant and Unionist parties, the UUP and the DUP, but also the cross-community Alliance, the results were similar to those of Scotland and Wales. With no or only one significant attitudinal correlate it is safe to say that there were few ideological correlates with attitudes towards them.

The findings were different for the two mainly Catholic and Nationalist/Republican parties. For both Sinn Fein (correlation 0.126, $p = 0.032$) and the SDLP (correlation 0.118, $p = 0.045$) there was only one significant correlate of attitudes towards them and this was the Xenophobia scale. In both instances there was the predictable finding that more xenophobic attitudes were associated with more antipathy towards these parties.

At the risk of forcing matters somewhat, a series of exploratory regression analyses (not shown here) were run with attitude towards each Northern Irish party as the dependant variable and the range of dimensions along with dummy variables for the various groups of respondents as the putative explanatory variables. When analysed in this manner there was a rather predictable finding but one which took things a little further than the findings of the partial correlation analyses above. For the Northern Irish parties the Xenophobia scale was a reoccurring predictor of some importance. In the cases of the mainly Protestant and Unionist parties, the DUP and the UUP, more xenophobic views were associated with less antipathetic attitudes towards the parties. In the cases of the mainly Catholic and Nationalist parties, Sinn Fein and the SDLP, but also the cross-community Alliance Party, more xenophobic views were associated with more antipathetic attitudes.

These findings robustly highlight the Unionist sympathies of our respondents. It might even speak of a degree of anti-Catholicism amongst some. However, although confessional background was one of the additional questions asked of ELCs, the small number of Catholic respondents makes further analysis impractical in this case.

Conclusion to Chapter 6

Looking at respondents' attitudes towards the other parties, the pattern seems clear. All of the mainland parties were disliked, but it was noticeable that the Liberal Democrats were more disliked than Labour across all groups of respondents. There was a more mixed view of the Northern Ireland parties, with those associated with Unionism viewed more favourably or at least less unfavourably.

Attitudinal associates of attitudes towards the Conservative Party's two main rivals, Labour and the Liberal Democrats, suggest a degree of universality in that attitudes towards the EU and economics were both significant. In both cases, attitudes on these scales were *negatively* associated with the other parties' generally perceived position. For example, respondents favouring free-market economics tended to be more antipathetic towards the Labour Party.

It should be noted what cannot be said from within the data. The results of the analyses in this chapter do not say much about why the Liberal Democrats were more disliked than Labour.

However, it was clear that when it came to parties rightly or wrongly identified as single-issue ones, the Green Party, the BNP and UKIP, then a major correlate was that scale most closely associated with the party concerned and that this association was *positively* correlated with the other parties' generally perceived position. For example, respondents favouring Euro-sceptic policies tended to be less antipathetic towards UKIP. In short, there was a qualitative difference between respondents' attitudes – or, rather, possible reasons for them – towards the two parties which were generally their main rivals on the one hand and the relatively minor parties on the other.

The only summary comment that can be made about attitudes towards the Celtic parties, or at least the Northern Irish ones, is that they strongly reflect the Unionism of our respondents.

7

The Wider World

A Research Question and Beyond

Whilst covering a range of issues concerned with the world outside of the UK, the main purpose of this chapter is to examine a particular – perhaps idiosyncratic – research question concerning the association between attitudes towards the EU, the USA and what is generally termed the Middle East. This is dealt with in the first section below.

After that, and using the same items from the questionnaire, the chapter tentatively investigates whether attitudes towards foreign affairs are associated with or cut across attitudes towards domestic ones.

Finally, to provide a more rounded sense of the views of respondents, additional data is analysed concerning attitudes towards the Commonwealth and the Islamic world.

Associated Attitudes about the Wider World?

The research question

This chapter does not intend to add to the many libraries' worth of material, academic or otherwise, concerning the Conservative Party and "Europe". Instead, it will look at a particular observation made by others around the time of the fieldwork and see, within the context of the data, whether there is any validity to the view expressed. No claim is made that these findings were particular to Conservative Party politicians in 2002. The aim here is to see whether, with the data to hand, any support can be given to the general observation.

Is it a case of "Euro-Sceptic, Atlanticist, Zionist, Economic Liberals' versus 'Euro-Enthusiast, Continentalist, Arabist, Economic Redistributionists"?

This observation, in whole or part, could be found in a variety of sources.[435] Closer inspection will reveal that most if not all of these sources are Euro-sceptic and/or pro-US and/or pro-Israeli and/or written from a libertarian or conservative perspective. However, whilst this may well bias the authors' perceptions it does not bias objective analysis.

The observation was that attitudes towards the EU, the USA and Israel were correlated with each other in that negative attitudes towards the first of these and positive attitudes towards the other two were associated with each other and vice-versa. (It is not the place here to discuss the view that a "pro-USA/anti-EU" stance is historically contradictory given the desire by successive US administrations for a "single phone number" when dealing with "Europe", the USA's post-War support for European integration[436] and the alleged actions that have been taken by US agencies to further this cause.[437])

There was also sometimes an additional observation that Euro-sceptic, pro-USA and pro-Israeli views tended to be correlated with support for free-market economics. In addition, it was claimed that younger people, particularly younger Conservatives, were more likely to be Euro-sceptic, pro-USA and pro-Israeli.

A variety of reasons have been put forward. Teasing out those most connected with this study, suggestions have included an "Arabist" romantic view of the Middle East and a degree of anti-Semitism; support for multiculturalism and/or an opposition to such things as a strong national and ethnic self-identity; regret at the displacement of a traditional and hierarchical society by a consumerist one; and anti-US or anti-Israeli views alongside an "enemy of my enemy" attitude towards the other.

---

[435] E.g. Applebaum, 12th September 2006; Craven, 17th January 2005; Davis, 25th May 2002; Duncan Smith, 18th September 2004; Hughes, 17th January 2005; Griffith, 12th February 2003; Hannan, 17th May 2006 & 12th August 2006; Joffe, 2002; Lowry, 19th January 2002; Pipes, 15th February 2005; Schroeder, February 2004; Steyn, 29th September 2001; Sullivan, 17th November 2002, *The Times*, 19th September 2002; Wooldridge, 31st May 2004; Yeor, 9th October 2002.
[436] Lundestad, 1997.
[437] Hitchens, 10th February 2009.

Whatever the validity of the explanations put forward, was there any evidence for the observation amongst respondents?

Analysing the observation with *CPRS 2002* data

A number of scales and single items in the questionnaire can be used to look at this observation. The Europeanism and Left-Right scales are encountered throughout this study, and ELCs were asked their age in the additional battery of items presented to them.

Respondents were also presented with two items dealing with the USA and also Israel and Arabia/Palestine. Regarding the former, respondents were presented with, "Britain should be more cautious in supporting the USA's foreign and military policies" along with a five-point Likert-type Agree strongly to Disagree strongly response set. (It will be remembered that the fieldwork took place after the terrorist attacks in the USA on the 11th September 2001 and the initial overthrow of the Taliban regime in Afghanistan but before the invasion of Iraq.) Regarding the latter, Respondents were presented with, "Thinking about the Middle East, how best would you describe yourself?" along with a five-point Likert-type "Very pro-Arab/Palestinian" to "Very pro-Israeli" response set.

Because of the speculative or exploratory nature of this chapter – and the fact that, as suggested above, it is as much to do with attitudes amongst the public – only the responses from local councillors in England, Scotland and Wales were analysed. ANOVA was first conducted and there were no significant between-groups differences on the three foreign affairs items concerning the EU as seen by the Europeanism scale ($p = 0.207$), the USA ($p = 0.095$) and the Middle East ($p = 0.967$), nor the Left-Right scale ($p = 0.402$).

The foreign affairs items

Univariate analysis of the combined responses from ELCs, SLCs and WLCs to the four main items or scales discussed above provides the figures set out in Tables 7.1a to 7.1d.

TABLE 7.1A: LEFT-RIGHT				
	Left	**Centre**	**Right**	
	5%	51%	44%	
Base				**346**

TABLE 7.1B: EUROPEANISM				
	Euro-enthusiast	**Euro-neutral**	**Euro-sceptic**	
	2%	46%	52%	
Base				**324**

TABLE 7.1C: THE MIDDLE EAST				
	Pro-Arab/Palestinian	**View both equally**	**Pro-Israeli**	
	17%	52%	31%	
Base				**348**

TABLE 7.1D: MORE CAUTIOUS IN SUPPORTING USA				
	Agree	**In between**	**Disagree**	
	60%	19%	21%	
Base				**354**

Local councillors – like other Conservative politicians at the time – were middling-to-free-marketeers regarding economics with very few displaying "leftist" views and were middling-to-sceptical towards the EU with very few enthusiasts.

Regarding the Middle East, respondents were more split with half (52%) viewing both sides equally but after that rather more favouring Israel. That said, within living memory there was an attitude amongst some Conservative politicians towards Israel that tended to be more anti-Zionist and arguably anti-Semitic than the other way around.[438] Near-contemporaneous opinion polling amongst the general public[439] indicated that Conservative supporters were less pro-Palestinian (23%) than either Labour (32%) or Liberal Democrat

---

[438] Defries, 2001: 193-197.
[439] Travis, 24th April 2002.

supporters (40%). Nevertheless, all were noticeably more pro-Palestinian than pro-Israeli, with the pro-Israeli figures for all three groups of supporters being between 11% and 14 %. In other words, Conservative politicians tended to be notably more pro-Israeli and somewhat less pro-Palestinian than even Conservative supporters.

Looking at attitudes towards the USA, local councillors were strongly inclined to Britain being more cautious in supporting the USA's foreign and military policies with well over a half – indeed, nearer two-thirds at 60% – reporting this against just a fifth (21%) who presumably wanted Britain to be at least as and perhaps more enthusiastic. This might seem surprising since the Conservative Party is generally seen as pro-US. However, there is a long-standing element of anti-US sentiment in the Conservative Party.[440]

Moving on, a series of bivariate analysis was conducted with the one-tailed hypothesis noted above.

TABLE 7.2: CORRELATION MATRIX OF FOREIGN AFFAIRS VARIABLES		Europeanism	Middle East	USA
Europeanism	Pearson correlation			
	One-tailed significance			
	Base			
Middle East	Pearson correlation	0.13		
	One-tailed significance	0.011		
	Base	318		
USA	Pearson correlation	0.179	0.288	
	One-tailed significance	<0.001	<0.001	
	Base	322	344	
Left-Right	Pearson correlation	0.124	0.087	0.171
	One-tailed significance	0.014	0.054	0.001
	Base	315	337	342

The results in the correlation matrix set out in Table 7.2 could hardly be more supportive of the overall hypothesis. All of the

---

[440] Finer, Berrington and Bartholomew, 1961: 8; Gamble, 1974: 162; Global Intelligence Company, 4th November 2002; Wooldridge, 31st May 2004.

foreign affairs items were significantly correlated with each other in, as further analysis indicated, the predicted direction. The supplementary economics variable – here using the Left-Right scale – was significantly correlated with both Europeanism and the USA item and only just fell short of being significantly correlated with the Middle East item.

What about the age of respondents? For this, only ELCs can be studied since this was the only group who were asked for this information. The results do not support this element of the observation. Even using a one-tailed hypothesis there was no significant correlation between age and Left-Right ($p = 0.11$), Europeanism ($p = 0.12$) or the Middle East item ($p = 0.42$). There was a significant correlation (one-tailed $p = 0.001$) between age and the USA item in the predicted direction. Younger ELCs wanted Britain to be at least as, and perhaps more even more supportive of the USA's foreign and military policies. Looking at the different results of the USA and Middle East items, bearing mind that ELCs ranged in age from 24 to 81 it might be tempting to suggest that if by 2002 the shadow of the anti-US feeling demonstrated by a number of Conservatives at the time of the Suez crisis[441] had lifted from ELCs vis-à-vis the USA, then that of the King David Hotel[442] vis-à-vis Israel had not.

As an aside, the finding just noted of there being no significant correlation between attitudes towards the EU and age suggests a secular change in the attitudes of Conservative Party politicians. Given that the Conservative Party became more Euro-sceptic over some years through fears of the state being re-imposed on an EU-level and the perceived threat to national sovereignty,[443] then a plausible hypothesis might have been that older respondents would have been less Euro-sceptic than younger ones.

Relating Foreign and Domestic Issues

Moving on from this specific research question, to what extent did attitudes towards foreign affairs correlate with or cut across attitudes

---

[441] *The Times*, 5th January 2009.

[442] Defries, 2001: 194-197.

[443] Webb, December 2008: 440.

towards domestic issues? To look at this, the same three foreign affairs variables were used which looked at in some fashion attitudes towards the EU, the USA and the Middle East. A series of partial correlation analyses was run, again using only local councillors in England, Scotland and Wales to keep a like-for-like comparison with the previous section. In the cases of the USA and the Middle East items each was tested one at a time alongside one of the multi-item scales whilst controlling for all the other multi-item scales. The procedure for the EU item was the same except, of course, that the Europeanism scale was removed from the set of control variables.

In all three cases there were a number of correlations that were significant at the two-tailed 5% level having controlled for responses to the other multi-item scales. In the case of the EU – tested here by using the Europeanism scale – these were (in descending order of strength of correlation): Traditional British Liberties (correlation = 0.232, p = 0.001), Optimism (correlation = -0.203, p = 0.003), Welfarism (correlation = -0.185, p = 0.008), Feminism (correlation = -0.166, p = 0.017) and Religiosity (correlation = -0.149, p = 0.032).

In the case of the USA these were: Environmentalism (correlation = -0.183, p = 0.009), Europeanism (correlation = 0.150, p = 0.0032), Postmaterialism (correlation = -0.147, p = 0.036) and Feminism (correlation = 0.141, p = 0.044).

In the case of the Middle East these were: Authoritarianism (correlation = -0.153, p = 0.029) and Traditional British Liberties (correlation 0.142, p = 0.043).

From this evidence, the answer to the question posed at the start of this section is that, on balance, attitudes to foreign affairs cut across attitudes towards domestic issues for this sub-set of respondents. No single multi-item scale was a reoccurring feature in all three sets of correlation analyses. Indeed, only Traditional British Liberties and Feminism appeared more than once. This suggests that any correlations between domestic and foreign attitudes were on a case-by-case basis and not an indication of a secular association of attitudes.

In the case of attitudes towards the EU as measured by the Europeanism scale, whilst a number of other scales were correlated with it having controlled for responses to the other scales it is also surely fair to note the reality of politics in Britain in the 2002, particularly regarding the Conservative Party. As is discussed elsewhere is this study, "Europe" was such a salient issue[444] that it can with justice be described as at least in part a domestic issue.

That said, the findings for the other two foreign affairs items can be fleshed out a little. The only issue significantly associated with the Middle East item were the two overlapping and themselves robustly correlated (one-tailed $p = 0.001$) scales of Authoritarianism and Traditional British Liberties. Further analysis indicates a correlation between "authoritarian" and pro-Israeli views. This perhaps goes against what was suggested above of pro-Arab views being associated with support for a more traditional view of society, but it is difficult to make much of this.

Of more interest was the analysis of the USA item. In the case of Europeanism it is a predictable finding that bivariate analysis indicates that Euro-sceptic respondents were more inclined to support the USA than less Euro-sceptic respondents. For many – rightly or wrongly – the USA and the EU were something of an either/or choice.[445]

Leaving that aside, it surely cannot be a coincidence that the other three significant correlations were with examples or tests of "new" values: Postmaterialism, Environmentalism and Feminism.[446] Bivariate analysis indicates that those tending to support such new values, particularly in the cases of Environmentalism and Postmaterialism, were more opposed to the USA or more specifically thought that Britain should be more cautious in supporting the USA's foreign and military policies. It can be suggested in general terms that supporters of "new" values viewed the USA as particularly at fault in its attitude towards (say) environmentalism. In more specific terms, it can be suggested that supporters of "new" values were inherently more suspicious of military and similar matters and that – although this is speculation since it is difficult from within this study's data to make any comparisons – the USA was particularly associated with such things.

The Commonwealth

A small number of other items in the questionnaire belong in this chapter. Two dealt with attitudes towards the UK's relationship with

---

[444] Burdett-Conway & Tether, 1997: 89-90; Cowley & Norton, 1999: 90.
[445] Laughland, 2ⁿᵈ January 2010.
[446] Inglehart, 1990; Nas, 1995; Lundmark, 1995.

the Commonwealth. Accompanied by a five-level "Agree strongly" to "Disagree strongly" response set, each question was prefaced with, "Britain should re-establish closer ties with…" with one continuing, "the former colonies in areas such as Australia, New Zealand, South Africa and Canada" and the other continuing, "the former colonies and existing dependencies in areas such as the Caribbean, Africa and Asia". In other words, those former parts of the British Empire often known as the "Old" – or, less politically correctly, "White" – Commonwealth and the "New" Commonwealth respectively.

TABLE 7.3: RE-ESTABLISH CLOSER TIES WITH THE COMMONWEALTH?	Old Commonwealth	New Commonwealth
Agree	75%	50%
Neither/nor	16%	27%
Disagree	9%	23%
Base	499	497

Using the undifferentiated datafile – since ANOVA and the Bonferroni post-hoc test with the two micro-groups omitted detected no significant between-groups differences – Table 7.3 shows that there was strong support for Britain forging closer ties with the Old Commonwealth with exactly three-quarters (75%) of all respondents agreeing with the item and only 9% disagreeing. There was less active enthusiasm for forging closer ties with the New Commonwealth, although even here twice as many wanted to (50%) than did not want to (23%).

Overall, and as might be predicted by the Conservative Party's post-War policy of maintaining Britain's position of influence in the Commonwealth,[447] there was considerable support for maintaining and strengthening ties with the former Empire. Whether the Commonwealth was consciously or unconsciously seen as some kind of substitute for the Empire cannot be ascertained from the data.[448]

Were attitudes towards the Commonwealth associated with other attitudinal measures? In some cases a causal relationship between the Commonwealth items and the multi-item scales might

---

[447] Buller, 1996: 222.
[448] Baker, Gamble & Seawright, 2002: 404.

reasonably by hypothesised. This is perhaps particularly true of those scales which clearly have a "foreign" component to them such as Xenophobia and Europeanism. But it other cases such a relationship is not at all obvious. Therefore this question was analysed by running a series of partial correlation analyses using these two Commonwealth items and the usual range of multi-item scales.

In both cases there were a number of significant bivariate associations between the two Commonwealth items and the scales having allowed for responses to all of the other scales. Perhaps the most predictable one was between the New Commonwealth item and the Xenophobia scale (correlation = 0.173, p = 0.002) where respondents with less xenophobic attitudes were more positive about forging closer ties.

There were only three scales which were significantly associated with both Commonwealth items: Europeanism (correlation = -0.224, p = <0.001 for the Old item and correlation = -0.167, p = 0.004 for the New item), Authoritarianism (correlation = 0.169, p = 0.003 for both items) and Pride in the Way the Nation Functions (correlation = -0.116, p = 0.043 for the Old item and correlation = -0.115, p = 0.056 for the New item).

More Euro-sceptic, more authoritarian and more nationally proud views were associated with wanting closer ties to both the Old and New Commonwealth.

In the case of Europeanism and Authoritarianism, respondents were similar to the general public at the same time. Analysis of relevant items from the *British Social Attitudes 2001* survey[449] (not shown here) indicates a similar attitude.

Overall, the findings concerning the Europeanism dimension make sense inasmuch as they might imply – as Euro-enthusiasts might be the first to argue – a sense of connection to, or even a nostalgia for, Britain's past global achievements and connections in a time before "Europe" came to dominant debate.

The case of Authoritarianism is more difficult to explain. If it had just been significantly associated with the Old Commonwealth and had been in the other direction then it might be explained in terms of Authoritarianism's overlap with the Xenophobia scale as this related to some historical Conservative Party attitudes towards

---

[449] NCSR, 29th October 2008[d].

immigrants.[450] However, it was in an "authoritarian = closer ties" direction. It must be admitted that it is hard to discern why those who tended to hold "authoritarian" or "traditionalist" views on matters such as the death penalty, censorship, homosexuality and the teaching to children of deference also tended to favour closer ties with both the Old and New Commonwealths, unless it was from some sense of nostalgia. It could simply have been "one of those things" thrown out by the wide array of analyses used in this study.

The case of the Pride in the Way the Nation Functions scale might also be an indication of pride not just in Britain at the time of the survey but again a nostalgic admiration for its past imperial history.

The Western and Islamic Worlds

A final relevant item in the questionnaire, again accompanied by a five-level "Agree strongly" to "Disagree strongly" response set, was "The Western and Islamic worlds can never truly be at peace with one another".

Of course, particularly in the years since the attacks in the USA on the 11th September 2001, the wars in Iraq and Afghanistan, and the bombings in London in July 2005, it would take a book-length work merely to act as an introductory bibliography to this subject. Here the aims are much more modest.

It should be acknowledged that this single item could as well have been included in Chapter 10 dedicated to religion. It depends upon one's view as to what, for example, "Islamic world" means. Implicit in the item is the notion – which may or may not be correct – that "the Western world" and "the Islamic world" offered different and competing world views.[451] However, it must be admitted that it is not clear what respondents understood by "The Western and Islamic worlds", especially the latter. Did it mean the geographical region of the world generally thought of as the Middle East and so on and "where the oil comes from"? Or perhaps it suggested an

---

[450] Gamble, 1974:181.
[451] Adams, 1993: 352; *BBC News*, 20th September 2001; Dougherty, 13th August 2002; Hague, 6th November 2000; Heywood, 1992: 5; Thatcher, 12th February 2002.

ideological/theological bloc, such as Iran after the 1979 Islamic Revolution? Closer to home, was it by then associated with terrorism? Or just "Those people that I saw when I was walking down Brick Lane and/or Edgware Road[452] the other day"? It was the "ideological/theological bloc" meaning that was intended but, upon reflection, this should have been made clearer in the questionnaire.

ANOVA with the post-hoc Bonferroni test indicated that ELCs were significantly more pessimistic (p = <0.001) about relations between the two worlds than some of the other groups. Over half (55%) of ELCs were pessimistic about relations between the two worlds against exactly a quarter (25%) who were optimistic. In the case of the other groups of respondents, the responses were more balanced – indeed, this was an item where there was little agreement amongst respondents – with 35% being pessimistic and 43% optimistic.

When run once for ELCs only and then for all other respondents, partial correlation analysis indicated that was only one multi-item scale that was significantly and indeed robustly associated with attitudes in both cases: the Xenophobia scale (correlation -0.256, p = 0.001 for ELCs and correlation -0.387, p = <0.001 for all others). In both cases, more xenophobic attitudes were associated with a more pessimistic view of relations between the Western and Islamic worlds. What this suggests is that those who viewed immigrants as tending to have a harmful impact on Briton in areas such as crime and the economy also tended to have a pessimistic view about the relationship between the Western and Islamic worlds. In other words, the findings perhaps indicated a view that "aliens" were bad for Britain and that furthermore Islam was notably alien.

There was a minor but still interesting finding concerning the analysis for all non-ELC respondents. Other than Xenophobia, the only other scale that was significantly associated with responses to this item was the Theocratism scale (correlation = 0.195, p = 0.028). Bivariate analysis indicated that those with more secularist attitudes – those who wanted to see little or no role for religion in public life – tended to be more pessimistic about relations between the Western and Islamic worlds.

---

[452] Centres respectively of Bangladeshi and Arab life in London: Gillan, 21st June 2001; Maysaloon, 27th August 2007.

Taking these findings together, it seems that for those agreeing with the item the main factor was the perceived harmful and alien nature of Islam along with – amongst most groups of respondents – a lesser but still significant belief that Islam was particularly and unacceptably insistent in its demands for a religious input into public life and governance. To turn it around, those who disagreed with the item tended not to have a problem with things and people that might be viewed as alien – and the Xenophobia scale does not specifically mention Islam – and/or they were more relaxed about an enhanced role for religion in public life even if this was not necessarily Christianity.

Conclusion to Chapter 7

Turning first to attitudes towards the Commonwealth, it was seen that respondents tended to support Britain establishing closer relations with both the Old and, albeit less so, New Commonwealths. If nothing else, this can perhaps be taken as evidence against the more extreme charges of xenophobia – although the presence and direction of the Xenophobia scale in one of the analyses was revealing – that were sometimes labelled against the Conservative Party at the time. Provided that, the cynic might suggest, the "others" stayed where they were.

Looking in more detail at statistically associated multi-item scales, the underlying theme that suggested itself was perhaps one of nostalgia for Britain's imperial past.

Turning to relations between the Western and Islamic words, attitudes were mixed. Local councillors in England were noticeably pessimistic about the prospects for peaceful relations between the two cultures whereas others tended, although not strongly, to be more optimistic.

Looking at associated attitudes, by far the most powerful one was the Xenophobia scale. For those taking a pessimistic view about relations between the two worlds there was the strong implication that Islam was viewed as both alien and malign. In addition, amongst some respondents there was a small but statistically significant indication of what may have been quite a complex view regarding

Islam and secularism.[453] It would seem that those who tended to take a pessimistic view about the relationship between the two worlds also tended to believe that the influence of religion in the world – beyond a purely personal one – should stop at the doors of the church or mosque.

A large part of this chapter was taken up with testing the validity within the context of Conservative Party politicians in 2002 of an observation made by many others. The core of it was that attitudes towards the EU, the USA and Israel were correlated with each other in a "negative, positive and positive" direction. The results robustly supported this observation at the level of bivariate analyses.

Following on from this, an admittedly tentative analysis using the same variables suggests that attitudes towards foreign affairs tended to cut across rather than be associated with attitudes towards domestic issues. A supplementary finding of note was that attitudes about Britain's relationship with the USA were most strongly associated with attitudes towards "new" values such as Environmentalism, Feminism and Postmaterialism rather than "old" values such as those measured by the economic Left-Right scale.

---

[453] Meek, May 2004.

8

National Identity

Aspects of National Identity

Throughout this study, reference has been made to local councillors in England, Scotland and Wales. All of these respondents were the same level of politician distinguished by the fact that they had been elected in three of the four countries making up the United Kingdom. It is attitudes towards various aspects of this Union that are analysed in this chapter before moving on to other aspects of national identity.

Respondents were presented with a number of items concerning attitudes about England, Scotland, Wales, the United Kingdom, the EU, devolution and so on and how these relate to each other.

Also briefly explored is a typology of national identity in a more general sense, and it is possible to compare these findings with those of the near-contemporaneous general public with reference to data from the *British Social Attitudes* series from which this particular typology was derived.

The electoral background to this study is a reminder of the irony that a party which had inserted "and Unionist" into its formal title to show its support for the Union had ended up after the May 1997 general election with not a single MP elected outside of England[454] and only one from Scotland after 2001.[455]

---

[454] Dyer, 2001; McLean, 1997: 145.
[455] Austin & Hames, 2001: 296.

Self-Identification

How respondents thought of themselves

Respondents were presented with two items based upon the Moreno national identity scale[456] analysing identification as British[457] as opposed to English, Scottish or Welsh and then European as opposed to British, English, Scottish or Welsh.

TABLE 8.1: SELF-IDENTIFICATION: BRITISH VERSUS INDIVIDUAL COUNTRIES							
	ELCs	Peers	MPs	SLCs	WLCs	MEPs	MSPs
More English/Scottish/Welsh than British	32%	17%	28%	20%	15%	29%	21%
Equally English/Scottish/Welsh and British	33%	21%	31%	33%	33%	43%	57%
More British than English/Scottish/Welsh	35%	62%	41%	48%	52%	29%	21%
Base	274	58	51	46	27	14	14

Table 8.1 presents a mixed picture, with opinion spread across the options. In all cases, at least a fifth and usually a third or more of respondents regarded themselves as equally British on the one hand and English, Scottish or Welsh as the case may have been on the other. Overall, there was evidence for a dual British and English/Scottish/Welsh identity. Looking at secondary data, this study's respondents from Scotland and Wales were conspicuously more likely to identify as equally or even more British than their compatriots amongst the Scottish and Welsh general public whereas ELCs and MPs much more closely matched the attitudes of the English general public.[458]

No table is provided for the other analysis which told a very different story. In practice there was a complete rejection of any sense of being European at the expense of being British and so on.

---

[456] Curtice & Heath, 2000: 157.

[457] It will be remembered that there were no respondents from Northern Ireland.

[458] Curtice & Syed, 2001: 236.

Only 1% of ELCs regarded themselves as more European than British, English, Scottish and/or Welsh and no respondents from any of the other groups did, not even MEPs. With the exception of MEPs (43%), there was generally a rejection of even a shared or equal identity with never more than 25% of any group citing this. There was little evidence of respondents from Scotland or Wales looking for an "umbrella" in the EU previously provided by Britain,[459] although given the nature of the respondents this is unsurprising.

The findings from the respondents can be compared to those of the public at the time set out in Table 8.2.

TABLE 8.2: SELF-IDENTIFICATION AMONGST PUBLIC: BRITISH VERSUS INDIVIDUAL COUNTRIES[460]			
	England	**Scotland**	**Wales**
More English/Scottish/Welsh than British	30%	74%	40%
Equally English/Scottish/Welsh and British	45%	14%	32%
More British than English/Scottish/Welsh	25%	12%	28%
Base	**1683**	**593**	**469**

Compared to the public at the time, it was noticeable that our explicitly Unionist respondents from above all Scotland and – albeit to a lesser extent even allowing for less Welsh self-identity in the first place – Wales were less inclined to regard themselves as more Scottish or Welsh than British. The responses from this study's English groups of ELCs and MPs were broadly in line with those of the public.

Within the context of being peripheral representatives of the Conservative and *Unionist* Party, that Scottish and Welsh local councillors were relatively more likely to emphasise their Britishness than their counterparts in England might be seen as indicating their status as beleaguered unionists.

---

[459] Clark, 22nd August 2000.
[460] *British Social Attitudes*, 2001.

The exercise is not repeated for the European aspect since the item was presented differently but also, like our respondents, there was little in the way of European self-identification amongst the British general public of the time.

There was another finding that indicated that in this respect respondents were similar to the general public. Amongst ELCs, stronger English as opposed to British identification was associated with *more* Euro-sceptic attitudes as measured by the Europeanism scale (one-tailed $p = 0.044$ using the chi^2 statistic). On the other hand, amongst SLCs stronger Scottish as opposed to British identification was associated with *less* Euro-sceptic attitudes as measured by the Europeanism scale (one-tailed $p = 0.023$ using the chi^2 statistic). This is the same pattern that was detected amongst the near-contemporary general public[461] and supports claims that Euro-scepticism, despite much talk of "Britain", was in reality more about a perceived threat to English identity, a view that had less resonance in Scotland or Wales or indeed in the rest of the EU.[462]

Other Issues Concerning the UK

In the following, all items were followed by a five-point "Agree strongly" to "Disagree strongly" response set.

"The cause of the centre-Right in Scotland and Wales has been damaged by its association with a Conservative Party that is often regarded as 'the English Party'" (as one Conservative MSP and other Conservatives would later publically state,[463] a view shared by some academics and other writers[464]). Responses to this item generally indicated uncertainty tending towards agreement and in no case did even a plurality disagree. Those most strongly agreeing were respondents from Scotland where 67% of SLCs and 86% of MSPs agreed. WLCs were less sure, although a plurality (38%) agreed with the statement. ELCs were the least convinced, but even here more agreed (31%) than disagreed (24%).

---

[461] Curtice & Heath, 2000: 167; Curtice & Syed, 2001: 240.
[462] Marquand, 2009: 326.
[463] *BBC News*, 22nd May 2005; Leslie, 19th January 2003.
[464] Mitchell, 1995: 1382; Stirling, 2012.

A belief amongst some Conservatives that this *had* been the case was one of the motivating factors behind the calls for a *"CSU"* option, named after the *Christlich-Soziale Union* which only operates in more identity-conscious Bavaria, leaving the rest of Germany to its sister party, the *Christlich Demokratische Union*.[465] The idea was that a linked but clearly separate "centre-right" party – not one merely renamed[466] – might do better.[467] However, many on the "right" of the Party rejected such an idea because it might lead to a shift toward the "centre" and become rather like the old Scottish Unionist Party that had existed as an independent force until merged into the Conservative Party in 1965.[468]

That this view from Scotland was not so robustly shared by councillors in Wales is perhaps surprising given claims that by the early 21st century anti-Conservatism was part of the Welsh national identity.[469] Nevertheless, on balance the view was clear and some senior Welsh Conservatives noted the vicious circle that with so few Welsh and to some extent Scottish Conservative representatives it was often English Conservatives to be seen in the media talking about Welsh and Scottish affairs. This served to reinforce the image of the Conservatives as an "English party",[470] something perhaps anyway apparent during the lengthy Thatcher and Major period when the Conservatives adopted a hard-line Unionism, moving away from an older belief that different policies in different places might be appropriate.[471]

"England should have its own parliament." Amongst all groups a majority disagreed with this item. ELCs were relatively the most in favour, with 42% agreeing against 51% actively disagreeing. On the other hand, their colleagues in Scotland and Wales were the most vehemently opposed, with 71% of SLCs and almost all (96%) WLCs disagreeing with this item. 59% of MPs,

---

[465] Stirling, 2012: 5.
[466] Linklater, 10th October 2002.
[467] Browne, 5th April 2007; Hamilton, 23rd May 2005; Nelson, 7th April 2007; Robertson & Black, 3rd June 2001.
[468] Lynch, 2003: 168-169; Stirling, 2012: 5.
[469] Charmley, 2009/2010; Wyn Jones, Scully & Trystan, 2002: 243.
[470] Evans, 2002: 18.
[471] Cooper, 1995: 1385; Hector, 2009/2010: 19; Peter Lynch, 1997: 564; Philip Lynch, 2000: 66; October 2004: 386; Mitchell, 1995: 1382; Stirling, 2012.

70% of Peers and 57% of MEPs also disagreed. Particularly with these latter groups, one must wonder how much this had anything to with national identity as such against how much it spoke of a more mundane fear of competition.

"The regions of England should have their own assemblies." Following on from the previous item, opposition to such a development was even more marked, with in most cases 80% or more of respondents from the different groups opposed to some degree. The two relative exceptions were respondents from Scotland where only 58% of SLCs and 50% of MSPs actively disagreed with this item. It is not clear why this should have been, unless it was a (relative) manifestation of a desire to "cut England down to size". Taking these last two items together, there was generally clear opposition to moves that might be seen as further splitting or federalising the UK.[472]

"The Scots and the Welsh have a more developed sense of national identity than the English." In every case a majority agreed with this item. Give or take two of three percentage points, two-thirds of Peers and MPs and three-quarters of ELCs, WLCs, MSPs and MEPs agreed as did exactly half of SLCs. Given the general direction of responses to this item and also the data in Tables 8.1a and 8.2, this again suggests a difference in the way that Celtic Conservatives perceived themselves when compared to the Scots and Welsh public.

"The extra public spending received by Scotland and Wales relative to England is often justified." The responses to this item were delightfully predictable. There had long been complaints from English Conservatives – particularly from the North of England – about the amount of public money that Scotland, Wales and Northern Ireland received via the Barnett Formula.[473, 474] This feeling appeared to increase following the creation of the devolved institutions in Wales and Scotland and their alleged "generosity" towards their own electorate at the expense of English taxpayers.[475] Robust majorities of ELCs (76%), MPs (75%) and Peers (65%) disagreed against equally

---

[472] Barnes, 1998.
[473] Kallenbach, 5th December 2001.
[474] Cooper, 1995: 1385-1390.
[475] Williams, 17th August 2002.

robust majorities of SLCs (74%), WLCs (68%) and MSPs (71%) who agreed. MEPs fell between these two groups, although a majority (57%) disagreed.[476]

The Legitimacy of the EU

Whilst there were no items in the survey looking explicitly at attitudes towards the overall "legitimacy"[477] of the political system as it pertained to the UK in 2002, there was one item in the Europeanism scale that is worth noting on its own in this context. It was one of the shortest items in the entire questionnaire and was part of the Europeanism scale: "Britain should withdraw from the EU". Within the context of anyway a tendency towards Euro-scepticism, substantial minorities of some groups of respondents went so far as to agree with this "nuclear option". This included 29% of ELCs, 26% of WLCs, 20% of SLCs and 22% of MPs and even three MEPs.

It is surely reasonable to argue that many respondents were not merely "unfriendly" towards the EU but did not accept its legitimacy at all. Given both that around this time the Conservative Party's perceived Euro-scepticism was one of the few areas where they more nearly represented the preferences of voters than did the other parties[478] and also what British opponents of the EU argued were the ever-increasing powers of the EU over its members states,[479] then perhaps this might be the source of some future "legitimation crisis" albeit on more straightforward nationalist grounds than sometimes suggested.[480]

---

[476] Further reading suggests that the assumptions behind this item may have been incorrect or at least slightly misleading and that it was/is not so much a case of England "propping up" Scotland and Wales but London, south-eastern and eastern England "propping up" much the rest of the UK including the rest of England. E.g. Allardyce, 11th January 2009; Farrer, 2nd November 2007; Hookham & Smith, 12th February 2012; Leask, 2nd November 2007; Orr, 27th August 2002.

[477] *European Social Survey*, 2007[g]: 327.

[478] Butler & Kavanagh, 2002[a]: 39.

[479] Campaign for an Independent Britain, 13th June 2008.

[480] Jary & Jary, 1991: 351-352.

On the other hand, it may be that the EU's "complicated, abstruse and intransparent multi-level network structures"[481] serve to diffuse any hostility.

A Revised Typology of National Identity

During background research for the *CPRS 2002,* further work was conducted on a study published in a *British Social Attitudes* report by Lizanne Dowds and Ken Young on the subject of 'national identity'.[482] In turn, they had based their work on items used in the 1995 *BSA* survey.

The original authors' aim was twofold. Firstly, to identify "dimensions of identity". They posited the existence of two different forms of nationalism: inclusive and exclusive. Inclusive nationalism ("national sentiment") they took to mean (i) pride in the nation's heritage and/or (ii) its functioning and place in the world. Exclusive nationalism ("exclusiveness") they took to mean protectionist or xenophobic tendencies towards (iii) foreign products and capital and/or (iv) foreigners themselves. These four elements were measured – and it is not the place here to look at how they developed these scales – by the Pride in Heritage & Culture, Pride in the Way the Nation Functions, Protectionism and Xenophobia dimensions respectively, and which are used throughout this book. The first and second and then the third and fourth of these dimensions were further combined into new dimensions: National Sentiment and Exclusiveness respectively although these combined dimensions were not used in this book except for the analysis now presented.

Second, they identified and operationalised distinct attitudinal typologies regarding national identity by combining these two new dimensions of identity into a fourfold typology. These four groups they described as follows:

- Supra-Nationalists: Low in exclusiveness and low in national sentiment.

- Patriots: Low in exclusiveness and high in national sentiment.

---

[481] *European Social Survey*, 2007[g]: 329.
[482] Dowds & Young, 1996.

- Belligerents: High in exclusiveness and low in national sentiment.

- John Bulls: High in exclusiveness and high in national sentiment.

The problem when analysing respondents to this present study was that because of the extreme loading on the two "Pride" scales – respondents tended to be very proud of Britain – there were effectively no Supra-Nationalists or Belligerents. Respondents were divided between the other two types depending upon their view of foreign people and things. The tendency was for "higher" representatives such as Peers, MPs, MSPs and MEPs but also SLCs to fall into the Patriot category whereas ELCs and WLCs were more inclined to fall into the John Bull category.

This typology was also used by the present author to analyse members of the British public using data from the 2003 *British Social Attitudes* survey.[483] The only finding of note was that approximately 10% of respondents could be described as Belligerents – misanthropes might be just as good a description – liking neither their own country nor foreign people and things.

Conclusion to Chapter 8

Looking first to how our respondents regarded themselves as being British or Scottish or European and so on, it was a tale of two parts. There was evidence for a dual/mixed British and English/Scottish/Welsh identity. Respondents were notably more inclined to think of themselves as British to some degree than their compatriots amongst the public. This is what would be expected from representatives of the Conservative and Unionist Party with its historical and explicit support for a British identity.[484]

That said, the findings confirm that Britain is one of those "countries [where] citizens do not have a single and evident national identity, but can choose between different more or less competing national identities".[485]

---

[483] *British Social Attitudes*, 18th April 2008.
[484] Seldon & Snowdon, 2001: 24-25.
[485] *European Social Survey*, 2007[i]: 400.

On the other hand, respondents were strongly inclined towards British/English/Scottish/Welsh rather than European identity, at least if the latter was at the expense of the former. Given the strongly Euro-sceptic attitudes reported throughout this book, this also comes as no surprise.

It also needs to be noted that no attempt was made to differentiate between notions of "citizenship" and "nationality" let alone "race". When a few years after 2002 the German-born Labour MP Gisela Stuart stated that the rise of Englishness was a threat to democracy,[486] a local Conservative councillor responded by saying, "I know people who are Scottish, Irish and Welsh and we are all proud British citizens, but if I was asked what nationality I was I would say English."

The array of stand-alone items cannot so easily be summarised. However, the main view seemed to be a continuing support for the Union much as it was by the time of the survey. In particular, whilst there was almost no support for outright Scottish or Welsh independence, there was support for some form of devolution. Even if they had been reluctant converts to devolution,[487] by 2002 few Conservative politicians advocated outright opposition to devolution anymore.[488] On the other hand, a bare majority opposed the creation of an English parliament which would arguably make the UK parliament redundant for all but policy areas such as foreign and military affairs and UK-level macroeconomics. There was also strong opposition to English regional assemblies. Overall, this might indicate opposition to what some would perceive as the further Balkanisation of the UK.

The typology of national identity was not a success in this case because of the particular nature of our respondents and their strong pride in Britain.

---

[486] Walker, 18th November 2005.
[487] Lynch, 2003: 164-165.
[488] Lynch, October 2004: 389.

9

The Free Market: "Necessary Evil" or "Good Thing"?

Pro-Free-Market, But Why?

As detailed in Appendix 4, respondents were very strongly disinclined towards "leftist" economic views as measured by the Left-Right dimension. Depending upon which group of respondents were examined, between a third to two-thirds fell into either the "in between" or "right" categories with almost all of the remainder falling into the other one.

However, this can also be seen as evidence of at least some support for a "mixed economy". Whereas the Labour Party has clearly been associated with socialist ideas, historically it had been the Liberals at least as much the Conservatives who supported, in this sense, "liberalism".[489] There has always been a strand of thinking within the Conservative Party that has been suspicious and sometimes critical of free-market liberalism,[490] arguing instead for "economic policies that stressed community and social cohesion rather than markets and individuals"[491] or that were designed to create a triangular economic system of government, organised labour and capital.[492]

That noted, economic liberalism was in the ascendancy within the Conservative Party by the 1980s[493] and respondents were at least inclined towards free-market economics.

---

[489] Heath *et al*, 1991: 5.
[490] Green, 2002.
[491] Evans, October 2004: 383.
[492] Marquand, 2009: 181.
[493] Bale, July 2006: 385.

In this brief chapter this was examined a little further. Did respondents regard the free market as "a necessary evil" that was just better than socialism at literally "delivering the goods", or as "a good thing" in itself?[494]

Private and Public: Efficiency and Worthiness

This was examined in an indirect but defensible manner. Respondents were presented with two items each with three response options. The first was a choice between, "The public sector is more efficient than the private sector", "The public and private sectors are equally efficient" and "The private sector is more efficient than the public sector". The other was a choice between, "The public sector is more worthy than the private sector", "The public and private sectors are equally worthy" and "The private sector is more worthy than the public sector". Between them, these two items analysed attitudes towards both the utilitarian and moral aspects of the free-market. As such, "private sector" was intended as a symbol for "market economics" and "public sector" as a symbol for "statist economics". Or to use the terminology of the associated dimension, "right" and "left".

Before proceeding, it was confirmed that both of these items were significantly correlated with the Left-Right dimension. Using the whole datafile and the Pearson statistic, there were two-tailed $p = 0.008$ and $p = 0.001$ for the "efficient" and "worthy" items respectively. Similarly there was a significant correlation of two-tailed $p = 0.009$ between the two items themselves in the predictable direction.

ANOVA detected no significant between-groups differences ($p = 0.7$) on the "worthiness" item. There were significant between-groups differences on the "efficiency" item but the finding was marginal ($p = 0.03$) and the post-hoc Bonferroni test failed to detect any significantly different pairs. It is probably safe to say that responses to these items were similar across all groups. Table 9.1 displays the results.

---

[494] O'Keeffe 2004; Rey, 1994.

TABLE 9.1: THE EFFICIENCY AND MORALITY OF THE PUBLIC AND PRIVATE SECTORS			
Efficiency		**Worthiness**	
The public sector is more efficient than the private sector	2%	The public sector is more worthy than the private sector	3%
The public and private sectors are equally efficient	11%	The public and private sectors are equally worthy	75%
The private sector is more efficient than the public sector	87%	The private sector is more worthy than the public sector	22%
Base	**492**	**Base**	**484**

This indicates a strong belief that the private sector was more efficient than the public sector with over four-fifths responding with this option. However, whilst almost no respondents believed that the public sector was more worthy than the private sector, three-quarters of respondents believed them to be equally so with the remainder opting for the private sector.

In short, there was some evidence for at least a mild version of the "necessary evil" attitude. This is because the results suggest that whilst the private sector was strongly regarded as being more efficient than the public it was generally not seen as more worthy even if the bias was towards thinking that it was.

Associations with Employment

One of the socio-demographic items asked of ELCs concerned which employment sector they worked in or had most recently worked in. The majority (71%) said that it was the private, a minority (20%) said that it was the public with the remainder saying that it was the voluntary or other sectors. Taking those from the private and public sectors only it is a reasonable hypothesis that this will correlate with attitudes towards the two sectors as seen in responses to the two items above.

In fact, in the case of the "efficiency" item there was little to choose between the two. Mostly this was because of the strongly one-sided loading of the responses. 88% of those who worked in the private sector believed that the private sector was more efficient than the public sector against "only" 82% of those who worked in the public sector.

The differences were more marked in the case of the "moral" item, as can be seen in Table 9.2.

TABLE 9.2: EMPLOYMENT AND ATTITUDES TOWARDS THE MORALITY OF THE PRIVATE AND PUBLIC SECTORS AMONGST ELCS		
	Private sector employment	**Public sector employment**
The public sector is more worthy than the private sector	3%	9%
The public and private sectors are equally worthy	73%	83%
The private sector is more worthy than the public sector	24%	8%
Base	**192**	**53**

Those who worked in the public sector were significantly less likely – crosstabs and the chi^2 statistic, two-tailed p = 0.009 – to believe in the superior worthiness of the private sector than their private sector colleagues. Whether this indicates an enduring belief that prompted such respondents to enter the public sector or a consequence of working within it and over time becoming more likely to believe in its worth – cause or effect – cannot be determined from the data.

Conclusion to Chapter 9

In looking at attitudes towards the public and private sectors, the bias in favour of the latter was confirmed. This must have been anticipated from responses to the Left-Right dimension. However, it also suggested that this tended to be on utilitarian rather than moral grounds. Or, if one prefers, pragmatic rather than dogmatic. Respondents did *not* typically regard the public sector as "unworthy" and this was particularly true amongst those who had recent experience of working in the public sector.

This combination of experience and attitude of some Conservative politicians might be of note if in the future the Party's leadership comes to believe that there really is a "tremendous political opportunity" in more actively canvassing for support amongst public sector workers.[495]

This focus on the utilitarian as opposed to moral claims of the free-market and the private sector reflected the debates on the subject both inside and outside of the Conservative Party. For example, looking at the national background, it has been argued that Conservative government's privatisations of the 1980s were not "ideological" so much as an economic necessity brought about the UK government's revenue as a proportion of GDP passing the apex of the Laffer Curve[496] resulting in collecting less tax against a background of rising demand for public services.[497] Also, the speeches and writings of senior Conservative politicians around the time of the study – particularly in the area of healthcare provision – often emphasised the alleged utilitarian benefits of the free-markets and the private sector.[498]

Nevertheless, others such as the Party leader at the time of the study, Iain Duncan Smith,[499] continued to make a moral claim. Others, such as senior Conservative MP Dr Liam Fox,[500] argued that strong emotional – arguably "moral" – attachment to the NHS had hampered rational debate about its efficiency at delivering healthcare provision.[501]

---

[495] Sanders, July 2006: 193.
[496] Sloman, 1991: 351.
[497] Whitehouse, 2002.
[498] Riddell, 8th October 2001.
[499] Kite, 6th February 2002.
[500] Fox, 23rd March 2002.
[501] Anderson, 18th May 2002: 26.

10

Religion

Meanings of Religion

It is beyond the scope of a single chapter in a wide-ranging survey to engage in a full sociological and attitudinal analysis of religious beliefs and practises.[502] Nevertheless, the questionnaire included a number of items on these matters. Batteries of questions were asked that formed two, multi-item scales. One was Religiosity that measured attitudes such as belief in God and behaviour such as religious observances.[503] The other was Theocratism that measured attitudes towards the role of religion and religious institutions in public life. Additionally, respondents were asked whether or not there should be an Established Church in any part of Britain and ELCs were asked about their confessional background even if they did not consider themselves to be personally religious.

After some scene setting, the initial part of this chapter provides an analysis of Religiosity and Theocratism on their own split by groups of respondents and then a two-way typology that uses both Religiosity and Theocratism. Next, confessional background is discussed and then the position of the Established Church. Then the two scales are analysed against socio-demographic data held for ELCs. Turning to further analysis, the predictive power of the two multi-item scales towards other attitudes is analysed, both by themselves using a series of bivariate correlation analyses and as but two of many variables using regression analysis.

---

[502] Arts & Halman, 2004: 283-386; *European Social Survey*, 2007[h].
[503] Interestingly, exactly these issues have been used in psychological studies of attitude-behaviour consistency: Cottam *et al*, 2010: 60.

It should be noted that "religion" can mean many things, sometimes simultaneously. It can be "institutional" in terms of (possibly notional) membership of a particular religious organisation or denomination. It can be "ideological" in the sense of describing beliefs about both this world and the next. It can also be a symbol for ethnic identity. The core of this chapter is taken up with the second – ideological – of these meanings. However, the others are touched on as well. For example, there are brief analyses concerning membership of the Roman Catholic Church and the position of Jews within the Conservative Party.

What is not covered by the two scales primarily analysed in this chapter are such things as the content of any religious doctrine adhered to by respondents.[504] Partly this was because this would involve too much detail in a study such as this. However, it was also because it was permissible to make some assumptions about the respondents. In particular, that most of them would come from Christian, usually Anglican, backgrounds and within this context detailed theological speculation did not seem relevant. For the same reason, the questionnaire did not provide an exhaustive list of all possible religious and denominational backgrounds from which respondents could choose. Instead, as far as the Religiosity scale was concerned, the focus was on non-denominational "personal devotion and experience"[505] and basic ritualistic elements concerning church (*sic*) attendance.

Religion in the UK

Politico-religious cleavages in the UK

Unlike in much of continental Europe, religious cleavages have been a relatively small factor in mainland British and certainly English party politics.[506] Similarly, there has never been the same anti-clerical tradition in British politics of the sort that continues to inform political debate in other members of the EU.[507]

---

[504] *European Social Survey*, 2007[h]: 350.
[505] *European Social Survey*, 2007[h]: 350 & 351.
[506] Gabriel, 1995: 379. However, a case can be made that the decade after the *CPRS 2002* fieldwork saw the emergence of such cleavages based upon high concentrations of Muslims in a number of geographically concentrated urban areas: Cohen, 1st April 2012; Gallagher, 30th March 2012; Gilligan, 30th March 2012.
[507] *Sunday Telegraph*, 11th April 2009.

Nevertheless, it is acknowledged that the Conservatives were once able to win considerable support in parts of Scotland, Wales and in English cities such as a Liverpool by appeals to Protestant "Orange" sensibilities, Anglicanism and an associated Unionism. However, these appeals had largely vanished by 2002.[508]

Christianity and the UK

Next, any discussion of religion and politics must be set against a decline in traditional Christian religious beliefs in much of Britain since the 1940s, alongside a static if minority adherence to non-traditional beliefs such as horoscopes, reincarnation and ghosts.[509] This was to such an extent that according to some measures and studies by 2002 Britain was one of the world's least religious countries.[510]

Some argued that by the start of the 21st century there was a noticeable reluctance on the part of mainstream British politicians and commentators to directly connect religion – or at least mainstream Christianity – and politics,[511] often treating it with embarrassment.[512] Indeed, it was argued by one British conservative commentator that by the start of the 21st century the highly secular nature of much of British society, and certainly of "opinion formers", led to a view of the rest of the being world distorted by being looked at through "a secularised prism, underplaying and denigrating the role of religion".[513]

This view was not confined to Conservatives. Tony Blair, who was the Prime Minister at the time of the *CPRS 2002* fieldwork, would later note that during his term in office he refrained from talking about his religious views for fear of being labelled "a nutter" whereas it was commonplace in the USA and elsewhere for politicians to talk about their religious convictions.[514]

---

[508] Bradley, 1996: 1751-1752; Catterall, 1994: 656; Cochrane, 29th August 2006; Wyn Jones, Scully & Trystan, 2002: 233; Stirling, 2012: 5.

[509] Gill, Hadaway & Marler, 1998: 509 & 513.

[510] Gledhill, 26th February 2004; King, 27th December 2004; but see for example Graaf & Need, 2000: 129; Reid, 13th September 2006.

[511] Assinder, 4th March 2006.

[512] Hobson, 2nd February 2002.

[513] Sherman, 2004: 13; and see also Browers, February 2005, for a worldwide perspective. However, see Sarler, 13th September 2007, for an alternative view, at least in terms of the more "illiberal" forms of religion.

[514] *BBC News*, 25th November 2007; Dutta, 15th May 2012.

Historically the Conservative Party had a religious background in that it was part of the "old nation" of the Anglican Church and the nobility.[515] However, the generally positive relationship between the Conservative Party and the Anglican Church as an institution was severely strained by the 1980s. The Church opposed many of the Thatcher government's economic policies[516] and was often seen as giving encouragement to more "socialistic" ideas[517] and as being actively hostile to the Conservative Party.[518] However, even if true, this was not a completely new phenomenon. When the then-famous preacher, suffragette, sometime pacifist and socialist Maude Royden made her famous call in 1917 that, "The Church should go forward along the path of progress and be no longer satisfied only to represent the Conservative Party at prayer"[519] it was with a view to moving the Church towards Royden's own socialist views.[520]

On social issues, a jaundiced view of what the Anglican Church had become was voiced by Norman Tebbit[521] when he said that that the modern Church has lost faith in its own Judeo-Christian ethics and "scarcely recognises any sins but racism, sexism, and homophobia."

Christianity and the Conservative Party

It was clear that for many Conservatives religion in some sense still mattered. It cannot be a coincidence that Margaret Thatcher's only House of Commons defeat was in April 1986 when she suffered a Conservative back-bench rebellion on the *Shops Bill* which was attempting to liberalise Sunday trading.[522] Relating religion to the Party's 2001 leadership contest, Iain Duncan Smith's victory was

---

[515] Blake, 1985: 93.

[516] Catterall, 1994: 638-641.

[517] Forrester, 1988: 44; Crouch, 2000: 101; Walters, 23rd June 2002.

[518] Willetts, 1996: 81.

[519] Partington, 1996: 549; but see Hilton, 20th March 2010, for an earlier provenance of the idea.

[520] Fletcher, 1989. By a coincidence, Agnes Maude Royden's personal papers are held at the Women's Library at London Metropolitan University where this study was conducted: reference 7AMR.

[521] Tebbit, 25th November 2000.

[522] Johnston, 10th April 2006.

welcomed by the Conservative Christian Fellowship,[523] a group promoted in official Party literature at the time.[524]

On the other hand, some commentators, often with a Conservative background, rejected the Party's involvement with religion, often because of views on issues such as homosexuality and marital status.[525]

All that can be said is that, around the time of this study's fieldwork, at least some Conservative and conservative politicians and commentators were still making the case that there was an active role for religion and religious institutions in British public life[526] and/or that political parties should not be shy in canvassing for support in specifically religious settings.[527]

Religiosity and Theocratism

Considered separately

Before proceeding, it should be noted that an analysis of the data that formed the core of Whiteley, Seyd and Richardson's work on Conservative Party members, *True Blues*,[528] suggests that religion was an area where the attitudes of local councillors were similar to that of ordinary Party activists. Whether this was still true a decade later cannot be answered directly here.

There is no need to rehearse in any detail the findings for Religiosity and Theocratism found in Appendix 4. Whilst it is the case that ANOVA detected significant between-groups differences ($p = 0.002$ for Religiosity and $p = <0.001$ for Theocratism), the patterns of distribution were the same. Regarding Religiosity, across all groups respondents tended to fall into either the "in between" or "devout" sectors. Conservative politicians in 2002 tended to be somewhat if not always fervently religious.

Regarding Theocratism, in every group a majority of respondents fell into the "in between" sector. However, there were

---

[523] Conservative Christian Fellowship, 18th September 2001.

[524] Conservative Party, 2001[a]: 18-19.

[525] E.g. Gledhill, 17th April 2000; Parris, 4th November 2000; Webster, 1st November 2000; and see for example Wilson, 25th January 2001.

[526] Gledhill, 25th September 2000; Bates, 2nd November 2000.

[527] Gledhill & Webster, 16th January 2001; Montgomerie, 24th January 2001.

[528] Whiteley, Seyd & Richardson, 1992; 1994.

differences either side with, in particular, Peers and MPs notably more inclined towards the "theocrat" category than the others. In other words, there was a tendency for members of all of groups of politicians to believe that there was at least *some* role for religion in public life.

There might be a somewhat cynical explanation of the finding that more respondents tended to fall into the "secularist" category of the Theocratism scale than the "sceptic" category of the Religiosity scale. The latter is about personal religious beliefs and practices. The former says something about political power, and implicitly the sharing of political power with others.

Comparison can be made of levels of religious belief between the near-contemporaneous English general public and their closest matches amongst our respondents, ELCs. The self-completion part of the 1998 *British Social Attitudes* survey[529] included identical items from the Theocratism scale and two of the three items from the Religiosity scale. To make the comparison as close as possible, as well as only using *BSA* respondents who lived in England only those respondents aged between 24 and 81 inclusive – the same age range as ELC respondents – were included.

Regarding Theocratism, the proportion of those members of the general public falling into the "theocrat" category was little different from ELCs: 6% (out of 491 valid cases) against 8% of ELCs. The difference was that an appreciably larger proportion of the English general public fell into the "secularist" category: 46% against only 30% of ELCs. The comparison for Religiosity is more difficult because there was a "missing" item from the *BSA* survey. However, a tentative analysis suggests that members of the general public were less devout than ELCs. In short, the English general public at the time tended to be less religious in both senses of the term used in this chapter compared to ELCs.[530]

---

[529] NCSR, 29th October 2008[b].

[530] See Spencer, 2006, for arguments in a UK-specific if not Conservative-specific context for the active engagement of religion in public life. The publishers of this report, Theos, also commissioned research by Communicate Research in 2006 which suggested that public opinion in the UK was on balance favourable to religion having a say in public life in the UK with a majority (58% against 37%) agreeing that "On balance, religion is a force for good in society".

Considered together

Having looked at Religiosity and Theocratism individually, to what extent were they correlated? Was it usually the case that strong personal religious views carried over into a desire to see religion and religious institutions play a role in public life or can we see evidence for some belief in a "separation of church and state" even amongst the personally devout?

A series of bivariate analyses was run between the two scales, broken down by group of respondent. As might be expected, the small numbers in some of the groups lessened the chances of obtaining statistically significant results (assuming a correlation in the first place). Nevertheless, using the Pearson statistic there was a one-tailed significant correlation at the 5% level or better in the anticipated "more Religious = more Theocratic" direction in the case of the four largest groups of ELCs, Peers, MPs and SLCs.

Table 10.1 displays a cross-tabulation of the two variables for ELCs only since this was only group large enough not to violate the assumptions of the chi^2 test.

TABLE 10.1: CROSS-TABULATION OF RELIGIOSITY AND THEOCRATISM FOR ELCs

| | | Religiosity | | | | |
		Sceptic	In between	Devout	Base	Total
Theocratism	Secularist	51%	33%	18%	81	31%
	In between	45%	63%	69%	164	62%
	Theocrat	4%	4%	13%	20	7%
	Base	49	116	100	265	100%
	Total	100%	100%	100%		

The results are in the direction that would be expected with "sceptic" views tending to be associated with "secularist" ones and the association is statistically significant: one-tailed p = 0.001.

However, there are two points of interest that might be seen as the mirror image of each other. The first is that by falling into the Theocratism's "in between" category, nearly half (45%) of all those identified as religious "sceptics" nevertheless believed that religion should have at least some role in public life. On the other hand, relatively few (13%) identified as "devout" held that religion should have a prominent role in public life. Indeed, slightly more (18%) religiously "devout" fell into the "secularist" category.

At the "extremes", out of the 265 valid cases 25 (9% of the total) fell into the "sceptic/secularist" cell indicating little or no personal religious beliefs and an opposition to religion having a say in public life. Only 13 (5% of the total) fell into the "devout/theocrat" cell indicating strong personal religious beliefs and support for religion having a say in public life. Rather endearingly, the most populated cell was the one in the middle, "in between" along both dimensions, which held 73 (28% of the total) respondents.

Confessional and Religious Background

Almost all (82%) ELCs came from an Anglican or Episcopal background, with a minority coming from non-Anglican Protestant (8%) or Roman Catholic (5%) backgrounds. (It is not the place here to engage in any discussion about whether the Anglican Church is "Protestant" or "Catholic" or something between or even unique.[531]) Only 4% – a small number of Jews and those who said that they had no religious or confessional background – stated that they came from an explicitly non-Christian background. (The predominance of Anglicans was also a feature of MPs at the time, particularly amongst Conservative MPs.[532])

To put this into context, the 2001 *National Census*[533] indicated that "only" about 72% of the population in England regarded themselves as Christians of any sort against no less than 96% of our respondents. Given that most non-Christians tended to live in urban areas at the time[534] and that this was where the Conservative Party was weakest, there are simple geographic reasons for this difference without having to suggest anti-minority prejudice on the part of candidate selection panels.

The *Census* figures suggest that the 1% of ELCs who came from a Jewish background accurately reflected the position of Jews in England

---

[531] Graaf & Need, 2000: 121.
[532] Brivati & Baston, 2002: 8.
[533] National Statistics, 11th October 2004; O'Beirne, March 2004: 6.
[534] Meek, May 2003: 8.

at the time in terms of both their numbers in the population[535] and their increasing post-Second World War support for the Conservative Party. (It also goes beyond the scope of this work to discuss any distinction between "Jew" *qua* religion and *qua* race.) This was something that had not happened amongst more recently-arrived racial minority groups which tended very strongly to back the Labour Party.[536] Given the geographical distribution of non-"Anglo-Saxons" and non-Christians vis-à-vis electoral support for the Conservatives, this in fact suggests – tentatively, since the numbers in absolute terms are so small – an "over-representation" of Jews amongst ELCs. This finding was not wholly unpredictable. Margaret Thatcher's preference for Jews, including some of her closest advisors, has been commented upon.[537] Although he tended to play down his background,[538] Michael Howard – who would take over the Party leadership from Iain Duncan Smith – was born to a father named Bernat Hecht.

The absolute numbers were very small, but it would seem that Roman Catholics amongst ELC respondents were markedly more religious in both senses used here. 60% of them fell into Religiosity's "devout" category against 40% of their Anglican colleagues. 27% of them fell into Theocratism's "theocrat" category against only 5% of their Anglican colleagues. T-tests indicated that these were statistically significant findings, with two-tailed $p = 0.026$ and $p = 0.002$ for Religiosity and Theocratism respectively. However, despite good reason to think that there might be similar significant differences along what might be regarded as some of this study's "core" dimensions such as Europeanism,[539] Left-Right[540] and Authoritarianism,[541] this was not found to be the case. In other words, Catholics were more religious but based on a handful of specimen variables this did not follow through into differences in other attitudes.

---

[535] National Statistics, 11th October 2004.

[536] Kotler-Berkowitz, 2001: 651 & 660.

[537] King, 2002: 446; Riddell, 27th February 2009.

[538] Roth, October 2004: 364.

[539] Boyes, 6th June 2003; Allen, 1st April 2005; Grennan, 1st July 2001; Nelson, Guth & Fraser, 2001; North, 3rd August 2009; Deloy, 21st September 2003.

[540] Glasman, 1996; Malcolm, 1996: 56; Meek, 2003.

[541] Browne, 28th October 2004.

The Established Church

Although it is often referred to as such, the Church of England has never been officially 'established' since its creation in 1534. It is simply part of the same organisation as the Crown.[542] For various reasons, the Church was disestablished in Ireland in 1871, in Wales in 1920 and was never established in Scotland.[543] The Church of Scotland is the national church of Scotland as guaranteed in the *Act of Union* of Scotland and England of 1707, but is not established (*sic*) like the Church of England and is "free… from civil interference in spiritual matters" unlike the Church of England.[544] Both the Church of Ireland and the Church in (*sic*) Wales have been independent members of the Anglican Communion since Disestablishment.[545]

Table 10.2 displays the responses to a single item in the questionnaire, originally using a five-point Likert-type response set, "There should no longer be an Established Church in any part of Britain".

TABLE 10.2: ATTITUDES TOWARDS DISESTABLISHMENT						
	ELCs	**SLCs**	**WLCs**	**Peers**	**MPs**	**MEPs**	**MSPs**
Agree	17%	36%	32%	30%	19%	54%	36%
Neither/nor	14%	9%	7%	15%	15%	0%	21%
Disagree	69%	55%	61%	55%	66%	46%	43%
Base	**280**	**47**	**28**	**60**	**52**	**13**	**14**

It can be seen that generally there was opposition to Disestablishment. Amongst all groups of local councillors, Peers and MPs a majority were opposed and amongst MSPs a plurality were. Only MEPs were marginally in favour. Given the Conservative Party's *historic* connection to the Established Church these results come as no surprise.

The number of Roman Catholics amongst ELC respondents was too small to allow for detailed analysis. Nevertheless, of the 15 who

---

[542] Church of England, 2004.
[543] Baldwin, 3rd December 2002.
[544] Church of Scotland, c. 2006a & 2006b.
[545] Anglican Communion, 2004.

responded to this item in the questionnaire 40% agreed to some degree against only 14% of those who identified their confessional background as Anglican. 33% Catholics disagreed with the item against 75% Anglicans. Again, it might be expected that there were a relatively high proportion of Catholics who were unhappy with their confessional-cum-constitutional position. On the other hand, a third of the admittedly small group of Catholic respondents were not unhappy with the situation.

Religion and Socio-Demographics

In Chapter 4 looking at ELC socio-demographics it was found that there was no significant correlation between age and either Religiosity or Theocratism. What about the other major measures used in this study: sex, marital status, level of formal education, type of school attended and the nature of the area that they represented?

Analysis indicated not a single statistically significant association between any of these measures and either Religiosity or Theocratism. This goes against some literature dealing with the British general public in the past,[546] but the findings stand. In short, the "type" of person that a respondent was, at least amongst ELCs, predicted no meaningful difference in religious attitudes and beliefs.

Religion as Predictors of Other Attitudes

A note about temporal causality

A few words need to be said about temporal causality[547] and these religion-based variables and their possible associations with other multi-item dimensions. First, of course, must be repeated the usual mantra that "correlation does not imply causation".

However, if there are causal relationships, it is intuitively probable that in any significant correlation between Theocratism and/or Religiosity and another attitudinal scale it is the religion-based variable that precedes the other in time. Apart perhaps for adherents

---

[546] E.g. Schweisguth, 1995: 339.

[547] Jary & Jary, 1991: 62-63.

of some form of natural theology,[548] it seems unlikely that views about (say) economics, taxation and welfare lead one to believe (or not) in God. It is, however, much more plausible that considerations of God and accompanying religious teachings might well lead someone to views about what makes up a "just" society regarding (say) taxation and welfare as well as about various moral issues. In other words, that there is clear direction to any causal relationship. This is one of the reasons that Religiosity and Theocratism are singled out for special treatment compared to most of the other multi-item scales.

As always, there may be exceptions to this temporal causality and one might – arguably – have been found in the following analysis.

Multivariate analysis

Rather than take up a great deal of space with exploratory bivariate analysis broken down by group of respondent, multivariate analysis was proceeded with directly by using regression analysis. One at a time each of the usual range of scales was treated as the dependent variable with all the other scales and dummy variables for the groups of respondents treated as putative explanatory variables.

Returning to the question of whether religious beliefs had any predictive power regarding other attitudes measured by this study's range of scales, then looking at the results the answer must be, "not really." In the cases of Europeanism, Intra-Party Elitism, Intra-Party Inclusivity, Optimism, Political Elitism, Postmaterialism, Pride in the Way Nation Functions, Protectionism, Traditional British Liberties and Xenophobia neither Religiosity nor Theocratism remained in the final, significant model.

Table 10.3 displays the results for those scales where either – but in fact never both – Religiosity or Theocratism remained in the final model. All of the figures are based upon the adjusted R^2 figure from the regression analysis.

---

[548] Cole, 2004: 1 & 3; Davies, 2004: 41 & 48.

TABLE 10.3: EXPLANATORY POWER OF RELIGIOSITY AND THEOCRATISM				
Scale	Religiosity	Theocratism	Total all variables	Base
Authoritarianism	2%	0%	47%	321
Environmentalism	5%	0%	17%	321
Feminism	0%	1%	21%	321
Left-Right	1%	0%	17%	321
Pride in Heritage & Culture	1%	0%	15%	321
Religiosity	n/a	12%	25%	321
Theocratism	12%	n/a	25%	321
Welfarism	2%	0%	32%	321

Excluding each other as might have been expected, in no case did either Religiosity or Theocratism appear as significant predictors accounting for even 10% of the variation in the dependent variable being tested.

In only one other case was Theocratism present at all as a significant predictor in a regression model. This was in the case of Feminism where it was the fifth (out of sixth) strongest predictive variable accounting for just 1% (out of a total power of the model of 21%) of the variation in Feminism. Detailed analysis indicated that Theocratism was positively associated with patriarchal attitudes. That those who wished to see religion play a strong role in public life had traditionalist views about the place of women in society probably comes as no surprise.[549] In short, beliefs about the influence that religion should have on public life had little impact on what that "public life" should be doing or not doing when other attitudes were taken into account.

Religiosity appeared more frequently as an element of other predictive models. However, with one exception this was also at a small if nevertheless statistically significant level.[550] It contributed 1% (out of 17%) towards predicting the Left-Right dimension, with Religiosity positively associated with economic right-wing attitudes. It also contributed 2% (out of a substantial 47%) towards predicting

---

[549] E.g. Clarkson, 1994; Gledhill, 19th April 2000.
[550] Gibbins & Reimer, 1995: 320.

Authoritarianism and Religiosity was positively associated with authoritarian attitudes.

Although marginal, these results make sense and can be plausibly explained. The connections between strong religious views and support for free-market economics (the Left-Right dimension) and/or socially conservative or traditionalist views (the Authoritarianism dimension) have certainly been demonstrated in the USA.[551] In the UK, regarding the former of these issues, senior Christian Conservatives have argued that there is no incompatibility between Christianity and support for a free-market economic system.[552] Regarding the latter of these issues, critics of the Conservative Party have certainly claimed a connection between strong religious views and traditionalist attitudes on issues such as homosexuality.[553]

Religiosity was a significant predictive variable for Welfarism, contributing 2% (out of 32%). In the light of some of the preceding – and also the "nasty party" hypothesis noted near the start of this book – this might come as a surprise because Religiosity was positively associated with welfarist attitudes. However, within the context of the British Conservative Party and British Christianity there has been a counter-argument that "a permissive, consumerist, competitive, market-orientated liberalism seems to undermine central Christian ideas of solidarity and community".[554] As such, there has existed within British conservatism a religiously-derived ethic that individuals should be protected to some degree against possible negative outcomes of free-market economics.[555] Indeed, it has been stated the Christian Conservative Fellowship was in part formed in 1990 to "reignite the party's compassion."[556]

Therefore it is not too surprising that those with stronger religious belief were more inclined to support state provision of welfare. In short, it could be argued that, at least amongst our respondents, holding stronger religious beliefs was associated with

---

[551] E.g. Laythe, Finkel & Kirkpatrick, March 2001; Brittan, 27ᵗʰ September 2002.

[552] Mawhinney, 1999: 288-229.

[553] Williams, 18ᵗʰ September 2002.

[554] McLellan, 1997: 172.

[555] Greenleaf, 1983: 196-262.

[556] Cook, 12ᵗʰ February 2010. This reinforces the point made above about temporal causality.

support for free-market economics but also the view that those who "fell through the cracks" should be supported by the taxpayer via the state.

Religiosity also contributed 1% (out of 15%) towards the predictive model for Pride in National Heritage and Culture, with Religiosity positively associated with higher levels of national pride. It might be conjectured that here can be seen evidence of an inner conflict within the Conservative Party between what one conservative writer termed "brutalist counting-house Toryism"[557] on the one hand and on the other a belief in "The conservation of what remains of rural England is the assertion of cultural references and national definition. What more important task can there be for a Conservative Party?" It is with this in mind, along with the "faith and flag" tradition within the Party[558] represented by the Cornerstone Group[559] of socially conservative or traditionalist Conservative MPs formed a while after this study's fieldwork, that this finding can be plausibly explained.

Religiosity and environmentalism

There was one dimension where the possible impact of religious belief was less trivial. Religiosity accounted for 5% (out of 17%) of the predictive power of the model and was the second most powerful (out of four) predictive variable of variation in Environmentalism. Bivariate analysis indicated that stronger religious beliefs were positively correlated with holding pro-green beliefs.

Using the terms of the debate, a plausible argument can be made that the more religious respondents came down on the "stewardship" view of Christian thinking vis-à-vis the environment rather than the "dominion" view.[560] It should be noted that there is no reason to think that this explanation might not apply to others. For example, it might be offered it as an explanation if a similar survey of Labour politicians also found a link between stronger religious beliefs and having more environmentalist attitudes.

---

[557] Lovibond, 2006: 24-25.
[558] Tempest, 22nd August 2005.
[559] Cornerstone Group, 2009.
[560] Santmire, 1985: 1-9; Gore, 1992: 243-244.

It was noted above of the likelihood of the religion-derived variables – inasmuch as there was any significant correlation let alone claimed causation – temporally preceding the more mundane ones. It might be argued that of all the other variables analysed Environmentalism was one where "earthly" values – literally in this case – could attain a transcendent quality. It is not the place here to discuss whether or not the environmentalist movement is or was some kind of ersatz religion.[561] However, there is a body of literature on, for example, pantheism that holds that "the Universe as a whole is worthy of the deepest reverence, and that only the Universe and Nature are worthy of that degree of reverence".[562] However, given the nature of our respondents in terms of confessional background and so on, this is probably unlikely to have been a consciously-held attitude amongst them.

Conclusion to Chapter 10

The findings in this chapter generally bear out what has been argued for some time.[563] That whilst many have argued for some essential connection between conservatism and religion, and that there is indeed a tradition of British conservative thought on religion that emphasises in particular original sin and the moral imperfection of human nature, there is also a tradition much more latitudinarian, Deist or simply secular and humanist.

As such, it is not surprising that the most comprehensive near-contemporaneous (to our fieldwork) document of the Conservative Party's beliefs, its 2001 General Election manifesto,[564] contains virtually no mention of religious matters. All that it does contain are a few comments about religious freedom and tolerance[565] and, perhaps more significantly given the association between Religiosity and Welfarism noted above, the pledge that "churches and other faith

---

[561] A formal ruling by a UK Employment Appeals Tribunal in November 2009 suggested that it was exactly that: Adams & Gray, 3rd November 2009; Samuel, 2010: 17.

[562] Harrison, 2004: 1.

[563] Quinton, 1978: 9-11.

[564] Conservative Party, 2001[b].

[565] Conservative Party, 2001[b]: 31-33.

communities"[566] would be allowed to set up schools. There was not a single mention of Christianity as such.

That said, nor was there in either the Labour (2001) or Liberal Democrat (2001) manifestos.[567] The same word of caution applies to much of this chapter. For example, it has been seen that there was some admittedly generally weak evidence for the continuing impact of religious beliefs on more secular issues. Another survey done at the same time might have been able to examine, for example, whether or not it was reasonable to talk of the continuing influence of "Christian socialism" amongst Labour Party politicians.[568]

Conservative politicians in 2002 were quite personally religious as measured by the Religiosity dimension. However, as measured by the Theocratism dimension, this did not strongly translate into a desire to see a role for religious institutions in public life and even less so as measured by the other dimensions into much of the way of religion-informed beliefs. Respondents were some way from being "American style" Christian Reconstructionists.[569] Taken as a group, these Conservative politicians could not be described as "fundamentalist".[570] Where, however, religious views were significantly associated with attitudes towards other issues, they were in a predictable or plausibly explained direction.

---

[566] Conservative Party, 2001[b]: 9.
[567] Labour Party, 2001; Liberal Democrats, 2001.
[568] E.g. Amber & Haslam, 1980; Thomas, 2005.
[569] Brinkley, 19th March 2006.
[570] Bealey, 1999: 140.

11

The Party-Political Institutions

The "Where" of Politics

The questionnaire contained a number of items concerned with the conduct and purpose of politics rather than attitudes towards issues and themes. Most of these were stand-alone items not specifically intended to form parts of multi-item scales.

That said, some of the scales set out in Appendix 3 were of a similar nature, most notably Political Elitism which says nothing about what "power" does but where respondents believed that it ought to reside. However, this is not covered again here.

There were also items concerning attitudes towards the powers of the various institutions overtly legislating in 2002 and it is with these that this chapters starts.

The Locus of Power

Power and responsibilities

Respondents were asked, "Relative to the present situation, what should be done about the powers of the following institutions?" followed by a list of institutions and a five-point "Increased a lot" to "Decreased a lot" Likert-type response set. The institutions were the Westminster Parliament, European Parliament, Scottish Parliament, Welsh Assembly, Northern Ireland Assembly, Greater London Assembly, principal local authorities and parish/town councils.

"Power" was meant in the everyday sense of the legislative powers of the various institutions rather than in any more philosophic sense.[571] This battery of items relied on a subjective "feel" for the institutions and their powers rather than relying on the expectation of a possibly unreasonable level of detailed, objective knowledge. Also implicit was the understanding that any desired change must be at least partly relative to the other institutions except in those cases where an increase or decrease was desired amongst all of the institutions.

It clear that politicians from the major parties did not always grasp these issues. For example, commentators in Scotland noted that the major parties were still campaigning at the 2001 general election as if devolution had not happened. They often argued about issues such as education, crime and healthcare that would have to wait until the 2003 Scottish parliamentary elections.[572]

The least surprising finding was that in every case where there was a direct comparison, members of an institution were the most inclined to want increased powers for that institution rather than leaving things as they were or decreasing them. Peers (53%) and particularly MPs (88%) most favoured increased power for the Westminster Parliament, MEPs (64%) for the European Parliament, MSPs (36%) for the Scottish Parliament and ELCs (71%) for principal local authorities. This was also true for the tiny number of respondents sitting in the Welsh and Greater London Assemblies, where both AMs and all four GLAs wanted to see their institutions possess increased powers.

Being in power in the institution was not the issue. For example, ELCs, many of whom would have sat as members of the ruling party in their local authorities, wanted increased powers for local authorities, but so did Conservative MPs at Westminster who were in opposition at the time.

---

[571] Jary & Jary, 1991: 490-492.

[572] Butler & Kavanagh, 2002[b]: 114. It seems that in the decade after the fieldwork, little changed. During the 2012 London Mayoral election, some of the candidates were standing on manifesto commitments which they candidly admitted were quite beyond the powers of that office: Szamuely, 12ᵗʰ April 2012.

The institutions compared

By looking across the results it can also be seen which institutions were generally held in esteem by respondents and which were not. This was done by subtracting the proportion of those who wanted to see a decrease in the powers of an institution from those who wanted to see an increase. A positive figure indicates an overall desire to see powers increased and a negative figure an overall desire to see powers decreased. The middle "Stay the same" option was retained in this calculation since omitting it exaggerates reported opinion.

TABLE 11.1: NET DESIRE TO SEE INCREASE OR DECREASE IN POWERS OF INSTITUTIONS[573]							
	ELCs	Peers	MPs	SLCs	WLCs	MEPs	MSPs
Westminster Parliament	25	48	87	17	8	43	0
European Parliament	-75	-41	-58	-79	-64	50	-43
Scottish Parliament	-45	-59	-34	-21	-46	-14	29
Welsh Assembly	-41	-38	-29	-23	-29	-21	25
Northern Ireland Assembly	-27	-28	-16	-5	-39	-7	25
Greater London Assembly	-48	-53	-52	-20	-59	-14	-8
Principal local authorities	66	26	63	40	52	64	-8
Parish/town councils	47	35	58	48	37	36	8

It can be seen from Table 11.1 that the institutions tended to break down into those where there was general support for increased powers – the Westminster Parliament and both principal and parish/town councils – and those where there was general support for decreased powers – all of the others except in the expected like-for-like instances noted above. MSPs stand out as being somewhat unusual in their coolness towards Westminster and their warmth towards the other Celtic devolved institutions in Wales and Northern Ireland but not of the Greater London Assembly.

---

[573] Since these represent 56 separate calculations, no bases are presented.

In short, there was support for what might be thought of as the traditional institutions at Westminster and also at a local level, but a general if not universal antipathy towards what were at the time the newer institutions in Scotland, Wales, Northern Ireland and London. And, of course, the European Parliament. This theme is also discussed in Chapter 8 that looks at aspects of national identity.

The Conservatives were opposed to the creation of the Scottish and the Welsh bodies, generally campaigning for a "No" result in the referenda in 1997.[574] This stance changed by the time of the Greater London Authority referendum in 1998[575] although this seems to have had little impact on the reported attitudes of respondents.

Whatever happened to "Rolling back the frontiers of the state"?

… as a young William Hague (amongst others) once said.[576] A notable finding from this battery of items was that so many respondents were happy to see the powers of at least some of these institutions remain the same or even increased. Amongst these, however, were there any respondents who wanted to see a *total* reduction of "state power" as demonstrated by a desire to see the powers and responsibilities of *every* level of government reduced, from the might of the "EU Directive" to the maintenance of the village clock?[577]

Indeed there were. *Three* out of 505 valid respondents. One Peer and two WLCs.

Representation at Westminster

Using data[578] to calculate the electorate-to-MP ratio at the 2001 general election, it can be demonstrated that Scotland and Wales were

---

[574] Brown, 11th September 1997; Donegan, 19th June 1997; MacAskill, White & Donegan, 12th September 1997; Travis, 10th October 1997.
[575] *BBC News*, 9th April 1998.
[576] Utley, 20th June 1997.
[577] Cheshire County Council, 1999; National Association of Local Councils, 5th September 2008.
[578] Austin & Hames, 2001: 296.

noticeably over-represented in the UK parliament compared to England. Each MP from Scotland and Wales represented between 55,000 and 56,000 electors whereas each MP from England represented almost 70,000 electors. This had been an issue in British politics for some time, particularly since the creation of the Scottish Parliament and the Welsh Assembly with their differing powers (itself a subject of debate[579]). It was noted that this over-representation of Scottish and Welsh MPs at Westminster was arguably compounded by the fact that England continued to be ruled – excepting, of course, those increasing areas covered by membership of the EU[580] – by a UK-wide parliament unlike Scotland, Wales and, in an erratic fashion at the time, Northern Ireland.[581]

This is also connected with the "West Lothian question", and was troubling to many in England who felt aggrieved at the situation where Scottish and Welsh MPs at Westminster could vote on matters that did not affect their own constituents.[582]

With a view to looking at these issues there was a stand-alone item that asked respondents to choose from four options concerning the level of Scottish and Welsh representation in the House of Commons at Westminster. The two "extreme" options of "Scotland and Wales should continue to return a relatively larger number of MPs to Westminster than England" and "Scotland and/or Wales should become independent countries" were chosen by almost no respondents. Whilst there was almost no appetite for Scottish and/or Welsh independence from the UK, in a post-devolution constitutional settlement there was a belief that things should not go on as they were.

As such, respondents were split between the two "middle" options of "The number of Westminster MPs returned by Scotland and Wales relative to England should be brought in line with their population" and "Scotland and Wales should return a proportionately smaller number of MPs to Westminster than England, commensurate with the autonomy of their devolved institutions". Furthermore, and just in words, the mainly English

---

[579] Melding, 14th August 2000.
[580] Kamall, November 2008.
[581] Curtice & Heath, 2000: 155-156.
[582] Hughes, 13th November 2000; Hurst, 8th March 20002.

respondents of ELCs and MPs were relatively if not absolutely more inclined to want to see taken into account the reality of the powers of the devolved institutions in Scotland and Wales. This was an area that would take on a concrete form shortly after the fieldwork where Scottish MPs allowed the Labour government to win a number of Commons votes that did not affect Scotland.[583] On the other hand, respondents from in particular Scotland wanted to see a less sophisticated arithmetical calculation and one might argue that this was a case of wanting to have their cake and eating it too.

Why become a Politician?

Types of reason

In this battery of ranked items respondents were prompted with "The following are some of the reasons why people decide to become politicians. Which for you is the *most* important? And the *next most* important? And the *least* important?" There was the assumption that this would elicit an autobiographical response rather than a more general one.

The wording of the three options was, "As someone concerned with social change or the promotion of certain beliefs", "As a representative of the electorate or public" and "As a necessary element within the machinery of stable, democratic government". These might be thought of as "ideological", "representational" and "constitutional" reasons respectively.

These three items were informed by Fenney.[584] However, it is not an exhaustive list. Crude self-interest might also be one reason.[585] Another might be a desire to seek out like-minded company.[586]

Only those who responded validly to all three parts of the item were counted. Looking at just the "Most important" reason, as can be seen in Table 11.2 there were differences between the types of respondent.

---

[583] Lynch, October 2004: 387.
[584] Fenney, 2000: 21.
[585] *Telegraph*, 2009.
[586] Mulé, 1995: 291.

TABLE 11.2: MOST IMPORTANT REASON FOR BECOMING A POLITICIAN							
	ELCs	Peers	MPs	SLCs	WLCs	MEPs	MSPs
As someone concerned with social change or the promotion of certain beliefs	27%	41%	64%	28%	26%	79%	62%
As a representative of the electorate or public	57%	19%	28%	65%	63%	21%	38%
As a necessary element within the machinery of stable, democratic government	16%	40%	8%	7%	11%	0%	0%
Base	**272**	**53**	**50**	**46**	**27**	**14**	**13**

Peers were different to MPs, MEPs and MSPs who in turn were different to local councillors. Peers were evenly split between the ideological and constitutional reasons – and were the only group who cited the latter reason in large numbers – with neither having a majority. MPs, MEPs and MSPs regarded the ideological reason as the most important, with a clear majority in each case opting for this. Local councillors primarily saw a career in politics as a representational calling.

Turning to the least important reason, either a plurality (ELCs and WLCs) or even an outright majority (MPs, SLCs, MEPs and MSPs) cited the constitutional reason as the least important. At least two reasons can be imagined. It might be because the concept of being "a necessary element within the machinery of stable, democratic government" was somewhat vague or high-flown compared to the other two. More optimistically, it could have been that respondents agreed with earlier writers such as Almond and Verba and believed that British democracy was anyway sufficiently secure.[587] As was noted, Peers were the exception. For them it was the representational reason that was the least important. Irrespective of their route into the House of Lords such as hereditary, appointee or former MP, given the unelected (by the general public) nature of the Lords this finding is not too surprising.

---

[587] Marquand, 2009: 155-156.

Ideological versus representational

Were there any attitudinal indicators about why someone cited either of the two most popular reasons for becoming a politician? In principle this can be analysed by creating two new binary variables indicating ideological/not ideological (the latter indicating those who cited either the representational or constitutional reasons) and representational/not representational (the latter indicating those who cited either the ideological or constitutional reasons).

There is, however, a problem because of what was detected in the preceding analysis: the strong influence of what group of politician respondents belonged to. Exploratory regression analysis (not shown here) with the entire dataset was conducted using these new binary variables and as the putative predictive variables the usual range of multi-item scales plus dummy variables for the type of respondent. In both cases these dummy variables featured heavily in the final model, particularly in the case of the ideological/not ideological item where they made up almost the entire model.

It is true that when a series of partial correlation analyses was conducted for these two binary items alongside the usual range of multi-item scales there were significant associations at the two-tailed 5% level. However, it is clear that what was of main importance about why respondents thought that people – whether or not themselves – became politicians was their representational level.

The socio-demographics of ELCs and "idealism"

In Chapter 4 on ELC socio-demographics, it was noted that most socio-demographic variables appeared to have little predictive power concerning attitudes. However, might they have had some association with "idealism" more generally, in this case as indicated by those who cited the ideological reason as being the most important? This particular regression analysis was re-run, but this time also using the range of socio-demographic items found in Chapter 4. The answer was "no" in any meaningful sense. Only one variable produced a significant (*sic*) model explaining 1% of the variability in this binary item.

Elections, Parties and Constitutional Power

With the aim of producing a wide-ranging snapshot of the attitudes of Conservative Party politicians, a number of stand-alone items relevant to this chapter were presented in the questionnaire. Because of the number of them, only some of the headline results are reported here. All items were presented alongside a five-point "Agree strongly" to "Disagree strongly" response set.

"There should be at least an element of proportional representation for general elections." There was a robust rejection of this idea, with only SLCs (55% disagreeing) and MEPs (64% disagreeing) displaying less than two-thirds disagreement to some degree. *"There should be at least an element of proportional representation for local authority elections."* Here there was also robust disagreement with the item, with again only SLCs (49% disagreeing) and MEPs (54% disagreeing) displaying less than two-thirds disagreement to some degree.

Taking these two items together, there was strong support for the first-past-the-post system with even those involved in a proportional representational system offering support. With some notable exceptions[588] there was a long tradition of Conservatives arguing against proportional representation on principle even when it had benefited them electorally.[589] Nevertheless, historically and based upon other research of Conservative *supporters*,[590] it is perhaps surprising that respondents from Scotland and Wales in particular were not more favourably inclined towards proportional representation.[591] In the 2001 general election[592] the Conservatives gained 21% of the popular vote in Wales – putting them in second place behind Labour – but did not win a single Westminster seat. Similarly, they captured 16% of the popular vote in Scotland which was equal to the Liberal Democrats, but whereas the latter won 10 seats the Conservatives won only one.

---

[588] Holroyd-Doveton, 1996: 77.
[589] Fraser, August/September 2002.
[590] Curtice, Seyd, Park & Thomson, 2000.
[591] Broughton, 2003: 204.
[592] Austin & Hames, 2001: 296.

On the other hand, aside from any principled objection to proportional representation there may have been reasons of overall self-interest. The first-past-the-post system had for years acted as a prop to the two main parties at the expense of the Liberal Democrats or other parties such as UKIP, the BNP and the Greens. In 1955 Labour and the Conservatives polled between them 91% of votes cast and in 1970 this was still 88%. But this fell throughout the 1980s and 1990s reaching 68% by 2005.[593] And yet Labour or the Conservatives continued to secure often substantial overall majorities, at least until 2010.

More dramatically, some commentators argued that any move towards proportional representation for Westminster elections represented a real threat to the existence of the Conservative Party.[594] This was particularly the case over the issue of "Europe" if "pro" and/or "anti" wings thought that they could gather sufficient votes by themselves to satisfy any minimum threshold needed to win seats.

"Local government is just as an appropriate arena for party politics as national government." This was a somewhat polarising item. A majority of all members of all groups agreed to some extent but often between a quarter and a third disagreed. Respondents from Scotland (SLCs 68% and MSPs 71% agreeing) and Wales (WLCs 71% agreeing) were the most "party political". In 2002 they were also the most electorally beleaguered. It is possible that being in such a position fostered a "No compromise with the electorate"[595] attitude.

This might seem like a rather naive item considering political history and local government in the UK in the years leading up to 2002. Consider, for example, the so-called "loony left" phenomenon and local government in London and Liverpool in the 1980s.[596] Yet within living memory there was a tradition within the Conservative Party whereby candidates would often stand at local elections as, for example, Ratepayers, "to imply that, unlike the Labour Party, they were non-political".[597] It also needs to be kept in mind that in 1979 two-party and three-party contests featured in only 41% and 17% respectively of wards although by 2002 local elections had become

---

[593] Aaronovitch, 23rd April 2010; Marquand, 2009: 154.
[594] 6, 1998: 15.
[595] Stone-Lee, 1st October 2002.
[596] Tyler, 16th May 2006.
[597] Hutchings, 1999: 81.

more competitive.[598] Many more experienced respondents, particularly ELCs, might have regarded "party politics" as just being opposed at all. It has also been argued that there was a major change after local government reorganisation in 1973 when much of "local government shifted from political control to managerial governance".[599] This left local councillors with less of the "deadly dull but vitally important issues of council management" so that "they devoted more and more time to party political bickering".

"Local campaigning makes little difference these days compared to the overall impression of the national party." This was a polarising item, with groups often split with at least a third on the less populated pole and with few in between. Only WLCs (64% disagreeing) strongly looked towards local campaigning. Conservative local councillors in Wales were in an unusual position in 2002 and indeed historically. The objective truth of this item is not an issue here. However, a number of authorities, making use of data from general elections either side of the fieldwork, have argued that local campaigning was certainly important to the overall performance of political parties.[600] For example, because successful local parties are more likely to have campaigning activists and parties in power locally are more likely to be visible to the local electorate and media and to be able to demonstrate their ability govern (or not).

"Single-issue groups are now a better way than political parties of advancing causes." There was general disagreement with this notion, with half to two thirds of each group of respondents disagreeing. MEPs were less certain – perhaps because of the long-term influence of groups such as the European Movement[601] – with opinion evenly divided with about a third agreeing or disagreeing. To turn the findings around, however, a fair number of respondents were at least sceptical about whether conventional political parties were still the best way of advancing causes. The reported rise in the influence of pressure groups as part of a rise in participation in "unconventional activity"[602] was also often cited in the context of environmentalism and the impact of

---

[598] Rallings, Thrasher & Johnston, 2002: 284-285.
[599] North, 27th September 2008.
[600] Fisher & Denver, October 2008; Rallings, Thrasher & Johnston, 2002: 272.
[601] North, 27th March 2012.
[602] Topf, 1995[b]: 78.

organisations such as Greenpeace and Friends of the Earth whose influence was held to have been greater than that of the Green Party.[603] Accordingly, responses to this item alongside the Environmentalism scale were analysed. However, there was no significant correlation. Nor was there any correlation between this item and whether or not respondents cited "As someone concerned with social change or the promotion of certain beliefs" as being the most important reason for becoming a politician.

"Political parties should be funded by the State and taxpayer rather than by individual donors, businesses, or unions." In every case at least a plurality disagreed with this idea. However, sizable minorities – often a quarter to a third – agreed with the proposition with all three groups of local councillors being the most receptive to the idea of state funding of political parties. The funding of political parties is an issue that never goes away, resurfacing for different reasons.[604] It arose around the time of the fieldwork[605] in part because of a decline in the membership of the major parties – which is why some of the smaller parties such as UKIP were particularly opposed to the idea[606] – as had certainly been the case with the Conservatives for some years.[607] At the time it was the position of the Conservatives to oppose any moves towards state funding of political parties[608] and this was explicitly stated by the then Chair of the Party, Theresa May[609] even though in the run-up to the 2001 general election the Conservatives were the poorer of the two main parties.[610]

"The House of Lords should be replaced by a wholly or mainly elected second chamber." This item indicated considerable disagreement both within and between groups. Never less than a quarter identified with one or either of the poles. MEPs, MPs and MSPs (69%, 69% and 64% respectively agreeing to some degree) were the most supportive of such constitutional change with, predictably, Peers (72%

---

[603] Matthews, 2008: 35; Sanders, 1997: 218.

[604] *BBC News*, 22nd November 2011, 26th March 2012; Gay, White & Kelly, 10th April 2007; *Guardian*, 11th October 2007.

[605] Hinsliff, 18th August 2002.

[606] Croucher, 8th June 2002.

[607] Conservative Party, 1998: 3; Watt, 5th January 2001.

[608] Fisher, October 2004: 409.

[609] Kite, 5th August 2002.

[610] Fisher, October 2004: 409.

disagreeing) and, less predictably, WLCs (71% disagreeing) the least supportive. When House of Lords of reform was debated in the House of Commons in February 2003, Conservative MPs were split over the five options where the House divided. [611] 43% supported a fully elected second chamber. 49% supported one that was 80% elected. 34% supported one that was 60% elected. 40% supported one that was fully appointed. Only two Conservative MPs (1%) supported outright abolition. Amongst MP respondents to this present study, support for a wholly or mainly elected second chamber apparently diminished somewhat in the intervening year.

"However a second chamber is elected or selected, it should always be subordinate to the House of Commons." In every case a plurality, and usually a majority, agreed with this idea. The responses from Peers were not markedly different from those of other groups. Taking this and the previous item together, amongst conservative commentators – amongst others – there had long been debate about the relationship between the Commons and a second chamber, the position of hereditary peers and so on.[612] Although the question was put in a different way – and the respondents self-selecting – a consultation process initiated by the Lord Chancellor's Department[613] also in 2002 suggested strong support for a second chamber that was wholly or mainly elected. This was also the position of Iain Duncan Smith after being elected as leader [614] and indeed MPs of all parties.[615] The consultation also indicated support for an increase in the powers of a second chamber however constituted.[616]

"Britain should become a republic." The negative responses to this item suggested very strong support for the monarchy – in almost every group those not actively disagreeing were limited to one or two individuals – and historically this had long been the case within the Conservative Party.[617] Opinion polls around the same time found that this was also the case amongst the general public.[618]

---

[611] Cowley & Stuart, October 2004: 357-359.
[612] Heathcoat-Amory, 1998.
[613] Lord Chancellor's Department, 2002: 16.
[614] Alderman & Carter, July 2002: 585; Duncan Smith, 13th January 2002.
[615] Perkins, 15th February 2002.
[616] Lord Chancellor's Department, 2002: 37.
[617] Whiteley, Seyd & Richardson, 1994: 180.
[618] Doughty, 14th April 2001; Harris & Millar, 12th June 2002.

Trust in Public Life

There was also an item looking at "trust", a common theme in social research. This was *"Public life in this country is generally honest."*

There was strong support for this belief with at least 70% agreeing to some degree. Although the results were marginal, local councillors (ELCs 80%, SLCs 70% and WLCs 71% agreeing) were relatively less sure than parliamentarians at a Westminster or European level (Peers 85%, MPs 92% and MEPs 85% agreeing). It cannot be said with certainty whether this item was measuring perceptions of their own and/or their immediate colleagues' standards, those of the political level at which they operated or of the UK when compared to abroad.[619] That SLCs had the most jaundiced view of the probity of public life might have been anticipated given allegations of corruption in a number of areas in Scotland.[620]

Elections – to take a headline aspect of public life – in Britain and the rest of the Western world were and are clearly qualitatively more honest than in many other parts of the world.[621] However, there has never been a time when the British public has fully trusted politicians, even at the height of the Second World War as indicated by a poll by Gallup in 1944. This tendency rose "inexorably" from the early 1990s and beyond under both Conservative and Labour governments.[622] Conservative politicians of the cohort targeted by the *CPRS 2002* must have had the often-alleged[623] impact of accusations of "Tory sleaze" engraved on their hearts;[624] the list of allegations against the Labour government even in the short time between 1997 and 2002 was already lengthening;[625] and there were concerns about the greater ease of postal voting introduced in 2000 and associated fraud, concerns which would multiply as the years went by.[626] Given this, that so many continued to believe in the probity of the conduct

---

[619] Rawnsley, 17th February 2002.
[620] Linklater, 17th October 2002.
[621] Topf, 1995[a]: 28.
[622] Thompson, 2008: 305.
[623] Sanders & Brynin, 1999: 223.
[624] Farrell, McAllister & Studlar, 1998: 92; Norton, 2002: 68.
[625] Dale & Fawkes, 2006.
[626] *BBC News*, 22nd March 2005; Electoral Reform Society, August 2007; Golds, 2nd March 2012; Greenhill & Shipman, 4th May 2010.

of public life was perhaps a little surprising. It is possible that they thought that many of these accusations were untrue or at least exaggerated by the media[627] or just "didn't apply to them".

The *British Social Attitudes* surveys provides a comparison with the public. In the 2004 survey[628] there was an item "Thinking of the last national election in Britain, how honest was it regarding the counting and reporting of the votes?" Of the 833 respondents to this item, only 7% thought that it was actively dishonest. In this respect, the public agreed with our own respondents.

Of course, any study touching upon "trust in public life" that is based upon date captured before the revelations about MPs' expenses published by the *Daily Telegraph*[629] from May 2009 onwards and the phone hacking scandals from the middle of the same decade onwards[630] must concede that responses to such items might latterly be very different. Unless, that it is, politicians of all sorts – and not just Westminster MPs – "just don't get it".

A Foray into Scale Building

The analyses within this book generally rely upon multi-item scales that either already existed or were created for the study. However, many of the items discussed in this chapter were not designed to form part of any such scale. But did they nevertheless?

This was analysed by taking these items and running a confirmatory factor analysis using varimax rotation, with principal components extraction, with a maximum of 25 iterations, rotated factor solution, with only Eigenvalues over 1 extracted, and with absolute values less than 0.3 suppressed. All respondents, undifferentiated by group, were used.

There is little need to go into detail when reporting this necessarily speculative and possibly highly context-dependant analysis. Most of the findings were to be expected. For example, the strongest factor (accounting for 21% of the variance between all variables) consisted mainly of the two obviously related items about

---

[627] Marr & Major, 16th July 2006.
[628] *British Social Attitudes* Information System, 2009.
[629] *Telegraph*, 2009.
[630] *Guardian*, 2012.

attitudes towards proportional representation at general and local elections. Similarly, the third strongest factor (accounting for 12% of the variance between all variables) mainly consisted of items concerned with attitudes towards the House of Lords and a second chamber.

However, there was also one interesting result. This was the second factor (accounting for 13% of the variance between all variables) consisting entirely of the items concerning the effectiveness of single-issue groups and local campaigning. Bivariate analysis indicated a robust association between these two variables (using the whole dataset and the Pearson statistic, two-tailed $p = <0.001$). Those who agreed that "Local campaigning makes little difference these days compared to the overall impression of the national party" also tended to agree that "Single-issue groups are now a better way than political parties of advancing causes". It suggests the beginnings of a scale tapping into a view of the efficacy of local and/or participatory politics. In other words, some idea of agreeing or disagreeing with the view that politics in terms of influence and power was increasingly in the hands of people and organisations at some remove from ordinary citizens and even the grass-roots activists of traditional mass-membership parties.

Conclusion to Chapter 11

Looking first at the powers of the various legislative bodies under study, there were three findings of note. First, and not too surprisingly, respondents tended to want a boost in the powers of the bodies in which they sat.

Next, with some unremarkable exceptions, the general trend was for respondents to have relatively little antipathy – as measured by a desire to reduce their powers – towards the more "traditional" bodies such as those at Westminster or local government level. It was the newer or less traditional bodies – the European Parliament, Scottish Parliament, Welsh Assembly, Northern Ireland Assembly and Greater London Assembly – that they tended to want to cut down to size. This might speak of nationalism, particularly British nationalism vis-à-vis the European Parliament, but might also speak of just "conservatism" and a resistance to change.

The third major finding was that, on the face of it, there was little desire to reduce the power of such institutions *overall*.

Regarding the level of representation of Scots and Welsh at Westminster – and without going as far as outright independence for these two countries – it is clear that respondents felt that something had to change in order to address the realities of the new institutions in Scotland and Wales and the numerical over-representation of Scots and Welsh at Westminster.

As to why people become politicians, there was a marked divide between parliamentarians of all sorts who tended to cite "ideological" reasons and local councillors who tended to cite "representational" reasons. It could be argued that parliamentarians viewed politics as acquiring power to implement ideological beliefs whereas local councillors viewed the profession of politics as representing the people *to* power. It was speculated that one of the reasons why the final proffered choice, the "constitutional" reason, was relatively infrequently cited was a belief in the enduring stability of British democracy.

Finally, from the brief foray into scale building, there was some evidence of the beginnings of a scale tapping into views about the efficacy of local and/or participatory politics.

12

The 2001 Leadership Contest

A Short-Lived Victory

In November 2003, after only 777 days as leader of the Conservative Party, Iain Duncan Smith was ejected from his position by a slim majority of MPs at Westminster.[631] The only candidate for the now-vacant post was Michael Howard who had come last in the MPs-only leadership ballot that followed John Major's resignation in 1997.[632] All those who had contested the 2001 leadership contest declined to stand again[633] and Michael Portillo took the opportunity to announce that he was standing down as an MP.[634] No other challenger came forward.[635] There was no confirmatory ballot of members which there had been in October 1997 when William Hague's election as leader by the Party's MPs had been confirmed 81% to 19% by the Party's general membership.[636] This time a ballot was not required under the Party's then rules since there was only one candidate.[637] Michael Howard became the Conservative Party's third leader in as many years.

By then, the Conservative Party's first experiment in choosing a new leader via a direct and competitive democratic consultation of the ordinary membership seemed a long time ago.

---

[631] Hughes, 30th October 2003.
[632] Cowley & Stuart, 2003: 68.
[633] Brogan, 1st November 2003.
[634] Tempest, 7th November 2003.
[635] Gilmour, 31st October 2003.
[636] Kelly, 2003: 88.
[637] Cowley & Stuart, October 2004: 360.

The 2001 Leadership Election

Following the Conservative Party's defeat at the general election in June 2001, William Hague resigned as leader. This initiated a leadership contest, the first held under the new rules introduced by Hague in 1998 via the *Fresh Future* document. This allowed Party members other than Westminster MPs a formal say on the new leader through casting a deciding vote between two candidates who had survived what was in effect an MPs-only primary.[638]

This chapter will not examine in detail the background to the rules changes made during Hague's leadership. However, it has been claimed that the "sexy" possibility of having a final vote between two candidates when choosing a leader hid a marked centralisation in power within the Conservative Party. It has been argued that this lure was successfully used as an inducement in getting the Party's members to approve Hague's internal reforms by an overwhelming (96%) majority in a ballot in February 1998.[639] Nevertheless, this was a move towards more direct membership participation in at least some aspects of the running of the Party,[640] and one which, by the time of the 2005 leadership contest, Hague was publicly regretting.[641]

Five Conservative MPs entered the 2001 contest: Michael Ancram, Kenneth Clarke, David Davis, Iain Duncan Smith and Michael Portillo. Kenneth Clarke was the only one of the five who had also stood during the leadership contest in 1997 when he had lost to William Hague. In that earlier contest he had led the first two stages but lost in the final round when virtually all of John Redwood's erstwhile support went to William Hague.[642]

Regarding the 2001 contest, precise details about who declared when and how they did it can be found elsewhere.[643] In brief, the first MPs-only round on the 10th July 2001 saw Portillo come out on top

---

[638] Conservative Party, 1998: 21; Alderman, 1999; Lees-Marshment & Quayle, April 2000; Quinn, 2005: 804.

[639] Lees-Marshment & Quayle, April 2000; Kelly, 2003: 86-89 & 98; *Telegraph*, 15th November 2004.

[640] Kelly, October 2004: 398-399.

[641] Bennett, 9th May 2005.

[642] Cowley & Stuart, 2003: 68.

[643] Conservative Party, September 2001; Alderman & Carter, 2002; Heppell & Hill, February 2010: 36-37.

with 49 votes (30%), followed by Duncan Smith with 39 votes (23%), Clarke with 36 votes (22%) and finally Ancram and Davis with 21 votes (13%) each.

Since there was a tie for last position, all five candidates went through to the next round held on the 12th July 2001. The results were similar to those of the first round. Portillo again come out on top with 50 votes (30%), followed by Duncan Smith with 42 votes (25%), Clarke with 39 votes (23%), Davis with 18 (11%) and finally Ancram with 17 votes (10%). This resulted in the exclusion of Ancram with Davis voluntarily withdrawing soon after. Both then pledged their support to Duncan Smith.[644]

A third ballot took place on the 17th July 2001 between the remaining candidates. This produced a very close result with Clarke receiving 59 votes (36%), followed by Duncan Smith with 54 votes (33%) and lastly Portillo with 53 votes (32%).

This resulted in the exclusion of Portillo to the shock of many commentators who had predicted a Portillo victory amongst MPs.[645] Accordingly, Duncan Smith and Clarke went forward to a final postal ballot of all Party members.[646]

This result was much less close. Duncan Smith received 155,933 votes (61%) against the 100,864 votes (39%) received by Clarke. Approximately 79% of eligible members voted. This was or would be more than in the leadership elections of Tony Blair (Labour Party in 1994), Charles Kennedy (Liberal Democrats in 1999) or Sir Menzies Campbell (Liberal Democrats in 2006) and surpassed all previous party postal ballots. In winning by the margin that he did, Duncan Smith secured a larger personal mandate from party members than Blair, Kennedy or Campbell in their respective parties' leadership elections[647] although not as large as David Cameron's 68% to 32% victory over David Davis in the Conservative Party's next *contested* leadership race in 2005.[648]

For the second time – first to Hague in 1997 and then to Duncan Smith in 2001 – the allegedly more electorally appealing and

---

[644] Alderman & Carter, 2002.
[645] Riddell, 14th June 2001.
[646] Alderman & Carter, 2002.
[647] Conservative Party, September 2001; Hurst, 3rd March 2006.
[648] *BBC News*, 6th December 2005.

certainly more politically experienced Clarke had lost to a less experienced candidate who was nevertheless more ideologically appealing to the Party if not necessarily to the wider electorate.[649]

Issues during the Contest

Throughout the leadership contest, there was no shortage of opinion expressed, whether by the mass media via editorials and opinion pieces, or the candidates themselves and their supporters and detractors. During the contest even the mass media had to concede that the "old labels" did not fit. Portillo was cited as an economic "Thatcherite" and yet was also now championing socially liberal policies. On the other hand, Clarke was seen as being on the Left because of his pro-EU views but had a track record in government of anti-trades unionism.[650]

Much commented upon was how the electorate perceived the Party. By the time of the contest, more "conservative" columnists were complaining that some senior Conservatives seemed to believe that the only reason that they had lost the 2001 general election was that they "didn't propose equal rights for serial cohabitant bisexual cocaine snorters".[651] On the other hand, some of those who defended the Conservatives against charges of *actual* extremism argued that it often *sounded* abrasive and extreme.[652]

This led on to considerations that it was not just *what* one said that mattered but the *way* one said it and *who* said it. For example, at an early stage one commentator backed Clarke over Portillo on the grounds that the public was not that interested in Portillo's new-found social liberalism but in everyday matters such as healthcare, education and law and order. Clarke, it was argued, was able to deploy a form of language that the public understood.[653] Certainly, opinion polls at the time seemed to indicate that members of the

---

[649] Heppell & Hill, April 2008: 89.
[650] Gove & Baldwin, 23rd June 2001.
[651] Phillips, 1st July 2001.
[652] Glover, 11th June 2001.
[653] Oborne, 16th June 2001.

public thought that out of the five candidates Clarke would do the best job of leading the Party.[654]

On the other hand, some supporters of Portillo argued that he should be backed because he was a man in the mould of Disraeli or Thatcher. He was someone "interesting", unlike the previous leader William Hague or then rival Duncan Smith.[655] Clarke and his supporters argued that it was a contest between ideological dogma, i.e. that of his opponents and in particular Duncan Smith, or electoral pragmatism, i.e. that of himself.[656]

Mixing the personal and political, some commentators, mistakenly assuming a final contest between Clarke and Portillo, argued that it would come down to whether some Conservatives were more "Europhobic" or "homophobic".[657] As noted below, Clarke continued to say this after the election. During the contest Portillo was certainly subjected to attack by sexual innuendo.[658] Portillo had gone public about his "homosexual experiences as a young person"[659] following his decision to stand for adoption as the Conservative candidate for the Kensington & Chelsea by-election that would see his return to Westminster.

Of course, the matter of the UK's membership of the EU could hardly be ignored. It had been an issue of remarkable saliency for Conservative Party internal debate for a great many years[660] if not always for the general public.[661] This was emphasised by the nature of some of the candidates, not least the "anti-Maastricht rebel" Iain Duncan Smith[662] as opposed to Kenneth Clarke, a supporter of the cross-party, pro-EU European Movement.[663]

It was also the case that the candidates measured up very differently in terms of their previous experience of political office,[664] a

---

[654] Mortimore, 20th July 2001.
[655] Rees-Mogg, 18th June 2001.
[656] *The Times*, 27th June 2001.
[657] Hames, 6th July 2001.
[658] Alderman & Carter, 2002: 579.
[659] *BBC News*, 9th September 1999.
[660] Burdett-Conway & Tether, 1997: 89-90; Cowley & Norton, 1999: 90.
[661] Baker, 2002: 321; Broughton, 2003: 208.
[662] Baker, 2002: 324-325.
[663] Baldwin, 15th May 2002; Tory Europe Network, c. 2002.
[664] Heppell & Hill, February 2010: 37.

factor regarded by many as important.[665] Looking at the final two candidates, Clarke had been an MP since 1970 and had been Chancellor of the Exchequer between 1993 and 1997. On the other hand, Duncan Smith had first been elected an MP only in 1992 and was perhaps best known as a backbench "irritant" during John Major's time as Prime Minister. Indeed, before becoming leader of the Party, Duncan Smith "had voted against his party's whip five times more than his four predecessors [as leader] put together".[666]

In amongst this were complex electoral issues that centred on the question of just how popular or unpopular the Party *really* was and hence its likely fortunes in the near future.[667] This in turn partly hinged on the answer to the long-running question of how accurately opinion polls were depicting levels of support for the various parties, and in particular whether the Conservatives were being sold short.[668] For example, on the same day in 2001 that the Party went down to a crushing general election defeat, it made gains in English county council elections at the expense of both Labour and the Liberal Democrats and became the biggest party in English local government.[669] There was also the issue of the use of anti-Conservative tactical voting. This meant that given between them Labour and the Liberal Democrats received support from approximately 35% of the electorate against the Conservative's 19%, the Conservatives had to "run to stand still" regarding the relationship between the proportion of the popular vote received and Westminster MPs returned.[670]

This chapter seeks to attenuate this "noise". In the end, what did members of the Conservative Party, or at least the *CPRS 2002's* particular subset of it, have in mind when casting their vote?

---

[665] Garnett, 2003[a]: 49.

[666] Cowley & Stuart, 2004/2005: 25.

[667] Norris & Lovenduski, 2004: 86.

[668] Glover, 9th February 2002; Worcester, 11th April 2010.

[669] Hetherington, 9th June 2001.

[670] Heathcoat Amory, 9th June 2001; Seldon & Snowdon, 2001: 3; Tyrie, 2001: 4 & 29-30.

Respondents' Behaviour and Attitudes

A section of the questionnaire focused on the 2001 leadership contest. All respondents were asked who they did support (if they were MPs) or who they would have supported (for the other groups of respondents) at all three major stages of the leadership contest.

Most respondents reported that they voted at the final stage with only 5% to 10% in some groups saying that they did not although this rose to over a fifth (22%) in the case of Peers. In most cases (75%) non-voting was due to "technical" reasons such as not receiving a ballot paper or being out of the country rather than a "none of the above" abstention.

Tables 12.1a to 12.1c detail respondents' support – actual or would-be – at the major stages of the contest. No distinction was made between the first and second ballots that featured all five candidates. The figures for MPs can be compared to the actual voting behaviour of Westminster MPs noted above. It would appear that there was a modest under-representation of Clarke and Portillo supporters and possibly an over-representation of Duncan Smith supporters amongst our respondents. This may be real or as a result of the well-known tendency for the proportion of those claiming to have voted for the winner in a past election to be somewhat higher than the proportion who actually did.[671]

TABLE 12.1A: REPORTED ACTUAL OR WOULD-BE SUPPORT FOR INITIAL FIVE CANDIDATES[672]							
Candidate	ELCs	Peers	MPs	SLCs	WLCs	MEPs	MSPs
Michael Ancram	9%	9%	17%	13%	15%	7%	14%
Kenneth Clarke	30%	37%	19%	36%	26%	29%	29%
David Davis	12%	7%	15%	15%	7%	14%	14%
Iain Duncan Smith	23%	19%	25%	23%	44%	21%	21%
Michael Portillo	18%	25%	25%	13%	7%	29%	21%
None of the above	8%	3%	0%	0%	0%	0%	0%
Base	275	59	48	47	27	14	14

---

[671] Mortimore, 3rd April 2001.

[672] Only MPs had an actual vote at this stage.

TABLE 12.1B: REPORTED ACTUAL OR WOULD-BE SUPPORT AT THE THIRD BALLOT[673]							
Candidate	ELCs	Peers	MPs	SLCs	WLCs	MEPs	MSPs
Kenneth Clarke	34%	42%	33%	47%	35%	29%	50%
Iain Duncan Smith	43%	31%	43%	43%	61%	43%	29%
Michael Portillo	19%	24%	24%	8%	4%	29%	21%
None of the above	4%	3%	0%	2%	0%	0%	0%
Base	278	59	49	47	26	14	14

TABLE 12.1C: REPORTED ACTUAL SUPPORT FOR THE FINAL TWO CANDIDATES[674]							
Candidate	ELCs	Peers	MPs	SLCs	WLCs	MEPs	MSPs
Kenneth Clarke	44%	55%	41%	51%	30%	50%	67%
Iain Duncan Smith	54%	43%	59%	49%	70%	50%	33%
Spoiled ballot paper	2%	2%	0%	0%	0%	0%	0%
Base	258	55	46	47	27	14	12

From these tables it can be seen that:

- In some cases there were considerable between-groups differences in expressed support.

- Kenneth Clarke's would-be support was relatively strong amongst MSPs, SLCs and Peers. At least initially, Clarke also had more support "out in the country" amongst local councillors than amongst his colleagues at Westminster who actually had a vote in the earlier stages.

- Iain Duncan Smith's support was remarkably strong amongst WLCs and – perhaps importantly as a possible indicator of grass-roots support in the Party's English heartland – to a lesser degree amongst the two "English" groups of ELCs and MPs. (There was only one Westminster MP representing a non-English constituency).

---

[673] Only MPs had an actual vote at this stage.
[674] This excludes those who were unable to vote for some reason.

- Michael Portillo's support flat-lined from the beginning, not least amongst MPs, which meant that he was unable to progress to the final ballot of all members. Whilst attracting considerable initial support he was the second choice of very few. Why this was is open to speculation. Some have argued that many MPs were angered by his apparent disloyalty to William Hague. Others claimed that he had "re-engineered"[675] his beliefs rather dramatically between losing his seat in 1997 and re-entering parliament in 1999 and moreover it was not too clear what his new beliefs actually were.[676] In any case, he was notably unpopular amongst Scottish and above all Welsh local councillors.

Supporters of Excluded Candidates

The destination of support for excluded candidates can also be analysed. Table 12.2 describes the destination of the small number of former Ancram and Davis supporters.

TABLE 12.2: DESTINATION OF MPS' SUPPORT OF FORMER ANCRAM AND DAVIS SUPPORTERS		
Candidate	Ex-Ancram supporters	Ex-Davis supporters
Kenneth Clarke	50%	29%
Iain Duncan Smith	50%	57%
Michael Portillo	0%	14%
Base	8	7

From this table it can be seen that:

- Iain Duncan Smith was the overall gainer, receiving at least half of each excluded candidate's former support amongst MPs.

- Kenneth Clarke was already loosing ground to Iain Duncan Smith inasmuch as the latter gained more support from former David Davis supporters.

---

[675] Denham & O'Hara, July 2007: 180.
[676] Cowley & Stuart, 2003: 78; Walters, 2001.

- Michael Portillo was the clear loser, unable to gather much new support amongst MPs: little from former supporters of David Davis and none at all from former supporters of Michael Ancram.

- Former supporters of either of the two excluded candidates did not necessarily follow in lock step with those candidates' declared support for Duncan Smith.

The subsequent, somewhat even destination of former Michael Portillo supporters is shown in Table 12.3.

TABLE 12.3: DESTINATION OF MPS' SUPPORT AT THE FINAL ROUND OF FORMER PORTILLO SUPPORTERS	
Kenneth Clarke	45%
Iain Duncan Smith	55%
Base	**11**

The Last Three Candidates

All three candidates

Returning to the penultimate stage, were there any differences between those who supported Kenneth Clarke, Iain Duncan Smith or Michael Portillo? This can be analysed following some of the methods of Cowley and Garry[677] in their analysis of the 1990 Conservative Party leadership contest eventually won by John Major.

A series of bivariate analyses were conducted identifying any significant differences or associations between those who supported a candidate and those who did not – i.e. who supported either of the other two candidates – and what those differences were.

Other techniques could have been used but the maximum base size of 52 made these impractical. Instead, the analyses were conducted using t-tests or the chi^2 statistic as appropriate using the full range of this study's multi-item scales and also items concerning the main challenger to their seat and the seat's perceived safeness (looking only at those who stated that it was either Labour or the

---

[677] Cowley & Garry, 1998.

Liberal Democrats). Only those variables where there was a significant difference or association at a two-tailed 5% level between supporters and non-supporters are reported in Tables 12.4a to 12.4c. In each case a line of explanation is provided.

TABLE 12.4A: CHARACTERISTICS OF PORTILLO SUPPORTERS AMONGST MPS				
Scale	Base	t	Two-tailed sig.	Greater support from those...
Feminism	49	-2.725	0.009	More in favour of female equality in society
Intra-Party Inclusivity	49	2.414	0.02	More in favour of advancing women etc. in the Conservative Party
Authoritarianism	49	-2.607	0.012	Less authoritarian
Theocratism	49	-2.249	0.029	More theocratic
Protectionism	47	2.828	0.007	Less protectionist
Pride in National Heritage & Culture	48	2.844	0.007	Less proud
Pride in Way Nation Functions	49	3.169	0.003	Less proud
Safeness of seat	48	-3.416	0.002	With a safer seat

TABLE 12.4B: CHARACTERISTICS OF CLARKE SUPPORTERS AMONGST MPS

Scale	Base	t	Two-tailed sig.	Greater support from those...
Environmentalism	48	3.936	0.001	More environmentalist
Europeanism	45	4.311	0.001	Less Euro-sceptic
Intra-Party Inclusivity	49	2.698	0.01	More in favour of advancing women etc. in the Conservative Party
Left-Right	49	2.083	0.043	Less economically right-wing (*sic*)
Optimism	47	-3.389	0.001	Less optimistic about the state of the Conservative Party
Pride in National Heritage & Culture	48	-2.361	0.023	Less proud
Pride in Way Nation Functions	49	-2.595	0.013	Taking a more middle position

TABLE 12.4C: CHARACTERISTICS OF DUNCAN SMITH SUPPORTERS AMONGST MPS

Scale	Base	t	Two-tailed sig.	Greater support from those...
Environmentalism	48	-3.347	0.002	Less environmentalist
Europeanism	45	-4.92	0.001	More Euro-sceptic
Intra-Party Inclusivity	49	-4.187	0.001	Less in favour of advancing women etc. in the Conservative Party
Left-Right	49	-2.381	0.021	More economically right-wing (*sic*)
Authoritarianism	49	3.619	0.001	More authoritarian
Optimism	47	3.081	0.004	More optimistic about the state of the Conservative Party
Xenophobia	47	-2.358	0.023	More protectionist
Protectionism	47	-2.737	0.009	More xenophobic

Further discussion can be found below concerning the meaning of the ultimate significant predictors of support for Clarke or Duncan Smith in the final, all-members ballot. However, with perhaps one exception noted in the next section, it would generally be agreed that the results shown in these tables tend to accord with the common perception at the time of the three candidates and their supporters, as well as that provided by the analyses of academic studies.[678]

Michael Portillo's exceptionalism

There is one finding in Table 12.4a that stands out as surprising. It will be noted that placement on the Theocratism scale was a significant distinguishing feature between those MPs who supported Michael Portillo and those who supported either of the other two candidates. Closer examination reveals that Portillo supporters were more "theocratic" and they were more supportive of the intervention of religious leaders and institutions in public and political life. There might be something to this or it might just be an example of a Type 1 error of a false positive always possible when running such a large number of bivariate analyses.

That aside, a study of the tables leads to another finding that ought to be highlighted and which separates Michael Portillo from both Kenneth Clarke and Iain Duncan Smith. Although many of the variables appear as significant findings in all three tables, what are conspicuously missing from the table analysing support for Michael Portillo are the economic issues tapped into by the Left-Right dimension and also the Europeanism dimension. (Whilst stating that he was personally opposed to the UK joining the single European currency, Portillo generally downplayed issues concerned with the EU.[679]) When compared to the other two candidates, Portillo's support was largely associated with attitudes towards cultural and social issues measured by scales such as Feminism, Intra-Party Inclusivity and Authoritarianism.

Additionally, and although referring to "would-be" rather than actual support, the findings from another item in the questionnaire revealed that Portillo was relatively popular amongst ELCs from

[678] Heppell & Hill, February 2010: 37, 46.
[679] Baker, 2002: 324.

London and south-east England. Overall, 42% of ELCs represented wards in London and south-east England. However, whereas 34% and 41% respectively of Kenneth Clarke's and Iain Duncan Smith's would-be ELC supporters came from this area, no less than 60% of Michael Portillo's would-be support came from ELCs representing wards in this area.

With this final piece of information in mind it is plausible to combine…

- that those issues that separated Portillo from the other two were neither "hard" economic issues nor the European issue;
- that Portillo supporters backed their man "from the off" but that he was unable to gather little actual or theoretical support during the leadership contest;
- that his would-be support "out in the country" was disproportionately to be found in London and the surrounding areas;

… into the view that there was evidence for the then existence of a group of often metropolitan-based "Portillistas": a substantial minority of Party members who were somewhat different from others and who supported Michael Portillo either as the "change" or "modernising" candidate and/or as much as a "personality" as for what he was perceived to believe or wished to do about "hard" issues to do with (say) the economy or the EU.[680]

The Final Ballot

All respondents

Using regression analysis, the significant predictive variables of support in the final ballot could be determined. Regression analysis was used because, even allowing for some affective reaction to the two candidates, it is surely the case that considerations of issues tapped into by the multi-item scales were more likely to impact on the decision who to vote for than the other way around. Also, in this case, with such a binary either/or dependant variable – the choice between the two men – regression provides a clear-cut result.

---

[680] Baldwin, 15ᵗʰ September 2001; Rogers, 14ᵗʰ August 2002.

The analysis was run with all respondents who said that they had voted for either Clarke or Duncan Smith (or would have voted if some purely technical reason such as not receiving a ballot paper had not prevented them) and then with ELCs only as detailed below. The analysis used the usual range of multi-item scales along with a binary item from the questionnaire asking whether respondents thought that the most important task of the party was to "unite internally" or "reach out externally". Dummy variables for the groups of respondents were not included since ANOVA indicated no significant between-groups (omitting the two micro-groups) difference (p = 0.226) in who respondents actually voted for in the final ballot.

The simplified Table 12.5 shows the predictors of variability left in the final, significant regression model. The percentage figures are based on the adjusted R^2 figure.

TABLE 12.5: SIGNIFICANT PREDICTORS OF VOTING BEHAVIOUR AT THE FINAL ROUND	
Variable	Variability explained
Europeanism	19%
Optimism	5%
Intra-Party Inclusivity	3%
Pride in Way Nation Functions	1%
Total	28%
Base	284

The final model predicted a substantial 28% of the variation in the choice between Iain Duncan Smith and Kenneth Clarke. One variable stood out in importance. Europeanism, which looked at attitudes about the UK's membership of the EU, predicted 19% of the total variation on its own. Some way behind this Optimism, which looked at attitudes about the state and likely fortunes of the Conservative Party, additionally provided 5% of the total. It is probably no coincidence that Intra-Party Inclusivity, which looked at attitudes towards the promotion of female, non-White and homosexual candidates within the Conservative Party, should also appear providing 3% of the total predictive power of the model. Pride in the Way Nation Functions provided a minor if statistically significant 1% of the total.

Irrespective of their direction, the salience of the Europeanism and Optimism scales confirms, for example, elements of an ICM poll of ordinary Conservative Party members conducted during the run-up to the final all-members ballot.[681] This indicated that, from a list of options, "Europe and the single currency" was the most important policy issue in deciding which candidate to support. 37% said that it was the most important issue against 28% who said that it was "Health" and 21% who said that it was "Law and order". No less than 86% of respondents said that the issue of Europe was "Very important" or "Quite important" in deciding which candidate to support. On the other hand, in a choice between whether liking a candidate the most or believing that he was more likely to win the next general election would help to decide their vote, the latter beat the former option by 66% to 25%.

Bivariate analysis for each of the significant predictors – omitting the trivial Pride in the Way Nation Functions – indicated the meaning of the results. Looking first at the dominant Europeanism dimension, outright Euro-sceptics were much more likely to have supported Duncan Smith, with Euro-centrists and almost all (88%) of the "stricken minority"[682] of outright Euro-enthusiasts much more likely to have supported Clarke.

Looking at the Optimism scale, those optimistic about the (then) present state and likely future fortunes of the Party were much more likely to have supported Duncan Smith, with those taking a more cautious or even pessimistic view were much more likely to have supported Clarke.[683] It will be recalled that in Chapter 5 Optimism was found to be a significant predictor of attitudes towards Iain Duncan Smith and this was in the same direction as found in this present analysis.

Finally, looking at Intra-Party Inclusivity it was found that outright "traditionalists" were much more likely to have supported Duncan Smith and outright "modernisers" were somewhat more likely to have supported Clarke.

In short, an "average" Iain Duncan Smith supporter was a socially conservative Euro-sceptic who was quite optimistic about how things stood for the Conservative Party or who simply denied

---

[681] Cracknell, 26th August 2001.

[682] *Guardian*, 14th September 2000.

[683] And see Peek, Henery, McDonald, Rozenburg & Baldwin, 8th November 2002.

that there were any serious problems.[684] An "average" Kenneth Clarke supporter had fewer distinguishing features in an active sense, generally taking a more middling position on these issues.

These results regarding the salience of those issues measured by the Europeanism and Optimism scales, although not necessarily their salience relative to each other, corresponds to the findings of polls carried out during the contest on members of local Conservative Party associations on the key determinants of support.[685]

What was also revealing about the findings of the regression analysis is what was missing. Variables concerning important issues such as the economy and welfare were absent as significant predictors of support. (Some have anyway argued that the Conservative's focus on economics during the last two or three decades of the 20th century was something of an aberration.[686]) So too was anything to do with moral or social or religious issues except in the case of how this applied to the Party internally.

Local councillors in England

The regression analysis was re-run just looking at ELCs. The same variables were included but so too were the range of socio-demographic data analysed in Chapter 4. The results are not further discussed here because they were almost identical to those found when analysing all respondents. There were three significant variables left in the model predicting a total of 22%. These were Europeanism (15% of the total), Optimism (4%) and Intra-Party Inclusivity (3%).

The only noteworthy finding was the negative one that, when taken together[687] with the study's range of attitudinal variables, who/what respondents were socio-demographically made no difference to voting behaviour in this instance.

---

[684] Cooper, 2001: 23.
[685] Lynch, 2003: 161.
[686] Scruton, 2001: viii.
[687] Heppell & Hill, February 2010: 47.

Commentary

The vote amongst MPs between Clarke, Duncan Smith and Portillo suggested something close to a three-way tie, with MPs "as a group" having little idea who they wanted to succeed William Hague.[688] However, looking at the final choice between Clarke and Duncan Smith, a straightforward question can be asked but only to receive a slightly less straightforward response. Was the 2001 Conservative Party leadership contest an internal referendum on Europe? At least as far as Conservative politicians were concerned, the answer must be, "Yes, *and…*"

Firstly, it has to be noted that the "and" must include the majority of the variation between a vote for Kenneth Clarke or Iain Duncan Smith not explained by the regression analyses noted above. One would not expect to explain 100% of human behaviour by such methods.[689] It is also fair to say that a unique event such as the final ballot in 2001 carries with it a substantial amount of situational context likely to interact with or even override more enduring attitudes.[690]

Nevertheless, within the limits of the variables under study, the analysis indicates that the EU was clearly the dominant issue. This is hardly surprising. Everyday observation and academic studies have indicated that "Europe" has been the most divisive issue amongst Conservatives since at least the 1970s but perhaps particularly after Margaret Thatcher's Bruges speech in 1988.[691]

However, a small number of other issues mattered as well. In particular, two other factors were significant predictors of the final choice between Clarke and Duncan Smith irrespective of what representational group respondents belonged to and, as far as it can be ascertained from ELCs, their socio-demographic status: Optimism and Intra-Party Inclusivity.

Regarding the latter, this accords with evidence that local associations had long resisted attempts by the Party to force them by some means to adopt a greater number of female and racial minority

---

[688] D'Ancona, 3rd November 2002.
[689] Sheehan, 23rd February 2006.
[690] Cottam *et al*, 2010: 14-15.
[691] Marquand, 2009: 311.

candidates in winnable seats.[692] Given this, the finding that those who took a "traditionalist" view on the promotion of women, racial minorities and homosexuals in the Party tended to back Duncan Smith makes sense. In Duncan Smith they saw themselves:[693] he was a "representative leader".[694]

It is likely that the meaning of the finding regarding the Optimism scale is that those who had a relatively less optimistic view of the Party's situation and prospects were more inclined to support the candidate generally perceived as being able to "reach out" to the electorate: Kenneth Clarke. Conversely, those who believed that Party was in good shape, held in reasonable esteem by the public and likely to do quite well in elections in the near-ish future were less concerned about this and more likely to support a candidate for "ideological" reasons: Iain Duncan Smith.

The directions of the findings on the Europeanism and Optimism scales were reflected in mass-media coverage and opinion at the time. In an editorial, *The Times* came out in favour of Duncan Smith for a number of ideological reasons but specifically because it could not accept Clarke's pro-EU and in particular pro-single-currency stance, views which sharply contrasted with that of the former leading Maastricht rebel Duncan Smith.[695] However, on the same day, the *Daily Mail* came out in favour of Clarke.[696] This was despite that newspaper's opposition to his pro-EU views, but instead because it believed that Duncan Smith's lack of charisma made him no match for Tony Blair and because Clarke was more capable of connecting with ordinary voters. Clarke was perceived by many as the man more likely to appeal to the general electorate. This was borne out by analysis conducted after the contest where Duncan Smith did better than Clarke amongst ordinary members in the remaining Conservative Party strongholds.[697]

---

[692] Cracknell, 3rd February 2002; Baldwin, 9th April 2002; *Guardian*, 7th December 2004.

[693] Parris, 25th August 2001.

[694] van Vugt, 2004: 276.

[695] *The Times*, 22nd August 2001; Baker, Gamble, Randall & Seawright, 2002: 1.

[696] *Daily Mail*, 22nd August 2001.

[697] Howard, 18th September 2001.

"A Word in Your Ear…"

Kenneth Clarke, echoed by others,[698] later claimed that MPs had been influenced in their choice between himself and Portillo by the relative strength in attitudes of some of their local activists about the EU and homosexuality.[699]

All respondents except MPs were asked whether during the MPs-only stages of the contest their opinion had been offered to or sought by a Westminster MP. It can be seen from Table 12.6 that this was often the case, with the likelihood seeming to be primarily influenced by how "high up" respondents were on the political "ladder": MEPs were the most likely followed by MSPs and Peers. WLCs and SLCs were the least likely, unsurprisingly given that the 2001 general election had seen the Party returning to Westminster only one MP from a Scottish constituency and none at all from Wales. Of course, the majority of English Conservative associations also did not have a sitting Conservative MP,[700] although it seems likely to suppose that the ones that *did* tended to have larger and hence potentially more influential memberships. Overall, it can be reasonably inferred that non-MP Conservative politicians had at least *some* informal input into the MPs-only stages of the contest.

TABLE 12.6: OPINION SOUGHT BY OR OFFERED TO AN MP BEFORE THE FINAL ALL-MEMBER BALLOT						
	Peers	**MEPs**	**MSPs**	**ELCs**	**SLCs**	**WLCs**
Yes	45%	38%	46%	39%	27%	15%
No	55%	62%	54%	61%	73%	85%
Base	**56**	**13**	**13**	**279**	**45**	**26**

Keeping in mind that there is no information about when in the process respondents had their informal input or how hard and how often they pressed their case, nevertheless what did they advise and could this have mattered? In other words, did those who caught the ear of MPs differ from those who did not about either which candidate – between

---

[698] Kelly, January 2002: 43.
[699] Eastham, 7th January 2002.
[700] Kelly, 2003: 99.

Clarke and Portillo – they supported and/or their views on the two issues that Clarke mentioned, the EU and homosexuality?

Looking at the contest between Clarke, Duncan Smith and Portillo, the first of these questions can be analysed by testing for any significant association between which candidate respondents "would-be supported" and whether or not they consulted or were consulted by an MP. Looking only at those groups where there were sufficient numbers not to violate the assumptions of the chi^2 test – ELCs and Peers – the answer is a resounding "no". With two-tailed significance values of $p = 0.89$ and $p = 0.77$ respectively, there was no association between whether or not respondents supported Kenneth Clarke or Michael Portillo and whether or not they had had some contact with an MP on the matter.

Nevertheless, looking only at those who *did* communicate with their MP during the MPs-only stages, did they differ in their attitudes towards the EU and/or homosexuality? Just looking at ELCs because of the small numbers involved, this can be tested by using an independent samples t-test with the multi-item Europeanism scale and the "Homosexual relationships are always wrong" item from the Authoritarianism scale as the test variables and which of these two candidates ELCs "would-be supported" as the grouping variable. Looking first at the issue of homosexuality, there was no significant difference (two-tailed $p = 0.16$) between would-be Clarke and Portillo supporters. Looking at the issue of the EU, there *was* a significant difference (two-tailed $p = 0.01$) between would-be supporters of these two candidates.

On balance, it has to be concluded that Clarke was wrong. What these results again demonstrate was the extraordinary importance of attitudes towards the EU during the contest. It is very hard to argue from these results for any evidence that "homophobia" amongst a particularly energetic group of activists – at least as far as it can be judged from the responses of ELCs – had any real impact.

"Europe", but not only "Europe"

Without agreeing with one commentator who argued that the result of the contest had demonstrated that the Party was no longer a political party at all but merely a single-issue, anti-EU pressure group,[701] by the 1990s the Conservative Party was "Euro-sceptic – and proud of it"[702] and the EU was by far the most significant ideological issue detected by this analysis when taking all of the others into account. The others were matters of electoral support or related to the running of the Party.

Andrew Gamble – writing just before Margaret Thatcher's resignation as Prime Minister in 1990 but already looking beyond her leadership – was possibly correct when he argued that within the Conservative Party "Attitudes towards Europe are rapidly becoming that litmus test, superseding old wet/dry divisions over economic management".[703] Subsequently, other commentators agreed,[704] and writing after the 2001 general election and Party leadership contest one was even more forthright in declaring that "For many Conservative MPs and party members, Euro-scepticism has become the defining feature of their political identity and the defence of British sovereignty the over-riding mission of their party".[705]

The *CPRS 2002* and this book concern Conservative politicians at the turn of the century. Nevertheless, it ought to be noted what a turnaround this Euro-scepticism was when analysed in an historical perspective. There are good grounds for saying that the Party as an institution – and certainly its oligarchic leadership irrespective of the views of its supporters, members or even elected politicians[706] – had been staunchly supportive of European integration – initially just with France but latterly with a view to a Europe-wide "democratic bloc" – since at least 1940. It was the Conservative Harold Macmillan who furthered the process which led to the UK joining in 1973, under another Conservative prime minister, Edward Heath, what was to become the European Union. After that, the transition to the European Union came about under another Conservative prime minister, John Major, in the shape of the *Maastricht Treaty*. It was the Labour party that was

---

[701] O'Farrell, 22nd September 2001.
[702] Bale, July 2006: 385-386.
[703] Gamble, 1990: 34.
[704] Heppell, 2002: 300.
[705] Lynch, 2003: 154.
[706] Hannan, 17th April 2012; McKenzie, 1964.

historically far more Euro-sceptic, at least until the 1980s or 1990s when the two parties swiftly swapped positions.[707]

The findings from the study suggest that, as far as it can be judged from the attitudes of Conservative representatives based upon their behaviour in the final leadership ballot in 2001, mass-media obsession at the time with "modernisers versus traditionalists" or "mods versus rockers"[708] along a range of policy issues was not an accurate description of what was uppermost in respondents' minds.

Nevertheless, during the leadership campaign the mass media often got it right when it came down to those issues that really mattered. (As therefore did Duncan Smith when he stated that Clarke's views on the EU were a minority within the Party.[709]) By some way, the most important issue was the debate about Britain's relationship with and perhaps even continuing membership of – given that 29% of ELCs *and even 23% of MEPs* agreed with the item in the questionnaire that Britain should withdraw from it – the EU. This was backed up to a lesser but still important degree with considerations of the state of the Party, both as an institution and in terms of the electorate's attitude towards it.

All about Europe? "Yes, *and…*"

Changing Saliency

Conservative MPs are not stupid. Just as with the "surprise" election of Margaret Thatcher as leader in 1975,[710] it is likely that more than anyone they knew what they were getting in Iain Duncan Smith.[711] Initially, Duncan Smith's leadership may well have rested on a Europe-shaped prop, but the significance of the *"and"* was not lost on MPs.

By the middle of 2003 the Party was still behind Labour in the opinion polls and, indeed, any disillusion with the Labour government and party often tended to benefit the Liberal Democrats

---

[707] North, 20th March 2012; Oborne, 21st April 2011.

[708] Baldwin, Webster & Watson, 5th October 2000.

[709] Alderman & Carter, 2002: 583; see also Gilby, Skinner & Atkinson, 22nd July 2001.

[710] Marquand, 2009: 260; Wickham-Jones, 1997.

[711] *Telegraph*, 15th November 2004.

rather than the Conservatives.[712] There was little indication that a more positive view of the Party in the minds of the electorate had been created.[713] For all of these, Duncan Smith's poor communication skills were widely blamed[714] and the matter assumed a new urgency as thoughts turned to the next general election.

It has been argued that "one of Iain Duncan Smith's few successes as leader had been to quarantine Europe from the main party agenda".[715] Certainly, compared to previous years, there was relatively little in the way of dissent amongst Conservative MPs as measured by votes cast against the Party whip.[716] There was thus the irony that by damping down the Party's internal debate on the EU[717] Iain Duncan Smith had dug his own political grave by negating *the* issue that had helped him to be elected in the first place.

At a fringe meeting during the Conservative Party's 2006 annual conference, commentator Christopher Booker noted that,

> *"The bizarre thing with IDS was that, although the main reason why he won such overwhelming support from the Tory grass roots in the leadership election was that he had a reputation for being a keen Eurosceptic, no sooner did he get into office than we heard almost nothing from him about it ever again. Although it was the very reason why he had been elected, it just seemed to vanish from his agenda – just as he was soon to vanish himself."[718]*

Our respondents were asked whether any future leadership contest should return to being formally decided by Westminster MPs alone. As Table 12.7 demonstrates, amongst all groups of representatives – even Westminster MPs – the answer was "no".

---

[712] Rallings & Thrasher, April 2004: 380.

[713] Broughton, October 2004: 352.

[714] Gove, 18th October 2003; King, 29th October 2003; but see also Pierce, 6th December 2004.

[715] Baker & Sherrington, 2004: 360.

[716] Cowley & Stuart, 2004/2005: 25-28.

[717] Hitchens, 4th October 2003; Jones, 29th October 2003; Portillo, 6th June 2004; Thomson, 30th October 2003.

[718] Booker, 3rd September 2006.

TABLE 12.7: FINAL DECISION IN ANY FUTURE LEADERSHIP CONTEST BY MPs ALONE							
	ELCs	Peers	MPs	SLCs	WLCs	MEPs	MSPs
Yes	16%	32%	30%	20%	11%	14%	38%
No	84%	68%	70%	80%	89%	86%	62%
Base	279	60	50	46	27	14	13

But by November 2003, little more than a year after the fieldwork, MPs and the Party generally appeared to have changed their minds. It was as if *Fresh Future* had never been published and that the campaign during the summer of 2001 had never taken place. It is true that some members – including some local councillors – complained to the press that MPs had betrayed the Party's internal electorate.[719]

However, others responded by saying that in 2001 MPs had presented members with a poor choice between Kenneth Clarke, regarded by many as far too "Europhile", and the largely unknown Iain Duncan Smith.[720]

After initially accepting ejection with good grace, Duncan Smith argued that it was ludicrous that a leader chosen by a majority of a 300,000-strong electorate could be deposed by a handful of MPs. He also said that he was unhappy with certain individuals with whom the new leader Michael Howard was associating.[721] He also later argued that, with almost no MPs from large swathes of the UK, Conservative *members* were more representative than MPs.[722]

However, by then nobody was listening and it was not until Howard's own resignation as leader in 2005 that the ordinary membership again had a formal say in the election of a new leader, this despite the best attempts of the Party's senior leadership to strip them of this power.[723]

---

[719] Forrest, 31st October 2003.
[720] Le Page, 31st October 2003; Scott, 4th November 2003.
[721] Kite, 4th December 2003; *Telegraph*, 15th November 2004.
[722] Duncan Smith, 24th May 2005.
[723] *BBC News*, 23rd May 2005; *BBC News*, 24th May 2005; *BBC News*, 28th September 2005.

13

The Public and Electoral Politics

Outside of the Political Bubble

Most of this book concerns itself with the attitudes of politicians, but from time to time there is mention in some context of the general public. Rather than deal with these issues in detail within the thematic chapters, they are brought together in this chapter.

First, some space is devoted to what our respondents thought were the main concerns facing Britain, what they thought the main concerns of the public were, and what those concerns actually were as far as can be known by analysis of secondary data.

Next, the analysis returns to attitudes towards the other parties, already discussed in some detail in Chapter 6. In this present chapter the focus is on the Conservative's two main national challengers, Labour and the Liberal Democrats, but with the addition of data looking at the impact of electoral competition on attitudes towards these parties.

Then the study returns to the PoliMap described in Chapter 3. In the present chapter the focus is on how the general public of the time were distributed on the PoliMap, how this compares with Conservative politicians, and – broadening the analysis somewhat – what this might say about the space for viable electoral competition and the constraints on political parties seeking popular support.

Main Concerns Facing Britain

Concerns across a range of issues

Respondents were asked to choose from a list of seven options what they considered to be the most pressing concern facing Britain and then asked to repeat the exercise by indicating what they thought was the public's main concern.

TABLE 13.1: MAIN CONCERN FACING BRITAIN: RESPONDENTS' OWN VIEW							
	ELCs	**Peers**	**MPs**	**SLCs**	**WLCs**	**MEPs**	**MSPs**
Economy and taxation	20%	25%	10%	28%	16%	43%	14%
Welfare, NHS, education, other public services	43%	31%	52%	46%	60%	29%	64%
Environment	1%	0%	0%	0%	4%	0%	0%
Europe	8%	12%	13%	17%	4%	14%	0%
Law and order	25%	19%	12%	7%	16%	7%	21%
International relations, defence and terrorism	3%	8%	13%	2%	0%	7%	0%
Civil liberties	1%	5%	0%	0%	0%	0%	0%
Base	**269**	**59**	**52**	**46**	**25**	**14**	**14**

Table 13.1 provides the responses for respondents' own views. It is clear that respondents strongly tended to view "Welfare, NHS, education and other public services" as the most important issues with, except in one case, a plurality and sometimes a majority citing this. "Economy and taxation" – which MEPs cited as the most important – "Europe" – where the responses from MEPs were not noticeably different from most of the other groups – and "law and order" were also cited quite often. "Environment" and "civil liberties" hardly rate a mention although a number of MPs cited "international relations, defence and terrorism" as the most important issue facing Britain.

Throughout this book, use has been made – not generally with much impact, it must be said – of Ronald Inglehart's Postmaterialism dimension.[724] Appendix 4 indicates that respondents tended towards a "mixed" position on the dimension. When asked about their main concerns in the manner presented in this chapter it would appear that respondents generally adhered to a "materialist" position. Certainly it can be argued that "Economy and taxation" and "Law and order" are materialist concerns. "Welfare, NHS, education and other public services" contains elements of both positions. Nevertheless, the two clearly postmaterialist concerns of "Environment" and "Civil liberties" were the main concerns of very few respondents.

Saliency and the multi-item scales

Asking respondents about their main concerns taps into the saliency of issues for them. That said, it might be reasonable to expect that saliency of issues as asked in the questionnaire was associated with those sets of attitudes most nearly associated with them.

To test this, a series of partial correlation analyses was run to see if there was an association between the multi-item scales and saliency. The test variables were created by recoding the responses to the original main concerns item into a series of new, binary items. For example, the first one differentiated between those who did and those who did not cite "Economy and taxation" as their main concern. Because of the small numbers of positive responses in some cases this was run for only the latter main concern and also for "Welfare, NHS, education, other public services", "Europe" and "Law and order".

The entire, undifferentiated dataset was used since ANOVA detected no significant between-groups differences at the conventional 5% confidence level in the cases of "Economy and taxation" ($p = 0.076$), "Welfare, NHS, education, other public services" ($p = 0.057$) or "Europe" ($p = 0.225$). There was a significant difference in the case of "Law and order" ($p = 0.036$) but the post-hoc Bonferroni test did not identify any pairs of significant differences.

Controlling for the other scales, in the case of "Economy and taxation" there were significant two-tailed associations between it and Europeanism ($p = 0.003$), Environmentalism ($p = 0.045$), Optimism

---

[724] Inglehart, 1990; 1997.

(p = 0.042), Protectionism (p = 0.04) and Traditional British Liberties (p = 0.04). In the case of "Europe" there were only significant two-tailed associations between it and Europeanism (p = 0.001) and Religiosity (p = 0.038).

In the case of those who cited either "Welfare, NHS, education, other public services" or "Law and order" as their main concern there were no significant associations between them and the multi-item scales controlling for attitudes towards the other scales.

Only in the case of "Europe" and the strong association with the Europeanism scale was there an obvious like-for-like saliency and attitude association. Detailed analysis indicates that those with more Euro-sceptic views were more likely to cite this as their main concern. It should be noted that the direction of this finding was not a foregone conclusion. For example, analysis in Chapter 5 indicated that it was the less Euro-sceptic respondents who were more inclined to want to see change in the Party's principles and beliefs.

On balance, what these results suggest is that knowing a respondent thought that such-and-such an issue was particularly important says little about what they thought about that issue. Broadly speaking, the hypothesis of this section was wrong.

The Real and Imagined Views of the Public

Main comparisons

From the same list, respondents were also asked what they believed to be the public's view of the main concerns facing Britain. Table 13.2a provides these latter responses and Table 13.2b provides the difference between Table 13.1 and Table 13.2a. Positive numbers in Table 13.2b indicate issues where respondents thought that they attached greater importance to them than did the public and negative numbers the opposite.

TABLE 13.2A: MAIN CONCERN FACING BRITAIN: RESPONDENTS' BELIEF ABOUT PUBLIC'S VIEW

	ELCs	Peers	MPs	SLCs	WLCs	MEPs	MSPs
Economy and taxation	9%	5%	4%	11%	12%	21%	7%
Welfare, NHS, education, other public services	70%	78%	79%	76%	71%	71%	86%
Environment	0%	0%	0%	0%	0%	0%	0%
Europe	1%	0%	0%	2%	0%	0%	0%
Law and order	20%	15%	15%	11%	17%	7%	7%
International relations, defence and terrorism	0%	2%	2%	0%	0%	0%	0%
Civil liberties	0%	0%	0%	0%	0%	0%	0%
Base	**269**	**59**	**52**	**46**	**24**	**14**	**14**

TABLE 13.2B: MAIN CONCERN FACING BRITAIN: DIFFERENCE BETWEEN VIEW OF RESPONDENTS AND THEIR BELIEF ABOUT VIEWS OF PUBLIC

	ELCs	Peers	MPs	SLCs	WLCs	MEPs	MSPs
Economy and taxation	11	20	6	17	4	22	7
Welfare, NHS, education, other public services	-27	-47	-27	-30	-11	-42	-22
Environment	1	0	0	0	4	0	0
Europe	7	12	13	15	4	14	0
Law and order	5	4	-3	-4	-1	0	14
International relations, defence and terrorism	3	6	11	2	0	7	0
Civil liberties	1	5	0	0	0	0	0
Base	**269**	**59**	**52**	**46**	**24**	**14**	**14**

It is clear that respondents believed that the public was much more concerned about "welfare, NHS, education, other public services" than they were. (Relatively so, since this was the issue that they most frequently cited themselves.) On the other hand, they believed that they were somewhat more concerned about the "economy and taxation" and "Europe" (something suggested by relative Euro-enthusiasts and others[725]).

---

[725] Baker, 2002: 321; Broughton, 2003: 208.

The findings in Table 13.2b make sense. Respondents – all of whom were at least semi-professional politicians – believed that more abstract or seemingly distant issues such as the economy and Europe were in fact more important than the public realised. On the other hand, they probably felt that the public were more concerned than they were about here-and-now issues such as finding a place for their children at a decent school or a relative needing a hip replacement operation.

The general public's own views

The beliefs of respondents about the main concerns of the general public can be compared with near-contemporary data from a range of other sources, and here data is used from the post-election part of the *British Election Panel Study 2001*.[726] The data from the *CPRS 2002* and the *BEPS 2001* data were recoded into a small number of as near-similar categories as possible. Because of the small numbers involved the only comparisons are between ELCs and the English general public as set out in Table 13.3.

TABLE 13.3: MAIN CONCERN FACING COUNTRY: ELCs AND ENGLISH PUBLIC				
	ELCs' own view	ELCs' belief about public's view	English public (all)[727]	English public (Strong Conservative identifiers)[728]
Economy, taxation, inflation, etc.	20%	9%	12%	13%
Welfare, NHS, education, pensions etc.	43%	70%	57%	39%
Europe, EU, Euro	8%	1%	17%	34%
Crime, law & order, dishonesty	25%	20%	8%	10%
Other	4%	0%	6%	5%
Base	**269**	**269**	**1475**	**226**

---

[726] *BEPS*, 4th December 2006.

[727] *BEPS*, 2001.

[728] *BEPS*, 2001.

On an ordinal level, the findings match. This was most obvious in that a plurality stated that "Welfare, NHS, education, pensions" was the main concern facing the country. However, our respondents somewhat overestimated the salience of this range of issues for the public: 70% compared with an actual reported proportion of 57% of the public citing this as their main concern.

Conversely – it might be said *perversely* – it would appear that respondents rather underestimated the salience of "Europe" for the public. This was particularly true when looking at their keenest supporters amongst strong Conservative identifiers. Some argued that during the 1990s and early 2000s the Conservatives undersold one of the few areas where their own views chimed with those of the electorate.[729] This was also true of "law and order".[730] However, caution is needed since, as noted above, knowing that someone feels strongly about something is not necessarily a guide to what they think about it.

The Experience of Electoral Politics

Fighting for their seat

This section starts where Chapter 6 on attitudes towards the other parties left off. Respondents – except for Peers in the case of the first battery of questions below – were asked a number of questions concerning their recent experience of electoral politics.

Specifically, they were asked to rate subjectively the following: who their main challenger was; how safe they felt that their seat was; and whether they had experienced any anti-Conservative tactical voting. Also included were two variables from the questionnaire specifically concerning the Labour and/or Liberal Democrat parties: "The Labour Party has genuinely shed its socialistic instincts" and "The Conservatives should be focusing their national campaigning efforts against the Liberal Democrats rather than Labour". (The emphasis was on "national" given both the impact of energetic or

---

[729] Evans, 1998, 2001: 249; McAllister & Studlar, 2000: 368; but see Baker, Gamble & Seawright, 2002: 405 for a view that the Party had used these areas to at least some benefit.
[730] Oborne, 22nd February 2003.

slack local campaigning[731] and that at a local level Conservative respondents might face different political situations.) Both were accompanied by a standard five-point "Agree strongly" to "Disagree strongly" response set.

TABLE 13.4: PERCEIVED MAIN CHALLENGER IN CONSTITUENCY, WARD OR REGION						
	ELCs	**MPs**	**SLCs**	**WLCs**	**MEPs**	**MSPs**
Labour	40%	58%	48%	76%	73%	54%
Lib Dem	53%	40%	15%	16%	18%	23%
Other	7%	2%	37%	8%	9%	23%
Base	**273**	**48**	**46**	**25**	**11**	**13**

Table 13.4 indicates a distinction between the "English" groups of ELCs and MPs (there was only one MP elected from a non-English constituency at the 2001 general election) and the exclusively or partially "Celtic" groups – including MEPs – regarding the perceived main challenger. In the case of ELCs and MPs, Labour and the Liberal Democrats accounted for 40% to 60 % each, and between them accounted for the vast majority of respondents' perceived main challengers. (Where there was occasional competition from other parties around this time such as from the BNP, UKIP or the Green Party[732] it tended to be in a very geographically limited area and/or a flash in the pan. It can rarely have been considered to have been a challenge to the Conservatives nationally however embarrassing it might have been at the time.)

In the case of the other groups of respondents, perceived competition from the Liberal Democrats was much less evident, hardly surprising given Labour's historic strength in Scotland and Wales. The only two groups where "Others" were a significant competitor were the exclusively Scottish groups of SLCs and MSPs and, of course, this was the SNP.

The same phenomenon was not found amongst WLCs vis-à-vis Plaid Cymru, but this says much about the geography of Welsh

---

[731] Denver, Hands & MacAllister, June 2004: 303-304.
[732] Baldwin, 13th July 2000; Carr, 23rd November 2002; Jenkins, 23rd November 2002; Riddell, 23rd April 2002; Sherman, 14th May 2003).

politics and the relative rarity of electorally meaningful first-past-the-post competition between the two parties.[733] (Although, as Conservative Party leader Iain Duncan Smith noted,[734] the Conservatives, despite not winning any seats, attained a greater share of the popular vote at the 2001 general election – but not at the 1999 Welsh Assembly election[735] – than either the Liberal Democrats or Plaid Cymru. Wales was certainly an area where the Conservatives suffered under the first-past-the-post electoral system.[736])

Next, respondents were asked how "safe" they felt was their seat as detailed in Table 13.5.

TABLE 13.5: PERCEIVED SAFENESS OF SEAT						
	ELCs	MPs	SLCs	WLCs	MEPs	MSPs
Very marginal	13%	10%	20%	32%	36%	21%
Somewhat marginal	21%	12%	43%	20%	27%	50%
Safe or fairly safe	66%	78%	37%	48%	36%	29%
Base	277	51	46	25	11	14

Again, the main difference was between the England-only groups of ELCs and MPs on the one hand and then the others, with the former tending to feel considerably more secure. Two-thirds (66%) and over three-quarters (78%) of ELCs and MPs respectively felt that their seat was at least fairly safe. This compared with at most just under a half in the other cases. The relaxed attitude found amongst the two England-only groups is perhaps understandable. In the case of MPs it is probably true to say that any Conservative MP elected at the landslide Labour general election victories of 1997 or 2001 had been fortunate enough to be selected to contest a "true blue" constituency. In Westminster terms – and excepting a profound alteration in England's political and/or ideological landscape probably last witnessed with the decline of the old Liberal Party in the 1920s[737] – the Conservatives were down to their bedrock.

---

[733] Evans, 2002: i.

[734] Duncan Smith, winter 2001: 1.

[735] Wyn Jones & Trystan, 2001: 712.

[736] Evans, 2002: 17-18.

[737] Adelman, 1995.

It might also speak of a fundamentally different political culture in England compared to Wales and Scotland. As one commentator put it, unlike in England, where historically the Conservative party has been at least nominally in favour of less interventionist government than Labour, "Scotland and Wales have openly statist governments working for ever more government spending and regulations – and openly statist oppositions, working for ever more government spending and regulations".[738]

Matters were a little different with ELCs. There was probably a degree of the same "true blue" effect, albeit at a ward level. But the Conservative Party's disastrous showing at the 1997 and 2001 general elections was not always reflected at local elections, even when these had been held on the same day. (This was sometimes true even in Scotland.[739])

The next question in this series asked whether respondents believed that they had experienced any anti-Conservative tactical voting by electors who might otherwise have supported other parties. This was a major political issue during the 1997 and 2001 general elections.

TABLE 13.6: PERCEIVED EXPERIENCE OF ANTI-CONSERVATIVE TACTICAL VOTING						
	ELCs	**MPs**	**SLCs**	**WLCs**	**MEPs**	**MSPs**
A great deal	13%	10%	17%	19%	25%	50%
Some	45%	43%	44%	50%	67%	43%
Very little or none	42%	47%	39%	31%	8%	7%
Base	**276**	**51**	**46**	**26**	**12**	**14**

As shown in Table 13.6, in every case a majority believed that they had experienced at least some anti-Conservative tactical voting in recent years, a phenomenon at all levels of political contest – parliamentary, local and so on – acknowledged in the literature.[740] Here, the most noticeable distinction was between those groups

---

[738] Marks, 13th August 2002; and see McLean, 1997: 152 for a more objective but similar view.

[739] Fraser, 29th December 2002.

[740] Broughton, 2003: 211; Butler, 6th May 2000; Evans, Curtice & Norris, 1998: 77; Seldon & Snowdon, 2001: 3.

elected by a first-past-the-post system and those elected via some type of proportional representation system, i.e. MEPs and MSPs. (The data does not allow a distinction to be made between those directly elected as constituency representatives and those elected via the party list.) The latter were very much more likely to believe that they had been hit by anti-Conservative tactical voting. Unfortunately, it is hard to take this observation much further given the different systems used to elect MEPs and MSPs.

(There was a final question in this series. This was the mirror to the previous item and asked if respondents believed that they had experienced any *pro*-Conservative tactical voting. Since often 90% and more within in each group of respondents said that they had not, no more is made of this item.)

Then there were the two other items from the questionnaire. The responses from Peers were also analysed out of a sense of completeness although they did not take part in public elections. In the case of "The Labour Party has genuinely shed its socialistic instincts" ANOVA detected a significant between-groups difference (p = 0.035) although the Bonferroni post-hoc test did not. That said, in every case a clear majority of respondents from all groups disagreed with this item and this was particularly true in case of both Peers (80%) and MPs (86%) at Westminster. In other words, respondents rejected the view that Labour had abandoned socialism although whether they thought that Labour had *ever* abandoned it and if so how consistently is another matter.[741]

ANOVA detected no between-groups differences (p = 0.909) in responses to "The Conservatives should be focusing their national campaigning efforts against the Liberal Democrats rather than Labour". Responses to this item were less clear-cut. Amongst most groups of respondents, around a half or a little more disagreed with the item as posed and instead thought that the Conservatives should indeed be focussing on Labour rather than the Liberal Democrats. MEPs were unique in that they tended to lean towards the Conservatives focussing on the Liberal Democrats.

---

[741] Baldwin, 28th January 2002[a]; Darwall, 2002: 1; *Evening Standard*, 12th June 2002; White, 20th July 2002.

More on attitudes towards Labour and the Liberal Democrats

First, what relationship, if any, was there between attitudes towards the two main parties and the degree of electoral challenge that respondents thought that they presented? Because of the small numbers in many of the groups, this analysis could only be carried out on ELCs.

Where the Labour Party was perceived to be the main challenger there was no significant difference (two-tailed $p = 0.580$ using the Pearson statistic) in attitudes towards either party. However, where the Liberal Democrats were perceived as the main challenger then there was a significant difference (two-tailed $p = 0.001$) in attitudes towards the two parties. The Liberal Democrats tended to be more disliked.

It will be remembered that all respondents under analysis in this sub-section were sitting local councillors. What this result suggests is that a Labour challenge was regarded with relative equanimity compared to a Liberal Democrat challenge which tended to be associated with a greater degree of dislike. Whether this was due to attitudes towards the Liberal Democrats *qua* institution, their perceived beliefs[742] or their campaigning practices[743] cannot be answered here.

TABLE 13.7: ELCS: PERCEIVED MAIN CHALLENGER AND SAFENESS OF SEAT		
Main challenger	**Labour**	**Lib Dems**
Very marginal	21%	8%
Somewhat marginal	22%	18%
Safe or fairly safe	57%	74%
Base	**109**	**144**

Moreover, as Table 13.7 indicates, it does not seem to have been due to the Liberal Democrats being seen as the more pressing challenger. Respondents associated (two-tailed $p = 0.005$) a more serious challenge from Labour with holding a *less* safe seat. In other words, the particularly negative attitude displayed towards the Liberal Democrats did not seem to be a result of them being seen as more of a threat.

---

[742] *Conservative Home*, 14th April 2006.
[743] Anderson, 13th March 2010; Methven, 24th July 2002.

Table 13.8 looks at who ELCs regarded as the main challenger and their perception of anti-Conservative tactical voting. It can be seen that there was a significant perception (two-tailed p = <0.001 using the Pearson statistic) that where the Liberal Democrats were the main challenger the greater was the degree of anti-Conservative tactical voting. Under half (45%) of those most pressed by the Labour party said that they had experienced any meaningful anti-Conservative tactical voting against well over two-thirds (71%) of those of those facing the Liberal Democrats. It cannot be said whether this indicated that the Liberal Democrats were better at marshalling the potential anti-Conservative vote, or whether notional Labour supporters were more willing to switch to aid the anti-Conservative cause, or whether it was a feature of the type of geographical area under analysis.

TABLE 13.8: ELCs: PERCEIVED MAIN CHALLENGER AND ANTI-CONSERVATIVE TACTICAL VOTING		
Main challenger	Labour	Lib Dems
A great deal	9%	16%
Some	36%	55%
Very little or none at all	55%	29%
Base	107	145

All of these analyses tend to reinforce the impression of the particular dislike respondents felt towards the Liberal Democrats.

It can also be seen whether attitudes about who the Conservatives should be directing their energies against were associated with who their main challenger actually was.

TABLE 13.9: ELCs: FOCUS CAMPAIGNING EFFORTS ON LIBERAL DEMOCRATS		
Main challenger	Labour	Lib Dems
Agree	17%	41%
Neither/nor	18%	19%
Disagree	65%	40%
Base	108	145

The results set out in Table 13.9 come as no surprise. There was a significant association (two-tailed p = <0.001 using the

Pearson statistic), with those respondents regarding the Liberal Democrats as their main challenger very much more likely to agree with the questionnaire item.

Attitudes and electoral experience together

It will be recalled from Chapter 6 that the only major attitudinal correlates with attitudes towards the Conservative Party's two main rivals, Labour and the Liberal Democrats, were the Europeanism and Left-Right scales. In both cases the findings were in the same direction, with the more Euro-sceptic and/or supportive of free-market economics respondents were then the more antipathetic they tended to be towards the two other parties. This was taken to indicate a relatively narrow, ideological assessment of the Party's two main UK-wide opponents.[744]

Looking again at these two parties, what can be said of the impact of electoral competition when taken alongside these more ideological considerations? To assess this, the partial correlation analyses were re-run for attitudes towards Labour and the Liberal Democrats. The undifferentiated dataset was used. However, only those respondents were analysed who said that either Labour or the Liberal Democrats were their closest challenger.

In addition to the usual range of attitudinal scales, the electoral items discussed in this present chapter were included. The item for whether Labour or the Liberal Democrats were the main challenger was included as were the items for the perceived safeness of their seat and experience of tactical voting. Also included were the two variables specifically concerning the Labour and/or Liberal Democrat parties: "The Labour Party has genuinely shed its socialistic instincts" and "The Conservatives should be focusing their national campaigning efforts against the Liberal Democrats rather than Labour".

The purpose of the analyses was to see if such electoral considerations – the struggle for political power – trumped more ideological considerations.

The answer, reasonably strongly, was "no". In the case of Labour, not a single one of these electoral items was significantly associated at the conventional 5% level with attitudes towards the party when attitudinal variables were controlled for. In the case of the Liberal

---

[744] The findings were very different for attitudes towards UKIP, the BNP and the Greens.

Democrats there was a single instance. This was the "The Labour Party has genuinely shed its socialistic instincts" item (correlation 0.164, two-tailed significance 0.015) which might suggest that attitudes towards the rival parties somewhat informed one another.

Looking solely at the Conservative Party's two main challengers, it seems clear that electoral politics had very little to do with attitudes towards them once more ideological measures were taken into account.

The General Public and the PoliMap

Using the PoliMap

In Chapter 3 the development of the PoliMap was discussed and then used to develop a picture of the ideological positions of Conservative Party politicians. Given that much was made of its aim being to help shed light on everyday political debate in way that was more meaningful than the flawed traditional left-right model, it can now be used to do just that. In this section the PoliMap is used to portray the general public and then to compare them with Conservative Party politicians.

Identifying comparators amongst the public

How did our respondents compare with their contemporaries amongst the general public? For reasons of sample size only ELCs were first compared with the English general public as a whole and then against those who were recorded as identifying with the Conservative Party, the Labour Party or the Liberal Democrats. To do this, data from the *British Social Attitudes 2001* survey[745] that also used the Left-Right and Authoritarianism dimensions was used. The Cronbach's alpha values found from the responses of the *BSA* respondents used here were a robust 0.87 for the Left-Right dimension and 0.74 for Authoritarianism.

Identifying the subsets of the *BSA* dataset was a simple matter. Only those listed as residing in one of the *BSA*'s regions in England were included. Similarly, the three types of party identifiers were noted as such in the relevant derived variable. Of those *BSA* respondents in

---

[745] NCSR, 29th October 2008[d].

England recorded as identifying with one of the three parties, 30% were Conservative identifiers, 54% were Labour identifiers, and 16% were Liberal Democrat identifiers. As a matter of historical record, at the June 2001 general election the Conservative Party received 37% of the votes cast in England for one of the three main parties, Labour 43%, and the Liberal Democrats 20%.[746]

Mapping the public

Table 13.10 displays the PoliMap distribution for ELCs and the English general public both undivided and split by party identification. Diagram 13.1 shows the PoliMap diagram for the undivided English general public by way of illustration and comparison with Diagram 3.3 in Chapter 3.

TABLE 13.10: POLIMAP DISTRIBUTIONS OF ELCS AND THE ENGLISH PUBLIC					
	ELCs	Public in England[747]	Conservative Identifiers[748]	Labour Identifiers[749]	Lib Dem Identifiers[750]
Northern	2%	<1%	0%	<1%	0%
North-Eastern	19%	5%	9%	2%	6%
Eastern	22%	2%	6%	1%	1%
South-Eastern	31%	17%	26%	13%	10%
Southern	5%	19%	13%	22%	16%
South-Western	2%	16%	8%	19%	17%
Western	0%	3%	0%	5%	5%
North-Western	1%	3%	<1%	3%	4%
Central	18%	35%	38%	35%	41%
Base	266	1498	373	683	203

---

[746] Austin & Hames, 2001: 296. It us unlikely that there would ever be an absolute match between the results of actual elections run under a first-past-the-post system and the "proportional representation" method of opinion polling and academic research such as the *BSA*.

[747] *BSA*, 2001.

[748] *BSA*, 2001.

[749] *BSA*, 2001.

[750] *BSA*, 2001.

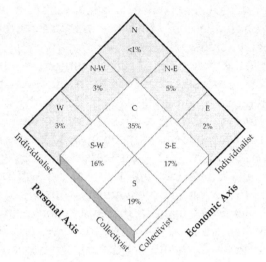

Diagram 13.1: PoliMap distribution of the English public

Looking first at the figures for the general public overall, it can be seen that they displayed a different distribution within the PoliMap than did ELCs. A plurality of them (35%) were located in the Centre sector, and most of the remainder (52% of the total) were distributed in the three Southern-most sectors. Amongst the general public in England there was very little support for either economic or personal individualism and instead considerable support for economic and personal collectivism. This can be seen from the small proportion (14% of the total) that mapped onto the Western, Eastern or any of the three Northern-most sectors.

This suggests that those Conservative or ex-Conservative activists and commentators at the time who felt aggrieved at the Party's new-found interest in "social liberalism" and/or longer-standing attachment to "market forces"[751] may have had popular or electoral grounds to support their view. It also literally illustrates the difference between the relatively unchangeable political "middle ground" which is the theoretical middle position between ideological "extremes" and the more changeable political "common ground" which is the point around which the largest number of individuals under analysis are located.[752] Whilst both the

---

[751] Rankin, 2001: 145-147; Scruton, 21st September 2002.
[752] Crewe & Särlvik, 1980: 247-248.

general public and the Conservative Party had a strong centrist element, the "gravitational influences" or the common ground for each group were somewhat different.

Looking at the three types of party identifier, it can be seen that, whilst there were differences between them, they were more similar to each other than were Conservative identifiers with ELCs. The most noticeable feature of all three groups is that, unlike ELCs, in each case a plurality of respondents mapped into the Centre sector.

Nevertheless, there was a difference between Conservative identifiers on the one hand and Labour and Liberal Democrat identifiers on the other. For example, whilst a mere 15% of Conservative identifiers mapped into the "capitalistic" sectors of Eastern, North-Eastern and Northern, even fewer Liberal Democrat (7%) and Labour (4%) identifiers did so. Conversely, whereas a substantial 21% of Conservative identifiers mapped into the "socialistic" sectors of Western, South-Western, and Southern – albeit mostly in the last of these – some 38% of Liberal Democrat and no less than 46% of Labour identifiers did so. At least to a relative degree these findings accord with perceptions of what the Conservative and Labour and possibly the Liberal Democrat[753] parties stood for at the time and why people tended to support one rather than the other.

(Surprisingly if some media reports and other opinions at the time were to be believed,[754] Conservative Party identifiers were the least wholly "authoritarian" – Southern, in the PoliMap's terms – of the three groups of identifiers.)

In short, whilst the distribution of Conservative identifiers was more similar to that of Labour and Liberal Democrat identifiers than ELCs, it was less dissimilar. Voter-to-party alignment was not completely random.

Tribalism and party realignment

It must again be noted that numbers of people with widely differing political views supported – albeit in this case identifying with if not actually joining let alone representing – the same political party.

---

[753] Parris, 19th May 2001; Riddle, 16th July 2001.
[754] Kent, 5th December 2001.

Indeed, this was perhaps especially true of Conservative identifiers where almost identical proportions of respondents mapped into the South-Western (8%) and North-Eastern (9%) sectors.

The reverse perspective was even truer. To know that someone was a Centrist according to the PoliMap was very little guide to which party they supported.

It goes beyond the bounds of this book to delve into this phenomenon in any detail, but it seems likely that party identification is often "tribal"[755] rather than ideological. If for some reason those tribal bonds weakened but there was no major ideological shift amongst the public, then the PoliMap indicates the viable space for identification with other, perhaps existing parties. To take a provocative example – and as others noted was true some years after the fieldowk[756] – an examination of the similarity of many of their respective social and particularly economic policies makes a large-scale desertion of electoral support from Labour to the BNP not at all implausible. Of more direct relevance to this study, the association between elements of Conservative Party and UKIP policies – or at least elements wished for by many of their supporters – has been remarked upon.[757]

Conclusion to Chapter 13

Regarding what respondents believed to be the most pressing concerns facing Britain today, it is perhaps admirable that they thought that they had at least somewhat different priorities to those of the public. They neither were arrogant enough to believe that "That they think like I do" nor supine enough merely to parrot the worries of the electorate.

As one conservative-inclined commentator argued,[758]

"If a multiparty democracy is to work properly, parties must march to the beats of drums that stand somewhat apart from the rhythm of the whole nation, agglomerated. It is not

---

[755] Lucas, 6th March 2010.
[756] Hannan, 22nd February 2009.
[757] *BBC News*, 6th September 2009.
[758] Parris, 2nd August 2008.

> *wrong for them to resonate to particular interests, instincts*
> *or opinions."*

In other words, there is at least something to be said for political parties *not* to operate along simple Downsian lines of party competition – which is that parties must converge on the median positions of aggregate voter distribution – since parties can shift voters' positions.[759]

That said, the apparent rejection by the Conservatives of such a Downsian approach was held by many to have been one of the many reasons for their lack of electoral success, most notably in 1997 and 2001.[760] How much this was a principled rejection of such an approach or simply a failure of senior Conservatives to understand what the public thought is unclear. Research by others using the *British Representation Survey* of 2001, the *British Social Attitudes* surveys of 1997 and 2001 and other sources has indicated that Conservative politicians were much less accurate than Labour and Liberal Democrat politicians when asked about their perceptions of voters' views on a range of policy issues compared to voters' actual views.[761]

Polling data from the 2001 general election indicated that voters were most interested in areas such as the NHS and education but that the Conservative Party, if by no means ignoring these issues, did not appear to focus on them.[762] The data from this chapter indicates that Conservative politicians were well aware of their importance, if nevertheless sincerely believing that some of these issues were not as important as the public thought.

The middle part of this chapter focused mainly on the experience of respondents in fighting for their seats, particularly against the Conservative Party's two main opponents, Labour and the Liberal Democrats. What was striking was the behaviour of voters: the majority of respondents from all groups had experienced at least some anti-Conservative tactical voting. The implications of the cessation of this – or, indeed, of another party being the victim of such behaviour[763] – are clear even without any increase in active support for the Conservatives.

---

[759] Ward, April 2000.
[760] Norris & Lovenduski, 2004: 97.
[761] Norris & Lovenduski, 2004: 98-99.
[762] Lees-Marshment, November 2001: 938.
[763] McFarlane, 9th April 2010.

Despite the parlous state of the Party and considerations of phenomena such as anti-Conservative tactical voting, the political situation in 2002 as far as our respondents were concerned needs to be reiterated. Anyone elected whilst wearing a blue rosette at this time would have been fortunate to have been selected in the first instance for what was probably a "true blue" constituency or ward. Indeed, only a minority of respondents said their seat could be described as very marginal. Such a place would in all likelihood contain a socio-demographic voter profile rather different from the country as a whole or even, for example, the swing seats lost in 1997 and which the Party needed to win back if it was ever to form a government.

Returning to the two main challengers, amongst ELCs the phenomenon noted in an earlier chapter of a particular and in part visceral or perhaps tribal dislike of the Liberal Democrats was reinforced. Nevertheless, further analysis indicated that, when taken alongside attitudinal measures, the experience of fighting elections had little impact on attitudes towards either of the two main challengers.

Turning to the PoliMap, it might be possible that the electorate becomes so profoundly disillusioned with *all of the major parties* that they accede to the attractions of one or more anti-political establishment parties[764] almost irrespective of what such parties stand for beyond that. This is not the same as a "throw the rascals out" disenchantment with *a party in office* where support will turn instead towards one or more of the existing major parties, as the Conservatives experienced only too well in 1997.

It is also possible that, for some reason, an issue outside of the PoliMap such as attitudes towards the EU becomes of overriding if perhaps temporary importance[765] or perhaps that one of the parties manages to buck the conventional Downsian model of positioning themselves to attract the median voter by inserting a different dominant issue into an election campaign.[766]

But absent of a major sea-change in political attitudes – and also accepting the salience of what are termed here the "Personal" and Economic" dimensions – then it is likely that for the foreseeable future any British political party that wishes to receive considerable

---

[764] Hayton, February 2010: 26.
[765] Micklethwait, 27th February 2003; Aaronovitch, 10th May 2005.
[766] Ward, April 2000.

electoral support has to be perceived as having its heart in a common ground which is the centre-to-collectivist area of politics measured in absolute terms.

Any desire to move away from this Centre-South common ground, whether this is the Conservative Party[767] or one of the other major parties,[768] whilst ideologically desirable from certain perspectives,[769] runs the risk of distancing that party from the electorate.[770] And, of course, this necessarily presents difficulties when, as has been seen, the ideological common ground of the Conservative Party at the time was somewhat different from that of the general public.

However, if the leaders of the major parties become ever-more concerned about the opinions of the public rather than those of their own members – particularly with increasing focus on regular opinion polling and a system of continuous campaigning – it calls into question the viability of ideologically distinct, mass-membership parties.[771] In this instance a more explicit move is possible towards the type of catch-all parties described in the 1960s which feature a strong leadership but a downgraded membership.[772]

Finally, it has been argued that it is a mistake to assume that there must be one major party on the "left" and another on the "right" by the reckoning of the conventional model.[773] If so, then the analysis presented here suggests that there is also no reason to think that at any particular moment all the sectors of the PoliMap must have or even can have their own electorally viable party[774] outside of a proportional representation system with a very low threshold for winning seats.[775]

---

[767] Ahmed, 4th March 2001.

[768] Baldwin, 28th January 2002[b],

[769] Parris, 4th August 2001.

[770] Norris & Lovenduski, 2004; but see also Crewe & Searing, 1988.

[771] Micklethwait, 24th April 2010.

[772] Pettitt, April 2007: 4.

[773] Hames, 22nd February 2002.

[774] Clarke, 1999; Meek, 1998; 1999: 14.

[775] Daems, 11th January 2010: para 44; Meek, August 2010.

14

Future Conservative Parliamentarians?

Generational Replacement

Eventually, sitting politicians must be replaced by new ones. After the 2001 general election, new MPs comprised 20% of the strength of the parliamentary Conservative party[776] although a concatenation of events at other times might considerably alter this proportion of newcomers.[777] What predictions can be made about the socio-demographic composition and attitudes of such replacements in the years following 2002?

In this chapter a method of identifying one group of possible replacements is first described before looking at the type of person who might replace existing parliamentarians and then analysing possible attitudinal changes between the generations.

There have, for example, been two general elections and two European Parliament elections between the *CPRS 2002* fieldwork and the publication of this book. This findings and predictions of this chapter, more than any other, are now open to empirical examination.

Identifying Potential Replacements

Around the time of the fieldwork, many higher-level Conservative politicians had served as local councillors before being elected to

---

[776] Criddle, 2002: 182.
[777] Riddell, 15th May 2009.

Parliament.[778] As shown in Table 14.1, responses to an item in the questionnaire indicated that a majority of Westminster MPs and other higher-level representatives had either been local councillors or had at least stood as local council candidates before attaining their present position. This was particularly true of MEPs who appear to have had more direct experience in local electoral politics experience than their all-UK or Scottish counterparts.

TABLE 14.1: EXPERIENCE IN ELECTED LOCAL GOVERNMENT BEFORE ATTAINING PRESENT POSITION			
	MPs	MEPs	MSPs
Had been a local councillor	35%	64%	38%
Had stood unsuccessfully at a local election	26%	7%	31%
Neither of the above	39%	29%	31%
Base	**49**	**14**	**13**

In addition, as shown in Table 14.2, a quarter (24%) of ELCs indicated that they would "definitely" consider a career "further up the political ladder" as an MP, MEP or member of the newer Scottish, Welsh or London institutions. Another fifth (19%) indicated that they "possibly" would.

TABLE 14.2: ELCs CONSIDERING A CAREER "FURTHER UP THE POLITICAL LADDER"	
Yes, definitely	24%
Yes, possibly	19%
Unlikely or not at all	57%
Base	**278**

Based upon these findings, an attempt can be made to describe the possible socio-demographic and attitudinal changes of incoming higher-level Conservative politicians in the years following the fieldwork. This can be done by comparing those current ELCs most likely to become higher-level politicians with such politicians at the

---

[778] Cowley & Melhuish, March 1997: 27; Landale & Peek, 15th March 2000.

time of the fieldwork. Because of the numbers involved, when looking at "higher-level politicians" only Westminster MPs will be considered.

Furthermore, "those sorts of current ELCs most likely to become higher-level politicians" needs to be defined more objectively. First, by looking at those who were already MPs around the time of the fieldwork, a defensible age-related cut-off point can be calculated beyond which someone is unlikely to be elected as an MP for the first time. Table 14.3 presents data collated from a convenient source[779] concerning age-related details of when individuals were first elected as a Conservative MP.

Analysis including a boxplot analysis in *SPSS* confirmed the presence of a solitary outlier at the upper end of the range of maximum age first elected as an MP. This individual was first elected as an MP at the age of 60 compared to the next oldest at 49. Accordingly, this individual was removed from the analysis although in practice it made little difference.

TABLE 14.3: AGE-RELATED DETAILS OF CONSERVATIVE MPs RETURNED AT 2001 GENERAL ELECTION	
Minimum age first elected as an MP	27
Maximum age first elected as an MP	49
Mean age first elected as an MP (rounded)	38
Standard deviation (rounded)	5
Base	**165**
Note: The outlier discussed in the text has been excluded from the figures in this table	

It is known that two standard deviations from the mean encompass over 95% of a normally distributed population. In practice, looking both at this and the simple maximum age of first being elected of those Conservative MPs returned at the 2001 general election, it means that the age of 49 can be accepted as the cut-off point for ELCs who harboured ambitions to climb the political ladder. Given that the fieldwork for this study was done in 2002 and there was in fact a general election three years later in 2005, this can be

---

[779] Austin & Hames, 2001.

qualified by excluding from further analysis any "ambitious" ELCs who were 47 or older at the time of the fieldwork.

When combining this calculation with the responses to the item about whether respondents would consider a career further up the political ladder, 30 ELCs are left who were "definitely" politically ambitious and were sufficiently young to entertain realistic hopes of advancement, at least for a few years.

The following analysis only included those who said that they were "definitely" ambitious rather than also including those who were "possibly" ambitious, even though the smaller base would make statistically significant findings less likely. This was because it was and is difficult just to be selected to contest a seat, let alone a winnable seat. Even allowing for a degree of diffidence on the part of respondents – if such a quality may be allowed for politicians – it was felt that only those prepared to say "definitely" were sufficiently keen.

In passing, it should be noted that our ELCs were often politically ambitious. Of the 51 ELCs who could be identified as being younger than 47 a mere seven indicated that they were unlikely or not at all likely to consider a career further up the ladder.

Of course, there are other routes to becoming an MP. However, an analysis of the 51 people who entered the House of Commons as Conservative MPs for the first time after the 2005 general election indicates that the "former local councillor route" remained an important one.[780] Of those 51 individuals, 40% could definitely be identified as having been local councillors. The analysis was done by reading the very brief biographies on the Conservative Party's website, so the number must be regarded as an approximation. Still, it suggests no great change either way in importance of the former-local-councillor route.

Socio-Demographics of Replacements

Before looking at what differences there might be between potential replacements drawn from ELCs and sitting MPs, a few things can be

---

[780] House of Commons Information Office, personal communication, 13th April 2007; Conservative Party, 2007.

said about what these replacements "look like". The following is an outline of the 30 ELCs identified above.

In much of the following the small number of respondents in absolute terms should be noted. The problem of reporting that 11% of potential replacements were cohabiting when this actually represents only three individuals is acknowledged.

Possible replacements were all white with not a single respondent checking the non-white option. They were also overwhelmingly male (87%).

By way of a check, those who were actually new entrants at the 2005 general election can be analysed. There were 51 new Conservative MPs. Of these, 12% – 9% of all Conservative MPs – were women, matching the proportion of potential replacements (13%) from our fieldwork almost exactly. More crudely, just by way of looking at names and photographs, only two could definitely be considered to be non-white.

Carrying on with the *CPRS 2002* respondents, they were generally married (68%) with few cohabiting with a partner (11%) with the rest noting that they were single. Most had attended a state secondary school (83%). Nevertheless, over two-thirds (69%) had attended university or had attained equivalent professional qualifications.

Three quarters (76%) were employed as opposed to self-employed, primarily working in the private sector (77% of those) and mainly in jobs that fell into the questionnaire's "service sector management or professions" category (70% of those) with "manufacturing or agriculture" accounting for much of the rest (13%). This accords with a simple analysis of the 51 individuals who were actually elected as MPs for the first time in 2005. Without creating a formal schema to quantify it, it was clear that the majority – at least two-thirds – had some significant occupational background in either the professions or the service sector, particularly law and finance.

Over two-thirds (69%) of the potential replacements viewed themselves as being "middle class" with most of the rest (21%) regarding themselves as belonging to no particular social class (as opposed to stating that they considered themselves to be "working class").

Nearly half (47%) had been in the Young Conservatives but very few (10%) said that they had been in the Federation of Conservative Students.

In short, and perhaps to no great astonishment, this is a picture of a fairly homogeneous group of white, middle-class, white collar, youngish-middle-aged males.

It says much about these respondents' dedication to the Conservative Party and/or public office and/or personal ambition that nearly half (45%) said that they had joined the Party before the age of 20 and exactly the same proportion said that they had become a local councillor before the age of 30.

Differences between Future and Sitting MPs

It was noted in Chapter 4 that analysed the socio-demographics of ELCs that there was much talk at the time of making the Conservative Party's MPs (and so on) more representative of the general public. Particular attention was paid to sex and race.

For the reasons noted in Chapter 2 concerning the methodology of this study, such items were not asked of any respondents *except* ELCs. However, some of this information about MPs of the time can be found in secondary sources. In 2002, 14 Conservative MPs were women, comprising 8% of the Party's total, and there were no non-white Conservative MPs.[781]

As already noted, of the possible replacement ELCs identified above, only 13% were female. This was hardly a dramatic increase in absolute terms. However, it would be a greater increase if female ELC respondents had been as keen to want to become MPs (and so on) as their male colleagues. But they were not. To turn the figures around, only 6% of *all* female ELC respondents fell into the group of possible future MPs compared to 12% of *all* male ELCs. Female ELCs were proportionately less likely than their male counterparts to fall into the group of potential replacements. Whether this was because of age, lack of political ambition or a belief that the selection system was biased against them – in short, the debate[782] about whether and to what extent it is "demand" or "supply" of female candidates that tends to be low – goes beyond this study.

As for race, it has already been seen that *every* ELC respondent ticked the box marked "White".

---

[781] Brivati & Baston, 2002: 8.
[782] Krook, May 2010.

It is of course true that elected local politicians are far from representing the whole pool of potential parliamentarians. That said, there was little evidence that replacement in terms of career advancement – as opposed to a more dramatic change in career – would have the apparently desired effect of markedly increasing the number of female and non-white candidates standing in general elections after the one in 2001. It seems likely that some form of positive discrimination would be needed.[783] That 92% of ELCs, 92% of SLCs and 89% of WLCs agreed with the statement "Local Conservative associations should retain control over parliamentary candidate selection" suggests that it would be in the teeth of local resistance.[784] Of course, some more senior female Conservative politicians around the time of the fieldwork also opposed positive discrimination.[785]

2010 General election update

The Conservative Party returned 49 female MPs at the 2010 general election, accounting for 16% of all Conservative MPs,[786] only three percentage points more than the potential replacements identified by this study in 2002.

However, the number of non-white MPs was notably higher. 11 non-white Conservative MPs were elected,[787] just under 4% of all Conservative MPs. This is still less than the non-white population of the UK as a whole. However, as was noted in Chapter 4 on ELC socio-demographics when looking at the idea of "representativeness", it is simply a fact that the Conservative Party was and is stronger in suburban and rural areas with a lower non-white population.

Attitudinal Differences

Looking at the range of multi-item scales used throughout this study, the attitudes of potential ELC replacements were compared with those of

---

[783] Sieghart, 20th December 2004.
[784] Walker, 4th August 2009.
[785] Villiers, 20th December 2004.
[786] Conservative Women's Organisation, 2012.
[787] Siddique, 7th May 2010.

existing MPs using the t-test procedure in *SPSS*. Of course, there can be little certainty about what attitudinal types of MP might *leave* the House of Commons thus creating a vacancy. In part, it depends upon matters such as the fortunes of the Conservative Party at elections and the size of majorities handed over to new parliamentary candidates. This analysis is meant only as a tentative guide.

The first result is that there was no significant difference at the conventional two-tailed 5% level between the two groups along most scales: Authoritarianism, Left-Right, Europeanism, Environmentalism, Welfarism, Feminism, Postmaterialism, Pride in the Way Nation Functions, Intra-Party Inclusivity, Political Elitism and Optimism. That there was no significant difference in attitudes between possible replacement ELCs and sitting MPs on some of the most important attitudinal scales – both politically and in terms of the analyses in this book – is surely of note.

Based upon other research undertaken some years after the study, commentators noted that, "For all his attempts to make the Conservative Party look to the future, a giant from the past looms over David Cameron. The next generation of Tory MPs are Thatcher's Children."[788]

However, there were seven scales where these were significant differences: Traditional British Liberties, Theocratism, Religiosity, Xenophobia, Protectionism, Pride in National Heritage & Culture and Intra-Party Elitism. These are set out in Table 14.4.

---

[788] Groves, 26ᵗʰ February 2010; Hall, 19ᵗʰ January 2010; Whitworth & Baldwin, 26ᵗʰ February 2010: 26.

TABLE 14.4: SIGNIFICANT DIFFERENCES BETWEEN SITTING MPs AND POSSIBLE ELC REPLACEMENTS

Scale	Base (MPs/ELCs)	t	Two-tailed sig.	Comments
Theocratism	52/28	3.882	<0.001	ELCs more inclined towards secularist attitudes
Religiosity	48/29	4.497	<0.001	ELCs more inclined towards non-religious attitudes
Traditional British Liberties	49/30	2.236	0.028	ELCs more inclined towards authoritarian attitudes
Xenophobia	49/29	-2.976	0.004	ELCs more inclined towards xenophobic views
Protectionism	50/29	-2.507	0.014	ELCs more inclined towards protectionist views
Pride in National Heritage & Culture	51/29	2.181	0.032	ELCs less proud
Intra-Party Elitism	51/30	4.614	<0.001	ELCs more inclined towards grass-roots control of Party

That members of our subset of ELCs tended to be more in favour of grassroots control of the Party than MPs hardly needs further comment. Whether they would have continued to do so after a few years at Westminster or Brussels is another matter.

That there were significant differences in the same direction in attitudes measured by both of the religion-based variables suggests a potential development of some substance. Religion was analysed more fully in Chapter 10, but this finding highlights the general secularisation of British – or at least English in this instance – public life.

The finding that the possible replacements were *less* proud of their country's heritage and culture than sitting MPs is at first sight puzzling. It might indicate a straightforward if unexpected finding about these relatively younger politicians' views about Britain's achievements and attributes. However, it might indicate a "going to hell in a handcart" view of how Britain was moving at the time after years of rule under a (to respondents) disliked Labour government and/of from an equally disliked "Brussels".

A study of the individual items detailed in Appendix 3 making up the Traditional British Liberties, Xenophobia and Protectionism suggests a degree of overlap. Correlation analysis (not shown here) using the Pearson statistic indicated significant bivariate, two-tailed correlations well below the conventional 5% level between all three scales. Given this, then the fact that the significant differences were all in the same direction – more "authoritarian" in some manner – again suggests a possible development of note. It can also be seen from Appendix 3 that the Xenophobia and Protectionism scales also dealt in some manner with economic issues. Overall, it may be defensible to argue that these findings suggest a shift towards economic and social/moral "populism", a reoccurring and sometimes electorally successful strand within Conservative thinking around the time of the study.[789] Indeed, if the preceding chapter's PoliMap analysis of the public is accurate, such attitudes might be in tune with the electorate.

That said, there were no significant difference between (then) current MPs and some of their most likely replacements along a whole range of important variables concerned with, for example, the EU and the environment. This is despite reputable claims to the contrary that there has been a continuing process amongst Conservative politicians of attitudinal change in some of these areas for many years.[790] In short, much like the findings for possible demographic changes, in many attitudinal areas of significance new Conservative MPs are likely to be similar to the existing ones around the time of this study's fieldwork. For good or ill, matters were unlikely to change unless the Party leadership actively promoted candidates to winnable seats at least in part on the basis of political views different to those held by the sitting MPs whom they hoped to replace.

The other qualification, already noted in the case of control of the Party, is that becoming an MP or MEP and so on might "refocus" points of view.

---

[789] Baker, Gamble & Seawright, 2002: 405; Cowley & Norton, 1999: 95-96; Norton, 2002: 86; Tyrie, 2001: 17.
[790] Webb, 2003; Heppell, 2005.

Conclusion to Chapter 14

Regarding socio-demographic changes amongst future higher-level politicians, it seemed that the proportion of non-whites was unlikely to increase by a great deal although the proportion of women might increase somewhat. This is backed up by an analysis of those who actually did enter the Commons in 2005. Matters had changed a little by 2010 although regarding non-white Conservative MPs this was arguably coming close to what a genuinely colour blind selection process – as opposed to an enthusiastic application of positive discrimination – could be expected to achieve.

Similarly, they are likely to possess a university (or equivalent) education and have a background in the service sector or the professions, particularly finance and law. In short, if the analysis holds any significant truth then for the next two or three general elections after 2005 then the "typical" new Conservative MP likely is likely to be a middle-class – although by no means "posh" when it is recalled that the majority of them did *not* attend a fee-paying school – white male with a background in law or finance. It is to be suspected that this appears very much like the picture that many would hold about Conservative politicians "as a group".

Regarding attitudinal changes, it has already been noted that if translated into reality – and "naively" assuming that the mere fact of becoming an MP did not result in real or professed attitudinal changes – a move towards more "authoritarian" or "populist" attitudes can be expected amongst Conservative parliamentarians.[791] However, it is seems probable that in many important areas replacements will share the views of those whom they have replaced.

To reiterate, this study conducted in 2002 suggests that neither the socio-demographic nor attitudinal profile of higher-level Conservative politicians would greatly change in the two or three general elections after 2002 absent of an active and centralising[792] policy by the Party leadership to force such a change.[793] This might include taking advantage

---

[791] Elliott, 30th April 2009; Montgomerie, 30th April 2009.
[792] Isaby, 30th July 2009.
[793] Montgomerie, 11th May 2006; but see Elliott & Coates, 28th April 2009; Isaby, 29th April 2009.

of unforeseen circumstances to remove less desirable sitting MPs[794] and/or, apparently paradoxically, giving members of the electorate from outside of the Party more say in the selection of candidates.[795]

Of course, assuming that any such changes were made at least partly in order to boost electoral popularity then there is still no guarantee that such changes would have the desired, causal result.[796]

Time and further research will tell.

---

[794] Montgomerie, 21st June 2009.
[795] Conservative Party, 10th July 2009; Hitchens, 9th August 2009.
[796] Bale, September 2008: 295.

15

Bringing the Findings Together

The Purpose of the Study Restated

To reiterate, this book is based upon a multi-focus study with a main aim of being an analysis of the attitudes, behaviour and socio-demographic background of Conservative politicians in 2002. It is the purpose of this concluding chapter to bring together the results so far presented but in a manner other than just rehearsing the concluding sections of the preceding thematic chapters.

Brief mention must also be made of the relationship between the Conservative Party as an institution on the one hand and the aggregate views, behaviour and background of its constituent parts on the other.

Finally, returning to a theme from Chapter 1, some further thoughts are presented as to why this study can plausibly be taken as an examination of Conservative Party politicians at or around a particular juncture in the history of the Party and of British politics.

The "Typical" Conservative Politician in 2002

Drawing a picture

It is possible to (almost) end this book with a flourish and draw together the findings into a comprehensible and succinct if "average" form.

Much of the work in the thematic chapters involved multivariate analysis and attempting to see what is associated with or predicts what. But if this is stripped away, and at the risk of providing an example of the ecological fallacy of making inferences about individuals from aggregate data[797] – and also being somewhat "generous" about combining results – a picture can be drawn of a typical Conservative politician in 2002. Needless to say, many of the actual respondents deviate a good deal from this exemplar.

In Chapter 1, an outline was provided of "conservatism" using a variety of approaches and sources. However, it was also noted that "conservatism" and the "Conservative Party" are not necessarily the same. This applies just as much to the distinction between the "Conservative Party" and individual "Conservative Party politicians". That said, there is clearly a link between all three. It would be foolish to claim that the following "Conservative Party politician" represents a definitive picture of "conservatism" in the UK at the turn of the 20th/21st centuries. But he *(sic)* is not too far away.

The Conservative politician in 2002

He – for he was likely to be a he rather than a she – was white, middle-aged and, at the time of the survey if not from birth, middle-class if not necessarily "posh". In most of this he differed little from his Labour and Liberal Democrat counterparts. Where he did differ from them was that his occupational background was more likely to have been in the private sector and also that he was more likely to represent a rural or suburban area rather than an urban one.

He was likely from an Anglican background. Although in his personal beliefs he was quite religious, these views were generally isolated from his secular attitudes and he was not convinced that religion should play a strong role in public life.

He believed in democracy and public engagement with governance, although this was tempered by an acknowledgement of elites and leaders in society. Similarly, he was quietly confident about the strength of British democracy, but when it came to what the purpose of that democracy was he was sometimes in two minds about whether the job of a politician was to be a representative of the people or to seek power to implement certain beliefs.

Looking at ideological attitudes, he held mixed-economy to free-market economic views although he did not necessarily have a principled objection to the public sector. Similarly, he believed in

---

[797] Bryman, 2008: 307.

some state provision of welfare to the needy but he was no believer in an all-embracing, cradle-to-grave Welfare State.

He held rather traditionalist or authoritarian views on morals and law and order.

However, turning to "new" values, he had some sympathy for environmentalist or green views and was certainly no dyed-in-the-wool adherent of "traditional" views about "a woman's place".

He was a patriot. He was generally proud of the way that Britain functioned although this was not without reservations. However, he showed almost unalloyed pride in Britain's heritage and culture. His attitude towards foreigners and foreign influences was middle-of-the-road, being neither notably welcoming nor hostile.

He was easy with thinking himself both British and English – since he was probably English – but was much less happy about seeing himself as both British and European. Unsurprisingly, he had at most "in Europe, not run by Europe" views tending towards outright hostility towards the EU. If for the sake of party unity and discipline he was quiet on the subject of "Europe", this might not always be the case...[798]

He took a "thus far and no further" attitude towards devolution, accepting the new institutions in Wales and Scotland but rejecting Celtic independence and possible developments such as an English parliament and particularly English regional assemblies. He held robustly Unionist sympathies as far as Northern Ireland was concerned and thought that the "peace process" – for he probably thought of it in inverted commas – had largely been a victory for the Republican side of the conflict.

Looking further afield, he was a little pessimistic about the prospect for peaceful relations between the West and the Islamic worlds. He was generally neutral between the Israelis on the one hand and the Palestinians and the Arab world in general on the other, although he inclined somewhat towards the Israelis. He was not inclined towards an enthusiastic Atlanticism inasmuch as this suggested subordination to the USA and he tended to believe that Britain should be more cautious in its support for the USA. He was generally keen to see Britain re-establish closer ties with the Commonwealth, particularly the "Old" Commonwealth.

---

[798] Webb, December 2008: 441.

When it comes to the Conservative Party, he believed in a mixture of Central Office and grass roots control of the Party. However, he felt that the Party's leadership sometimes went too far in watering down some principles and beliefs for fear that they would be unacceptable to the floating voter or sections of the mass media. He was uncertain about attempts to "modernise" the Party vis-à-vis advancing women, racial minorities and homosexuals.

As far as the other major political parties were concerned, whilst he liked neither he had a particularly strong dislike of the Liberal Democrats when compared to Labour although these attitudes seemed as much visceral as ideological. The only party in the UK that he had active sympathy for was the historically closely associated Ulster Unionist Party. His views about those rightly or wrongly perceived to be single-issue parties – the Greens, UKIP and the BNP – was shaped by his own attitudes towards those same single issues. The more he sympathised with their signature stance, the less hostile he was towards them.[799]

He was, to be blunt, wildly overoptimistic about the Party's condition and short to medium-term prospects. This attitude, along with his Euro-scepticism, was why he probably voted for the hapless Iain Duncan Smith in the 2001 leadership contest.

And as of 2002, his attitude towards Margaret Thatcher still approached fervent worship.

The Attitude of the Party as an Institution

That said, and turning matters completely around, there are reasons to predict that there would be differences between the aggregated and averaged views of Conservative politicians as recorded by the study and described in this book on the one hand and the Party as an institution on the other.

(It is beyond the scope of this chapter to engage in an in-depth study of Conservative Party documents such as general election manifestos[800] to ascertain the values of the Party as an institution. This would be a different study altogether.)

---

[799] In a high-profile case shortly before this book was published, a particularly Euro-sceptic Conservative MEP defected to UKIP: Helmer, 4th March 2012.

[800] Conservative Party 2001[b]; Conservative Party, 2005; Klingemann *et al*, 2006.

In the 1960s, Robert McKenzie[801] argued that the main parties were oligarchical in nature and that this was a positive quality in that ordinary party members – as opposed to the leadership – were more "extreme" than ordinary voters. (Revisiting McKenzie, it was argued that between 1997 and 2001 the Conservative Party at least for a while moved somewhat away from such an oligarchical structure towards more direct membership participation. This was particularly seen in the election as leader by the mass membership of Iain Duncan Smith, a man who was never overwhelmingly popular amongst MPs.[802])

The concept of "Downsianism"[803] must again be mentioned: the tendency of political parties to move towards the political "centre" in an attempt to attract votes. (Of course, in reality this would often apply to the public utterances of politicians who were toeing the party line irrespective of what they personally believed.)

In short, it is likely that if such a like-for-like comparison could be done – if the Conservative Party itself was a respondent to the study, so to speak – then it would tend to fall at least relatively nearer the middle of the range of multi-item scales used here than the average actual respondent.

The Study as a Picture at a Point in Time

A case can be made that *CPRS 2002* fieldwork took place during a period with a claim to be distinctive. This period represented a nadir in the Party's fortunes.

An extended account of this period can be considered as starting in September 1992 following the events of Black Wednesday when the Conservative government was forced to withdraw the pound from the European Exchange Rate Mechanism and after which popular support for the Party collapsed.[804] This period also witnessed the rise of New Labour.[805] The end date was May 2010 when the Conservatives under

---

[801] McKenzie, 1964; Kelly, 2004: 398.
[802] Kelly, 2004: 398-399.
[803] Lees-Marshement & Quayle, 2000; Ward, 2000.
[804] Pattie & Johnston, 1996; Norton, 2002: 68; Travis, 27th April 2002.
[805] Worcester & Mortimer, 1999.

David Cameron formed a new government, albeit in coalition with the Liberal Democrats under Nick Clegg.[806]

A shorter period starts in May 1997 when the Conservatives succumbed to the Labour landslide at the general election.[807] The slightly less distinct end date for this period is around December 2007 or January 2008 when the Conservatives under David Cameron were at last routinely ahead of Labour in the polls[808] even if this was substantially based on hostility to Labour rather than a positive endorsement of the Conservatives.[809]

However, an even narrower period can be defined. The start date for this is still May 1997 when the Conservative Party lost office. The end date is November 2003 – a year and a half after the fieldwork – when Michael Howard replaced Iain Duncan Smith as leader of the Conservatives and was seen by many as steadying the ship before leading the Party to a still losing but more respectable performance at the 2005 general election.[810] The latter events seemed to draw a line – albeit a somewhat indistinct one – under a long period of national electoral and institutional misery and decline for the Party.

It is this period of five or six years, May 1997 to November 2003, which neatly bisects the 20th and 21st centuries, into which the study falls. Revisionist analyses of the sort noted in Chapter 1 notwithstanding, by most common metrics of British politics, and above all from the results of general elections, this was a period of unique gloom in the history of the modern Conservative Party. It was out of office and with no immediate prospect of return. It was going through a parade of unsuccessful leaders. Furthermore, and perhaps as strikingly indicated by the attitudes of respondents towards the Iron Lady in Chapter 5, for good or ill its politicians – and its lay members, it is to be expected – were still looking backwards to the perceived golden age of Margaret Thatcher's period in office.

The main purposes of the study included providing a wide-ranging picture of the attitudes, behaviour and socio-demographic

---

[806] *BBC News*, 12th May 2010.

[807] Worcester & Mortimore, 1999.

[808] *BBC News*, 6th December 2005; Marquand, 2009: 398-399.

[809] *Political Studies Association News*, March 2009: 30.

[810] Dyke & Bale, 28th January 2010; King, 30th July 2004.

background and culture of Conservative Party politicians with – as is discussed in the following chapter – the additional purpose of the creation of a dataset that would allow analysis and comparison by future researchers.

It is true that some of the younger respondents and their colleagues elsewhere in the country – particularly those who were local councillors – are likely to continue to have an overt role in the Party for many years after the fieldwork. In short, some of the younger respondents or those like them might be targets for a *CPRS 2022* or even a *CPRS 2032*.

From responses to items in the questionnaire, we have seen that 2002 was a time when the Party was still looking back to the glory days of Margaret Thatcher's time and yet was becoming aware that things had changed externally and perhaps had to change internally as a result.

If one tries hard enough almost any point in time can be described as "pivotal" in some manner or other. Nevertheless, for the reasons just rehearsed, the period around 2002 seems a defensible time to call *finis* on the "turn of the century Conservative Party".

16

Beyond the *CPRS 2002*

Further Analysis of the *CPRS 2002* Data

However, it is not necessary to call *finis* on the data collected by the *CPRS 2002* and then used for this book. The study captured in excess of 100,000 items of raw data – over 500 individuals responding to over 200 questionnaire items – even before considering the calculation of derived variables such as the multi-item scales or the PoliMap. The preceding thematic chapters can only describe so much and there was insufficient space and/or justification within the remit of the original study to analyse every single variable alone or in combination. For example, there are a small number of items – such as about the running of the Party, about religion and about general attitudes towards the state – which are not analysed in this book, often because they could not be successfully developed as elements of multi-item dimensions.

In addition to this, for the reasons explained at the start of this study the range of statistical techniques used to analyse the data was limited and there are others that might be used with profit. Similarly, other researchers might wish to examine different theoretical questions and hypotheses such as an empirical analysis of elements of the synthesised description of conservatism found at the start of Chapter 1.

In short, other researchers might want to interrogate the data in ways besides those described in this book.

Re-Running the Study

The study captured data at a point in time. For a number of reasons such as a desire to answer specific questions or as a necessary step towards constructing a time-series dataset some or all of the items in the questionnaire might be used again with future Conservative politicians. Or others, of course, since many of the items are universal in nature.

For the reasons noted in Chapter 2 it was not possible to pilot the main questionnaire. If one could treat the *CPRS 2002* itself as a pilot study then it is possible to suggest certain amendments, omissions and additions. In short, to improve upon it.

Trivially, other than out of a sense of completeness one wonders whether there is any point in sending questionnaires – assuming for the sake of argument a similar form of deployment – to members of the Greater London Assembly or Welsh Assembly. The number of potential respondents is so small. (The counter argument might be, "In which case, why not?")

Looking at the items in the questionnaire, the most obvious candidates for removal would be those making up the multi-item scales Pride in Heritage and Culture, Pride in the Way the Nation Functions, Protectionism and Xenophobia used to create a typology of national identity. In terms of analysis of the Conservative Party the typology, and indeed the individual scales, added very little. Similarly, the Postmaterialism scale was rarely of great importance and, because of its manner of presentation, caused some confusion amongst a minority of respondents leading to a noticeably lower response rate. Between them, these five scales consisted of 24 items. The removal of these would lead to a considerable saving of space.

There are certainly some topics and items that could be cleaned up or added. As just suggested, areas of the questionnaire dealing with national identity and foreign affairs were not as strong as they could have been and/or were used to answer what some might see as idiosyncratic questions such as the relationships between attitudes towards the EU, the USA and Israel/Middle East. Other researchers will have different interests. The Religiosity scale, although valid and reliable, was accompanied by an unusual response set which meant that statistical standardisation had to be used. It is possible to devise a scale with otherwise similar items using a more typical Likert-type response set.

In the questionnaire there should have been more on traditional media consumption. However, a future survey would also likely go into more detail about use of the Internet, social media and so on. The fieldwork for this study was conducted just as broadband was taking off in the UK[811] and before the launching of social media such as Facebook (2004), Twitter (2006) or LinkedIn (2003).[812]

Over time, attitudes towards, and the salience of, various topics will likely change. For example, May 2010 witnessed the formation of a Conservative and Liberal Democrat coalition government along with a commitment by David Cameron to offer a referendum on some form of change to the voting system – which was rejected by the public in a referendum[813] in May 2011 – as a price for Liberal Democrat support.[814] It might be of interest to revisit but in more detail the robust aversion expressed in 2002 by Conservative politicians to both the Liberal Democrats and proportional representation after their experiences of coalition.

Some important issues did not feature in the questionnaire. For example, the Conservative Party's long-standing support for an independent British nuclear deterrent was taken for granted.[815] This assumption was almost certainly correct, but it is well to examine one's assumptions.

When looking at socio-demographic issues it would be advisable to employ more orthodox and hence comparable measures such as the Goldthorpe Class Schema[816] or NRS social grades[817] (the famous "C1s" and "C2s").

One can also think of other techniques that would capture not just more but also different information. For example, with greater resources in terms of money, technology and personnel, the use of at least some face-to-face interviews would be of profit.

For understandable reasons, the survey was very party-centric. There were many items asking about political parties and the various legislative bodies in which their representatives sat. Other than an item about pressure groups, there was little about attitudes towards other political activism on the one hand or the power of the

---

[811] *Telegraph*, 31st March 2010.
[812] Smarty, November 2011.
[813] *BBC News*, 7th May 2011.
[814] *Telegraph*, 12th May 2010.
[815] Marquand, 2009: 184.
[816] Goldthorpe & Heath, 1992.
[817] National Readership Survey, 2008.

"mandarinate"[818] of the civil service and other elements of what has been called "managerialism"[819] on the other. It would be proper to address this. This is particularly the case given that chapter 11 tentatively suggested the presence of an attitude dimension tapping into the idea that political power was increasingly in the hands of people and organisations at some remove from traditional mass-membership parties let alone ordinary citizens.

Indeed, it might be reasonable to claim that the *CPRS 2002* was itself inherently somewhat managerialist or at least oligarchic in its approach. At the other end of the scale, so to speak, a re-run of this study ought to include more about the experiences of politicians in their wide range of direct dealings[820] with those whom they are notionally meant to represent: the public.[821]

All of that said, the *CPRS 2002* captured a wide array of reliable and valid quantitative data about the attitudes, behaviour and socio-demographic background of Conservative politicians. It seems likely that future researchers could do worse than to use the study's questionnaire and the data captured – and this book – as at least a starting point.

---

[818] Carswell, 15ᵗʰ March 2012; Forsyth, 21ˢᵗ April 2012.

[819] Moore, 11ᵗʰ May 2012; North, 12ᵗʰ May 2012.

[820] The informal sponsor of the *CPRS 2002*, Eric Forth, was well-known – to his opponents, notoriously so – for not holding regular constituency surgeries: *Daily Mail*, 19ᵗʰ May 2006. One Conservative local councillor of my acquaintance once described a fair proportion of those who contacted him as "mendicants". As a political activist in my own small way, a fair proportion of those who have taken the trouble to contact me over the years are clearly "green inkers".

[821] One hesitates to say "electorate" for a number of reasons. Many cannot vote because they are too young or ill yet are surely affected by decisions that politicians make. On top of this, there was a substantial fall in voter turnout at, for example, the 2001 general election although this trend reversed somewhat in 2005 and 2010. Nevertheless, turnout at local elections was falling: Tizard, 4ᵗʰ May 2012; UK Political Info, 2010. That said, the assumption that low turnouts are inherently bad or that high turnouts are inherently good is itself contentious: Saunders, June 2012.

Bibliography

3EBNUT, 'Politics in a Third Dimension', *Kuro5hin*, 15th June 2003, retrieved 9th April 2004, http://www.kuro5hin.org/story/2003/6/14/45425/6208.

Perri 6, *On The Right Lines: The Next Centre-Right in the British Isles*, London, Demos, 1998.

David AARONOVITCH, 'So, some people think I'm rightwing...', *Guardian*, 10th May 2005, retrieved 10th May 2005, http://www.guardian.co.uk/Columnists/Column/0,5673,1480192,00.html.

—, 'How did the far Left manage to slip into bed with the Jew-hating Right?', *The Times*, 28th June 2005, p. 18.

—, 'Voters have been waiting for this for years', *The Times*, 23rd April 2010, p. 31.

Guy ADAMS, 'Conservatives to field their first transsexual', *Telegraph*, 14th March 2002, retrieved 14th March 2002, http://www.telegraph.co.uk/opinion/main.jhtml?xml=%2Fopinion%2F2002%2F03%2F14%2Fdp1401.xml.

Ian ADAMS, *Political Ideology Today*, Manchester, Manchester University Press, 1993.

Stephen ADAMS & Louise GRAY, 'Climate change belief given same legal status as religion', *Telegraph*, 3rd November 2009, retrieved 4th March 2010, http://tinyurl.com/yexj5fu.

Paul ADELMAN, *The Decline of the Liberal Party, 1910-31* (2nd ed.), Harlow, Pearson Education, 1995.

ADVOCATES FOR SELF-GOVERNMENT, *World's Smallest Political Quiz*, Cartersville, GA, Advocates for Self-Government, 1995.

—, 'World's Smallest Political Quiz: The Original Internet Political Quiz', *Advocates for Self-Government*, circa 2003, retrieved 13th January 2004, www.theadvocates.org/quiz.html.

Kamal AHMED, 'Despairing Tories want Hague out', *Guardian*, 4th March 2001, retrieved 10th February 2012, http://www.guardian.co.uk/politics/2001/mar/04/ Whitehall.uk.

Keith ALDERMAN, 'Revision of Leadership Election Procedures in the Conservative Party', *Parliamentary Affairs*, Vol. 52, No. 2, 1999, pp. 260-274.

Keith ALDERMAN & Neil CARTER, 'The Conservative Leadership Election of 2001, *Parliamentary Affairs*, Vol. 55, No. 3, July 2002, pp. 569-585.

Jason ALLARDYCE, 'Scotland on a par with Cuba for state largesse', *Sunday Times*, 11th January 2009, retrieved 13th January 2009, http://www.timesonline.co.uk/tol/news/uk/article5489654.ece.

John ALLEN, 'How the Vatican views Europe', *National Catholic Reporter*, 1st April 2005, p. 17.

Rex AMBLER & David HASLAM (eds.), *Agenda for Prophets: Towards a Political Theology for Britain*, London, The Bowerdean Press, 1980.

Michael ANCRAM, Speech to Conservative Women's Conference, Conservative Party website, 29th November 2001, retrieved 13th August 2006, http://www.conservatives.com/tile.do?def=news.story.page&obj_id=20954&speeches=1.

Bruce ANDERSON, 'Ten years on, Mr Major's achievements look more impressive than ever', *The Spectator*, Vol. 285, No. 8990, 25th November 2000, p. 10.

—, 'Knickers to Kelvin', *The Spectator*, Vol. 288, No. 9067, 18th May 2002, pp. 25-26.

—, 'Nick Clegg's only true allegiance is to his belief in a federal Europe', *The Spectator*, Vol. 312, No. 9472, 13th March 2010, p. 15.

ANGLICAN COMMUNION, 'Member Churches of the Anglican Communion', Anglican Communion website, 2004, retrieved 7th February 2007, http://www.anglicancommunion.org/tour/index.cfm.

Anne APPLEBAUM, 'Stop blaming America for terrorism', *Telegraph*, 12th September 2006, retrieved 12th September 2006, http://tinyurl.com/6d4s5z.

Terry ARTHUR, 'Free Enterprise: Right or Left', *Governance*, No. 126, April 2004, pp. 10-12.

Wil ARTS & Loek HALMAN (eds.), *European Values at the Turn of the Millennium*, Leiden, Brill, 2004.

Michael ASHCROFT, *Smell the Coffee: A Wakeup Call for the Conservative Party*, London, Politico's, 2005.

Nick ASSINDER, 'Bringing God into politics', *BBC News*, 4th March 2006, retrieved 4th March 2006, http://news.bbc.co.uk/1/hi/uk_politics/4773852.stm.

ASSOCIATION OF PROFESSIONAL OPINION POLLING ORGANISATIONS, 'Polls Confound Sceptics', MORI website, 8th June 2001, retrieved 11th April 2002), www.mori.com/polls/2001/apopo.shtml.

Tim AUSTIN & Tim HAMES (eds.), *The Times Guide to the House of Commons, June 2001*, London, Times Books, 2001.

Penny BABB, *A Summary of Focus on Social Inequalities*, Office for National Statistics, London, 2005.

David BAKER, 'Britain and Europe: More Blood on the Euro-Carpet', *Parliamentary Affairs*, Vol. 55, No. 2, April 2002, pp. 317-330.

David BAKER & Imogen FOUNTAIN, 'Eton Gent or Essex Man? The Conservative Parliamentary Elite', 1996, in Steve LUDLUM & Martin SMITH (eds.), *Contemporary British Conservatism*, Basingstoke, Macmillan Press, 1996, pp. 86-97.

David BAKER, Andrew GAMBLE & Steve LUDLUM, '1846 ... 1906 ... 1996? Conservative Splits and European Integration', *The Political Quarterly*, Vol. 64, No. 4, 1993, pp. 420-434.

—, 'The Parliamentary Siege of Maastricht 1993: Conservative Divisions', *Parliamentary Affairs*, Vol. 47, 1994[a], pp. 37-58.

—, 'Mapping Conservative Fault Lines: Problems of Typology', *Contemporary Political Studies*, 1994[b], pp. 278-297.

David BAKER, Andrew GAMBLE, Nick RANDALL & David SEAWRIGHT, *British Conservative Scepticism towards European Union Re-examined*, Association Francaise de Science Politique, date unknown, retrieved 9th June 2002, http://www.afsp.msh-paris.fr/activite/cyberdte/textes/bakergamble.pdf.

David BAKER, Andrew GAMBLE & David SEAWRIGHT, *Mapping Changes in British Parliamentarians' Attitudes to European Integration*, (computer file No. 4001), Colchester, Essex, UK Data Archive, 1998.

David BAKER, Andrew GAMBLE & David SEAWRIGHT, 'Sovereign Nations and Global Markets: Modern British Conservatism and Hyperglobalism', *British Journal of Politics and International Relations*, Vol. 4, No. 3, October 2002, pp. 399-428.

David BAKER & Philippa SHERRINGTON, 'Britain and Europe: Europe and/or America?', *Parliamentary Affairs*, Vol. 57, No. 2, April 2004, pp. 347-365.

Tom BALDWIN, 'Hague warned over support for racist groups', *The Times*, 13th July 2000, p. 15.

—, 'Portillo quits Tory group over leak', *The Times*, 2nd November 2000, p. 1.

—, 'Calamity forces fractious party to sense of perspective', in *The Times*, 15th September 2001, pp. 14-15.

—, 'New Labour loses its shine as members depart in droves', *The Times*, 28th January 2002[a], p. 10.

—, 'Kennedy shifts to the right on tax cuts', *The Times*, 28th January 2002[b], p. 10.

—, 'Leadership pushes for more Tory women MPs', *The Times*, 9th April 2002, p. 12.

—, 'Clarke tackles Duncan Smith to kick off euro campaign', No Campaign, 15th May 2002, retrieved 29th April 2004, http://www.no-euro.com/mediacentre/dossiers/display.asp?IDNO=551.

—, 'Tories delay showdown on 'gold list' for minority candidates', *The Times*, 21st October 2002, p. 10.

—, 'How the Church may loosen its historic ties with the State', *The Times*, 3rd December 2002, p. 10.

Tom BALDWIN, Philip WEBSTER & Roland WATSON, ''Mods and Rockers' fight for power', The Times, 5th October 2000, p. 9.

Tim BALE, 'Between a soft and a hard place? The Conservative Party, Valence Politics, and the Need for a New "Eurorealism"', July 2006, *Parliamentary Affairs*, Vol. 59, No. 3, July 2006, pp. 385-400.

—, ''A Bit Less Bunny-Hugging and a Bit More Bunny Boiling'? Qualifying Conservative Party Change Under David Cameron', *British Politics*, Vol. 3, No. 3, September 2008, pp. 270-299.

Alan BALL, *Modern Politics and Government* (4th ed.), Basingstoke, Macmillan, 1988.

John BARNES, *Federal Britain: No Longer Unthinkable?*, Centre for Policy Studies, 1998, retrieved 25th August 2002, www.cps.org.uk/fedbrit.htm.

Steven BARNETT, 'Trust Survey for *The Political Quarterly*', *The Political Quarterly*, Vol. 79, No. 3, July-September 2008, pp. 321-323.

Robert BARON & Don BYRNE, *Social Psychology* (7th ed.), Boston, MA, Allyn & Bacon, 1994.

James BARTHOLOMEW, *The Welfare State We're In*, London, Politico's, 2004.

Stephen BATES, 'You tackle social problems, Hague tells churches', *Guardian*, 2nd November 2000, retrieved 20th May 2001, http://www.guardian.co.uk/guardianpolitics/story/0,,391275,00.html.

Gerard BATTEN, 'Batten in Brussels', *Freedom Today*, January/February 2005, p. 7

BBC NEWS, 'Conservative proposals for London', *BBC News*, 9th April 1998, retrieved 28th July 2008, http://news.bbc.co.uk/1/hi/special_report/1998/ london_referendum/75990.stm.

—, 'Vote 99', *BBC News*, May 1999, retrieved 11th April 2009, http://news.bbc.co.uk/hi/english/static/vote_99/during/index.stm.

—, 'Portillo begins comeback', *BBC News*, 9th September 1999, retrieved 30th April 2004, http://news.bbc.co.uk/1/hi/uk_politics/442422.stm.

—, 'Leak warns 'out of touch' Tories', *BBC News*, 8th August 2000, retrieved 16th March 2006, http://news.bbc.co.uk/1/hi/uk_politics/871060.stm.

—, 'UK Muslims condemn 'lunatic fringe'', *BBC News*, 20th September 2001, retrieved 9th September 2002, http://news.bbc.co.uk/2/hi/uk/1554177.stm.

—, 'Broadband access leaps ahead', *BBC News*, 19th March 2003, retrieved 5th March 2009, http://news.bbc.co.uk/1/hi/technology/2863939.stm.

—, 2004 local election results in Wales, *BBC News*, 15th June 2004, retrieved 5th March 2006, http://news.bbc.co.uk/1/hi/wales/north_east/3808087.stm.

—, 'Tory MSP in party breakaway call', *BBC News*, 22nd May 2005, retrieved 24th January 2009, http://news.bbc.co.uk/1/hi/scotland/4570921.stm.

—, 'Tories agree leader election plan', *BBC News*, 23rd May 2005, retrieved 23rd May 2005, http://news.bbc.co.uk/1/hi/uk_politics/4571907.stm.

—, 'Duncan Smith warns over changes', *BBC News*, 24th May 2005, retrieved 24th May 2005, http://news.bbc.co.uk/1/hi/uk_politics/4574685.stm.

—, 'Tory rule change bid is defeated', *BBC News*, 28th September 2005, retrieved 1st January 2006, http://news.bbc.co.uk/1/hi/uk_politics/4285182.stm.

—, 'Cameron chosen as new Tory leader', *BBC News*, 6th December 2005, retrieved 3rd March 2006, http://news.bbc.co.uk/1/hi/uk_politics/4502652.stm.

—, 'Blair feared faith 'nutter' label', *BBC News*, 25th November 2007, retrieved 25th November 2007, http://news.bbc.co.uk/1/hi/uk_politics/7111620.stm.

—, 'Private pupils grab top courses', *BBC News*, 27th November 2007, retrieved 5th June 2008, http://news.bbc.co.uk/1/hi/education/7113607.stm.

—, 'The John Bercow story', 24th June 2009, retrieved 1st February 2012, http://news.bbc.co.uk/1/hi/uk_politics/8114399.stm.

—, ''Most Tories' back UKIP over EU', *BBC News*, 6th September 2009, retrieved 21st April 2010, http://news.bbc.co.uk/1/hi/8240318.stm.

—, 'Judge hits out at postal voting', *BBC News*, 22nd March 2010, retrieved 6th May 2010, http://news.bbc.co.uk/1/hi/england/west_midlands/4373719.stm.

—, 'England council elections: Labour make gains', *BBC News*, 8th May 2010, retrieved 8th May 2010, http://news.bbc.co.uk/1/hi/uk_politics/election_2010/ 8663247.stm.

—, 'David Cameron's coalition government sets to work', *BBC News*, 12th May 2010, retrieved 12th May 2010, http://news.bbc.co.uk/1/hi/uk_politics/election_2010/ 8676607.stm.

—, 'Vote 2011: UK rejects alternative vote', *BBC News*, 7th May 2011, retrieved 13th February 2012, http://www.bbc.co.uk/news/uk-politics-13297573.

—, 'Political parties 'should get more taxpayer funding'', *BBC News*, 22nd November 2011, retrieved 28th March 2012, http://www.bbc.co.uk/news/uk-politics-15822333.

—, 'Tory treasurer Peter Cruddas donation row explained', *BBC News*, 26th March 2012, retrieved 28th March 2012, http://www.bbc.co.uk/news/uk-politics-17504261.

Frank BEALEY, *The Blackwell Dictionary of Political Science*, Oxford, Blackwell, 1999.

Rosemary BENNETT, 'Tory plan to bring women forward', *The Times*, 26th June 2003, p. 2.

—, 'Grassroots fight plan to deny them vote on leader', *The Times*, 9th May 2005.

Bruce BERG, Qualitative *Research Methods for the Social Sciences* (2nd ed.), Needham Heights, MA, Simon & Schuster, 1995.

David BERGLAND, *Libertarianism in One Lesson* (6th ed.), Costa Mesa, CA, Orpheus Publications, 1993.

Hugh BERRINGTON, 'After the Ball was Over ... The British General Election of 2001', *West European Politics*, Vol. 24, No. 4, October 2001, pp. 206-215.

Andrew BILLEN, 'I searched in vain for Tory Boy', *Evening Standard*, 5th April 2000, pp. 29-30.

Eben BLACK, 'Sex trials of the Labour women', *Sunday Times*, 3rd February 2002, p. 11.

Robert BLAKE, *The Conservative Party from Peel to Thatcher*, London, Fontana, 1985.

Michael BLASTLAND, 'What the survey didn't say...', *BBC News*, 5th August 2008, retrieved 26th August 2008, http://news.bbc.co.uk/1/hi/magazine/7542886.stm.

John BLUNDELL & Brian GOSSCHALK, *Beyond Left and Right: The New Politics of Britain*, London, Institute of Economic Affairs, 1997.

Norberto BOBBIO, *Left and Right: The Significance of a Political Distinction* (trans. 2nd ed.), Cambridge, Polity Press, 1996.

Christopher BOOKER, 'Talking rubbish', *EU Referendum*, 3rd September 2006, retrieved 4th October 2006, http://eureferendum2.blogspot.com/2006/10/talking-rubbish.html.

Judith BOSER, 'Variations in Mail Survey Procedures: Comparison of Response Rates and Cost', paper presented at the Annual Meeting of the American Educational Research Association, Boston, MA, April 1990, retrieved 5th May 2009, http://www.eric.ed.gov/ERICWebPortal/contentdelivery/servlet/ERICServlet? accno=ED319803.

Roger BOYES, 'Gunman kills right-wing leader', *The Times*, 7th May 2002, p. 1.

—, 'Poland's Catholic shun membership of 'Godless' EU', *The Times*, 6th June 2003, p. 21.

Joseph BRADLEY, 'Some Aspects of Orangeism in Contemporary Scotland: Religion and Politics', *Contemporary Political Studies*, 1996, pp. 1750-1758.

Alan BRINKLEY, 'Clear and Present Dangers', *New York Times*, 19th March 2006, retrieved 15th November 2008, http://tinyurl.com/5fyqhj.

BRITISH ELECTION PANEL STUDY 2001, dataset supplied by Professor Richard Topf, London Metropolitan University. See also information on the corresponding dataset SN 4620 lodged at the UK Data Archive, 4th December 2006, retrieved 23rd September 2008, http://www.data-archive.ac.uk/findingData/snDescription.asp? sn=4620#doc.

BRITISH SOCIAL ATTITUDES INFORMATION SYSTEM, analyse variable for *BSA* 2004 'HONELEC', 2009, retrieved 5th January 2009, http://www.britsocat.com/ BodySecure.aspx?control=BritsocatMarginals&var=HONELEC&surveyid=336.

BRITISH SOCIAL ATTITUDES SURVEY 1995, dataset supplied by Professor Richard Topf, London Metropolitan University. See also information on the corresponding dataset SN 3764 lodged at the UK Data Archive, 29th October 2008, retrieved 15th February 2009, http://www.data-archive.ac.uk/findingdata/snDescription.asp? sn=3764&key=BRITISH+social+attitudes+1995.

BRITISH SOCIAL ATTITUDES SURVEY 2001, dataset supplied by Professor Richard Topf, London Metropolitan University. See also information on the corresponding dataset SN 4615 lodged at the UK Data Archive, 29th October 2008, retrieved 2nd March 2009, http://www.data-archive.ac.uk/findingdata/snDescription.asp?sn=4615& key=BRITISH+social+attitudes+2001.

BRITISH SOCIAL ATTITUDES 2003, dataset supplied by Professor Richard Topf, London Metropolitan University, September 2008. See also information on the corresponding dataset

SN 5235 lodged with the UK Data Archive, 18th April 2008, retrieved 23rd September 2008, http://www.data-archive.ac.uk/findingData/ snDescription.asp?sn=5235.

Samuel BRITTAN, *Left or Right: The Bogus Dilemma*, London, Secker & Warburg, 1968.

—, *Capitalism and the Permissive Society* (altered ed.), London, Macmillan, 1976.

—, 'Humanitarianism without illusions', *Samuel Brittan*, 27th September 2002, retrieved 17th October 2002, www.samuelbrittan.co.uk/text124_p.html.

Brian BRIVATI & Lewis BASTON, 'It's not like it was, Ma'am. Nowadays it's a game played by professionals', *Parliamentary Brief*, Vol. 8, No. 5, June 2002, pp. 7-9.

Benedict BROGAN, 'It's Howard unopposed as Clarke stands aside', *Telegraph*, 1st November 2003, retrieved 17th August 2009, http://www.telegraph.co.uk/news/ uknews/1445653/Its-Howard-unopposed-as-Clarke-stands-aside.html.

David BROUGHTON, 'The 2001 General Election: So, No Change There Then?', 2003, in Mark GARNETT & Philip LYNCH (eds.), *The Conservatives in Crisis*, Manchester, Manchester University Press, 2003, pp. 198-216.

—, 'Doomed to Defeat? Electoral Support and the Conservative Party', *The Political Quarterly*, Vol. 75, No. 4, October 2004, pp. 350-355.

Michaelle BROWERS, 'The secular bias in ideology studies and the case of Islamism', *Journal of Political Ideologies*, Vo. 10, No. 1, February 2005, pp. 75-93.

David BROWN, 'Tories to bring a taste of the country to party conference', *Telegraph*, 11th September 2000, retrieved 20th May 2001, http://www.telegraph.co.uk/ news/main.jhtml?xml=/news/2000/09/11/nfair11.xml.

Derek BROWN, 'Davies warns of 'last chance'', *Guardian*, 11th September 1997, retrieved 28th July 2008, http://www.guardian.co.uk/politics/1997/sep/11/ wales.devolution.

Michael BROWN, 'Eric Forth' [obituary], *Independent*, 20th May 2006, retrieved 10th January 2009, http://www.independent.co.uk/news/obituaries/eric-forth-478940.html.

Anthony BROWNE, 'Europe's new far Right', *The Times*, T2, 1st January 2003, p. 19.

—, 'How one man fell foul of bigger forces', *The Times*, 28th October 2004, p. 11.

—, 'Conservatives may split Scottish arm into separate party', *The Times*, 5th April 2007, retrieved 1st March 2009, http://www.timesonline.co.uk/tol/news/ politics/article1615771.ece.

Alan BRYMAN, *Social Research Methods*, Oxford, Oxford University Press, 2001.

—, *Social Research Methods* (3rd ed.), Oxford, Oxford University Press, 2008.

Alan BRYMAN & Duncan CRAMER, *Quantitative Data Analysis with SPSS Release 8 for Windows*, London, Routledge, 1999.

Emily BUCHANAN, 'Black church celebrates growth', *BBC News*, 6th July 2000, retrieved 16th November 2008, http://news.bbc.co.uk/1/hi/uk/822200.stm.

Jim BULLER, 'Foreign Policy and Defence Under Thatcher and Major', 1996, in Steve LUDLUM and Martin SMITH (eds.), *Contemporary British Conservatism*, Basingstoke, Macmillan Press, 1996, pp. 222-243.

Angela BURDETT-CONWAY & Philip TETHER, 'Conservative Conflict and European Integration', *Renewal*, Vol. 5, No. 3/4, Autumn 1997, pp. 89-99.

John BURNS & Alan COWELL, 'British Parties Jockey to Form Governing Alliance', *New York Times*, 7th May 2010, retrieved 8th May 2010, http://tinyurl.com/25t7nrj.

David BUTLER, 'Labour needs a drop in the opinion polls', *Daily Mail*, 6th May 2000, p. 7.

David BUTLER & Dennis KAVANAGH, 'Conservatives', 2002[a], in David BUTLER & Dennis KAVANAGH (eds.), *The British General Election of 2001*, Basingstoke, Hampshire, Palgrave, 2002, pp. 37-93.

—, 'The National Campaign', 2002[b], in David BUTLER & Dennis KAVANAGH (eds.), *The British General Election of 2001*, Basingstoke, Hampshire, Palgrave, 2002, pp. 91-120.

Vincent CABLE, *The World's New Fissures*, London, Demos, 1994.

CAMPAIGN FOR AN INDEPENDENT BRITAIN, 'Key Questions & Answers about Britain and the European Union', CIB website, 13th June 2008, retrieved 27th February 2009, http://www.eurofaq.freeuk.com/eurofaq/.

Rosie CAMPBELL, 'Ideology and Issue Preference: Is There Such a Thing as a Political Women's Interest in Britain?', *British Journal of Politics & International Relations*, Vol. 6, No. 1, February 2004, pp. 20-44.

Brian CAPLAN, 'Libertarian Purity Test', *Bryan Caplan*, circa 1997, retrieved 3rd January 2004, http://www.bcaplan.com/cgi/purity.cgi.

David CARR, 'Conservatives up the creek', *Samizdata*, 11th October 2002, retrieved 13th October 2002, www.samizdata.net/blog/archives/002202.html#002202.

—, 'Ignore no more', *Samizdata*, 23rd November 2002, retrieved 24th November 2002, http://www.samizdata.net/blog/archives/002527.html#002527.

Douglas CARSWELL, 'The triumph of the mandarinate', Douglas Carswell's blog, 15th March 2012, retrieved 11th April 2012, http://www.talkcarswell.com/ disqus.aspx?id=2293.

Bill CASH, 'No stability, no growth, no pact. It is time to confront the Euro disaster zone', *The Times*, 5th January 2005, p. 18.

Sue CATLING, 'Reform needed for victory' [letters to the editor], *Telegraph*, 8th March 2002, retrieved 4th August 2009, http://tinyurl.com/n4ev5x.

Peter CATTERALL, 'The Party and Religion', 1994, in Anthony SELDON & Stuart BALL (eds.), *Conservative Century: The Conservative Party since 1900*, Oxford, Oxford University Press, 1994, pp. 637-670.

Karen CELIS & Sarah Childs, 'The Substantive Representation of Women: What to Do with Conservative Claims?', *Political Studies*, Vol. 60, No. 1, March 2012, pp. 213-225.

Gerard CHARMLEY, 'The House of Dynevor and Conservative Politics 1910-38', *Conservative History Journal*, Winter 2009/2010, pp. 29-32.

David CHARTER, 'Tories recoil from 'nasty' plot to oust Lord Tebbit', *The Times*, 12th October 2002, p. 9.

CHESHIRE COUNTY COUNCIL, 'Cheshire Parish & Town Councils', Cheshire County Council website, 1999, retrieved 19th July 2000, http://www.cheshire.gov.uk/ parish/home.htm.

Sarah CHILDS & Julie WITHEY, 'Women Representatives Acting for Women: Sex and the Signing of Early Day Motions in the 1997 British Parliament', *Political Studies*, Vol. 52, 2004, pp. 552-564.

CHURCH OF ENGLAND, ARCHBISHOPS' COUNCIL OF THE, 'The History of the Church of England', Church of England website, 2004, retrieved 7th February 2006, http://www.cofe.anglican.org/about/history.

CHURCH OF SCOTLAND, 'History', Church of Scotland website, c. 2006[a], retrieved 7th February 2006, http://www.churchofscotland.org.uk/organisation/ orghistory.htm.

—, 'Queen, State and Kirk, Church of Scotland website, c. 2006[b], retrieved 7th February 2006, http://www.churchofscotland.org.uk/organisation/orgqueen.htm.

CITIZENS ONLINE, 'Digital Divide is not old news!', Citizens Online website, 26th July 2007, retrieved 7th August 2008, http://www.citizensonline.org.uk/conline/news/display?contentId=4686.

Jonathan CLARK, 'Why we shouldn't say sorry for being English', *The Times*, 22nd August 2000, p. 18.

Alistair CLARKE, 'The Location of Power in Scotland's Post-Devolution Political Parties: An Exploratory Analysis', paper for Political Studies Association Annual Conference April 2002, retrieved 24th January 2009, http://www.psa.ac.uk/journals/ pdf/5/2002/clark.pdf.

Antoine CLARKE, *The Independent Libertarian Party: An Idea Whose Time Has Come (Being Among Other Things, A Reply to Nigel Meek)*, London, Libertarian Alliance, 1999.

Charles CLARKE, 'Foreword by the Secretary of State for Education and Skills', *The Future of Higher Education*, Department for Education and Skills, 22nd January 2003, retrieved 26th March 2006, http://www.dfes.gov.uk/hegateway/strategy/hestrategy/ foreword.shtml.

Greg CLARKE & Scott KELLY, 'Echoes of Butler? The Conservative Research Department and the Making of Conservative Policy', October 2004, *The Political Quarterly*, Vol. 75, No. 4, October 2004, pp. 378-382.

Frederick CLARKSON, 'Theocratic Dominionism Gains Influence. Part 1: Overview and Roots', *The Public Eye Magazine*, Vol. VIII, Nos. 1 & 2, March/June 1994, retrieved 23rd October 2004, www.publiceye.org/magazine/chrisre1.html.

Frances CLEGG, *Simple Statistics*, Cambridge, Cambridge University Press, 1982.

Alan COCHRANE, 'Sectarianism in Labour's rotten burghs', *Telegraph*, 29th August 2006, retrieved 29th August 2006, http://tinyurl.com/2f3bhx.

Nick COHEN, 'Galloway and Livingstone: twins in so many ways', *Observer*, 1st April 2012, retrieved 1st April 2012, http://tinyurl.com/cac84fd.

Peter COLE, *Philosophy of Religion* (2nd ed.), London, Hodder & Stoughton, 2004.

COLOMBO PLAN, 2005, retrieved 22nd April 2010, http://www.colombo-plan.org.

COMMUNICATE RESEARCH, 'Religious Faith Survey', 2006, retrieved 14th September 2007, http://www.communicateresearch.com/poll.php?id=89.

Tim CONGDON, 'Tories can't buck the market' [letters to the editor], *The Spectator*, Vol. 285, No. 8979, 9th September 2000, p. 28.

CONSERVATIVE CHRISTIAN FELLOWSHIP, 'Listening to Britain's Churches Continues Under Conservative Party's New Catholic Leader', CCF website, 18th September 2001, retrieved 17th January 2002, http://ourworld.compuserve.com/homepages/CCFHUB/IDS_LTBC.HTM.

CONSERVATIVE HOME, 'Menzies thinks *we* are "still unpleasant"', *Conservative Home*, 14th April 2006, retrieved 2nd May 2010, http://tinyurl.com/25fohdk.

CONSERVATIVE PARTY, *The Next Five Years* [1959 General Election manifesto], 1959, Richard Kimber's Political Science Resources, retrieved 22nd April 2010, http://www.politicsresources.net/area/uk/man/con59.htm.

—, *The Fresh Future*, London, Conservative Central Office, 1998.

—, *An Introduction to the Conservative Party*, London, Conservative Party, 2001[a].

—, *Time for Common Sense* [2001 General Election manifesto], London, Conservative Party, 2001[b].

—, 'Leadership Result', Conservative Party website, September 2001, retrieved 1st December 2001, http://www.conservatives.com/leadership.cfm.

—, 'Letwin urges more legal rights for same-sex couples', Conservative Party website, 25th January 2002, retrieved 26th January 2002, http://www.conservatives.com/show_news_item.cfm?obj_id=23480&PS=1.

—, *Are You Thinking What We're Thinking?* [2005 General Election manifesto], London, Conservative Party, 2005.

—, 'Open primary and-all-postal ballot to be held in Totnes', Conservative Party website, 10th July 2009, retrieved 7th August 2009, http://tinyurl.com/m664et.

CONSERVATIVES IN NORTHERN IRELAND, 'A Matter of Governance', Conservatives NI website, c. 2002, retrieved 1st May 2002, http://www.conservativesni.com/html/government.html.

—, 'A Matter of Governance', Conservatives NI website, 26th February 2009, retrieved 27th February 2009, http://conservativesni.net/2009/02/26/now-for-change/.

CONSERVATIVE WOMEN'S ORGANISATION, 'Conservative Women and Parliament', Conservative Women's Organisation website, 2012, retrieved 11th February 2012, http://www.conservativewomen.org.uk/women_parliament.asp.

Jean CONVERSE & Stanley PRESSER, *Survey Questions: Handcrafting the Standardized Questionnaire*, Beverly Hills, CA, Sage Publications, 1986.

Chris COOK, 'Christian Tories rewrite party doctrine', *Financial Times*, 12th February 2010, retrieved 4th March 2010, http://www.ft.com/cms/s/2/12400596-16ac-11df-aa09-00144feab49a.html.

Andrew COOPER, 'A Party in a Foreign Land', 2001, in Edward VAIZEY, Nicholas BOLES & Michael GOVE (eds.), *A Blue Tomorrow: New Visions for Modern Conservatives*, London, Politico's Publishing, 2001, pp. 9-29.

James COOPER, 'The Scottish Problem: English Conservatives and the Union with Scotland in the Thatcher and Major Eras', *Contemporary Political Studies*, 1995, pp. 1384-1393.

Colin COPUS, 'Councillors' Attitudes Towards Citizen Participation, Protest, and Pressure: The Civic Culture and the Modernising Agenda', paper for the Political Studies Association Annual Conference, April 2000, retrieved 3rd January 2009, http://www.psa.ac.uk/journals/pdf/5/2000/Copus%20Colin.pdf.

CORNERSTONE GROUP, 'Who we are', Cornerstone Group website, 2009, retrieved 1st March 2009, http://cornerstonegroup.wordpress.com/about/.

Dan COSSINS, 'When were the terms 'leftwing' and 'rightwing' first used politically, and by whom?', *BBC History Magazine*, Vol. 13, No. 5, May 2012, p. 94.

Martha COTTAM, Beth DIETZ-UHLER, Elena MASTORS & Thomas PRESTON, *Introduction to Political Psychology* (2nd ed.), Hove, East Sussex, Psychology Press, 2010.

Colin COULTER, 'The Origins of the Northern Ireland Conservatives', *Irish Political Studies*, 2001, Vol. 16, pp. 29-48.

Philip COWLEY & JOHN GARRY, 'The British Conservative Party and Europe: The Choosing of John Major', *British Journal of Political Science*, Vol. 28, No. 3, 1998, pp. 473-499.

Philip COWLEY & David MELHUISH, 'Peers' Careers: Ministers in the House of Lords, 1964-1995', *Political Studies*, Vol. 45, No. 1, March 1997, pp. 21-35.

Philip COWLEY & Philip NORTON, 'Rebels and Rebellions: Conservative MPs in the 1992 Parliament', *British Journal of Politics and International Relations*, Vol. 1, No. 1, 1999, pp. 84-105.

Philip COWLEY & Mark STUART, 'The Conservative Parliamentary Party', 2003, in Mark Garnett & Philip Lynch (eds.), *The Conservatives in Crisis*, Manchester, Manchester University Press, 2003, pp. 66-81.

—, 'Mapping Conservative Divisions Under Michael Howard', *Revolts*, 2004, retrieved 1st January 2005, www.revolts.co.uk/Conservative%20splits.pdf.

—, 'Still Causing Trouble: The Conservative Parliamentary Party', *The Political Quarterly*, Vol. 75, No. 4, October 2004, pp. 356-361.

—, 'Conservative Backbench Dissent Under Iain Duncan Smith', *Conservative History Journal*, No. 4, Winter 2004/2005, pp. 25-28.

David CRACKNELL, 'Poll shows Europe is the main issue for Conservatives', *Telegraph*, 26th August 2001, retrieved 4th August 2009, http://tinyurl.com/lxttl9.

—, 'Tory candidates to reflect racial mix of constituencies, *Sunday Times*, 3rd February 2002, p. 11.

Richard CRACKNELL, *Social background of MPs*, Standard Note 1528, Houses of Parliament website, 17th November 2005, retrieved 11th May 2009, www.parliament.uk/commons/lib/research/notes/snsg-01528.pdf.

Auslan CRAMB, 'Young Tories host a 14-pint pub crawl', *Telegraph*, 15th September 2000, retrieved 10th February 2012, http://tinyurl.com/89cmjv7.

Nick CRAVEN, 'The muddled mind of a treacherous Mr Nobody', *Daily Mail*, 17th January 2005, p. 11.

Ivor CREWE & Bo SÄRLVIK, 'Popular Attitudes and Electoral Strategy', 1980, in Zig LAYTON-HENRY (ed.), *Conservative Party Politics*, London, Macmillan Press, 1980, pp. 244-275.

Ivor CREWE & Donald SEARING, 'Ideological Change in the British Conservative Party', *American Political Science Review*, Vol. 82, No. 2, June 1988, pp. 361-384.

Byron CRIDDLE, 'MPs and Candidates', 2002, in David BUTLER & Dennis KAVANAGH (eds.), *The British General Election of 2001*, Basingstoke, Hampshire, Palgrave, 2002, pp. 182-207.

Richard CRISP, 'Social Categorisation: Blurring the Boundaries', *The Psychologist*, Vol. 15, No. 12, 2002, pp. 612-615.

Mark CROUCHER, 'State funding for our political parties' [letters to the editor], *The Times*, 8th June 2002, p. 27.

Patrick CROZIER, *The Pamphlet is Dead: Long Live the Web Page*, Tactical Notes No. 27, London, Libertarian Alliance, 2000.

John CURTICE & Anthony HEATH, 'Is the English lion about to roar?', 2000, in Roger JOWELL, John CURTICE, Alison PARK, Katarina THOMSON, Lindsey JARVIS, Catherine BROMLEY & Nina STRATFORD (eds.), *British Social Attitudes*, The 17th Report: Focusing on Diversity, London, SAGE Publications, 2000, pp. 155-174.

John CURTICE & Ben SEYD, 'Is devolution strengthening or weakening the UK?', 2001, in Alison PARK, John CURTICE, Katarina THOMSON, Lindsey JARVIS & Catherine BROMLEY (eds.), *British Social Attitudes, The 18th Report: Public Policy, Social Ties*, London, SAGE Publications, 2001, pp. 227-244.

John CURTICE, Ben SEYD, Alison PARK & Katarina THOMSON, 'Wise after the Event? Attitudes to Voting Reform Following the 1999 Scottish and Welsh Elections', *Contemporary Political Studies*, proceedings of the 2000 PSA Annual Conference held at the University of London, 2000, retrieved 22nd August 2008, http://www.psa.ac.uk/journals/pdf/5/2000/Curtice%20John%20et%20al.pdf.

DAILY MAIL, 'Time to end the insanity' [editorial], *Daily Mail*, 22nd August 2001, pp. 1 & 10.

DAILY MAIL, 'An almost crazy pleasure in offending the mainstream', *Daily Mail*, 19th May 2006, retrieved 15th May 2012, http://tinyurl.com/7m2thsd.

Iain DALE & Guido FAWKES (eds.), *The Little Red Book of New Labour Sleaze*, Tunbridge Wells, Politico's Media, 2006.

Matthew D'ANCONA, 'The Conservative Party has become a serial killer', *Telegraph*, 3rd November 2002, retrieved 10th February 2012, http://tinyurl.com/73mc2s2.

James DANZIGER, *Understanding the Political World: A Comparative Introduction to Political Science* (4th ed.), New York, Longman, 1998.

Rupert DARWALL, *Paralysis or Power? The Centre Right in the 21st Century*, London, Centre for Policy Studies, 2002.

Brian DAVIES, *An Introduction to the Philosophy of Religion* (3rd ed.), Oxford, Oxford University Press, 2004.

Jon DAVIES, 'The Future Doesn't Last Long: How the decline of mass membership parties has made Tony Blair and David Cameron possible - and why it means that both their appeal is transient', Social Affairs Unit blog, 6th January 2006, retrieved 11th April 2009, http://www.socialaffairsunit.org.uk/blog/archives/000716.php.

Douglas DAVIS, 'Why I won't talk to the BBC', *The Spectator*, Vol. 288, No. 9068, 25th May 2002, pp. 22-23.

J. DEANS, 'Trimble to battle on after his poll debacle', *Daily Mail*, 23rd September 2000, p. 2.

Harry DEFRIES, *Conservative Party Attitudes to Jews, 1900-1950*, London, Frank Cass, 2001.

Nan Dirk DE GRAFF & Ariana NEED, 'Losing Faith: Is Britain Alone?', 2000, in Roger JOWELL, John CURTICE, Alison PARK, Katarina THOMSON, Lindsey JARVIS, Catherine BROMLEY & Nina STRATFORD (eds.), *British Social Attitudes, The 17th Report: Focusing on Diversity*, London, Sage Publications, 2000, pp. 119-136.

Perry DE HAVILLAND, 'More musings on the Political Compass', *Samizdata*, 21st May 2003, retrieved 8th November 2003, http://www.samizdata.net/blog/ archives/003522.html.

James DELINGPOLE, 'Liberals are the true heirs of the Nazi spirit', *The Spectator*, Vol. 309, No. 9418, 28th February 2009, pp. 18-19.

Corinne DELOY, 'Referendum on the European Union in Poland: a round up just a few days before the election', *European Elections Monitor*, 6th June 2003, retrieved 21st September 2003, www.robert-schuman.org/anglais/oee/pologne/referendum/ default2.htm.

Andrew DENHAM & Kieron O'HARA, 'The Three 'Mantras': 'Modernization' and The Conservative Party', *British Politics*, Vol. 2, No. 2, July 2007, pp. 167-190.

Mike DENHAM, 'Freedom for the South-east!', *The Spectator*, Vol. 290, No. 9094, 23rd November 2002, p. 31.

David DENVER, Gordon HANDS & Iain MACALLISTER, 'The Electoral Impact of Constituency Campaigning in Britain, 1992-2001', *Political Studies*, Vol. 52, No. 2, June 2004, pp. 289-306.

David DENVER, James MITCHELL, Jonathan BRADBURY & Lynn BENNIE, *Major Party Candidates in the Scottish Parliament and Welsh Assembly Elections*, (computer file No. 4058), Colchester, Essex, UK Data Archive, 1999[a].

David DENVER, James MITCHELL, Jonathan BRADBURY & Lynn BENNIE, *Major Party Council Candidates in the Scottish Parliament and Welsh Assembly Elections*, (computer file No. 4057), Colchester, Essex, UK Data Archive, SN 4057, 1999[b].

Jan van DETH, 'Introduction: The Impact of Values', 1995, in Jan van DETH & Elinor SCARBROUGH (eds.), *The Impact of Values*, Oxford, Oxford University Press, 1995/1998, pp. 1-18.

David DE VAUS, *Surveys in Social Research* (4th ed.), London, UCL Press, 1996.

Don DILLMAN, *Mail and Telephone Surveys: The Total Design Method*, New York, John Wiley & Sons, 1978.

Lawrence DONEGAN, 'Who will speak for those who say 'No'?', *Guardian*, 19th June 1997, retrieved 28th July 2008, http://www.guardian.co.uk/politics/1997/jun/19/constitution.comment.

Peter DOREY, 'Conservative Policy Under Hague', 2003, in Mark Garnett & Philip Lynch (eds.), *The Conservatives in Crisis*, Manchester, Manchester University Press, 2003, pp. 125-145.

Stephen DORRELL, Can the Conservative Party be a Liberal Party?', *Connect*, 13th March 2002, retrieved 15th March 2002, http://www.connectweb.org/news/07.html.

Jon DOUGHERTY, 'Muslim leaders pledge to 'transform West'', *World Net Daily*, 13th August 2002, retrieved 13th August 2002, www.worldnetdaily.com/news/article.asp?ARTICLE_ID=28589.

Steve DOUGHTY, 'Yes, we still want the monarchy', *Daily Mail*, 14th April 2001, pp. 1 & 4.

Lizanne DOWDS & Ken YOUNG, 'National Identity', 1996, in Roger JOWELL, John CURTICE, Alison PARK, Lindsay BROOK & Katarina THOMSON, K. (eds.), *British Social Attitudes: The 13th Report*, Aldershot, Social & Community Planning Research, 1996, pp. 141-160.

Iain DUNCAN SMITH, 'Wales key to future election success', *Blue Dragon*, no. 1, Winter 2001, p. 1.

—, 'Trust the people: that's the Tory message', *Daily Telegraph*, 13th January 2002, retrieved 10th February 2012, http://tinyurl.com/7dubekd.

—, 'Saddam is a threat to Britain we cannot ignore', *Sunday Times*, 1st September 2002, p. 17.

—, 'Restore balance to the Northern Ireland process', speech to the 2002 Ulster Unionist Conference, Conservative Party website, 19th October 2002, retrieved 24th October 2002, www.conservatives.com/news/article.cfm?obj_id=42394&speeches=1.

—, 'Why I'm backing Bush', *The Spectator*, Vol. 296, No. 9189, 18th September 2004, pp. 14-15.

—, 'The Tory grassroots are more in touch with the real world', *Telegraph*, 24th May 2005, retrieved 10th February 2012, http://tinyurl.com/882g6pb.

Bobby DUFFY, 'Response Order Effects: How Do people Read', *Research in Focus: The Newsletter of the MORI Research Methods Unit*, 2004, p. 6.

Patrick DUNLEAVY, 'The Political Parties', 1993, in Patrick DUNLEAVY, Andrew GAMBLE, Ian HOLLIDAY & Gillian PEELE (eds.), *Developments in British Politics 4*, Basingstoke, Macmillan Press, 1993, pp. 123-153.

Martin DURHAM, 'The Thatcher Government and the 'Moral Right'', *Parliamentary Affairs*, Vol. 43, 1989, pp. 58-71.

Kumal DUTTA, 'Humility is deeply important, says Blair as he 'does God'', *i*, 15th May 2012: 7.

Michael DYER, 'The Evolution of the Centre-Right and the State of Scottish Conservatism', *Political Studies*, Vol. 49, No. 1, March 2001, pp. 3-50.

Joe DYKE & Tim BALE, 'Interview with Tim Bale', *Total Politics*, 28th January 2010, retrieved 26th April 2010, http://tinyurl.com/yeyae3m.

Paul EASTHAM, 'Prejudice cost Portillo leadership, says Clarke, *Daily Mail*, 7th January 2002, p. 8.

ECONOMIC & SOCIAL DATA SERVICE, 'About the Economic and Social Data Service', ESDS website, 19th June 2006, retrieved 2nd February 2012, http://www.esds.ac.uk/about/about.asp.

Keith EDKINS, 'Local Authority By-election Results', 2005, last consulted 30th January 2005, http://www.gwydir.demon.co.uk/byelections/index.htm.

ELECTORAL REFORM SOCIETY, 'Alternative Voting Methods: Postal Voting', August 2007, retrieved 24th April 2009, http://www.electoral-reform.org.uk/article.php?id=44.

Francis ELLIOTT, 'Greenhorns with no green credentials: Tory wannabes push party to the right', *The Times*, 29th April 2009, pp. 20-21.

Francis ELLIOTT & Sam COATES, 'How David Cameron's conference stage has become a women-free zone', *The Times*, 28th April 2009, pp. 16-17.

EMPLOYERS' ORGANISATION FOR LOCAL GOVERNMENT, *National Census of Local Authority Councillors in England and Wales 2001: Results by Party Representation*, circa 2001, retrieved 27th February 2005, http:/www.lg-employers.gov.uk/documents/diversity/councillors/party01.pdf.

—, *Survey of Newly Elected Local Authority Councillors 2003: Newly Elected Results 2003*, circa 2003, retrieved 27th February 2005, http:/www.lg-employers.gov.uk/documents/diversity/councillors/newelected_res03.pdf.

Matthew ENGEL, 'The strange, slow death of the Tories', *Guardian*, 2nd January 2001, retrieved 30th April 2001, http://www.guardian.co.uk/Columnists/Column/0,,416854,00.html.

EPPING FOREST CONSERVATIVES, 'Epping Forest Conservative Future', Epping Forest Conservatives website, 7th March 2006, retrieved 12th January 2009, http://tinyurl.com/8zthma.

EUROPEAN DEMOCRATS, 'Member parties, European Democrats website, c. 2007, retrieved 12th December 2007, www.epp-ed.eu/europeandemocrats/ed-memberparties.asp.

EUROPEAN SOCIAL SURVEY, 'Chapter 1: European Social Survey Core Questionnaire Development', *European Social Survey* website, 2007[a], retrieved 13th April 2010, http://tinyurl.com/y8tpvtk.

—, 'Chapter 2: How to ascertain the socio-structural position of the individual in the society', *European Social Survey* website, 2007[b], retrieved 13th April 2010, http://tinyurl.com/yc6yfft.

—, 'Chapter 4: Media and communications questions', *European Social Survey* website, 2007[c], retrieved 13th April 2010, http://tinyurl.com/ybuw76o.

—, 'Chapter 5: Opinions about political issues', *European Social Survey* website, 2007[d], retrieved 13th April 2010, http://tinyurl.com/y4y6uu7.

—, 'Chapter Chapter 6: The measurement of socio-political orientations', *European Social Survey* website, 2007[e], retrieved 13th April 2010, http://tinyurl.com/ybk6522.

—, 'Chapter 7: A proposal for measuring value orientations across nations', *European Social Survey* website, 2007[f], retrieved 13th April 2010, http://tinyurl.com/y8wad4b.

—, 'Chapter 8: Shifts in governance', *European Social Survey* website, 2007[g], retrieved 13th April 2010, http://tinyurl.com/yyc34us.

—, 'Chapter 9: Proposal for questions on religious identity', *European Social Survey* website, 2007[h], retrieved 13th April 2010, http://tinyurl.com/y5bkd9k.

—, 'Chapter 10: Questions about national, subnational and ethnic identity', *European Social Survey* website, 2007[i], retrieved 13th April 2010, http://tinyurl.com/yyl7yks.

—, 'Improving response', *European Social Survey* website, 2007[j], retrieved 13th April 2010, http://tinyurl.com/yydjcq7.

—, 'Funding', *European Social Survey* website, 2007[k], retrieved 13th April 2010, http://tinyurl.com/yyfqawq.

Geoffrey EVANS, 'Euroscepticism and Conservative Electoral Support: How an Asset Became a Liability', *British Journal of Political Science*, Vol. 28, 1998, pp. 573-590.

—, 'The Conservatives and Europe: Waving or drowning?', 2001, in Alison PARK, John CURTICE, Katarina THOMSON, Lindsey JARVIS & Catherine BROMLEY (eds.), *British Social Attitudes, The 18th Report: Public Policy, Social Ties*, London, SAGE Publications, 2001, pp. 245-262.

—, 'In search of tolerance', 2002, in Alison PARK, John CURTICE, Katarina THOMSON, Lindsey JARVIS & Catherine BROMLEY (eds.), *British Social Attitudes, The 19th Report*, London, SAGE Publications, 2002, pp. 213-230.

Geoffrey EVANS, John CURTICE & Pippa NORRIS, 'New Labour, New Tactical Voting? The Causes and Consequences of Tactical Voting in the 1997 General Election', 1998, in David DENVER, Justin FISHER, Philip COWLEY & Charles PATTIE (eds.), *British Elections and Parties Review*, Vol. 8, London, Frank Cass, 1998, pp. 65-79.

Geoffrey EVANS & Anthony HEATH, 'The Measurement of Left-Right and Libertarian-Authoritarian Values: A Comparison of Balanced and Unbalanced Scales', *Quality & Quantity*, No. 29, 1995, pp. 191-206.

Geoff EVANS, Anthony HEATH & Mansur LALLJEE, 'Measuring Left-Right and Libertarian-Authoritarian Values in the British Electorate', *British Journal of Sociology*, Vol. 47, No. 1, 1996, pp. 93-112.

Jonathan EVANS, *The Future of Welsh Conservatism*, Cardiff, Welsh Academic Press, 2002.

Timothy EVANS, *Conservative Radicalism: A Sociology of Conservative Party Youth Structures and Libertarianism 1970-1992*, Oxford, Berghahn Books, 1996.

—, 'Conservative Economics and Globalisation', *The Political Quarterly*, Vol. 75, No. 4, October 2004, pp. 383-385.

EVENING STANDARD, 'Glib phrasemaking', *Evening Standard*, 12th June 2002, p. 11.

Hans EYSENCK, *The Psychology of Politics*, London, Routledge, 1954.

David FARRELL, Ian MCALLISTER & Donley STUDLAR, 'Sex, Money, and Politics: Sleaze and the Conservative Party in the 1997 Election', in David DENVER, Justin FISHER, Philip COWLEY & Charles PATTIE (eds.), *British Elections and Parties Review*, Vol. 8, London, Frank Cass, 1998, pp. 80-94.

David FARRER, 'Will this smash or save the Union?', *Freedom and Whisky* blog, 2nd November 2007, retrieved 15th September 2008, http://tinyurl.com/65uvjm.

Ron FENNEY, *Essential Local Government 2000* (9th ed.), London, LGC Information, 2000.

Samuel Edward FINER, Hugh BERRINGTON & David BARTHOLOMEW, *Backbench Opinion in the House of Commons 1955-1959*, Oxford, Pergamon Press, 1961.

Justin FISHER, 'Money Matters: The Financing of the Conservative Party', *The Political Quarterly*, Vol. 75, No. 4, October 2004, pp. 405-410.

Justin FISHER & David DENVER, 'From foot-slogging to call centres and direct mail: A framework for analysing the development of district-level campaigning', *European Journal of Political Research*, Vol. 47, No. 6, October 2008, pp. 794-826.

Sheila FLETCHER, *Maude Royden: A Life*, Oxford, Blackwell, 1989.

Richard FORD, 'Number of crimes falls 7% in a year, but police admit public doesn't trust figures', *The Times*, 23rd April 2010, p. 17.

Ronald FORREST, 'Conservative leadership turmoil tests grassroots support' [letters to the editor], *The Times*, 31st October 2003, p. 31.

Duncan FORRESTER, *Theology and Politics*, Oxford, Basil Blackwell, 1988.

James FORSYTH, 'Cameron and the civil service coup', *Spectator*, Vol. 318, No. 9582, 21st April 2012, p. 12.

Liam FOX, 'Labour will fail on health', speech to Conservative Spring Forum 2002, Conservative Party website, 23rd March 2002, retrieved 29th March 2002, www.conservatives.com/news_article.cfm?obj_id=27498&speeches=1.

Jonathan FOX & Shmuel SANDLER, 'Regime Types and Discrimination against Ethnoreligious Minorities: A Cross-Sectional Analysis of the Autocracy-Democracy Continuum', *Political Studies*, Vol. 51, No. 3, October 2003, pp. 469-489.

Chava FRANKFORT-NACHMIAS & David NACHMIAS, *Research Methods in the Social Sciences* (5th ed.), London, Arnold, 1996.

Douglas FRASER, 'Labour face council loss', *Sunday Herald*, 29th December 2002, retrieved 31st December 2002, www.sundayherald.com/30318.

Murdo FRASER, 'Proportional Representation: The Enemy of Freedom', *Freedom Today*, August/September 2002, pp. 14-15.

Jeffrey FRIEDMAN, 'Primitive Judgement', *Libertarian Party News*, October 1999, p. 8.

Marshall FRITZ, 'Hope for the Politically Homeless', 1988, in ADVOCATES FOR SELF-GOVERNMENT, *Nolan Chart Reader*, Atlanta, GA, Advocates for Self-Government, 1995, between pp. 1 & 2.

Sean GABB, 'Not Arrogance but Genius', *Tech Central Station*, 21st June 2004, retrieved 22nd June 2004, www.techcentralstation.be/062104G.html.

—, 'What's Wrong With British Conservatism?', *Free Life Commentary*, 16th February 2005, retrieved 16th March 2010, http://www.seangabb.co.uk/flcomm/flc130.htm.

—, *Literary Essays*, London, Hampden Press, 2011.

Oscar GABRIEL, 'Political Efficacy and Trust', 1995, in Jan VAN DETH & Elinor SCARBROUGH, (eds.), *The Impact of Values*, Oxford, Oxford University Press, 1995/1998, pp. 357-389.

Tom GALLAGHER, 'A talented agitator exploits Britain's dangerous social fracture', *Commentator*, 30th March 2012, retrieved 1st April 2012, http://tinyurl.com/7ht3fu5.

Andrew GAMBLE, *The Conservative Nation*, London, Routledge & Kegan Paul, 1974.

—, 'The Great Divide', *Marxism Today*, October 1990, pp. 34-37.

—, 'An Ideological Party', 1996, in Steve Ludlum & Martin Smith (eds.), *Contemporary British Conservatism*, Basingstoke, Macmillan Press, 1996, pp. 19-36.

Ron GARLAND, 'The Mid-Point on a Rating Scale: Is it Desirable?', *Marketing Bulletin*, No. 2, Research Note No. 3, 1991, pp. 66-70.

Jonathan GARDNER & Andrew OSWALD, 'Internet use: the digital divide', 2001, in Alison PARK, John CURTICE, Katarina THOMSON, Lindsey JARVIS & Catherine BROMLEY (eds.), *British Social Attitudes, The 18th Report: Public Policy, Social Ties*, London, SAGE Publications, 2001, pp. 159-174.

Mark GARNETT, 'Win or Bust: The Leadership Gamble of William Hague', 2003[a], in Mark Garnett & Philip Lynch (eds.), *The Conservatives in Crisis*, Manchester, Manchester University Press, 2003, pp. 49-65.

—, 'A Question of Definition: Ideology and the Conservative Party, 1997-2001', 2003[b], in Mark GARNETT & Philip LYNCH (eds.), *The Conservatives in Crisis*, Manchester, Manchester University Press, 2003, pp. 107-124.

—, 'The Free Economy and the Schizophrenic State', *The Political Quarterly*, Vol. 75, No. 4, October 2004, pp. 367-372.

Mark GARNETT & Philip LYNCH, 'Bandwagon Blues: The Tory Fightback Fails', *Political Quarterly*, Vol. 73, No. 1, January 2002, pp. 29-37.

Oonagh GAY, Isobel WHITE & Richard KELLY, *The Funding of Political Parties*, Research Paper 07/34, London, House of Commons Library, 10th April 2007.

John GIBBINS, 'Contemporary Political Culture: An Introduction', 1989, in John GIBBINS (ed.), *Contemporary Political Culture: Politics in a Postmodern Age*, London, Sage, 1989, pp. 1-30.

John GIBBINS & Bo REIMER, 'Postmodernism', 1995, in Jan VAN DETH & Elinor SCARBROUGH, (eds.), *The Impact of Values*, Oxford, Oxford University Press, 1995/1998, pp. 301-331.

Nicholas GILBY, Gideon SKINNER & Simon ATKINSON, 'Constituency Chairmen Poll', MORI report, 22nd July 2001, retrieved 2nd October 2004, http://www.mori.com/polls/2001/ms010721.shtml.

Mark GILL, Simon ATKINSON & Sara DAVIDSON, 'Political Attitudes in Great Britain', MORI website, 10th April 2002, retrieved 11th October 2004, www.mori.com/polls/2002/t020326.shtml.

Robin GILL, C. Kirk HADAWAY & Penny Long MARLER, 'Is Religious Belief Declining in Britain?', *Journal for the Scientific Study of Religion*, Vol. 37, No. 3, 1998, pp. 507-516.

Audrey GILLAN, 'From Bangladesh to Brick Lane', *Guardian*, 21st June 2002, retrieved 10th April 2012, http://www.guardian.co.uk/uk/2002/jun/21/religion.bangladesh.

Andrew GILLIGAN, 'A runaway victory for George Galloway – and all praise to Allah', *Telegraph*, 30th March 2012, retrieved 1st April 2012, http://tinyurl.com/c437q8e.

Ian GILMOUR, 'Only MPs should have a say in who leads the Conservatives', *Telegraph*, 31st October 2003, retrieved 4th August 2009, http://tinyurl.com/latw7a.

Maurice GLASMAN, *Unnecessary Suffering: Managing Market Utopia*, London, Verso, 1996.

Ruth GLEDHILL, 'Hague takes Tory gospel to Church', *The Times*, 17th April 2000, p. 8.

—, 'Is the Bible Belt here?', *The Times*, T2, 19th April 2000, pp. 3-4.

—, 'Hague turns to religious leaders', *The Times*, 25th September 2000, p. 10.

—, 'God gets short shrift in nation of unbelievers', *The Times*, 26th February 2004, p. 12.

Ruth GLEDHILL & Philip WEBSTER, 'Tories put faith in church appeal', *The Times*, 16th January 2001, p. 13.

GLOBAL INTELLIGENCE COMPANY, 'The British Geopolitical Enigma', *Stratfor*, 4th November 2002, retrieved 6th November 2002, www.stratfor.biz/Story.neo? storyId=207355.

Julian GLOVER, 'Tories end 30 years of bipartisanship on Northern Ireland', *Guardian*, 18th December 2001, retrieved 5th December 2007, http://www.guardian.co.uk/Northern_Ireland/Story/0,,620567,00.html.

—, 'Tories in bid for minority MPs', *Guardian*, 9th April 2002, retrieved 16th April 2002): http://politics.guardian.co.uk/conservatives/story/0,9061,681370,00.html.

Stephen GLOVER, 'Oh, please let the Tories be normal again', *Daily Mail*, 11th June 2001, p. 10.

—, 'MORI does not mean better: why *The Times* has decided to stop using the polling organisation', *The Spectator*, Vol. 288, No. 9053, 9th February 2002, p. 32.

—, 'If you want to see Labour getting a soft ride, look no further than the news pages of *The Times*', *The Spectator*, Vol. 289, No. 9072, 22nd June 2002, p. 12.

Jonah GOLDBERG, 'What Primaries Are For: Right, Left, and Whatever', *National Review Online*, 28th January 2004, retrieved 30th January 2004, http://www.nationalreview.com/goldberg/goldberg200401281036.asp.

—, *Liberal Fascism: The Secret History of the Left from Mussolini to the Politics of Meaning*, London, Penguin, 2009.

Peter GOLDS, 'Nothing being done to stop massive electoral fraud in Tower Hamlets', *Conservative Home* blog, 2nd March 2012, retrieved 5th March 2012, http://tinyurl.com/6w2mxqa.

John GOLDTHORPE & Anthony HEATH, 'Revised Class Schema 1992', Centre for Research into Elections and Social Trends (CREST), March 1992, retrieved 5th March 2010, http://www.crest.ox.ac.uk/p13.htm.

Al GORE, *Earth in the Balance: Forging a New Common Purpose*, London, Earthscan Publications Ltd., 1992.

Teresa GORMAN, *The Bastards: Dirty Tricks and the Challenge to Europe*, London, Pan Books, 1993

Michael GOVE, 'The World is Still Divided Between Competing Ideologues', *The Times*, 1st January 2000, p. 42.

—, 'Red flag flies again', *The Times, T2*, 15th January 2002, pp. 2-3.

—, 'The Maggie and Tony and Iain show', *The Spectator*, Vol. 290, No. 9088, 12th October 2002, pp. 12-13.

—, 'Terminal depression', *The Spectator*, Vol. 293, No. 9141, 18th October 2003, pp. 14 & 15.

Michael GOVE & Tom BALDWIN, 'Portillistas start uncivil war in quest for New Model Party', *The Times*, 23rd June 2001, pp. 18-19.

Paul GRAY, 'How to Win the Next General Election', Connect website, 2001, retrieved 15th March 2002, www.connectweb.org/papers/howto.htm.

E.H.H. GREEN, *Ideologies of Conservatism*, Oxford, Oxford University Press, 2002.

Sam GREENHILL & Tim SHIPMAN, 'Postal vote fraud: 50 criminal inquiries nationwide amid fears bogus voters could swing election', *Daily Mail*, 4th May 2010, retrieved 6th May 2010, http://tinyurl.com/2eql4r2.

W.H. GREENLEAF, *The British Political Tradition, Vol. 2, The Ideological Heritage*, London, Routledge, 1983.

Gunnar GRENDSTAD, 'Comparing Political Orientations: Grid-Group Theory Versus the Left-Right Dimension in the Five Nordic Countries', *European Journal of Political Research*, Vol. 42, No. 1, 2003, pp. 1-21.

Sinéad GRENNAN, (2001, 1st July) 'Pope unhappy with Nice No', *Irish Independent*, 1st July 2001, retrieved 1st June 2002, www.unison.ie/irish_independent/ stories.php3?ca=9&si=463541&issue_id=4765.

James GRIFFITH, 'Confession of a former Palestinian sympathiser', *Griffany Online*, 12th February 2003, retrieved 21st September 2002, http://homepage.ntlworld.com/ griffany/james/021203.htm.

Richard GRIFFITHS, 'The Perils of Principle', 1996, in Kenneth MINOGUE (ed.), *Conservative Realism: New Essays on Conservatism*, London, HarperCollins, 1996, pp. 68-79.

Jason GROVES, 'More than two-thirds of new Tories are sceptical about climate change', *Daily Mail*, 26ᵗʰ February 2010, retrieved 27ᵗʰ February 2010, http://tinyurl.com/yz5wmuy.

GUARDIAN, 'Marginal Tories' [editorial], *Guardian*, 9ᵗʰ September 2000, retrieved 3ʳᵈ April 2004, http://www.guardian.co.uk/leaders/story/0,3604,366244,00.html.

—, 'Annual memberships of political parties and other national organisations', *Guardian*, January 2002, retrieved 2ⁿᵈ February 2002, http://politics.guardian.co.uk/specialreports/tables/0,9071,641234,00.html.

—, 'Tory MP condemned for DUP move', *Guardian*, 3ʳᵈ October 2002, retrieved 5ᵗʰ October 2002, http://politics.guardian.co.uk/conservatives/story/0,9061,803772,00.html.

—, 'Tories need central power' [editorial], *Guardian*, 7ᵗʰ December 2004, retrieved 7ᵗʰ December 2004, www.guardian.co.uk/leaders/story/0,3604,1367796,00.html.

—, ''Cash-for-honours' timeline', *Guardian*, 11ᵗʰ October 2007, retrieved 28ᵗʰ March 2012, http://www.guardian.co.uk/politics/2007/oct/11/partyfunding.uk.

—, 'Phone hacking', *Guardian*, 2012, retrieved 6ᵗʰ February 2012, http://www.guardian.co.uk/media/phone-hacking.

Peter GUNDELACH, 'Grass-Roots Activity', 1995, in Jan van DETH & Elinor SCARBROUGH (eds.), *The Impact of Values*, Oxford, Oxford University Press, 1995/1998, pp. 357-389.

Barrie GUNTER & Adrian FURNHAM, *Consumer Profiles: An Introduction to Psychographics*, London, Routledge, 1992.

Mads HAAHR, 'Web Interface to the True Random Numbers', *Random.org*, July 1999, last consulted 7ᵗʰ February 2005, http://www.random.org/nform.html.

William HAGUE, Speech by William Hague to 'Faith in Future' Celebration, Conservative Party website, 7ᵗʰ July 2000, retrieved 19ᵗʰ August 2000, www.conservative-party.org.uk.

—, Statement by William Hague MP, Conservative Party Leader, at the launch of Islam Awareness Week, Conservative Party website, 6ᵗʰ November 2000, retrieved 27ᵗʰ July 2007, http://www.conservatives.com/tile.do?def=news.story.page&obj_id=315&speeches=1.

Marion HALCOMBE, review in *Free Life*, No. 26, December 1996, pp. 11-12, of David CAPITANCHIK & Michael WHINE, *The Governance of Cyberspace: The Far Right on the Internet*, London, Institute for Jewish Policy Research, 1996.

Macer HALL, 'David Cameron faces green rebellion from Tory MPs', *Daily Express*, 19ᵗʰ January 2010, retrieved 4ᵗʰ March 2010, http://tinyurl.com/yaue2u6.

Tim HAMES, 'How to Lose Elections', *The Spectator*, Vol. 285, No. 8983, 7ᵗʰ October 2000, pp. 14-15.

—, 'Why Ken is really Tony's preferred Tory leader', *The Times*, 6ᵗʰ July 2001, p. 18.

—, 'What's yellow and black and about to sting?', *The Times*, 22ⁿᵈ February 2002, p. 24.

—, 'The older generation, what a bunch of Commies' *The Times*, 12ᵗʰ January 2004, p. 16.

Duncan HAMILTON, 'Go-it-alone Scots Tories will need much more than a change of name', *The Scotsman*, 23ʳᵈMay 2005, retrieved, 23ʳᵈ May 2005, http://news.scotsman.com/index.cfm?id=561032005.

Daniel HANNAN, 'Worldwide: How Europe unwittingly fuels bloodshed in Israel', *Telegraph*, 17ᵗʰ May 2006, retrieved 20ᵗʰ May 2006, http://tinyurl.com/5ezdpv.

—, 'When we question Israel, we question democracy itself', *Telegraph*, 12ᵗʰ August 2006, retrieved 12ᵗʰ August 2006, http://tinyurl.com/5wvmnp.

—, 'There's nothing Right-wing about the BNP', *Telegraph*, 22ⁿᵈ February 2009, retrieved 21ˢᵗ April 2010, http://tinyurl.com/y5emt2m.

—, 'As long as the Eurosceptic vote is fragmented, the Euro-enthusiasts will keep winning', *Telegraph*, 17th April 2012, retrieved 18th April 2012, http://tinyurl.com/cluyfcv.

Ed HARRIS & Chris MILLAR, 'Young voters want William to become king, not Charles', London *Evening Standard*, 12th June 2002, p. 9.

J.W. HARRIS, 'Botched USA Weekend Political Quiz Draws Criticism', *The Liberator*, Summer 1996, Vol. 12 No. 3, pp. 7 & 11.

Paul HARRISON, *Elements of Pantheism* (2nd ed.), Coral Springs, FL, Llumina Press, 2004.

Friedrich HAYEK, *The Constitution of Liberty*, London, Routledge, 1960.

John HAYES, 'Freedom is not enough', *The Spectator*, Vol. 204, No. 9162, 13th March 2004, p. 26.

Richard HAYTON, 'Towards the Mainstream? UKIP and the 2009 Elections in the European Parliament', *Politics*, Vol. 30, No. 1, February 2010, pp. 26-35.

—, 'Dr Richard Hayton', profile page on University of Huddersfield website, 2012, retrieved 15th May 2012, http://tinyurl.com/6u6m9fu.

Anthony HEATH, Geoffrey EVANS, Mansur LALLJEE, Jean MARTIN & Sharon WITHERSPOON, *The Measurement of Core Beliefs and Values*, Working Paper No. 2, Oxford, Social & Community Planning Research, 1991.

Anthony HEATH, Roger JOWELL & John CURTICE, *How Britain Votes*, Oxford, Pergamon Press, 1985.

—, *British Election Panel Study 1997-1998*, (computer file, No. 4028), Colchester, Essex, UK Data Archive, October 1999.

Anthony HEATH, Roger JOWELL, Bridget TAYLOR & Katarina THOMSON, 'Euroscepticism and the Referendum Party', 1998, in David DENVER, Justin FISHER, Philip COWLEY & Charles PATTIE (eds.), *British Elections and Parties Review Vol. 8*, London, Frank Cass, 1998, pp. 95-110.

Anthony HEATH, Catherine ROTHON & Lindsey JARVIS, 'English to the core?', 2002, in Alison PARK, John CURTICE, Katarina THOMSON, Lindsey JARVIS & Catherine BROMLEY (eds.), *British Social Attitudes, The 19th Report*, London, SAGE Publications, 2002, pp. 169-183.

Anthony HEATH & Richard TOPF, 'Educational Expansion and Political Change in Britain: 1964-1983', *European Journal of Political Research*, Vol. 14, 1986, pp. 543-567.

—, 'Political Culture', 1987, Roger JOWELL, Sharon WITHERSPOON & Lindsay BROOK (eds.), *British Social Attitudes: The 1987 Report*, Aldershot, Gower, 1987, pp. 51-67.

Edward HEATHCOAT-AMORY, *Lords a'Leaping*, London, Centre for Policy Studies, 1998.

—, 'And the winner is: The Stay at Home Party', *Daily Mail*, 9th June 2001, p. 6.

Gordon HECTOR, 'Where there is error, let us bring truth', *Conservative History Journal*, Winter 2009/2010, pp. 16-19.

Simon HEFFER, 'Power to the people', *The Spectator*, Vol. 289, No. 9074, 6th July 2002, pp. 14-15.

—, 'Enough of this craven self-hatred', *Daily Mail*, 12th October 2002, p. 15.

Timothy HELLWIG, 'Explaining the salience of left–right ideology in postindustrial democracies: The role of structural economic change', *European Journal of Political Research*, Vol. 47, No. 6, October 2008, pp. 687-709.

Roger HELMER, 'Kippers in Skegness', personal blog, 4th March 2012, retrieved 5th March 2012, http://rogerhelmermep.wordpress.com/2012/03/04/kippers-in-skegness/.

Timothy HEPPELL, 'The Ideological Composition of the Parliamentary Conservative Party 1992-1997', *Political Studies*, Vol. 4, No. 2, June 2002, pp. 299-324.

—, 'Ideology and Ministerial Allocation in the Major Government 1992-1997', *Politics*, Vol. 25, No 3, September 2005, pp. 144-152.

—, 'Research & Scholarships', University of Huddersfield, School of Human & Health Sciences, 2009, retrieved 6th January 2009, http://www2.hud.ac.uk/staffprofiles/staffcv.php?staffid=305#research.

—, 'Dr Timothy Heppell', profile page on University of Leeds website, 2012, retrieved 15th May 2012, http://tinyurl.com/798nxqd.

Timothy HEPPELL & Michael HILL, 'Ideological Typologies of Contemporary British Conservatism', *Political Studies Review*, Vol. 3, No. 3, September 2005, pp. 335-355.

—, 'The Conservative Party Leadership Election of 1997: An Analysis of the Voting Motivations of Conservative Parliamentarians', *British Politics*, Vol. 3, No. 1, April 2008, pp. 63-91.

—, 'The Voting Motivations of Conservative Parliamentarians in the Conservative Party Leadership Election of 2001', *Politics*, Vol. 30, No. 1, February 2010, pp. 36-51.

Susan HERBST, *Reading Public Opinion: How Political Actors View the Democratic Process*, Chicago, University of Chicago Press, 1998.

Peter HETHERINGTON, 'Tories buck trend with county gains', *Guardian*, 9th June 2001, retrieved 27th January 2002, http://www.guardian.co.uk/Archive/Article/0,4273,4201400,00.html.

Andrew HEYWOOD, *Political Ideologies: An Introduction*, Basingstoke, Macmillan, 1992.

Kevin HICKSON (ed.), *The Political Thought of the Conservative Party Since 1945*, Basingstoke, Palgrave Macmillan, 2005.

—, 'Dr Kevin Hickson', profile page on University of Liverpool website, 2012, retrieved 15th May 2012, http://tinyurl.com/d73s8l6.

Adrian HILTON, 'Whiggish derision' [letter to the editor], *The Spectator*, Vol. 312, No. 9473, 20th March 2010, p. 27.

Gaby HINSLIFF, '£12m ceiling on election cash planned', *The Observer*, 18th August 2002, retrieved 23rd August 2008, http://www.guardian.co.uk/politics/2002/aug/18/uk.partyfunding.

Peter HITCHENS, 'A party split from top to toe', *The Spectator*, Vol. 293, No. 9139, 4th October 2003, pp. 12-13.

—, 'Down with the Special Relationship', *Mail on Sunday*, 10th February 2009, retrieved 10th February 2009, http://hitchensblog.mailonsunday.co.uk/2009/02/down-with-the-special-relationship.html.

—, 'Dancing to Dave's tune: Sarah and the Cameronettes', *Mail on Sunday*, 9th August 2009, p. 25.

Theo HOBSON, 'Losing our religion', *The Spectator*, Vol. 288, No. 9052, 2nd February 2002, pp. 20-21.

John HOLROYD-DOVETON, *Young Conservatives: A History of the Young Conservative Movement*, Bishop Auckland, The Pentland Press, 1996.

Mark HOOKHAM & David SMITH, 'Scots rejoice as subsidy junkie myth laid to rest', *Sunday Times*, 12th February 2012, p. 16.

Anthony HOWARD, 'Why the Tories are 'the stupid party'', *The Times*, 18th September 2001.

Michael HOWARD, 'An end to the cancer of paramilitarism', Conservative Party website, 3rd February 2004, retrieved 8th February 2008, http://www.conservatives.com/tile.do?def=news.show.article.page&obj_id=87240.

David HUGHES, "Why I would be forced to silence Scots MPs', by Hague', Daily Mail, 13th November 2000, p. 35.

—, 'Coronation of King Howard', Daily Mail, 30th October 2003, pp. 1-2.

—, 'Tory traitor 'sells out for a peerage'', Daily Mail, 17th January 2005, p. 10.

Greg HURST, 'Lib Dems to consider Scots vote ban', The Times, 8th March 2002, p. 12.

—, 'Lib Dems fall short on women', The Times, 28th December 2002, p. 16.

—, "Safe pair of hands' ready to take risks for the Lib Dems', The Times, 3rd March 2006, p. 2.

Roger HUTCHINGS, Crystal Palace Vistas, The Book Guild, Sussex, 1999.

ICM RESEARCH, 'Guardian Afghanistan Poll October 2001', ICM Research website, 2005, retrieved 16th March 2010, http://tinyurl.com/yarrqjt.

IMPROVEMENT AND DEVELOPMENT AGENCY, National Census of Local Authority Councillors in England and Wales 2001, 2001, retrieved 11th April February 2002, http://www.idea.gov.uk/member/census2001.pdf.

Ronald INGLEHART, 'Observations on Cultural Change and Postmodernism', 1989, in John R. GIBBINS (ed.), Contemporary Political Culture: Politics in a Postmodern Age, London, Sage, 1989, pp. 251-256.

—, Culture Shift in Advanced Industrial Society, Princeton, NJ, Princeton University Press, 1990.

—, Modernisation and Postmodernisation: Cultural, Economic, and Political Change in 43 Societies, Princeton, NJ, Princeton University Press, 1997.

IMPROVEMENT AND DEVELOPMENT AGENCY, National Census of Local Authority Councillors in England and Wales 2001, 2001, retrieved 11th April February 2002, www.idea.gov.uk/member/census2001.pdf.

INDEPENDENT SCHOOLS COUNCIL, 'Facts & Figures, Independent Schools Council, 2006, retrieved 13th March 2006, http://www.isc.co.uk/index.php/5.

INTERNATIONAL INSTITUTE FOR DEMOCRACY AND ELECTORAL ASSISTANCE, 'Global Database of Quotas for Women', IDEA website, 2006, retrieved 21st August 2006, http://www.quotaproject.org/countryPolitical.cfm.

INTERNATIONAL SOCIAL SURVEY PROGRAMME, Religion 1991, (computer file, SN 3062), Colchester, Essex, UK Data Archive, 29th January 1996, http://www.data-archive.ac.uk/findingdata/snDescription.asp?sn=3062&key=3062.

Jonathan ISABY, 'Where are the original A-Listers now?', Conservative Home blog, 29th April 2009, retrieved 29th April 2009, http://tinyurl.com/mhjw3y.

—, 'Lots of councillors... lots of lawyers... lots of people who have fought for their seats more than once... meet the next parliamentary Conservative party', Conservative Home blog, 1st July 2009, retrieved 1st July 2009, http://tinyurl.com/m47a8b.

—, 'Pickles and CCHQ gain unprecedented power over shortlists for autumn selections', Conservative Home blog, 30th July 2009, retrieved 7th August 2009, http://tinyurl.com/l2kcuw.

Brian JANISKEE, 'The Legend of the Social Liberal-Fiscal Conservative', The Claremont Institute, 15th October 2003, retrieved 24th November 2003, http://www.claremont.org/writings/janiskee031015.html.

Krista JANSSON, British Crime Survey: Measuring Crime for 25 Years, London, Home Office, 2007.

David JARY & Julia JARY, *Dictionary of Sociology*, London, HarperCollins, 1991.

Russell JENKINS, 'Another northern town turns to the BNP', *The Times*, 23rd November 2002, p. 14.

Simon JENKINS, 'The strange dearth of liberal England', *The Times*, 17th May 2002, p. 22.

—, 'A decent chap lost in an era of charisma', *The Times*, 9th October 2002, p. 20.

JK, untitled cartoon, *The Times*, 11th January 2000, p. 10.

Josef JOFFE, 'The Axis of Envy: Why Israel and the United States both strike the same European nerve', *Foreign Policy*, September/October 2002, retrieved 12th October 2002, www.foreignpolicy.com/issue_septoct_2002/axisofenvy.html.

Philip JOHNSTON, 'We don't need more Sunday shopping', *Telegraph*, 10th April 2006, retrieved 10th April 2006, http://tinyurl.com/yofw35.

George JONES, 'Let battle commence: plotters put IDS to the test of his political life', *Telegraph*, 29th October 2003, retrieved 17th August 2009, http://tinyurl.com/r6poyg.

Charles JUDD, Eliot SMITH & Louise KIDDER, *Research Methods in Social Relations* (6th ed.), Forth Worth, TX, Harcourt Brace Jovanovich, 1991.

Michael KALLENBACH, 'Yesterday in Parliament', *Telegraph*, 5th December 2001, retrieved 4th August 2009, http://tinyurl.com/kuovco.

Syed KAMALL, *Pocket Guide to the EU and Local Government*, Kingston-upon-Thames, November 2008.

Richard KELLY, 'The Party Didn't Work: Conservative Reorganisation and Electoral Failure', *The Political Quarterly*, Vol. 73, No. 1, January 2002, pp. 38-43.

—, 'Organisational Reform and the Extra-Parliamentary Party', 2003, in Mark Garnett & Philip Lynch (eds.), *The Conservatives in Crisis*, Manchester, Manchester University Press, 2003, pp. 82-106.

—, 'The Extra-Parliamentary Tory Party: McKenzie Revisited', *The Political Quarterly*, Vol. 75, No. 4, October 2004, pp. 398-404.

Justin KEMPLEY, 'How far was the Falklands War the main reason for Thatcher's 1983 General Election victory?', *Conservative History Journal*, Winter 2009/2010, pp. 38-40.

Andrew KENNY, 'The end of left and right', *The Spectator*, Vol. 297, No. 9209, 5th February 2005, p. 18-19.

Nick KENT, 'The party I joined was full of nice old people; today it is full of nasty old people', *Guardian*, 5th December 2001, retrieved 27th January 2002, http://www.guardian.co.uk/Archive/Article/0,4273,4313477,00.html.

George KEREVAN, 'Beware dangerous new Romantics of the Left', *The Scotsman*, 5th May 2003, retrieved 5th May 2003, http://thescotsman.co.uk/opinion.cfm?id=512162003.

—, 'SSP faces factious times after Tommy Sheridan', *The Scotsman*, 18th November 2004, retrieved 18th November 2004), http://news.scotsman.com/archive.cfm?id=1327062004.

Tessa KESWICK, Rosemary POCKLEY & Angela GUILLAUME, *Conservative Women*, London, Centre for Policy Studies, 1999.

KEYSTROKE KNOWLEDGE, website, c. 2008, retrieved 18th November 2008, http://www.keystroke-knowledge.co.uk.

Richard KIMBER, 'British Governments and Elections since 1945', 3rd November 2008, Richard Kimber's Political Science Resources, retrieved 1st March 2009, http://www.psr.keele.ac.uk/area/uk/uktable.htm.

—, 'Party manifestos', 17th April 2010, Richard Kimber's Political Science Resources, retrieved 22nd April 2010, http://www.politicsresources.net/area/uk/man.htm.

Anthony KING, 'The Outsider as Political Leader: The Case of Margaret Thatcher', *British Journal of Political Science*, Vol. 32, Part 3, July 2002, pp. 435-454.

—, 'The brutal truth facing whoever leads party at the next election', *Telegraph*, 29th October 2003, retrieved 4th August 2009, http://tinyurl.com/l9u4wd.

—, 'Mr Howard's worst rating is still better than Iain Duncan Smith's best', *Telegraph*, 30th July 2004, retrieved 17th August 2009, http://tinyurl.com/l4mgw4.

—, 'Britons' belief in God vanishing as religion is replaced by apathy', *Telegraph*, 27th December 2005, retrieved 4th August 2009, http://tinyurl.com/m25367.

Melissa KITE, 'Trimble is keen to forge closer links', *The Times*, 10th October 2001, p. 16.

—, 'Tories 'biased against women MPs'', *The Times*, 17th January 2002, p. 12.

—, 'Health service is dictatorship, says Duncan Smith', *The Times*, 6th February 2002, p. 10.

—, 'Tories will oppose state funds for parties', *The Times*, 5th August 2002, p. 2.

—, 'Accept the Bridget Jones lifestyle Willetts tells Tories', *The Times*, 18th September 2002, p. 4.

—, 'Tories back Bill for women MPs', *The Times*, 25th October 2002, p. 18.

—, 'Duncan Smith threat to Howard', *The Times*, 4th December 2003, p. 12.

Melissa KITE, Tom BALDWIN & Alice MILES, 'Only women can save us, says Duncan Smith', *The Times*, 19th January 2002, pp. 1-2.

Peter KLASSEN, 'Variance', 12th September, 2008, retrieved 11th March 2009, http://www.documentingexcellence.com/stat_tool/variance.htm.

Hans-Dieter KLINGEMANN, Andrea VOLKENS, Judith BARA, Ian BUDGE & Michael MCDONALD (eds.), *Mapping Policy Preferences II: Estimates for Parties, Electors, and Governments in Eastern Europe, European Union and OECD 1990-200*, Oxford, Oxford University Press, 2006.

Laurence KOTLER-BERKOWITZ, 'Ethnicity and Politics: Cohesion, Division, and British Jews', *Political Studies*, Vol. 49, No. 4, 2001, pp. 648-669.

Mona Lena KROOK, 'Why Are Fewer Women Than Men Elected? Gender and the Dynamics of Candidate Selection.', *Political Studies Review*, Vol. 8, No. 2, May 2010, pp. 155-168.

LABOUR PARTY, *Ambitions for Britain* [2001 General Election manifesto], London, Labour Party, 2001.

Gary LACHMAN, *A Dark Muse: A History of the Occult*, New York, NY, Thunder's Mouth Press, 2003/2005.

James LANDALE, 'Members had a real party in the Fifties', *The Times*, 21st April 2000, p. 6.

—, 'No stopping decline of the party faithful', *The Times*, 13th March 2001, p. 4.

James LANDALE & Tom BALDWIN, 'Tory troops desert on eve of battle', *The Times*, 13th March 2001, p. 1.

John LAUGHLAND, 'Why the "Anglosphere" Is No Alternative for the EU', *The Brussels Journal*, 2nd January 2010, retrieved 4th April 2010, http://www.brusselsjournal.com/node/2821.

Brian LAYTHE, Deborah FINKEL & Lee KIRKPATRICK, 'Predicting Prejudice from Religious Fundamentalism and Right-Wing Authoritarianism: A Multiple-Regression Approach', *Journal for the Scientific Study of Religion*, Vol. 40, No. 1, March 2001, pp. 1-10.

Jonathan LEAKE, 'Greenpeace withers as its members quit', *Sunday Times*, 30th July 2000, p. 5.

Davis LEASK, 'Why the figures peddled by Scotland's critics don't add up', *The Herald*, 2nd November 2007, retrieved 15th September 2008, http://tinyurl.com/56kjbk.

Matthew LEEKE, *UK Election Statistics: 1945-2003*, Research Paper 03/59, Houses of Parliament website, 1st July 2003, retrieved 11th April 2009, http://www.parliament.uk/commons/lib/research/rp2003/rp03-059.pdf.

Jennifer LEES-MARSHMENT, 'Marketing the British Conservatives 1997-2001', *Journal of Marketing Management*, Vol. 17, Nos. 9-10, November 2001, pp 929-941.

—, 'Mis-Marketing the Conservatives: The Limitations of Style Over Substance', *The Political Quarterly*, Vol. 75, No. 4, October 2004, pp. 392-397.

Jennifer LEES-MARSHMENT & Stuart QUAYLE, 'Spinning the Party or Empowering the Members? The Conservative Party reforms of 1998', paper for the Political Studies Association Annual Conference, April 2000, retrieved 27th October 2001, http://www.psa.ac.uk/cps/2000/Lees-Marshment%20Jennifer%20&%20Quayle%20Stuart.pdf.

Adam LENT & Matthew SOWEMIMO, 'Remaking the Opposition?', 1996, in Steve LUDLUM & Martin SMITH (eds.), *Contemporary British Conservatism*, Basingstoke, Macmillan Press, 1996, pp. 121-142.

Russell LE PAGE, 'Conservative leadership turmoil tests grassroots support' [letters to the editor], *The Times*, 31st October 2003, p. 31.

Paul LESLIE, 'Tories have learned little from decline in Scotland' [letters to the editor], *Scotland on Sunday*, 19th January 2003, retrieved 24th January 2003, http://scotlandonsunday.com/letters.cfm?id=70152003.

Jan LESTER, *The Political Compass: Why Libertarianism is Not Right-Wing*, London, Libertarian Alliance, 1995.

Shirley LETWIN, 'British Conservatism in the 1990s', 1996, in Kenneth MINOGUE (ed.), 1996, *Conservative Realism: New Essays on Conservatism*, London, HarperCollins, 1996, pp. 173-180.

Steven LEVITT, 'Newspeak: When Words Can Kill', *The Individual*, No. 34, May 2003, pp. 2-3.

LIBERAL DEMOCRATS, *Freedom, Justice, Honesty*, [2001 General Election manifesto], Richard Kimber's Political Science Resources, 2001, retrieved 4th March 2007, http://www.psr.keele.ac.uk/area/uk/e01/man/libdem/Fed2001.htm.

LIBERTARIAN ALLIANCE, 'History and Purpose', Libertarian Alliance website, 2009, retrieved 23rd January 2009, http://www.libertarian.co.uk/about/about.htm#History%20and%20Purpose.

LIBERTY LEAGUE, 'Compass', Liberty League website, date n/k, retrieved 25th February 2012, http://uklibertyleague.org/resources/compass/.

Liz LIGHTFOOT, 'State pupil numbers at university are still going down', *Telegraph*, 21st July 2006, retrieved 27th September 2007, http://tinyurl.com/6y3wgg.

Stuart LILIE & William MADDOX, 'An Alternative Analysis of Mass Belief Systems: Conservative, Liberal, Populist, and Libertarian, 1981, in ADVOCATES FOR SELF-GOVERNMENT, *Nolan Chart Reader*, Atlanta, GA, Advocates for Self-Government, 1995, pp. 60-82.

Gary LILIEN, Philip KOTLER & K. Sridhar MOORTHY, '4 Ps of marketing', Institute for Manufacturing, University of Cambridge, originally published 1992, retrieved 4th February 2012, http://www.ifm.eng.cam.ac.uk/dstools/paradigm/4pmark.html.

Magnus LINKLATER, 'There is more than one set of extremists in Europe', *The Times*, 25th April 2002, p. 20.

—, 'A Conservative Party by any other name will still seem just as unappealing', *The Times*, 10th October 2002, p. 22.

—, 'Corruption is an old vice for a young institution', *The Times*, 17th October 2002, p. 22.

Sam LISTER, Clare MCDONALD, Emma HARTLEY & Chris JOHNSTON, 'Sadly, she is no longer one of us, say Tories', *The Times*, 22nd March 2002, p. 12.

John LOPEZ, 'Libertarian Politics: An Oxymoron', *The Libertarian Enterprise*, No. 188, 26th August 2002, retrieved 20th January 2004, http://www.webleyweb.com/tle/libe188-20020826-02.html.

LORD CHANCELLOR'S DEPARTMENT, *The House of Lords: Completing the Reform*, London, Lord Chancellor's Department, 2002.

David LOVIBOND, 'True Blues, True Greens', *The Salisbury Review*, Vol. 24, No. 4, Summer 2006, pp. 24-25.

Suzanne LOWRY, 'Are the French 'a sh**tty lot'?', *The Spectator*, Vol. 288, No, 9050, 19th January 2002, pp. 20 & 22.

Caroline LUCAS, 'What would it take for you to leave your Party?', personal blog, 6th March 2010, retrieved 2nd April 2010, http://tinyurl.com/yb9w3ml.

Steve LUDLUM, 'The Spectre Haunting Conservatism: Europe and Backbench Rebellion', 1996, in Steve LUDLUM & Martin SMITH (eds.), *Contemporary British Conservatism*, Basingstoke, Macmillan Press, 1996, pp. 98-120.

Geir LUNDESTAD, *"Empire" by Integration: The United States and European Integration, 1945-1997,* Oxford, Oxford University Press, 1997.

Carina LUNDMARK, 'Feminist Political Orientations', 1995, in Jan van DETH & Elinor SCARBROUGH (eds.), *The Impact of Values*, Oxford, Oxford University Press, 1995, pp. 250-274.

Peter LYNCH, 'Regional Party Organisations and Territorial Politics in Britain', *Contemporary Political Studies*, 1997, pp. 559-566.

—, 'The Scottish Conservatives, 1997-2001: From Disaster to Devolution and Beyond', 2003, in Mark GARNETT & Philip LYNCH (eds.), *The Conservatives in Crisis*, Manchester, Manchester University Press, 2003, pp. 164-181.

—, 'The Conservative Party and Nationhood', *The Political Quarterly*, Vol. 71, No. 1, 2000, pp. 59-67.

—, 'The Conservatives and Europe, 1997-2001', 2003, in Mark Garnett & Philip Lynch (eds.), *The Conservatives in Crisis*, Manchester, Manchester University Press, 2003, pp. 146-163.

—, 'Saving the Union: Conservatives and the 'Celtic Fringe'', *The Political Quarterly*, Vol. 75, No. 4, October 2004, pp. 386-391.

Ewen MACASKILL, Michael WHITE & Lawrence DONEGAN, 'Scotland says Yes', *Guardian*, 12th September 1997, retrieved 28th July 2008, http://www.guardian.co.uk/politics/1997/sep/12/constitution.uk.

R. MADHOK, R. MCEWAN, R. BHOPAL & A. MCCALLUM, 'Anonymous postal surveys' [letters to the editor], *Journal of Epidemiology and Community Health*, No. 44, 1990, p. 253.

Noel MALCOLM, 'Conservative Realism and Christian Democracy', 1996, in Kenneth Minogue (ed.), *Conservative Realism: New Essays on Conservatism*, London: HarperCollins, 1996, pp. 44-67.

John MAJOR, Welcome page, 1990-1997 Conservative administration web-site, 1990, retrieved 3rd April 2006, http://www.johnmajor.co.uk.

N. Gregory MANKIW, *Principles of Economics* (2nd ed.), Orlando, FL, Harcourt College Publishers, 2001.

Karl MANNHEIM, *Ideology and Utopia: An Introduction to the Sociology of Knowledge* (expanded ed.), New York, Harvest Books, 1936.

Catherine MARSH, *Exploring Data*, Cambridge, Polity Press, 1988.

Paul MARKS, 'England is normal, Scotland and Wales are not', *Samizdata*, 13th August 2002, retrieved 13th August 2002, www.samizdata.net/blog/archives/ 001749.html#001749.

David MARQUAND, *Britain Since 1918: The Strange Career of British Democracy* [paperback ed.], London, Phoenix, 2009.

Andrew MARR & John MAJOR, 'Government sleaze' [an interview of Sir John Major by Andrew Marr], *BBC News*, 16th July 2006, retrieved 22nd August 2008, http://news.bbc.co.uk/1/hi/programmes/how_euro_are_you/5184602.stm.

Simon MATTHEWS, 'Kiss me on the apocalypse! Some reflections on the life and times of Sir James Goldsmith', *Lobster*, No. 55, Summer 2008, pp. 32-36.

MAYSALOON, "Edgware Road nights...", *Maysaloon* blog, 27th August 2007, retrieved 5th April 2010, http://maysaloon.blogspot.com/2007/08/edgware-road-nights.html.

Francis MAUDE, 'Male, white, straight – and doomed to extinction if we don't change', *The Times*, 24th June 2002, p. 20.

Brian MAWHINNEY, *In the Firing Line: Politics, Faith, Power and Forgiveness*, London, HarperCollins, 1999.

Ian MCALLISTER & Donley STUDLAR, 'Conservative Euroscepticism and the Referendum Party in the 1997 British General Election', *Party Politics*, Vol. 6, No. 3, 2000, pp. 359-371.

Stuart MCANULLA, 'Fade to Grey? Symbolic Politics in the Post-Thatcher Era', *Contemporary Political Studies*, 1997, pp. 315-323.

Andrew MCFARLANE, 'Will tactical voting swing 2010 general election?', BBC Election 2010 website, 9th April 2010, retrieved 2nd May 2010, http://news.bbc.co.uk/1/hi/uk_politics/election_2010/8612463.stm.

Robert MCKENZIE, *British Political Parties: The Distribution of Power Within the Conservative and Labour Parties* (2nd ed.), London, Heinemann, 1964.

Robert MCKENZIE & Allan SILVER, *Angels in Marble: Working Class Conservatives in Urban England*, London, Heinemann, 1968.

Iain MCLEAN, 'The Semi-Detached Election: Scotland', 1997, in Anthony KING (ed.), *New Labour Triumphs: Britain at the Polls*, Chatham, NJ, Chatham House Publishers, 1997, pp. 145-176.

David MCLELLAN, *Political Christianity: A Reader*, London, Society for Promoting Christian Knowledge, 1997.

David MELDING, 'More power for Welsh Assembly?' [letters to the editor], *The Times*, 14th August 2000, p. 17.

Nigel Gervas MEEK, *The Libertarian Party of Great Britain: An Idea Whose Time Has NOT Come*, London, Libertarian Alliance, 1998.

—, *Personal and Economic Ideology: British Party Politics and the Political Compass*, London, Libertarian Alliance, 1999.

—, 'The Conservative Party and One Libertarian: The Story of an Estrangement', *Free Life*, No. 32, July 1999, pp. 5-7

—, 'The assassination of Pim Fortuyn' [letters to the editor], 9th May 2002, *The Times*, p. 25.

—, *The Nature Of Christian Democracy*, Libertarian Alliance, London, 2003.

—, 'The March for Evil', *Samizdata*, 17th February 2003, retrieved 10th January 2009, http://www.samizdata.net/blog/archives/2003/02/the_march_for_evil.html.

—, 'The UK is Not A "Multiracial, Multicultural" Country', *The Individual*, May 2003, pp. 7-10.

—, 'The Rise of Blogging!', *The Individual*, September 2003, pp. 2-3.

—, 'An Atheist Libertarian's Appreciation of Christianity', *The Individual*, May 2004, pp. 14-15.

—, *The Backlash Campaign: Defending S&M is Defending Individual Freedom*, Libertarian Alliance, London, 2006.

—, 'At the Margins of Politics: The Prevalence (and Irrelevance?) of Libertarian Attitudes in the UK', *The Individual*, August 2010, pp. 2-7.

—, *Conservative Party Representatives Study, 2002*, datafile SN 6552, Economic and Social Data Service, 27th August 2010, retrieved 2nd February 2012, http://www.esds.ac.uk/findingData/snDescription.asp?sn=6552&key=conservative+party.

Adam MELLOWS-FACER, *General Election 2005*, Research Paper 05/33, Houses of Parliament website, 17th May 2005, retrieved 8th April 2009, http://www.parliament.uk/commons/lib/research/rp2005/rp05-033.pdf.

Paul MERCER, *Directory of British Political Organisations 1994*, Harlow, Longman, 1994.

Charlie METHVEN, 'Lib Dem website links 'racist Tories' to BNP', *Telegraph*, 24th July 2002, retrieved 30th July 2002, www.telegraph.co.uk/opinion/main.jhtml?xml=/opinion/2002/07/24/dp2401.xml.

Brian MICKLETHWAIT, *Losing, Blogging and Winning*, Personal Perspectives No. 17, London, Libertarian Alliance, 2002.

—, 'The War Against Terror: How Conservative fortunes could finally be changing', *Samizdata*, 27th September 2003, retrieved 27th February 2003, http://www.samizdata.net/blog/archives/003054.html#003054.

—, 'On the impact of opinion polls', *Samizdata*, 24th April 2010, retrieved 25th April 2010, http://www.samizdata.net/blog/archives/2010/04/on_the_impact_o.html.

Ludwig von MISES, 'The Source of Hitler's Success', Ludwig von Mises Institute, 1940/2004, retrieved 19th December 2004, http://www.mises.org/fullstory.aspx?Id=1691.

James MITCHELL, 'Unionism, Assimilation, and the Conservatives', *Contemporary Political Studies*, 1995, pp. 1376-1383.

Tim MONTGOMERIE, 'Tories reach out to Christian voter' [letter to the editor], *The Times*, 24th January 2001, p. 17.

—, 'Who is on the A-list?', *Conservative Home* blog, 11th May 2006, retrieved 29th April 2009, http://conservativehome.blogs.com/goldlist/2006/05/as_promised_thi.html.

—, 'Thatcher revolution inspires this generation', *The Times*, 30th April 2009, p. 21.

—, 'The grim mood of the Parliamentary Conservative Party', *Conservative Home* blog, 21st June 2009, retrieved 3rd August 2009, http://tinyurl.com/mmbfum.

Brian MONTEITH, 'Horror show points way for Scots Tories', *Edinburgh Evening News*, 31st October 2003, retrieved 1st November 2003, www.edinburghnews.com/opinion.cfm?id=1202232003.

—, 'Great sulk spoiled memory of Heath', *Edinburgh Evening News*, July 22nd 2005, retrieved 11th April 2010, http://www.selsdongroup.co.uk/article.asp?id=80.

Charles MOORE, 'Bloodless bean-counters rule over us – where are the leaders?', *Telegraph*, 11th May 2012, retrieved 13th May 2012, http://tinyurl.com/7yx8zzz.

Bryn MORGAN, *By-election results: 1997-2000*, Research Paper 01/36, Houses of Parliament website, 29th March 2001, retrieved 11th April 2009, http://www.parliament.uk/commons/lib/research/rp2001/rp01-036.pdf.

MORI, 'Political Attitudes in Great Britain', MORI website, 10th April 2002, retrieved 11th April 2002, www.mori.com/polls/2002/t020326.shtml.

—, 'Voting Intention in Great Britain' [May 1979 to March 2009], Ipsos MORI website, March 2009, retrieved 11th April 2009, http://www.ipsos-mori.com/content/voting-intention-in-great-britain-all.ashx.

Roger MORTIMORE, 'How did you vote?', MORI report, 3rd April 2001, retrieved 25th November 2004, http://www.mori.com/mrr/2001/c010403.shtml.

—, 'Tory Leadership', MORI report, 20th July 2001, retrieved 2nd October 2004, http://www.mori.com/mrr/2001/c010720.shtml.

Claus MOSER & Graham KALTON, *Survey Methods in Social Investigation* (2nd ed.), Aldershot, Dartmouth Publishing, 1971.

Rosa MULÉ, 'Party Competition and the Hierarchy of Goals', *Contemporary Political Studies*, 1995, pp. 284-294.

Rachel NAKASH, Jane HUTTON, Ellen JØRSTAD-STEIN, Simon GATES & Sarah LAMB, 'Maximising response to postal questionnaires: A systematic review of randomised trials in health research', *BMC Medical Research Methodology*, Vol. 6, No. 5, 2006, retrieved 5th May 2009, http://wrap.warwick.ac.uk/587/1/WRAP_Lamb_Maximising_Response.pdf.

Masja NAS, 'Green, Greener, Greenest', 1995, in Jan van DETH & Elinor SCARBROUGH (eds.), *The Impact of Values*, Oxford, Oxford University Press, 1995, pp. 275-300.

NATION MASTER, 'Economy Statistics: GDP (2002) by country', *Nation Master*, 2009, retrieved 11th January 2009, http://www.nationmaster.com/graph/eco_gdp-economy-gdp-nominal&date=2002.

NATIONAL ASSOCIATION OF LOCAL COUNCILS, *What Can Local Councils Do?*, National Association of Local Councils website, 5th September 2008; retrieved 4th May 2009, http://www.nalc.gov.uk/Document/Download.aspx?uid=079806d3-0e69-4588-9a32-ef02c91598df.

NATIONAL CENTRE FOR SOCIAL RESEARCH, *British Social Attitudes Survey 1997*, (computer file, SN 4072), UK Data Archive, 29th October 2008[a], retrieved 5th May 2009, http://www.data-archive.ac.uk/findingdata/snDescription.asp?sn= 4072&key=4072.

—, *British Social Attitudes Survey 1998*, (computer file, SN 4131), UK Data Archive, 29th October 2008[b], retrieved 5th May 2009, http://www.data-archive.ac.uk/findingdata/snDescription.asp?sn=4131&key=4131.

—, *British Social Attitudes Survey 1999*, (computer file, SN 4318), UK Data Archive, 29th October 2008[c], retrieved 5th May 2009, http://www.data-archive.ac.uk/findingdata/snDescription.asp?sn=4318&key=4318.

—, *British Social Attitudes Survey 2001*, (computer file, SN 4615), UK Data Archive, 29th October 2008[d], retrieved 5th May 2009, http://www.data-archive.ac.uk/findingdata/snDescription.asp?sn=4615&key=4615.

NATIONAL READERSHIP SURVEY, 'Lifestyle Data', NRS website, 2008, retrieved 5th March 2010, http://www.nrs.co.uk/lifestyle.html.

NATIONAL STATISTICS, 'Adults who have used the Internet by their characteristics: Individual Internet Access', National Statistics website, c. 2003, retrieved 27th May 2008, http://www.statistics.gov.uk/downloads/theme_commerce/ Internet_Access_Datasets_pre-Apr03.zip.

—, 'Graduation rates from first university degrees: EU comparison, 2001: Social Trends 34', National Statistics website, 4th February 2004, retrieved 25th March 2006, http://www.statistics.gov.uk/StatBase/Expodata/Spreadsheets/D7311.xls.

—, 'Religious Populations', National Statistics website, 11th October 2004, retrieved 18th July 2006, http://www.statistics.gov.uk/cci/nugget.asp?id=954.

—, 'Usual resident population, Census 2001: Key Statistics for the rural and urban area classification 2004', National Statistics website, 2005, retrieved 24th August 2006, http://www.statistics.gov.uk/StatBase/Expodata/Spreadsheets/D8914.xls.

—, 'Cohabitation amongst non-married people aged 16 to 59, 2000-02: Regional Trends 38', National Statistics website, 2nd March 2005, retrieved 14th March 2006, http://www.statistics.gov.uk/STATBASE/Expodata/Spreadsheets/D7677.xls.

—, 'All people Part 1: Census 2001, National Report for England and Wales - Part 2', National Statistics website, 21st March 2005, retrieved 28th April 2006, http://www.statistics.gov.uk/StatBase/Expodata/Spreadsheets/D7547.xls.

—, '(a) Household type by tenure, (b) Tenure by household type: General Household Survey 2003', National Statistics website, 29th March 2005, retrieved 19th March 2006, http://www.statistics.gov.uk/STATBASE/Expodata/Spreadsheets/D8731.xls.

—, 'Age structure, Census 2001: Key Statistics for the rural and urban area classification 2004, 30th March 2005, National Statistics website, retrieved 15th March 2006, http://www.statistics.gov.uk/StatBase/Expodata/Spreadsheets/D8915.xls.

—, 'Age distribution: Cohabiting couples are youngest families', National Statistics website, 7th July 2005, retrieved 14th March 2006, http://www.statistics.gov.uk/cci/nugget.asp?id=1165.

—, 'Public Sector Employment: 1 in 5 of all workers', National Statistics website, 28th October 2005, retrieved 21st March 2006, http://www.statistics.gov.uk/cci/nugget.asp?ID=1292&Pos=2&ColRank=2&Rank=1000.

—, 'Use of the Internet: 6 in 10 Internet users go online daily', National Statistics website, 15th March 2007, retrieved 27th May 2008, http://www.statistics.gov.uk/cci/nugget.asp?id=1711.

—, 'Population Estimates: UK population grows to 60.6 million', National Statistics website, 22nd August 2007, retrieved 11th August 2008, http://www.statistics.gov.uk/cci/nugget.asp?ID=6.

—, Internet Access 2007: Households and Individuals, National Statistics website, 28th August 2007, retrieved 27th May 2008, http://www.statistics.gov.uk/pdfdir/ inta0807.pdf.

—, 'Internet Access', National Statistics website, 26th August 2008, retrieved 5th March 2009, http://www.statistics.gov.uk/CCI/nugget.asp?ID=8&Pos=1&ColRank= 2&Rank=448.

—, 'Labour Market Statistics: 1983-2008', (computer file No. TZ258596011), National Statistics website, 11th December 2008, retrieved 11th January 2009, http://www.statistics.gov.uk.

Brent NELSON, James GUTH & Cleveland FRASER, 'Does Religion Matter?', *European Union Politics*, Vol. 2, No. 2, 2001, pp. 191-217.

Fraser NELSON, 'Revealed: How the Conservative party is planning to split', *The Spectator*, Vol. 303, No. 9321, 7th April 2007, pp. 14-15.

Simon NIXON, 'Why the Tories backed the war', *The Spectator*, Vol. 292, No. 9119, 17th May 2003, pp. 18-19.

David NOLAN, 'Classifying and Analysing Politico-Economic Systems, 1971, in ADVOCATES FOR SELF-GOVERNMENT, *Nolan Chart Reader*, Atlanta, GA, Advocates for Self-Government, 1995, pp. 3-9.

Pippa NORRIS, 'The *British Representation Study 1997*', 1997, retrieved 30th January 2005, http://ksghome.harvard.edu/~pnorris/Data/Data.htm.

Pippa NORRIS & Joni LOVENDUSKI, 'Why Parties Fail to Learn: Electoral Defeat, Selective Perception and British Party Politics', *Party Politics*, Vol. 10, No. 1, January 2004, pp. 85-104.

Richard NORTH, 'They still don't get it', *EU Referendum* blog, 14th June 2004, retrieved 14th June 2004, http://www.eureferendum.blogspot.com/#108722301705096279.

—, 'While the children play', *EU Referendum* blog, 27th September 2008, retrieved 27th September 2008, http://eureferendum.blogspot.com/2008/09/while-children-play.html.

—, 'A litany of contradictions', *EU Referendum* blog, 12th April 2009, retrieved 13th April 2009, http://eureferendum.blogspot.com/2009/04/litany-of-contradictions.html.

—, 'Make politics local', *EU Referendum* blog, 28th May 2009, retrieved 29th May 2009, http://eureferendum.blogspot.com/2009/05/make-politics-local.html.

—, *Ministry of Defeat 2003-2009: The British in Iraq*, London, Continuum, 2009.

—, 'From the authors of the inquisition ...', *EU Referendum* blog, 3rd August 2009, retrieved 4th August 2009, http://eureferendum.blogspot.com/2009/08/from-authors-of-inquisition.html.

—, 'Clearing the backlog', *EU Referendum* blog, 22nd April 2010, retrieved 23rd April 2010, http://eureferendum.blogspot.com/2010/04/clearing-backlog.html.

—, 'Whack-a-mole', *EU Referendum* blog, 27th October 2010, retrieved 3rd February 2012, http://eureferendum.blogspot.com/2010/10/whack-mole.html.

—, 'Europe is domestic policy', *EU Referendum* blog, 9th February 2012, retrieved 10th February 2012, http://eureferendum.blogspot.com/2012/02/europe-is-domestic-policy.html.

—, 'Tories "enthusiastically supported" wartime Euro-integration', *EU Referendum* blog, 20th March 2012, retrieved 20th March 2012, http://eureferendum.blogspot.co.uk/2012/03/tories-enthusiastically-supported.html.

—, 'The Old Swan Manifesto' *EU Referendum* blog, 27th March 2012, retrieved 28th March 2012, http://eureferendum.blogspot.co.uk/2012/03/old-swan-manifesto.html.

—, 'He finally noticed', *EU Referendum* blog, 12th May 2012, retrieved 13th May 2012, http://www.eureferendum.com/blogview.aspx?blogno=82656.

NOTHERN IRELAND OFFICE, 'The Agreement', Northern Ireland Office website, 2007, retrieved 10th January 2009, http://www.nio.gov.uk/the-agreement.

Philip NORTON, '"The Lady's Not For Turning' But What About the Rest? Margaret Thatcher and the Conservative Party 1979-1989', *Parliamentary Affairs*, Vol. 43, 1990, pp. 41-58.

—, 'The Conservative Party from Thatcher to Major', in Anthony KING (ed.), *Britain at the Polls 1992*, Chatham, NJ, Chatham House Publishers, 1992, pp. 29-69.

—, 'The Conservative Party: In Office but Not in Power', 1997, in Anthony KING (ed.), *New Labour Triumphs: Britain at the Polls*, Chatham, NJ, Chatham House Publishers, 1997, pp 75-112.

—, 'The Conservative Party: Is There Anyone Out There?', in Anthony King (ed.), *Britain at the Polls 2001*, London, Chatham House Publishers, 2002, pp. 68-94.

—, 'The Future of Conservatism', *The Political Quarterly*, Vol. 79, No. 3, July-September 2008, pp. 324-332.

Marija NORUŠIS, *SPSS 10.0 Guide to Data Analysis*, Upper Saddle River, NJ, Prentice Hall, 2000.

Maria O'BEIRNE, *Religion in England and Wales: Findings from the 2001 Home Office Citizenship Survey*, London, Home Office Research, Development and Statistics Directorate, March 2004.

Peter OBORNE, 'The problem is simple: Tony's a pretty straightforwardly devious sort of guy', *The Spectator*, Vol. 285, No. 8981, 23rd September 2000, p. 8.

—, 'Why it's got to be Ken', *The Spectator*, Vol. 286, No. 9019, 16th June 2001, pp. 12-13.

—, 'If the Tories want to win the asylum debate, they must trust their own instincts', *The Spectator*, Vol. 291, No. 9104, 1st February 2003, p. 9.

—, 'This week Iain Duncan Smith finally turned his back on the media/political class', *The Spectator*, Vol. 291, No. 9107, 22nd February 2003, p. 9.

—, 'It's taken decades, but Labour has seen the light on Europe', *Telegraph*, 21st April 2011, retrieved 20th March 2012, http://tinyurl.com/3bvr93m.

—, 'As the landscape starts to shift, Ukip can create political havoc', *Telegraph*, 2nd November 2011, retrieved 25th February 2012, http://tinyurl.com/6jzp4sr.

Peter OBORNE & Frances WEAVER, *Guilty Men*, London, Centre for Policy Studies, 2011.

Christina ODONE, 'All-female short lists? Not if Tory Woman has her way', *Guardian*, 26th January 2003, retrieved 26th January 2003, http://politics.guardian.co.uk/conservatives/comment/0,9236,882697,00.html.

John O'FARRELL, 'It's official: Tories are bonkers', *Guardian*, 22nd September 2001, retrieved 7th October 2001, http://www.guardian.co.uk/comment/story/ 0,3604,556118,00.html.

Dennis O'KEEFFE (ed.), *Economy and Virtue: Essays on the Theme of Markets and Morality*, London, Institute of Economic Affairs, 2004.

A.N. OPPENHEIM, *Questionnaire Design, Interviewing and Attitude Measurement* (new ed.), London, Pinter Publishers, 1992.

James ORR, 'Achievements of an economically independent Scotland' [letters to the editor], *The Times*, 27th August 2002, p. 17.

John O'SULLIVAN, *Conservatism, Democracy and National Identity*, London, Centre for Policy Studies, 1999.

—, 'Magical Mystery Tour: David Cameron and the need for nastiness', *National Review*, 9th March 2009, retrieved 17th August 2009, http://tinyurl.com/arudby.

Matthew PARRIS, 'What in God's name is Hague doing?', *The Times*, 4th November 2000, p. 28.

—, 'If you want to vote for the forces of moderation, forget the Lib Dems', *The Spectator*, Vol. 286, No. 9015, 19th May 2001, p. 10.

—, 'Think Tory, think Iain', *The Times, Times2*, 10th July 2001, pp. 2-3.

—, 'Ministers pander to a misguided populace', *Curmudgeon*, 4th August 2001, retrieved 21st March 2004, http://members.lycos.co.uk/curmudgeon/misc/ art_misguided.html.

—, 'You don't have to be mad to vote for Iain', *The Times*, 25th August 2001.

—, 'A new Prime Minister needs a new mandate', *The Times*, 2nd August 2008, p. 17.

Angela PARTINGTON (ed.), *The Oxford Dictionary of Quotations* (revised 4th ed.), Oxford, Oxford University Press, 1996.

Charles PATTIE & Ron JOHNSTON, 'The Conservative Party and the Electorate', in Steve LUDLUM & Martin SMITH (eds.), *Contemporary British Conservatism*, Basingstoke, Macmillan Press, 1996, pp. 37-62.

Christine PAUL, Raoul WALSH & Flora TZELEPIS, 'A monetary incentive increases postal survey response rates for pharmacists' (online short report), *Journal of Epidemiology and Community Health*, No 59, 2005, retrieved 5th May 2009, http://jech.bmj.com/cgi/content/abstract/59/12/1099.

Robert PAXTON, *The Anatomy of Fascism*, London, Allen Lane, 2004

Laura PEEK, Michelle HENERY, Claire MCDONALD, Gabriel ROZENBURG & Tom BALDWIN, 'We've no chance but we want no change, say Tories', *The Times*, 8th November 2002, p. 17.

Gillian PEELE, 'Political Parties', 1997, in Patrick DUNLEAVY, Andrew GAMBLE, Ian HOLLIDAY & Gillian PEELE (eds.), *Developments in British Politics 5*, Basingstoke, Macmillan Press, 1997, pp. 89-109.

Anne PERKINS, 'MPs say reformed Lords should be 60% elected', *Guardian*, 15th February 2002, retrieved 18th February 2002, www.guardian.co.uk/Archive/Article/0,4273,4356375,00.html.

Robin PETTITT, 'Revisiting Michels' 'Iron Law of Oligarchy': an examination of membership influence in political parties', Paper prepared for EPOP Panel on The Changing Nature and Structure of Political Parties, 57th Political Studies Association Annual Conference, University of Bath, April 2007, PSA website, retrieved 2nd May 2010, http://www.psa.ac.uk/journals/pdf/5/2007/pettitt.pdf.

Melanie PHILLIPS, 'These tolerant Tories lack courage as well as conviction', *Sunday Times*, 1st July 2001, p. 17.

Andrew PIERCE, 'Norris calls for gay leader', *The Times*, 23rd October 2000, p. 10.

—, 'Tories plunge £15m into red as polls point to loss of faith', *The Times*, 6th December 2004, p. 2.

Bruce PILBEAM, 'The Conservative Party and the Problem of Contemporary Conservatism', *Contemporary Political Studies*, 1998, pp. 279-287.

—, 'Natural Allies? Mapping the Relationship between Conservatism and Environmentalism', *Political Studies*, Vol. 51, No. 3, October 2003, pp. 490-508.

Daniel PIPES, 'Anti-Semitism Evolves', *New York Sun*, 15th February 2005, retrieved 1st February 2006, http://www.danielpipes.org/article/2412.

Efraim PODOKSIK, 'Overcoming the Conservative Disposition: Oakeshott vs. Tönnies', *Political Studies*, Vol. 56, No. 4, December 2008, pp. 857-880.

Robertas POGORELIS, Bart MADDENS, Wilfried SWENDEN & Elodie FABRE, 'Issue salience in regional and national party manifestos in the UK', *West European Politics*, Vol. 28, No. 5, November 2005, pp. 992-1014.

POLITICAL COMPASS, 'The Political Compass: Take the Test'', *PoliticalCompass*, 2004[a], retrieved 15th February 2004, http://www.digitalronin.f2s.com/politicalcompass/questionnaire.pl?page=1.

—, 'A Few Words about 'The Extreme Right'', *PoliticalCompass*, 2004[b], retrieved 15th February 2004, http://www.digitalronin.f2s.com/politicalcompass/extremeright.html.

POLITICAL STUDIES ASSOCIATION NEWS, 'Cameron's Conservatives: Approaching Government?', *Political Studies Association News*, Vol. 20, No.1, March 2009, pp. 30-31.

Michael PORTILLO, Another slow Tory crash into the buffers of Europe, *Sunday Times*, 6th June 2004, p. 21.

Jerry POURNELLE, 'All Ends of the Spectrum: An Appendix', 1986, retrieved 1st January 2009: http://www.baen.com/chapters/axes.htm.

Thomas QUINN, 'Leasehold or Freehold? Leader Eviction Rules in the British Conservative and Labour Parties', *Political Studies*, Vol. 53, No. 4, December 2005, pp. 793-815.

Daniel QUINTILIANI, 'The World's Most Honest Political Quiz', 2004, retrieved 1st October 2004, http://danq.lunarpages.com/polquiz/index.html.

Anthony QUINTON, *The Politics of Imperfection: The Religious and Secular Traditions of Conservative Thought in England from Hooker to Oakeshott*, London, Faber & Faber, 1978.

Colin RALLINGS & Michael THRASHER, 'Elections and Public Opinion: Conservative Doldrums and Continuing Apathy', *Parliamentary Affairs*, Vol. 56, No. 2, April 2003, pp.. 270-282.

—, 'Elections and Public Opinion: Leaders Under Pressure', *Parliamentary Affairs*, Vol. 57, No. 2, April 2004, pp. 380-395.

Colin RALLINGS, Michael THRASHER & Ron JOHNSTON, 'The Slow Death of a Governing Party: The Erosion of Support of Conservative Local Electoral Support in England 1979-1997', *Political Studies*, Vol. 4, No. 2, June 2002, pp. 271-298.

Aidan RANKIN, 'Church of the Poisoned Mind', 2001, in Edward VAIZEY, Nicholas BOLES & Michael GOVE (eds.), *A Blue Tomorrow: New Visions for Modern Conservatives*, London, Politico's Publishing, 2001, pp. 142-150.

Glen RAPHAEL, 'A Non-Non-Libertarian FAQ: Responses to Mike Huben', *Liberals & Libertarians*, 1996, retrieved 13th January 2004, http://www.impel.com/liblib/NNLibFAQ.html.

Andrew RAWNSLEY, 'The corruption of Tony Blair', *Guardian*, 17th February 2002, retrieved 23rd February 2002, www.observer.co.uk/comment/story/0,6903,651583,00.html.

RAEDWALD, 'Sleazy MPs - what's changed?', *Raedwald*, 14th May 2012, retrieved 15th May 2012, http://tinyurl.com/8xuodbw.

John REDWOOD, 'New Right', 2005, in Kevin HICKSON (ed.), *The Political Thought of the Conservative Party Since 1945*, Basingstoke, Palgrave Macmillan, 2005, pp. 202-208.

William REES-MOGG, 'This hooded eagle among Tory owls', *The Times*, 18th June 2001.

Tim REID, 'America is revealed as one nation under four faces of God', *The Times*, 13th September 2006, p. 46.

Jo REVILL, 'Blair plans amnesty for 30 IRA terrorists', *Evening Standard*, 6th March 2002, p. 22.

Joshua REY, *Cognitive Dissonance, Markets and the Labour Party: Why Labour Must Accept Market Economics*, Economic Notes No. 61, London, Libertarian Alliance, 1994.

Peter RIDDELL, 'Tory Unity Collapses as Labour is Reborn', in Tim AUSTIN (ed.), *The Times Guide to the House of Commons, May 1997*, London, Times Books, 1997, pp. 17-19.

—, 'Don't be misled by notions of left and light', *The Times*, 9th December 1997, p. 10.

—, 'Town and country are divided', *The Times*, 29th March 2001, p. 4.

—, 'First task: to win back 5.7 million missing voters', *The Times*, 14th June 2001, p. 6.

—, 'Howard relishes return to front line of politics', *The Times*, 8th October 2001, p. 16.

—, 'Threat of the Right in Britain remains local, rather than national', *The Times*, 23rd April 2002, p. 15.

—, 'Most voters think Labour has swung right', *The Times*, 20th September 2004, p. 2.

—, 'It's the person, not the post, who merits a title', *The Times*, 27th February 2009, p. 5.

—, 'Now MPs must face the music back at home', *The Times*, 15th May 2009, p. 9.

Paul Craig ROBERTS, 'America the Unfree', *LewRockwell.com*, 28th January 2004, retrieved 14th February 2004, http://www.lewrockwell.com/roberts/roberts27.html.

Duncan ROBERTSON, 'Why we'd vote Thatcher back into Number 10', *Daily Mail*, 7th April 2008, p. 19.

Joanne ROBERTSON & Eben BLACK, 'Scots split as Tories admit defeat', *Sunday Times*, 3rd June 2001, retrieved 10th June 2001, www.sunday-times.co.uk.

Bendict ROGERS, 'Five years on and the Tories have changed for the better', *Daily Telegraph*, 14th August 2002, retrieved 12th April 2010, http://tinyurl.com/yac5a45.

Richard ROSE & Ian MCALLISTER, *The Loyalties of Voters: A Lifetime Learning Model*, London, Sage, 1990.

Kelley L. ROSS, 'Positive and Negative Liberties in Three Dimensions', *Friesian School*, 2004, retrieved 3rd March 2004, http://www.friesian.com/quiz.htm.

Andrew ROTH, 'Michael Howard: The First Jewish Prime Minister?', *The Political Quarterly*, Vol. 75, No. 4, October 2004, pp. 362-366.

Andrew ROTH & Michael WHITE, 'Eric Forth' [obituary], *Guardian*, 19th May 2006, retrieved 17th November 2008, http://www.guardian.co.uk/news/2006/may/19/guardianobituaries.conservatives.

Catherine ROTHON & Anthony HEATH, 'Trends in Racial Prejudice', 2003, in Alison PARK, John CURTICE, Katarina THOMSON, Lindsey JARVIS & Catherine BROMLEY (eds.), *British Social Attitudes*, 20th report, London, National Centre for Social Research, 2003, pp. 189-214.

Gabriel ROZENBURG, 'Find your political colours with *The Times* quiz', *The Times: Election 2005, A Survival Guide*, 6th April 2005, p. 15.

Mark RUPRIGHT, 'The World's Smallest Political Hook', *Mike Huben*, 1997, retrieved 3rd January 2004, http://world.std.com/~mhuben/rupright.html.

John RUST & Susan GOLOMBOK, *Modern Psychometrics* (2nd ed.), London, Routledge, 1999.

Jens RYDGREN, 'Immigration sceptics, xenophobes or racists? Radical right-wing voting in six West European countries', *European Journal of Political Research*, Vol. 47, No. 6, October 2008, pp. 737-765.

Adrian SACKMAN, 'The Political Marketing Organisation Model and the Modernisation of the Labour Party, 1983-87', *PSA Conference Proceedings*, 1994, pp. 465-478, retrieved 7th April 2012, http://www.psa.ac.uk/journals/pdf/5/1994/sack.pdf.

Juliet SAMUEL, 'Over the rainbow: How radical environmentalists thwarted Copenhagen', in Peter WHITTLE (ed.), *A Sorry State: Self-denigration in British culture*, London, New Culture Forum, 2010: 15-34.

David SANDERS, 'The New Electoral Battleground', 1997, in Anthony KING (ed.), *New Labour Triumphs: Britain at the Polls*, Chatham, NJ, Chatham House Publishers, 1997, pp. 209-248.

—, 'Reflections on the 2005 General Election: Some Speculations on How The Conservatives Can Win Next Time', *British Politics*, Vol. 1, No. 2, July 2006, pp. 170-194.

David SANDERS & Malcolm BRYNIN, 'The Dynamics of Party Preference Change in Britain, 1991-1996', *Political Studies*, XLVII, 1999, pp. 219-239.

Paul SANTMIRE, *The Travail of Nature: The Ambiguous Ecological Promise of Christian Theology*, Philadelphia, Fortress Press, 1985.

Roger SAPSFORD, *Survey Research*, London, Sage Publications, 1999.

Carol SARLER, 'Enough religion. Stop shoving it down my throat', *The Times*, 13th September 2007, retrieved 17th August 2007, http://tinyurl.com/yt4pbo.

Ben SAUNDERS, 'The Democratic Turnout 'Problem'', *Political Studies*, Vol. 60, No. 2, June 2012, pp. 306-320.

Elinor SCARBROUGH, *Political Ideology and Voting*, Oxford, Clarendon Press, 1984.

—, 'Materialist-Postmaterialist Value Orientations', 1995, in Jan VAN DETH & Elinor SCARBROUGH (eds.), *The Impact of Values*, Oxford, Oxford University Press, 1995/1998, pp. 123-159.

—, 'The British Election Study and Electoral Research', *Political Studies*, Vol. 48, No. 3, June 2000, pp. 391-414.

Norman SCHOFIELD, Gary MILLER & Andrew MARTIN, 'Critical Elections and Political Realignments in the USA: 1860-2000', *Political Studies*, Vol. 51, No. 2, June 2003, pp. 217-240.

Ilka SCHROEDER, 'The War against Israel and Growing European Nationalism', *The Sprout*, February 2004, retrieved 11th June 2007, http://www.travelbrochuregraphics.com/extra/the_war_against_israel.htm.

Shalom SCHWARTZ, 'Value orientations: Measurement, antecedents and consequences across nations', 2007, in Roger JOWELL, Caroline ROBERTS, Rory Fitzgerald & Gillian EVA (eds.), *Measuring Attitudes Cross-Nationally*, London, Centre for Comparative Social Surveys, 2007, pp. 169-203.

Etienne SCHWEISGUTH, 'Status Tensions', 1995, in Jan VAN DETH & Elinor SCARBROUGH (eds.), *The Impact of Values*, Oxford, Oxford University Press, 1995/1998, pp. 332-354.

Nora SCOTT, 'We have been betrayed by the party we loved' [letters to the editor], *Daily Mail*, 4th November 2003, p. 56.

Roger SCRUTON, *The Meaning of Conservatism* (3rd ed.), Basingstoke, Palgrave, 2001.

—, 'My life beyond the pale', *The Spectator*, Vol. 290, No. 9085, 21st September 2002, pp. 16-17.

—, 'Brain drain', *The Spectator*, Vol. 318, No. 9577, 17th March 2012, pp. 18-19.

Anthony SELDON & Stuart BALL (eds.), *Conservative Century: The Conservative Party Since 1900*, Oxford, Oxford University Press, 1994.

Anthony SELDON & Peter SNOWDON, *A New Conservative Century?*, London, Centre for Policy Studies, 2001.

—, *The Conservative Party*, Stroud, Sutton Publishing Limited, 2004.

Patrick SEYD, 'Factionalism in the 1970s', 1980, in Zig LAYTON-HENRY (ed.), *Conservative Party Politics*, London, Macmillan Press, 1980, pp. 231-243.

James SHEEHAN, 'Fools Put Faith in Data Alone', Ludwig von Mises Institute website, 23rd February 2006, retrieved 28th February 2006, http://www.mises.org/story/2056.

Alfred SHERMAN, 'The Missing Dimension: Religion in World Affairs', *The Salisbury Review*, Vol. 22, No. 3, Spring 2004, pp. 13-15.

Jill SHERMAN, 'Big cities remain Tory-free zones despite gains', *The Times*, 14th May 2003, p. 12.

Martin SHIPTON, 'Poll suggests support for Plaid and Labour up', *WalesOnline*, 16th October 2008, retrieved 20th October 2008, http://tinyurl.com/6m2nvy.

Haroon SIDDIQUE, 'Election results: Black politics 'comes of age' in Britain', *Guardian*, 7th May 2010, retrieved 11th February 2012, http://www.guardian.co.uk/politics/blog/2010/may/07/election-reaults-black-politics-britain.

Mary Ann SIEGHART, 'Where is the team that women can support?', *The Times*, 11th August 2000, p. 20.

—, 'More women Tory MPs? It's still jobs for the boys', *The Times, T2*, 20th December 2004, pp. 4-5.

Peter SIMINSKI, 'Order Effects in Batteries of Questions', *Quality & Quantity*, No. 42, 2008, pp. 477-490.

Peter SIMPLE, End Column, *Telegraph*, 1st February 2002, retrieved 26th July 2008, http://tinyurl.com/6dd9gh.

Mark SKOUSEN, 'Neither Left nor Right', *Ideas on Liberty*, Vol. 50, No. 7, July 2000, pp. 52-53.

John SLOMAN, *Economics*, Hemel Hempstead, Harvester Wheatsheaf, 1991.

Ann SMARTY, 'The Evolution of Three Home Pages: Facebook, Twitter and LinkedIn', Seo Smarty website, November 2012, retrieved 13th February 2012, http://tinyurl.com/7lucu6z.

David SMITH, 'Labour moves back into poll lead', *Sunday Times*, 15th October 2000, p. 12.

SOCIETY FOR INDIVIDUAL FREEDOM, 'SIF Beliefs', Society for Individual Freedom website, 27th October 2004, retrieved 13th February 2012, http://tinyurl.com/7voplmq.

SPECTATOR, 'Portillo's Fall' [editorial], *The Spectator*, vol. 287, no. 9024, 21st July 2001, p. 9.

—, 'Right war: Wrong reason', *The Spectator*, Vol. 294, No. 9157, 7th February 2004, p. 7.

Herbert SPENCER, *The Man Versus The State*, Harmondsworth, Middlesex, Pelican, 1884/1969.

Nick SPENCER, *"Doing God": A Future for Faith in the Public Square*, London, Theos, 2006.

Michael SPICER, *A Treaty Too Far: A New Policy for Europe*, London, Fourth Estate, 1992.

SPSS, 'SPSS Data Entry Builder', *SPSS* website, 2006, retrieved 8th May 2006, http://www.spss.com/Data_Entry/data_entry_builder.

STATSOFT, 'Multidimensional Scaling', StatSoft website, 2003, retrieved 21st January 2005, http://www.statsoft.com/textbook/stmulsca.html.

Stewart STEVEN, 'Where are the Tebbits who'll rescue Tories?', 28th July 2002, *The Mail on Sunday*, p. 55.

Mark STEYN, 'The war between America and Europe', *The Spectator*, Vol. 287, No. 9047, 29th December 2001, pp. 18-19.

William STIRLING, 'Act of Disunion', *Salisbury Review*, Vol. 30, No. 3, spring 2012, pp. 4-6.

Ollie STONE-LEE, 'Mandelson on his communist days', *BBC News*, 1st October 2002, retrieved 4th July 2008, http://news.bbc.co.uk/1/hi/uk_politics/2289501.stm.

Andrew SULLIVAN, 'Media Bias: It's real and it's even worse in Britain', *andrewsullivan.com*, 17th November 2002, retrieved 5th January 2003, http://www.andrewsullivan.com/main_article.php?artnum=20021117.

SUNDAY TELEGRAPH, 'Christians face a new persecution' [editorial], *Sunday Telegraph*, 11th April 2009, retrieved 17th August 2009, http://tinyurl.com/ccwovm.

SUTTON TRUST, *The Educational Backgrounds of Members of the House of Commons and House of Lords*, London, Sutton Trust, 2005.

—, *The Educational Backgrounds of Members of Parliament in 2010*, London, Sutton Trust, 2010.

Helen SZAMUELY, 'It is all soooo boring', *Your Freedom and Ours* blog, 16th March 2010, retrieved 16th March 2010, http://yourfreedomandours.blogspot.com/2010/03/it-is-all-soooo-boring.html.

—, 'Really, it is not hard to work out', *Your Freedom and Ours* blog, 12th April 2012, retrieved 15th April 2012, http://yourfreedomandours.blogspot.co.uk/2012/04/really-it-is-not-hard-to-work-out.html.

Abul TAHER, 'Quiz hits out left, right and centre', *Sunday Times*, 24th October 2004, p. 9.

Stephen TANSEY, *Politics:The Basics*, London, Routledge, 1995.

V. TAYLOR, *Municipal Yearbook 2000, Vol. 2*, London, Newman Books, 2000.

Norman TEBBIT, 'There is such a thing as society', *The Spectator*, Vol. 285, No. 8990, 25th November 2000, p. 16.

TELEGRAPH, 'The future of the Tories', *Telegraph*, 15th June 2001, retrieved 26th July 2008, http://tinyurl.com/58ees5.

—, 'The future of the Tories', *Telegraph*, 16th June 2001, retrieved 26th July 2008, http://tinyurl.com/6r9xma.

—, 'Eric Forth' [obituary], *Telegraph*, 19th May 2006, retrieved 18th April 2012, http://tinyurl.com/7m5vvfb.

—, 'Only Tory MPs should elect their party leader' [editorial], *Telegraph*, 26th July 2008, retrieved 15th November 2004, http://tinyurl.com/57pzmt.

—, 'Councils of despair', *Telegraph*, 4th September 2006, retrieved 26th July 2008, http://tinyurl.com/5tpcap.

—, 'MPs' expenses' [main page], *Telegraph*, 2009, retrieved 20th June 2009, http://www.telegraph.co.uk/news/newstopics/mps-expenses/.

—, 'Ten years of broadband in Britain', *Telegraph*, 31st March 2010, retrieved 13th February 2012, http://tinyurl.com/ydoqsyq.

—, 'Antony Flew' [obituary], *Telegraph*, 13th April 2010, retrieved 14th April 2010, http://tinyurl.com/y8x5grm.

—, 'Out of confusion comes David Cameron and clarity', *Telegraph*, 12th May 2010, retrieved 12th May 2010, http://tinyurl.com/2wepfdb.

Matthew TEMPEST, 'Portillo to quit as MP', *Guardian*, 7th November 2003, retrieved 28th December 2003, http://politics.guardian.co.uk/conservatives/story/0,9061,1080339,00.html.

—, 'Tories seek flagbearer for faith and family', *Guardian*, 22nd August 2005, retrieved 31st July 2006, http://politics.guardian.co.uk/conservatives/story/0,,1554153,00.html.

Margaret THATCHER, 'Islamism is the new bolshevism', *Guardian*, 12th February 2002, retrieved 19th February 2002, www.guardian.co.uk/bush/story/0,7369,648935,00.html.

Kevin THEAKSTON & Mark GILL, 'Rating 20th Century British Prime Ministers', *British Journal of Politics & International Relations*, Vol. 8, No. 2, May 2006, pp. 193-213.

Clifford THIES, 'Understanding the RLC LiberGraph', *Republican Liberty Caucus*, 2000, retrieved 31st January 2004, http://www.republicanliberty.org/libdex/LiberGraph.htm.

Bev THOMAS, 'A welcome from Bev Thomas, Chair of CSM', Christian Socialist Movement, 2005, retrieved 30th May 2006, http://www.thecsm.org.uk/aboutus.html.

Mark THOMPSON, 'The Trouble with Trust', *Political Quarterly*, Vol. 79, No. 3, July-September 2008, pp. 303-313.

Peter THOMPSON, 'The PDS: Marx's Baby or Stalin's Bathwater?', in Peter BARKER (ed.), *The GDR and Its History*, Amsterdam, Rodopi, 2000, pp. 97-112.

Alice THOMSON, 'It looks as if their luck has finally changed', *Telegraph*, 4th August 2009, retrieved 30th October 2003, http://tinyurl.com/mrs2ty.

—, 'Balancing act tripped up the Quiet Man', *Daily Telegraph*, 30th October 2003, retrieved 4th August 2009, http://tinyurl.com/mwckl2.

James TILLEY, 'Political Generations and Partisanship in the UK, 1964-1997', *Journal of the Royal Statistical Society*, Series A, Vol. 165, Part 1, 2002, pp. 121-135.

THE TIMES, 'Looking forward: An inevitable but necessary split on the Tory Right' [editorial], *The Times*, 3rd November 2000, p. 23.

—, 'The disunity candidate' [editorial], *The Times*, 27th June 2001.

—, 'The Tory choice' [editorial], *The Times*, 22nd August 2001, p. 13.

—, 'Shades of blue' [editorial], *The Times*, 19th September 2002, p. 23.

—, 'Eric Forth' [obituary], *The Times*, 19th May 2006, retrieved 17th November 2008, http://www.timesonline.co.uk/tol/comment/obituaries/article721288.ece.

—, 'The Earl of Lauderdale' [obituary], *The Times*, 5th January 2009, p. 51.

John TIZARD, 'Local elections: the turnout trauma', *Public Finance*, 4th May 2012, retrieved 15th May 2012, http://tinyurl.com/cqt9lz3.

Richard TOPF, 'Political Change and Political Culture in Britain 1959-1987', 1989, in John GIBBINS (ed.), *Contemporary Political Culture: Politics in a Postmodern Age*, London, Sage, 1989, pp. 52-80.

—, 'Party manifestos', 1994, in Anthony HEATH, Roger JOWELL & John CURTICE (eds.), *Labour's Last Chance?: The 1992 Election and Beyond*, Aldershot, Dartmouth Publishing, 1994, pp. 149-172.

—, 'Electoral Participation', 1995[a], in Hans-Dieter KLINGEMANN & Dieter FUCHS (eds.), *Citizenship and the State*, Oxford, Oxford University Press, 1995, pp. 27-51.

—, 'Beyond Electoral Participation', 1995[b], in Hans-Dieter KLINGEMANN & Dieter FUCHS (eds.), *Citizenship and the State*, Oxford, Oxford University Press, 1995, pp. 52-91.

TORY EUROPE NETWORK, 'Why we support the Tory Europe Network', c. 2002, retrieved 29th April 2004, http://www.toryeuropenetwork.org.uk/oursupporters.htm.

TORY REFORM GROUP, 'Lessons from the 2001 General Election: Winning Back the Missing Conservatives', Tory Reform Group, 11th June 2001, retrieved 28th March 2006, http://core2.trg.org.uk/publications/missingconservatives.html.

Gawain TOWLER, Emmanuel BORDES & Lee ROTHERHAM, *Bloc Tory: A New Party for Europe?*, London, Centre for Policy Studies, 2001.

TRADING ECONOMICS, 'United Kingdom GDP Growth Rate', *Trading Economics*, 2009, retrieved 11th January 2009, http://www.tradingeconomics.com/Economics/GDP-Growth.aspx?Symbol=GBP.

Alan TRAVIS, 'Poll shock for Welsh home rule', *Guardian*, 10th October 1997, retrieved 28th July 2008, http://www.guardian.co.uk/politics/1997/oct/10/wales.devolution.

—, 'More Britons support Palestinians, says poll', *Guardian*, 24th April 2002, retrieved 29th April 2002, www.guardian.co.uk/Archive/Article/0,4273,4400330,00.html.

—, 'Most popular PM of the past 100 years: Unprecedented domination of opinion polls goes back nine years', *Guardian*, 27th April 2002, retrieved 29th April 2002, www.guardian.co.uk/Archive/Article/0,4273,4402702,00.html.

—, 'Old story is bad news for Howard', *Guardian*, 18th November 2004, retrieved 21st November 2004, http://www.guardian.co.uk/guardianpolitics/story/ 0,3605,1353511,00.html.

Alan TRAVIS & Michael WHITE, 'Poll shows UKIP will split Tory vote', *Guardian*, 15th June 2004, retrieved 2nd October 2004, http://politics.guardian.co.uk/polls/story/0,11030,1239111,00.html.

David TRIMBLE, Address to the 2001 Conservative Party Conference, David Trimble's website, 10th October 2001, retrieved 12th December 2007, http://www.davidtrimble.org/speeches_toryparty2001.htm.

Benjamin TUCKER, *Instead of a Book by a Man Too Busy to Write One: A Fragmentary Exposition of Philosophical Anarchism*, New York, NY, Haskell House Publishers, 1987/1969.

Richard TYLER, 'Firms told not to fear loony Left', *Telegraph*, 16th May 2006, retrieved 10th February 2012, http://tinyurl.com/84382a9.

Andrew TYRIE, *Back from the Brink*, London, Parliamentary Mainstream, 2001.

UK INDEPENDENCE PARTY, 'Free Country' (as long as you're a Tory), says *Telegraph*', UKIP website, 9th July 2002, retrieved 11th July 2002, www.independence.org.uk/press/messages/14/14.html?1026230271.

UK POLITICAL INFO, 'General election turnout 1945 – 2010', UK Political Info website, 2010, retrieved 15th May 2012, http://www.ukpolitical.info/Turnout45.htm.

UK POLLING REPORT, 'ICM Voting Intention since 2005', UK Polling Report website, March 2009, retrieved 11th April 2009, http://ukpollingreport.co.uk/blog/voting-intention/icm.

—, 'Voting Intention since 2005', UK Polling Report website, May 2009, retrieved 13th May 2009, http://ukpollingreport.co.uk/blog/voting-intention.

—, 'Bromley and Chislehurst, UK Polling Report website, 2010, retrieved 9th February 2012, http://ukpollingreport.co.uk/guide/seat-profiles/bromley/.

Tom UTLEY, 'Tory Boy grows up to be the Best Man', *Telegraph*, 20th June 1997, retrieved 23rd July 2008, http://www.telegraph.co.uk/htmlContent.jhtml?html=/archive/1997/06/20/nboy120.html.

Ed VAIZEY, 'Kiss goodbye to B'Stard', *Sunday Times, News Review*, 9th June 2002, p. 7.

Mark VAN VUGT, 'Follow the Leader… But at What Cost', *The Psychologist*, Vol. 17, No. 5, May 2004, pp. 274-277.

Theresa VILLIERS, 'Attracting women? Honestly, we're getting better', *The Times, T2*, 20th December 2004, p. 5.

C. WALKER. 'Paisley's man gets support from two Tories', 20th September 2000, *The Times*, p. 14.

Kirsty WALKER, 'Backlash over Cameron's plan to parachute in 30 candidates', *Daily Mail*, 4th August 2009, p. 26.

Jonathan WALKER, 'Being English is bad for you, insists MP', *Birmingham Post*, 18th November 2005, retrieved 17th November 2008, http://tinyurl.com/6aap4k.

Simon WALTERS, *Tory Wars*, London, Politicos, 2001.

Hugh WARD, 'If the Party Won't go to the Median Voter, then the Median Voter Must Come to the Party: A Spatial Model of Two-Party Competition with Endogenous Voter Preferences', paper for the Political Studies Association Annual Conference, April 2000, retrieved 3rd January 2009, http://www.psa.ac.uk/journals/pdf/5/2000/Ward%20Hugh.pdf.

Stephen WARD & Rachel GIBSON, 'On-line and on message? Candidate websites in the 2001 General Election', *British Journal of Politics and International Relations*, Vol. 5, No 2, May 2003, pp. 188-205.

Bruno WATERFIELD, 'The Eurocratic assault on democracy', *Spiked*, 8th February 2012, retrieved 10th February 2012, http://www.spiked-online.com/index.php/site/article/12058/.

Nicholas WATT, 'Grassroots snub Hague plea for more women MPs', *Guardian*, 8th February 2000, retrieved 17th August 2000, http://www.guardian.co.uk/guardianpolitics/story/0,,236356,00.html.

—, 'Labour scorned for failing to select women', *Guardian*, 16th October 2000, retrieved 20th May 2001, http://www.guardian.co.uk/guardianpolitics/story/0,,383161,00.html.

—, 'Tories lag in race to raise £15m fund for election', *Guardian*, 5th January 2001, retrieved 23rd August 2008, http://www.guardian.co.uk/uk/2001/jan/05/labour.politics2.

—, 'Tories signal Ulster retreat', 5th January 2001, retrieved 12th December 2007, *Guardian*, http://www.guardian.co.uk/guardianpolitics/story/0,,418147,00.html.

—, 'Portillo group launched at secret meeting', *Guardian*, 25th June 2002, retrieved 29th June 2002, http://politics.guardian.co.uk/conservatives/story/0,9061,743397,00.html.

Paul WAUGH, 'Alan Duncan comes out as first gay Tory MP', *Independent*, 29th July 2002, retrieved 3rd July 2009, http://tinyurl.com/l2jmo6.

Paul WEBB, 'Parties and Party System: Prospects for Realignment', *Parliamentary Affairs*, Vol. 56, No. 2, April 2003, pp. 283-296.

—, 'The Attitudinal Assimilation of Europe by the Conservative Parliamentary Party', *British Politics*, Vol. 3, No. 4, December 2008, pp. 427-444.

Philip WEBSTER, 'Hague promises all-faiths crusade for marriage', *The Times*, 1st November 2000, p. 15.

Benjamin WEGG-PROSSER, 'Conservative Future gets a make-over', 12th October 2001, retrieved 28th February 2009, *Guardian*, http://www.guardian.co.uk/politics/2001/oct/12/conservatives.uk.

Guy WEIR, 'Self-employment in the UK labour market', *Labour Market Trends*, September 2003, pp. 441-451.

Michael WHARTON, *Peter Simple's Century*, London, Claridge Press, 1999.

—, *Peter Simple's Domain*, London, New European Publications, 2003.

Lynn WHITE, 'The Historical Roots of Our Ecological Crisis', 1967, retrieved 18th June 2006, http://web.lemoyne.edu/~glennon/LynnWhitearticle.pdf. The article originally appeared in *Science*, Vol. 155, No, 3767, March 1967, pp. 1203-1207.

Michael WHITE, 'Left challenges 'stale' New Labour', *Guardian*, 20th July 2002, retrieved 30th July 2002, http://politics.guardian.co.uk/labour/story/0,9061,758701,00.html.

Ian WHITEHOUSE, *A Private Service: The Possible Privatisation of Britain's Armed Forces*, London, Libertarian Alliance, 2002.

Paul WHITELEY, Patrick SEYD & Jeremy RICHARDSON, *True Blues: The Politics of Conservative Party Membership*, Oxford, Clarendon Press, 1994.

—, *Survey of Conservative Party Members* (computer file No. 3286), Colchester, Essex, The Data Archive (distributor), 1992, lodged 13th March 1995. See also more recent documentation, 17th June 2005, retrieved 16th May 2009, http://www.data-archive.ac.uk/findingdata/snDescription.asp?sn=3286&key=3286.

Andy WHITTLES, 'Repeat after me: Right-wingers are the root of all evil', *Biased BBC*, 11th January 2004, retrieved 3rd March 2004, http://www.biased-bbc.blogspot.com/2004_01_01_biased-bbc_archive.html.

Damian WHITWORTH & Tom BALDWIN, 'Maggie rules For Thatcher's Children, with a gay martyr', *The Times*, 26th February 2010, pp. 26-27.

Mark WICKHAM-JONES, 'Right Turn: A Revisionist Account of the 1975 Conservative Party Leadership Election', *Twentieth Century British History'*, Vol. 8, No. 1, 1997, pp. 74-89.

David WILLETTS, 'The Free Market and Civic Conservatism', 1996, in Kenneth MINOGUE (ed.), *Conservative Realism: New Essays on Conservatism*, London, HarperCollins, 1996, pp. 80-87.

Hywel WILLIAMS, 'Preaching and prying bigots: The wrath Anglicans and Tories visit on gays shows their squalor', *Guardian*, 18th September 2002, retrieved 29th September 2002, http://politics.guardian.co.uk/conservatives/comment/0,9236,794166,00.html.

Tim WILLIAMS, 'Robbing Jack to pay Jock', *The Spectator*, Vol. 289, No. 9080, 17th August 2002, p. 34.

Andy WILLIAMSON, *MPs Online: Connecting With Constituents*, London, Hansard Society, 2009.

Glen WILSON, 'Projective Aggression and Social Attitudes', 1973, in Hans EYSENCK & Glen WILSON (eds.), *The Psychological Basis of Ideology*, Lancaster, MTP Press, 1978, pp. 183-186.

Graeme WILSON, 'Top Tory splits the party with call to pray for ban on abortion', *Daily Mail*, 25th January 2001, p. 19.

Michael WOODS, 'Was There a Rural Rebellion? Labour and the Countryside in the 2001 General Election', 2002, in Lynn DENNIE, Colin RALLINGS, Jonathan TONGE & Paul WEBB (eds.), *British Elections and Parties Review, Volume 12: The 2001 General Election*, London, Frank Cass, 2002, pp. 206-228.

Adrian WOOLDRIDGE, 'The Michael Moore Conservatives: Meet Britain's anti-American Tories', *The Weekly Standard*, 31st May 2004, retrieved 17th August 2009, http://tinyurl.com/lpmvdj.

Robert WORCESTER, 'Tories hold a steady lead, but 'magic 40%' is still beyond them', *Observer*, 11th April 2010, retrieved 12th April 2010, http://www.guardian.co.uk/politics/2010/apr/11/election-polls-review.

Robert WORCESTER & Roger MORTIMER, *Explaining Labour's Landslide*, London, Politico's Publishing, 1999.

Richard WYN JONES, Roger SCULLY & Dafydd TRYSTAN, 'Why Do the Conservatives Always Do (Even) Worse in Wales?', 2002, in Lynn DENNIE, Colin RALLINGS, Jonathan TONGE & Paul WEBB (eds.), *British Elections and Parties Review, Volume 12: The 2001 General Election*, London, Frank Cass, 2002, pp. 229-245.

Richard WYN JONES & Dafydd TRYSTAN, 'Wales', *Parliamentary Affairs*, Vol. 54, No. 4, 2001, pp. 712-724.

Patricia WYNN DAVIES, 'Fear of defeat fuels Conservative clear-out', *Independent*, 5th February 1996, retrieved 13th May 2012.

Bat YEOR, 'Eurabia: The road to Munich', *National Review*, 9th October 2002, retrieved 18th October 2002, www.nationalreview.com/comment/comment-yeor100902.asp.

Ross YOUNG, *By-election results 2001-05*, Research Paper 05/34, Houses of Parliament website, 11th May 2005, retrieved 11th April 2009, http://www.parliament.uk/commons/lib/research/rp2005/rp05-034.pdf.

Jean YULE, 'Women Councillors and Committee Recruitment', *Local Government Studies*, Vol. 26, No. 3, autumn 2000, pp. 31-54.

APPENDIX 1

SEPTEMBER 2000 PILOT STUDY

As described in Chapter 2, a small-scale pilot study was conducted in September 2000. The questionnaire contained a number of items that were intended to assess two multi-item scales: the new "Judeo-Christian Concerns" dimension and a new way of operationalising the PoliMap, a concept described in greater detail in Chapter 3.

The following sets out the preface for each set of items and the wording for each item. It also describes the response option sets used for the two scales. All original text is in italics.

Question 1

"Below are five issues that often appear as matters of public and political discussion. Some people think that, whilst accepting that any or all of them may not always cause problems for every single individual, in general they represent serious and immediate moral and physical dangers to civilised society as a whole. Other people think that, whilst accepting that any or all of them may well cause problems for some individuals, in general their importance and impact for civilised society as a whole has been subject to exaggeration and scaremongering. In each case, where would you put your own view? Please place only one tick per row."

Each of the five items below was presented along with the following five-point Likert-style response set: "Very serious danger to society", "Fairly serious danger to society", "Somewhere in between", "Somewhat exaggerated danger to society" and "Very much exaggerated danger to society".

- *"Drug use, especially amongst young people".*
- *"The weakening of the traditional family, particularly seen in increased divorce and single-parenthood".*

- *"The availability of violent and pornographic material through videos and the internet".*

- *"Crime and the fear of crime".*

- *"Removing barriers to the promotion in schools of homosexuality and other non-conventional relationships".*

Question 2

"Below you will find ten pairs of opposing statements concerning ten separate issues. Some people will fully agree with one of the pair, some the other, and others will have a view somewhere in between. Between each pair of statements you will also find a row of five boxes. People who fully agree with either one of the pair of statements would place a tick in the box at the end of the row closest to that statement. People who tend to agree with one of the statements but with reservations would place a tick in one of the boxes second in from the end of the row closest to that statement. People who take a neutral position between the two statements would use the middle or third box. In each case, please place a tick in the box that most nearly reflects your own opinion. Please place only one tick per row."

In the original questionnaire, between each opposing statement there were five boxes into which respondents would place their mark depending upon how close (or equidistant) to either was their own view. Here are only presented the opposing pairs.

"It is the duty of the state to provide through taxation for all the educational, health, and welfare needs of its citizens" **versus** *"It is up to individuals themselves, their families, or charitable organisations to provide for all of a person's educational, health, and welfare needs".*

"The success or failure of businesses and the fate of their employees should be left entirely to the workings of the free market" **versus** *"The government should not hesitate to regulate, subsidise, or take into public ownership businesses if this is necessary to ensure their survival or to safeguard jobs".*

"Adults should be allowed to engage in any form of private, consensual sexual activity they wish" **versus** *"The only form of sexual activity that is acceptable is between a man and woman who are married to each other".*

"Within the criminal justice system the emphasis should always be on the rights of the victim" **versus** *"Within the criminal justice system the emphasis should always be on the rights of the accused".*

"The level and standards of wages and working conditions should be solely a matter of negotiation between employers, employees, or their respective representatives" **versus** *"The government should set legally enforceable levels and standards for wages and working conditions".*

"The government should take whatever measures are necessary to protect domestic industry and jobs from foreign competition even if this means limiting consumer choice" **versus** *"The freedom of consumers to purchase goods and services from anywhere they wish, including from abroad, overrides any considerations of protecting domestic industry and jobs".*

"Adults are responsible for their own bodies and should be able to consume whatever drugs they wish" **versus** *"For their own good, the government should use all its powers to stop people taking drugs".*

"Key industries and utilities such as public transport and power generation and supply need to be in public ownership to ensure their use for the good of the nation as a whole" **versus** *"Industries and utilities such as public transport and power generation and supply are no different from any other businesses and should be in private hands competing in the free market".*

"If adults wish to read or watch material of a pornographic or extremely violent nature that is entirely up to them" **versus** *"To protect decent society and vulnerable individuals, the government needs to stop the distribution of material of a pornographic or extremely violent nature".*

"The young people of this country, and the country itself, would benefit from the reintroduction of some form of compulsory national service, whether of a military or civilian form" **versus** *"Any form or compulsory national service, whether of a military or civilian form, is simply enforced servitude of a sort unacceptable in a civilised, peacetime society".*

APPENDIX 2

LETTER FROM ERIC FORTH

The following is the text of the signed letter originally written on the Right Honourable Eric Forth MP's House of Commons notepaper. Copies of this letter were sent to all respondents along with the questionnaire.

14th March 2002

Dear Colleague,

I have pleasure in introducing the enclosed survey from Nigel Meek, a researcher at London Guildhall University.

As well as his work at London Guildhall, Nigel has been an activist in what is now the Bromley & Chislehurst Conservative Association since the mid-1980s. He has served on its Executive Committee and various candidate selection panels, and was a member of the former London South-East European Constituency Council.

I think that one of the striking aspects of contemporary political reporting is the often poor coverage given to the Conservative Party itself. At times, this may be due to the political inclinations of many in the media. However, even when well-intentioned, reports often derive from anecdote and gossip on the one hand, or serious study which is nevertheless partial or out of date on the other.

Nigel's work is important for two reasons. First, being both an academic and a member of the Party, he is able to bring to bear objective analysis on an institution that he is part of and understands. Second, the outcome will enable serious commentators to draw upon reliable, up-to-date, and wide-ranging data about the Conservative Party's "front-line" representatives.

These days, some politicians are deluged with surveys of one sort or another. Others seem comparatively ignored. In either case, please see if you can spare the time to complete and return the enclosed questionnaire.

Yours faithfully,

Eric

APPENDIX 3

CONTENT OF SCALES

The following are the multi-item scales or dimensions used throughout the study and discussed in Chapter 2. Unless otherwise indicated, all items were introduced with "How much do you agree or disagree with each of the following?" Unless otherwise indicated, respondents were presented with a five-point, Likert-type "Agree strongly" to "Disagree strongly" response set. The direction of the wording of the individual items is as found in the original *CPRS 2002* questionnaire set out in Appendix 5 below. Where necessary, the direction of individual items was reversed to compute the final multi-item scale.

Authoritarianism

- Young people today don't have enough respect for traditional British values
- People who break the law should be given stiffer sentences
- For some crimes, the death penalty is the most appropriate sentence
- Schools should teach children to obey authority
- The law should always be obeyed, even if a particular law is wrong
- Censorship of films and magazines is necessary to uphold moral standards

In the *CPRS 2002* questionnaire the following item was used to identify attitudes towards gays and lesbians:

- Homosexual relationships are always wrong

In the *BSA 2001* questionnaire a different item was used to identify attitudes towards gays and lesbians:

- Do you think they would be right or wrong to refuse a job to an applicant only because he or she is gay or lesbian?

Environmentalism

- The government should do more to protect the environment, even if it leads to higher taxes
- Industry should do more to protect the environment, even if it leads to lower profits and fewer jobs
- Ordinary people should do more to protect the environment, even if it means paying higher prices
- People should be allowed to use their cars as much as they like, even if it causes damage to the environment
- Many of the claims about mankind's damage to the environment are exaggerated

Europeanism

- The UK should embrace the concept of a federal Europe
- Membership of the Euro is crucial for Britain's future prosperity
- The EU's budget should be enlarged
- A single European Army would undermine rather than underpin the security of the UK
- Britain should withdraw from the EU
- The strength of national identities rules out parliamentary democracy on a European scale for the foreseeable future
- Conservative MEPs should remain committed members of the EPP/ED group

Feminism

- Government should make sure that women have an equal chance to succeed
- Men and women are equally suited emotionally for politics

- All in all, family life suffers when the woman has a full-time job
- Being a housewife is just as fulfilling as working for pay
- A husband's job is to earn the money; a wife's job is to look after the home and family

Intra-Party Elitism

(Members of the Conservative Party should have more influence in...)
- Basic principles and beliefs of the Party
- Formulation of Party policy and writing of manifestos
- Running and administering the Party and its finances

Intra-Party Inclusivity

(More should be done to advance members of the following groups within the Conservative Party...)
- Women
- Racial minorities
- Homosexuals and lesbians

Left-Right

- Government should redistribute income from the better-off to those who are less well off
- Big business benefits owners at the expense of workers
- Ordinary working people do not get their fair share of the nation's wealth
- There is one law for the rich and one for the poor
- Management will always try to get the better of employees if it gets the chance

Optimism

- People do not trust Conservative politicians at a national level
- People do not trust Conservative politicians at a local level
- The Conservative Party can win the next general election

- The Conservative Party can win the next-but-one general election
- The Conservative Party as an institution is in better shape than many seem to think
- Opinion polls underestimate the level of support for the Conservatives amongst ordinary people
- The Conservative Party should change its name
- The view that the Conservative Party is culturally and socially "out of touch" is exaggerated
- The Conservative period in office between 1979 and 1997 brought about a major change in public attitudes
- Depictions in recent years of the Conservative Party as being "extreme" have some validity

Political Elitism

- Ordinary citizens should have more say in the decisions made by government
- More should be done to interest people in government
- More should be done to involve ordinary people in decision making
- It is for politicians rather than the public to make decisions on issues and priorities

Postmaterialism

(First and second most important aims of the country in the coming years)
- Maintaining order in the nation
- Giving people more say in important government decisions
- Fighting rising prices
- Protecting freedom of speech

Pride in Heritage and Culture

(How proud or not are you of Britain in each of the following? "Very proud", "Somewhat proud", "Not very proud" or "Not proud at all")

- Its armed forces
- Its history
- Its achievements in sports
- Its achievements in arts and literature
- Its scientific and technological achievements

Pride in the Way the Nation Functions

(How proud or not are you of Britain in each of the following? "Very proud", "Somewhat proud", "Not very proud" or "Not proud at all")

- Its political influence in the world
- Its social security system
- The way its democracy works
- Its economic achievements

The individual items making up this scale and Pride in Heritage & Culture were furthermore designed by the original researchers[822] to be combined into a single multi-item scale, National Sentiment (alpha = 0.69, n = 484).

Protectionism

- Britain should limit the import of foreign products to protect its national economy
- British television should give preference to British films and programmes
- Foreigners should be allowed to buy land in Britain as easily as British people
- Britain should follow its own interests, even if this leads to conflicts with other nations

---

[822] Dowds & Young, 1996.

- People do not have to share British customs and traditions to become fully British

Religiosity

- How close do you feel to God most of the time? [5-point scale.]
- How often do you attend a religious service? (Excluding weddings & funerals etc.) [4-point scale.]
- Which of the following comes closest to your own view? [6-point scale.]

Because each individual item possessed a different response option set, the Religiosity scale was computed from the three items after they had been standardised using *SPSS*.

Theocratism

- Religious leaders should not try to influence how people vote in elections
- Religious leaders should not try to influence government decisions
- Churches and religious organisations in this country have too much power

Traditional British Liberties

- Britain should introduce compulsory identity cards
- Jury trials should be reserved only for the most serious of criminal charges
- The "double jeopardy" principle should be abolished for the most serious crimes
- Successive governments have been right to place stricter controls on the ownership of firearms

Welfarism

- The welfare state makes people nowadays less willing to look after themselves

- People receiving social security are made to feel like second class citizens
- The welfare state encourages people to stop helping each other
- The government should spend more money on welfare benefits for the poor, even if it leads to higher taxes
- Around here, most unemployed people could find a job if they really wanted one
- Many people who get social security don't really deserve any help
- Most people on the dole are fiddling in one way or another
- If welfare benefits weren't so generous, people would learn to stand on their own two feet

Xenophobia

- Immigrants take jobs away from people who were born in Britain
- Immigrants increase crime rates
- Immigrants are generally good for Britain's economy
- Refugees who have suffered political repression in their own country should be allowed to stay in Britain
- Immigrants make Britain more open to new ideas and culture
- British schools should make much more effort to teach foreign languages properly
- The number of immigrants allowed into Britain nowadays should be increased
- Race relations will improve over the next few years [added for the *CPRS 2002*]

The individual items making up this scale and Protectionism were furthermore designed by the original researchers[823] to be combined into a single multi-item scale, Exclusiveness (alpha = 0.85, n = 478).

---

[823] Dowds & Young, 1996.

APPENDIX 4

RESPONSES TO SCALES

The following tables display the observed distribution of responses to the multi-item scales detailed in Appendix 3. The responses are split by group of respondent: MPs, Peers and so on but omitting the two micro-groups of AMs and GLAs. The raw scales – i.e. the (re-ordered where necessary) sum of all responses to each scale's constituent items – have been recategorised into three levels measured in absolute terms, i.e. the lowest, middle and highest thirds of the aggregate scores along each multi-item scale. Where it was not mathematically possible to divide the scale data into three equal categories the middle category alone was altered to accommodate this calculation. This also applies to the use of such categories in the chapters above.

Little detail is gone into here since these scales are discussed in the text. However, since they are all in one place, sometimes one or two additional pieces of information are included. One-way ANOVA tests were run in *SPSS* for each uncategorised scale, with the factor being the type of respondent, again excluding AMs and GLAs. In formal terms, the null hypothesis was tested that there were no significant differences in attitudes between the groups of respondents. In those cases where the null hypotheses could be rejected – two-tailed $p < 0.05$ – this is stated below the table along with the significance figure. At the same time, the Bonferroni post-hoc multiple comparison procedure was run to determine if any significant between-groups differences between pairs of types of respondent could be identified. Where such differences are present, these are highlighted along with the significance figure.

Both the ANOVA and Bonferroni tests are sensitive to the sizes of the groups being compared. However, this also means that significant differences between smaller groups such as MEPs and WLCs in the case of Authoritarianism can be considered robust.

As suggested, these inferential statistical analyses are here to add flavour to the descriptive data provided by the tables themselves.

As such, the assumptions of ANOVA and/or non-parametric alternatives such as the Kruskal-Wallis test are not considered[824] nor are the full workings for the ANOVA and Bonferroni tests shown.

There is also the matter of nomenclature of the categories within each scale. To take one example, at the time of the survey to be seen as "Green" was "a good thing" whereas to be regarded as "Not Green" was generally regarded as "a bad thing". However, it forms no part of this study to argue for or against the "goodness" of any beliefs and as such neutrality in terminology has been strived for.

AUTHORITARIANISM							
	ELCs	**Peers**	**MPs**	**SLCs**	**WLCs**	**MEPs**	**MSPs**
Authoritarian	58%	35%	31%	47%	59%	29%	36%
In between	40%	63%	67%	53%	41%	71%	64%
Libertarian	2%	2%	2%	0%	0%	0%	0%
Base	**275**	**57**	**52**	**47**	**27**	**14**	**14**

ANOVA: p < 0.001. Bonferroni: ELCs & Peers, p = 0.023; ELCs & MPs, p = 0.011; ELCs & MEPs, p = 0.02; MPs & WLCs, p 0.044; WLCs & MEPs, p = 0.016.

ENVIRONMENTALISM							
	ELCs	**Peers**	**MPs**	**SLCs**	**WLCs**	**MEPs**	**MSPs**
Green	26%	21%	23%	24%	26%	21%	8%
In between	65%	65%	67%	71%	67%	71%	92%
Not green	9%	14%	10%	4%	7%	7%	0%
Base	**270**	**58**	**51**	**45**	**27**	**14**	**13**

EUROPEANISM							
	ELCs	**Peers**	**MPs**	**SLCs**	**WLCs**	**MEPs**	**MSPs**
Euro-enthusiast	2%	4%	4%	2%	9%	33%	0%
In between	44%	54%	26%	54%	50%	25%	71%
Euro-sceptic	54%	43%	70%	44%	41%	42%	28%
Base	**259**	**56**	**47**	**43**	**22**	**12**	**14**

ANOVA: p = 0.007.

---

[824] Norušis, 2000: 263 & 334.

FEMINISM							
	ELCs	**Peers**	**MPs**	**SLCs**	**WLCs**	**MEPs**	**MSPs**
Patriarchist	5%	2%	6%	8%	0%	14%	0%
In between	72%	76%	72%	69%	63%	71%	67%
Feminist	23%	22%	22%	23%	37%	14%	33%
Base	**276**	**55**	**51**	**48**	**27**	**14**	**12**

INTRA-PARTY ELITISM							
	ELCs	**Peers**	**MPs**	**SLCs**	**WLCs**	**MEPs**	**MSPs**
Grass-roots control	57%	36%	22%	42%	61%	57%	21%
In between	41%	59%	53%	50%	39%	36%	57%
Central control	3%	5%	25%	8%	0%	7%	21%
Base	**281**	**59**	**51**	**48**	**28**	**14**	**14**

ANOVA: $p < 0.001$. Bonferroni: ELCs & Peers, $p = 0.001$; ELCs & MSPs, $p = 0.001$; Peers & MPs, $p = 0.012$; MPs & SLCs, $p < 0.001$; MPs & WLCs, $p < 0.001$; MPs & MEPs, $p = 0.04$; WLCs & MSPs, $p = 0.034$.

INTRA-PARTY INCLUSIVITY							
	ELCs	**Peers**	**MPs**	**SLCs**	**WLCs**	**MEPs**	**MSPs**
Moderniser	18%	25%	38%	26%	7%	29%	29%
In between	57%	60%	48%	52%	68%	57%	64%
Traditionalist	25%	15%	14%	22%	25%	14%	7%
Base	**275**	**60**	**52**	**46**	**28**	**14**	**14**

ANOVA: $p = 0.008$.

LEFT-RIGHT							
	ELCs	**Peers**	**MPs**	**SLCs**	**WLCs**	**MEPs**	**MSPs**
Left	7%	0%	0%	0%	0%	0%	0%
In between	49%	43%	39%	51%	67%	36%	46%
Right	44%	57%	61%	49%	33%	64%	54%
Base	**274**	**58**	**51**	**45**	**27**	**14**	**13**

ANOVA: $p < 0.001$. Bonferroni: ELCs & Peers, $p = 0.004$.

OPTIMISM							
	ELCs	**Peers**	**MPs**	**SLCs**	**WLCs**	**MEPs**	**MSPs**
Optimistic	53%	58%	67%	53%	64%	43%	50%
In between	46%	42%	33%	47%	36%	57%	50%
Pessimistic	1%	0%	0%	0%	0%	0%	0%
Base	**271**	**55**	**49**	**47**	**28**	**14**	**14**

POLITICAL ELITISM							
	ELCs	**Peers**	**MPs**	**SLCs**	**WLCs**	**MEPs**	**MSPs**
Democrat	38%	34%	25%	27%	50%	21%	15%
In between	55%	64%	65%	64%	50%	79%	77%
Elite	7%	2%	10%	9%	0%	0%	8%
Base	**277**	**58**	**52**	**45**	**28**	**14**	**13**

Bonferroni: MPs & WLCs, $p = 0.044$. There was no significant difference result on the initial ANOVA procedure. However, like the Bonferroni result, this was marginal but the other side of the standard significance level: $p = 0.055$.

POSTMATERIALISM							
	ELCs	**Peers**	**MPs**	**SLCs**	**WLCs**	**MEPs**	**MSPs**
Materialist	17%	19%	12%	17%	5%	17%	20%
Mixed	77%	77%	88%	71%	90%	58%	70%
Postmaterialist	6%	4%	0%	12%	5%	25%	10%
Base	**248**	**48**	**49**	**42**	**21**	**12**	**10**

PRIDE IN HERITAGE AND CULTURE							
	ELCs	**Peers**	**MPs**	**SLCs**	**WLCs**	**MEPs**	**MSPs**
Not proud	0%	0%	0%	0%	0%	0%	0%
In between	8%	11%	8%	17%	0%	14%	8%
Proud	92%	89%	92%	83%	100%	86%	92%
Base	**274**	**57**	**51**	**47**	**27**	**14**	**13**

PRIDE IN WAY THE NATION FUNCTIONS							
	ELCs	Peers	MPs	SLCs	WLCs	MEPs	MSPs
Not proud	3%	0%	0%	0%	0%	0%	0%
In between	61%	65%	65%	64%	68%	86%	69%
Proud	36%	35%	35%	36%	32%	14%	31%
Base	275	57	52	47	25	14	13

PROTECTIONISM							
	ELCs	Peers	MPs	SLCs	WLCs	MEPs	MSPs
Not protectionist	9%	21%	28%	9%	7%	29%	21%
In between	66%	78%	68%	74%	64%	71%	71%
Protectionist	25%	2%	4%	17%	29%	0%	7%
Base	278	58	50	47	28	14	14

ANOVA: $p < 0.001$. Bonferroni: ELCs & Peers, $p < 0.001$; ELCs & MPs, $p < 0.001$; ELCs & MEPs, $p < 0.001$; Peers & WLCs, $p = 0.036$; MPs & SLCs, $p = 0.043$; MPs & WLCs, $p = 0.005$; WLCs & MEPs, $p = 0.014$.

RELIGIOSITY							
	ELCs	Peers	MPs	SLCs	WLCs	MEPs	MSPs
Sceptic	19%	7%	4%	17%	12%	15%	21%
In between	43%	37%	29%	30%	46%	31%	21%
Devout	38%	56%	67%	52%	42%	54%	57%
Base	267	57	48	46	26	13	14

ANOVA: $p = 0.002$. Bonferroni: ELCs & MPs, $p = 0.002$.

THEOCRATISM							
	ELCs	Peers	MPs	SLCs	WLCs	MEPs	MSPs
Secularist	30%	12%	8%	38%	29%	29%	14%
In between	62%	64%	69%	50%	64%	57%	71%
Theocrat	8%	24%	23%	12%	7%	14%	14%
Base	275	58	52	48	28	14	14

ANOVA: $p < 0.001$. Bonferroni: ELCs & Peers, $p < 0.001$; ELCs & MPs, $p < 0.001$; Peers & SLCs, $p = 0.001$; MPs & SLCs, $p < 0.001$; MPs & WLCs, $p = 0.013$.

Traditional British Liberties							
	ELCs	**Peers**	**MPs**	**SLCs**	**WLCs**	**MEPs**	**MSPs**
Authoritarian	48%	29%	4%	48%	42%	36%	36%
In between	44%	55%	63%	40%	58%	50%	50%
Libertarian	8%	16%	33%	12%	0%	14%	14%
Base	**271**	**55**	**49**	**42**	**26**	**14**	**14**

ANOVA: p < 0.001. Bonferroni: ELCs & MPs, p < 0.001; Peers & MPs, p = 0.006; MPs & SLCs, p < 0.001; MPs & WLCs, p < 0.001.

Welfarism							
	ELCs	**Peers**	**MPs**	**SLCs**	**WLCs**	**MEPs**	**MSPs**
Self-help	36%	32%	27%	28%	36%	43%	15%
In between	62%	66%	73%	70%	64%	57%	85%
Welfarist	2%	2%	0%	2%	0%	0%	0%
Base	**275**	**59**	**52**	**46**	**28**	**14**	**13**

Xenophobia							
	ELCs	**Peers**	**MPs**	**SLCs**	**WLCs**	**MEPs**	**MSPs**
Not xenophobic	12%	26%	25%	17%	4%	29%	29%
In between	66%	65%	71%	72%	85%	57%	71%
Xenophobic	22%	9%	4%	11%	11%	14%	0%
Base	**272**	**54**	**49**	**47**	**27**	**14**	**14**

ANOVA: p < 0.001. Bonferroni: ELCs & Peers, p = 0.001; ELCs & MPs, p = 0.002; ELCs & MSPs, p = 0.034.

APPENDIX 5

THE *CPRS 2002* QUESTIONNAIRE

The following is a resized facsimile of the questionnaire sent to local councillors in England (ELCs) in April 2002. The questionnaire sent to all other respondents was the same except that the final two pages of socio-demographic items were omitted and replaced with a "thank you" notice at the foot of page 18 and "This page deliberately blank" notices on the final two pages.

An A4 PDF version of the questionnaire can be downloaded from the *CPRS 2002* entry[825] (SN 6552) on the Economic and Social Data Service website.

[825] Meek, 27th August 2010.

**CONSERVATIVE PARTY
REPRESENTATIVES STUDY 2002**

LONDON GUILDHALL
Introduction
UNIVERSITY

Dear Sir/Madam,

It would be kind of you if you could spare the time to complete the enclosed questionnaire and to return it in the SAE supplied.

The purpose of this study, part of a PhD thesis, is to obtain an objective measure of the views of the Conservative Party's 'public' or 'statutory' representatives. The responses will then be used to answer questions concerning a wide range of abstract political, economic, social, and religious beliefs on the one hand, and more concrete matters on the other. Some of the issues and questions are 'tried and tested' and you may have encountered them before. Others have been developed for this study.

Aside from the scope of the questions, another feature is the range of individuals being surveyed. Versions of this questionnaire are being sent to all Conservative Westminster MPs, Peers, MEPs, Scottish MPs, Welsh AMs, members of the GLA, local councillors in Scotland and Wales, and a 10% sample of local councillors in England. Altogether, this is one of the most comprehensive academic studies of the Conservative Party for a decade.

Please note that this survey is anonymous. Nowhere are you asked to give your name, address, or the exact area that you represent.

I am grateful to my own member of parliament, the Rt. Hon. Eric Forth MP, for introducing this survey. However, this work has no formal connection with the Conservative Party, but instead is part of an academic project being undertaking at London Guildhall University.

With thanks for your help,

Nigel Meek
(Department of Politics & Modern History)

Instructions

This questionnaire should only be answered by the person to whom it has been sent.

The following questions take a number of forms, but you should find them reasonably easy to answer. There are no 'right' or 'wrong' answers. All you need to do is put a tick in the box that you select. Please use either a black or a blue pen. If at times you find that none of the provided answers exactly fits what you think, please choose the one that comes closest to your views.

Except where instructions in block capitals indicate otherwise, all questions are for everyone. For example, there are a number of questions concerning Scotland and Wales on the one hand, or England on the other. The views of everyone are important.

Please go to the first question on page 3

1

This page deliberately blank

The United Kingdom

How much do you agree or disagree with each of the following?

1		Agree strongly	Agree	Neither agree nor disagree	Disagree	Disagree strongly
A	The cause of the centre-Right in Scotland and Wales has been damaged by its association with a Conservative Party that is often regarded as 'the English Party'	❏	❏	❏	❏	❏
B	England should have its own parliament	❏	❏	❏	❏	❏
C	The regions of England should have their own assemblies	❏	❏	❏	❏	❏
D	All three major mainland UK political parties should organise and campaign in their own right in Northern Ireland	❏	❏	❏	❏	❏
E	The Scots and the Welsh have a more developed sense of national identity than the English	❏	❏	❏	❏	❏
F	The extra public spending received by Scotland and Wales relative to England is often justified	❏	❏	❏	❏	❏
G	The government was right to allow Sinn Fein MPs to make use of Commons facilities	❏	❏	❏	❏	❏

2 **Who do you think has benefited most from the recent Northern Ireland peace process?**

◯ The Unionist or Loyalist community

◯ Both equally

◯ The Nationalist or Republican community

3 **Which one of the following comes closest to your own view?**

◯ Scotland and Wales should continue to return a relatively larger number of MPs to Westminster than England

◯ The number of Westminster MPs returned by Scotland and Wales relative to England should be brought in line with their population

◯ Scotland and Wales should return a proportionately smaller number of MPs to Westminster than England, commensurate with the autonomy of their devolved institutions

◯ Scotland and/or Wales should become independent countries

The Environment

How much do you agree or disagree with each of the following?

4		Agree strongly	Agree	Neither agree nor disagree	Disagree	Disagree strongly
A	The government should do more to protect the environment, even if it leads to higher taxes	❑	❑	❑	❑	❑
B	Industry should do more to protect the environment, even if it leads to lower profits and fewer jobs	❑	❑	❑	❑	❑
C	Ordinary people should do more to protect the environment, even if it means paying higher prices	❑	❑	❑	❑	❑
D	People should be allowed to use their cars as much as they like, even if it causes damage to the environment	❑	❑	❑	❑	❑
E	Many of the claims about mankind's damage to the environment are exaggerated	❑	❑	❑	❑	❑

Business, Labour Relations, Welfare, and the Economy

How much do you agree or disagree with each of the following?

5		Agree strongly	Agree	Neither agree nor disagree	Disagree	Disagree stongly
A	Government should redistribute income from the better-off to those who are less well off	❑	❑	❑	❑	❑
B	Big business benefits owners at the expense of workers	❑	❑	❑	❑	❑
C	Ordinary working people do not get their fair share of the nation's wealth	❑	❑	❑	❑	❑
D	There is one law for the rich and one for the poor	❑	❑	❑	❑	❑
E	Management will always try to get the better of employees if it gets the chance	❑	❑	❑	❑	❑
F	In general, the trades unions have been tamed	❑	❑	❑	❑	❑

6   Which of the following comes closest to your own view?

○ The public sector is more efficient than the private sector

○ The public and private sectors are equally efficient

○ The private sector is more efficient than the public sector

7   Which of the following comes closest to your own view?

○ The public sector is more worthy than the private sector

○ The public and private sectors are equally worthy

○ The private sector is more worthy than the public sector

How much do you agree or disagree with each of the following?

8		Agree strongly	Agree	Neither agree nor disagree	Disagree	Disagree strongly
A	The welfare state makes people nowadays less willing to look after themselves	❏	❏	❏	❏	❏
B	People receiving social security are made to fee like second class citizens	❏	❏	❏	❏	❏
C	The welfare state encourages people to stop helping each other	❏	❏	❏	❏	❏
D	The government should spend more money on welfare benefits for the poor, even if it leads to higher taxes	❏	❏	❏	❏	❏
E	Around here, most unemployed people could find a job if they really wanted one	❏	❏	❏	❏	❏
F	Many people who get social security don't really deserve any help	❏	❏	❏	❏	❏
G	Most people on the dole are fiddling in one way or another	❏	❏	❏	❏	❏
H	If welfare benefits weren't so generous, people would learn to stand on their own two feet	❏	❏	❏	❏	❏

Britain, Europe, and the Wider World

If all were equally possible, which of the following would you MOST prefer Britain to seek? And the NEXT MOST preferred? And the LEAST preferred?

9		Greater British independence at the expense of ties with both the EU and the USA	Closer ties to the USA at the expense of British independence and ties with the EU	Closer ties to the EU at the expense of British independence and ties with the USA
A	Most preferred	❏	❏	❏
B	Next most preferred	❏	❏	❏
C	Least preferred	❏	❏	❏

10 Thinking about the Middle East, how best would you describe yourself?

○ Very pro-Arab/Palestinian

○ Somewhat pro-Arab/Palestinian

○ View both sides equally

○ Somewhat pro-Israeli

○ Very pro-Israeli

Commentators sometimes talk about 'Euro-enthusiasts' and 'Euro-sceptics'. Using the following scale, where 1 means Euro-enthusiast and 10 means Euro-sceptic, where would you place:

11		1 - Enthusiast	2	3	4	5	6	7	8	9	10 - Sceptic
A	Yourself	❏	❏	❏	❏	❏	❏	❏	❏	❏	❏
B	Conservative Party	❏	❏	❏	❏	❏	❏	❏	❏	❏	❏
C	Labour Party	❏	❏	❏	❏	❏	❏	❏	❏	❏	❏
D	Liberal Democrats	❏	❏	❏	❏	❏	❏	❏	❏	❏	❏
E	Scottish National Party	❏	❏	❏	❏	❏	❏	❏	❏	❏	❏
F	Plaid Cymru	❏	❏	❏	❏	❏	❏	❏	❏	❏	❏

12 **Which of the following statements best describes how you see yourself?**

O English/Scottish/Welsh not British

O More English/Scottish/Welsh than British

O Equally English/Scottish/Welsh and British

O More British than English/Scottish/Welsh

O British not English/Scottish/Welsh

O None of these

13 **Which of the following statements best describes how you see yourself?**

O British/English/Scottish/Welsh not European

O More British/English/Scottish/Welsh than European

O Equally British/English/Scottish/Welsh and European

O More European than British/English/Scottish/Welsh

O European not British/English/Scottish/Welsh

O None of these

How much do you agree or disagree with each of the following?

14		Agree strongly	Agree	Neither agree nor disagree	Disagree	Disagree strongly
A	Britain should re-establish closer ties with the former colonies and existing dependencies in areas such as the Caribbean, Africa, and Asia	❏	❏	❏	❏	❏
B	Britain should re-establish closer ties with the former colonies in areas such as Australia and New Zealand, Southern Africa, and Canada	❏	❏	❏	❏	❏
C	Britain should be more cautious in supporting the USA's foreign and military polices	❏	❏	❏	❏	❏
D	The Western and Islamic worlds can never truly be at peace with one another	❏	❏	❏	❏	❏

How much do you agree or disagree with each of the following?

15

		Agree strongly	Agree	Neither agree nor disagree	Disagree	Disagree strongly
A	The UK should embrace the concept of a federal Europe	❏	❏	❏	❏	❏
B	Membership of the Euro is crucial for Britain's future prosperity	❏	❏	❏	❏	❏
C	The EU's budget should be enlarged	❏	❏	❏	❏	❏
D	A single European Army would undermine rather than underpin the security of the UK	❏	❏	❏	❏	❏
E	Britain should withdraw from the EU	❏	❏	❏	❏	❏
F	The strength of national identities rules out parliamentary democracy on a European scale for the foreseeable future	❏	❏	❏	❏	❏
G	Conservative MEPs should remain committed members of the European People's Party and European Democrats (EPP-ED) group in the European Parliament	❏	❏	❏	❏	❏

Ethnicity, Citizenship, and National Image

How much do you agree or disagree with each of the following?

16

		Agree strongly	Agree	Neither agree nor disagree	Disagree	Disagree strongly
A	Britain should limit the import of foreign products to protect its national economy	❏	❏	❏	❏	❏
B	British television should give preference to British films and programmes	❏	❏	❏	❏	❏
C	Foreigners should be allowed to buy land in Britain as easily as British people	❏	❏	❏	❏	❏
D	Britain should follow its own interests, even if this leads to conflicts with other nations	❏	❏	❏	❏	❏
E	People do not have to share British customs and traditions to become fully British	❏	❏	❏	❏	❏
F	Immigrants are generally good for Britain's economy	❏	❏	❏	❏	❏
G	Immigrants increase crime rates	❏	❏	❏	❏	❏

How proud or not are you of Britain in each of the following?

17		Very proud	Somewhat proud	Not very proud	Not proud at all
A	Its armed forces	❏	❏	❏	❏
B	Its history	❏	❏	❏	❏
C	Its achievements in sports	❏	❏	❏	❏
D	Its achievements in arts and literature	❏	❏	❏	❏
E	Its scientific and technological achievements	❏	❏	❏	❏
F	Its political influence in the world	❏	❏	❏	❏
G	Its social security system	❏	❏	❏	❏
H	The way its democracy works	❏	❏	❏	❏
I	Its economic achievements	❏	❏	❏	❏

How much do you agree or disagree with each of the following?

18		Agree strongly	Agree	Neither agree nor disagree	Disagree	Disagree strongly
A	Refugees who have suffered political repression in their own country should be allowed to stay in Britain	❏	❏	❏	❏	❏
B	Immigrants make Britain more open to new ideas and culture	❏	❏	❏	❏	❏
C	British schools should make much more effort to teach foreign languages properly	❏	❏	❏	❏	❏
D	Immigrants take jobs away from people who were born in Britain	❏	❏	❏	❏	❏
E	The number of immigrants allowed into Britain nowadays should be increased	❏	❏	❏	❏	❏
F	Race relations in Britain will improve over the next few years	❏	❏	❏	❏	❏

Society and Culture

How much do you agree or disagree with each of the following?

19		Agree strongly	Agree	Neither agree nor disagree	Disagree	Disagree strongly
A	Men and women are equally suited emotionally for politics	❏	❏	❏	❏	❏
B	All in all, family life suffers when the woman has a full-time job	❏	❏	❏	❏	❏
C	Being a housewife is just as fulfilling as working for pay	❏	❏	❏	❏	❏
D	Government should make sure that women have an equal chance to succeed	❏	❏	❏	❏	❏
E	A husband's job is to earn the money; a wife's job is to look after the home and family	❏	❏	❏	❏	❏

How much do you agree or disagree with each of the following?

20

		Agree strongly	Agree	Neither agree nor disagree	Disagree	Disagree strongly
A	Young people today don't have enough respect for traditional British values	❏	❏	❏	❏	❏
B	People who break the law should be given stiffer sentences	❏	❏	❏	❏	❏
C	For some crimes, the death penalty is the most appropriate sentence	❏	❏	❏	❏	❏
D	Schools should teach children to obey authority	❏	❏	❏	❏	❏
E	The law should always be obeyed, even if a particular law is wrong	❏	❏	❏	❏	❏
F	Censorship of films and magazines is necessary to uphold moral standards	❏	❏	❏	❏	❏
G	Homosexual relationships are always wrong	❏	❏	❏	❏	❏

How much do you agree or disagree with each of the following?

21

		Agree strongly	Agree	Neither agree nor agree	Disagree	Disagree strongly
A	Britain should introduce compulsory identity cards	❏	❏	❏	❏	❏
B	Jury trials should be reserved only for the most serious of criminal charges	❏	❏	❏	❏	❏
C	The 'double jeopardy' principle should be abolished for the most serious crimes	❏	❏	❏	❏	❏
D	Successive governments have been right to place stricter controls on the ownership of firearms	❏	❏	❏	❏	❏
E	The idea that social and cultural matters in Britain are dominated by a 'Left-liberal, London-based metropolitan elite' is much exaggerated	❏	❏	❏	❏	❏
F	Detention without trial is not justified in peacetime	❏	❏	❏	❏	❏

The Conduct of Politics

We often talk about what the main aims of the country should be in the coming years. If you had to chose between the following items, which one seems the MOST important and which one the NEXT most important to you?

22

		Most Important	Next most important
A	Maintaining order in the nation	❏	❏
B	Giving people more say in important government decisions	❏	❏
C	Fighting rising prices	❏	❏
D	Protecting freedom of speech	❏	❏

Relative to the present situation, what should be done about the powers of the following institutions?

23		Increased a lot	Increased somewhat	Stay the same	Decreased somewhat	Decreased a lot
A	Westminster Parliament	❏	❏	❏	❏	❏
B	European Parliament	❏	❏	❏	❏	❏
C	Scottish Parliament	❏	❏	❏	❏	❏
D	Welsh Assembly	❏	❏	❏	❏	❏
E	Northern Ireland Assembly	❏	❏	❏	❏	❏
F	Greater London Assembly	❏	❏	❏	❏	❏
G	Principal local authorities	❏	❏	❏	❏	❏
H	Parish/town councils	❏	❏	❏	❏	❏

How much do you agree or disagree with each of the following?

24		Agree strongly	Agree	Neither agree nor disagree	Disagree	Disagree strongly
A	There should be at least an element of proportional representation for general elections	❏	❏	❏	❏	❏
B	There should be at least an element of proportional representation for local authority elections	❏	❏	❏	❏	❏
C	Local government is just as an appropriate arena for party politics as national government	❏	❏	❏	❏	❏
D	Local campaigning makes little difference these days compared to the overall impression of the national party	❏	❏	❏	❏	❏
E	Single-issue groups are now a better way than political parties of advancing causes	❏	❏	❏	❏	❏
F	Public life in this country is generally honest	❏	❏	❏	❏	❏

How much do you agree or disagree with each of the following?

25		Agree strongly	Agree	Neither agree nor disagree	Disagree	Disagree strongly
A	Political parties should be funded by the State and taxpayer rather than by individual donors, businesses, or unions	❏	❏	❏	❏	❏
B	The House of Lords should be replaced by a wholly or mainly elected second chamber	❏	❏	❏	❏	❏
C	However a second chamber is elected or selected, it should always be subordinate to the House of Commons	❏	❏	❏	❏	❏
D	There should no longer be an Established Church in any part of Britain	❏	❏	❏	❏	❏
E	Britain should become a republic	❏	❏	❏	❏	❏

10

How much do you agree or disagree with each of the following?

26		Agree strongly	Agree	Neither agree nor disagree	Disagree	Disagree strongly
A	The scope and power of the State over the individual should be much reduced	❏	❏	❏	❏	❏
B	A strong State is necessary for the preservation of a peaceful social order	❏	❏	❏	❏	❏
C	The State should be an active agency for social change and development	❏	❏	❏	❏	❏
D	Ordinary citizens should have more say in the decisions made by government	❏	❏	❏	❏	❏
E	More should be done to interest people in government	❏	❏	❏	❏	❏
F	More should be done to involve ordinary people in political decision making	❏	❏	❏	❏	❏
G	It is for politicians rather than the public to make decisions on issues and priorities	❏	❏	❏	❏	❏

The Political Parties

How much do you agree or disagree with each of the following?

27		Agree strongly	Agree	Neither agree nor disagree	Disagree	Disagree strongly
A	In recent years, it has not always been clear what the Conservative Party stands FOR	❏	❏	❏	❏	❏
B	In recent years, it has not always been clear what the Conservative Party stands AGAINST	❏	❏	❏	❏	❏
C	The Conservative Party is not an ideological party	❏	❏	❏	❏	❏
D	The Conservative period in office between 1979 and 1992 brought about a major change in public attitudes about issues such as the economy, taxation, public services, and welfare	❏	❏	❏	❏	❏
E	Depictions in recent years of the Conservative Party as being 'extreme' have some validity	❏	❏	❏	❏	❏

How much do you agree or disagree with each of the following?

28		Agree strongly	Agree	Neither agree nor disagree	Disagree	Disagree strongly
A	Conservative constituency agents should be employed and deployed by the Party centrally	❏	❏	❏	❏	❏
B	Local Conservative associations should retain control over parliamentary candidate selection	❏	❏	❏	❏	❏

How much do you agree or disagree with each of the following?

29		Agree strongly	Agree	Neither agree nor disagree	Disagree	Disagree strongly
A	People do not trust Conservative politicians at a national level	❏	❏	❏	❏	❏
B	People do not trust Conservative politicians at a local level	❏	❏	❏	❏	❏
C	The Conservative Party can win the next general election	❏	❏	❏	❏	❏
D	The Conservative Party can win the next-but-one general election	❏	❏	❏	❏	❏
E	The Conservative Party as an institution is in better shape than many seem to think	❏	❏	❏	❏	❏
F	Opinion polls underestimate the level of support for the Conservatives amongst ordinary people	❏	❏	❏	❏	❏
G	The Conservative Party should change its name	❏	❏	❏	❏	❏
H	The media is generally hostile towards the Conservative Party	❏	❏	❏	❏	❏
I	The view that the Conservative Party is culturally and socially 'out of touch' is exaggerated	❏	❏	❏	❏	❏

How much do you agree or disagree that more should be done to advance members of the following groups within the Conservative Party?

30		Agree strongly	Agree	Neither agree nor disagree	Disagree	Disagree strongly
A	Women	❏	❏	❏	❏	❏
B	Racial minorities	❏	❏	❏	❏	❏
C	Homosexuals and lesbians	❏	❏	❏	❏	❏

How would you rate the following leaders of the Conservative Party?

31		Very positively	Positively	Neither positively nor negatively	Negatively	Very Negatively
A	Edward Heath	❏	❏	❏	❏	❏
B	Margaret Thatcher	❏	❏	❏	❏	❏
C	John Major	❏	❏	❏	❏	❏
D	William Hague	❏	❏	❏	❏	❏
E	Iain Duncan Smith	❏	❏	❏	❏	❏

32 **All mass political parties that seek to be both honest and electorally successful need to reconcile two tasks: INTERNALLY to unite the party, and EXTERNALLY to reach out to the electorate. Of the two, which do you think is the most urgent task for the Conservative Party at the moment?**

○ To unite internally   ○ To reach out externally

Do you agree or disagree with the idea that the members of the Conservative Party should have more influence in...

33

		Agree strongly	Agree	Neither agree nor disagree	Disagree	Disagree strongly
A	Basic principles and beliefs of the Party	❏	❏	❏	❏	❏
B	Formulation of Party policy and writing of manifestos	❏	❏	❏	❏	❏
C	Running and administering the Party and its finances	❏	❏	❏	❏	❏

The defeats at the 1997 and 2001 general elections show that the Conservative Party...

34

		Agree strongly	Agree	Neither agree nor disagree	Disagree	Disagree strongly
A	Needs to change its principles and beliefs	❏	❏	❏	❏	❏
B	Needs to change its style and presentation	❏	❏	❏	❏	❏

How much do you agree or disagree with each of the following?

35

		Agree strongly	Agree	Neither agree nor disagree	Disagree	Disagree strongly
A	The Labour Party has genuinely shed its socialistic instincts	❏	❏	❏	❏	❏
B	The Conservatives should be focusing their national campaigning efforts against the Liberal Democrats rather than Labour	❏	❏	❏	❏	❏

36 **FOR LOCAL COUNCILLORS IN ENGLAND AND WESTMINSTER MPs IN ENGLAND ONLY. In which part of England is the constituency, ward, or region that you represent located?**

○ North   ○ Midlands   ○ East   ○ South-West

○ South-East (excluding Greater London)   ○ Greater London

13

How do you feel towards the following mainland British political parties?

37

		Strongly sympathetic	Sympathetic	In between	Antipathetic	Strongly antipathetic	Don't know enough to say
A	Labour Party	❑	❑	❑	❑	❑	❑
B	Liberal Democrats	❑	❑	❑	❑	❑	❑
C	Plaid Cymru	❑	❑	❑	❑	❑	❑
D	Scottish National Party	❑	❑	❑	❑	❑	❑
E	UK Independence Party (UKIP)	❑	❑	❑	❑	❑	❑
F	British National Party	❑	❑	❑	❑	❑	❑
G	Green Party	❑	❑	❑	❑	❑	❑
H	Socialist Alliance/Scottish Socialist Party	❑	❑	❑	❑	❑	❑

How do you feel towards the following Northern Ireland political parties?

38

		Strongly sympathetic	Sympathetic	In between	Antipathetic	Strongly antipathetic	Don't know enough to say
A	Ulster Unionist Party (led by David Trimble)	❑	❑	❑	❑	❑	❑
B	Democratic Unionist Party (led by Ian Paisley)	❑	❑	❑	❑	❑	❑
C	Sinn Fein	❑	❑	❑	❑	❑	❑
D	Social Democratic & Labour Party (SDLP)	❑	❑	❑	❑	❑	❑
E	Alliance Party of Northern Ireland	❑	❑	❑	❑	❑	❑

39 FOR ALL EXCEPT PEERS. How marginal or safe is the constituency, ward, or region that you represent?

○ Very marginal   ○ Somewhat marginal   ○ Safe or fairly safe

40 FOR ALL EXCEPT PEERS. Who is the MAIN challenger in the constituency, ward, or region that you represent?

○ Labour   ○ Liberal Democrat   ○ Ratepayer/Residents/Regionalist/Independent
○ SNP   ○ Plaid Cymru   ○ Other

41 FOR ALL EXCEPT PEERS. In recent years, have you experienced ANTI-Conservative tactical voting by supporters of other parties in the constituency, ward, or region that you represent?

○ Yes, a great deal   ○ Yes, some   ○ Very little or none at all

42 FOR ALL EXCEPT PEERS. In recent years, have you experienced PRO-Conservative tactical voting by supporters of other parties in the constituency, ward, or region that you represent?

○ Yes, a great deal   ○ Yes, some   ○ Very little or none at all

The 2001 Conservative Party Leadership Election

43 If you had been able to vote and had been presented with all five original candidates, who would you have voted for (or did vote for if you are a Westminster MP)?

- O Michael Ancram
- O Kenneth Clarke
- O David Davis
- O Iain Duncan Smith
- O Michael Portillo
- O None of the candidates

44 And from the 'almost final' three, who would you have voted for (or did vote for if you are a Westminster MP)?

- O Kenneth Clarke
- O Iain Duncan Smith
- O Michael Portillo
- O None of the candidates

45 FOR ALL EXCEPT WESTMINSTER MPs. At any time during the MPs-only stages of the contest, was your opinion offered to, or sought by, a Westminster MP?

- O Yes
- O No

46 Did you cast your vote in the final ballot of all members?

- O Yes *[Please go to Q48]*
- O No *[Please go to Q47]*

47 If no, was this because…

- O I could not support either of the two candidates
- O Some other practical reason such as not receiving a ballot paper, being ill or out of the country, etc.

48 Who did you vote for (or would have voted for had some practical reason not prevented you)?

- O Kenneth Clarke
- O Iain Duncan Smith
- O Deliberately spoiled the ballot paper or wrote in another's name

49 In any future leadership contest, should the final decision return to being one for Westminster MPs alone?

- O Yes *[Please go to Q52]*
- O No *[Please go to Q50]*

50 Do you nevertheless think that Westminster MPs should retain the task of narrowing down the final candidates to two or three?

- O Yes
- O Don't know
- O No

51 Do you think that all paid-up Party members should have the final say or just the demonstrably activist membership?

- O All members
- O Activists only

52 Irrespective of who you think ought to make the final choice, do you think that it would be a good idea to introduce a method whereby votes for a second-choice candidate might count in some way?

- O Yes
- O Don't know
- O No

Religion

53   **Which one of the following comes closest to your own view?**

○ I don't believe in God

○ I don't know whether there is a God and I don't believe there is any way to find out

○ I don't believe in a personal God, but I do believe in a Higher Power of some kind

○ I find myself believing in God some of the time, but not at others

○ While I have doubts, I feel that I do believe in God

○ I know God really exists and I have no doubts about it

54   **How close do you feel to God most of the time?**

○ Don't believe in God

○ Not close at all

○ Not very close

○ Somewhat close

○ Extremely close

55   **How often do you attend a religious service? (Excluding weddings and funerals etc.)**

○ At least once a week

○ At least once a month

○ At least once a year

○ Never

How much do you agree or disagree with each of the following?

56

		Agree strongly	Agree	Neither agree nor disagree	Disagree	Disagree strongly
A	Politicians who do not believe in God are unfit for public office	❏	❏	❏	❏	❏
B	Religious leaders should not try to influence how people vote in elections	❏	❏	❏	❏	❏
C	It would be better for Britain if more people with strong religious beliefs held public office	❏	❏	❏	❏	❏
D	Religious leaders should not try to influence government decisions	❏	❏	❏	❏	❏
E	Churches and religious organisations in this country have too much power and influence	❏	❏	❏	❏	❏

A Few Questions About Yourself

57   Were you ever a member of one or more of the following Conservative Party youth or younger persons' organisations? **Please tick any that apply.**

A | Young Conservatives (YCs)

B | Federation of Conservative Students (FCS)

C | Conservative Collegiate Forum (CCF)

D | Federation of University Conservative and Unionist Associations (FUCUA)

E | National Association of Conservative Graduates (NACG)

F | Conservative Future (CF)

The following are some of the reasons why people decide to become politicians. Which for you is the MOST important? And the NEXT MOST important? And the LEAST important?

58

		As someone concerned with social change or the promotion of certain beliefs	As a representative of the electorate or public	As a necessary element within the machinery of stable, democratic government
A	Most important	❑	❑	❑
B	Next most important	❑	❑	❑
C	Least important	❑	❑	❑

59   FOR ALL LOCAL COUNCILLORS ONLY. Would you consider a career 'further up' the political ladder, i.e. as an MP, MEP, or member of the Scottish, Welsh, and London institutions?

○ Yes, definitely   ○ Yes, possibly   ○ Unlikely or not at all

60   FOR ALL EXCEPT LOCAL COUNCILLORS. Before attaining your present position, did you have any experience as a local councillor?

○ I was a local councillor   ○ I stood unsuccessfully as a local council candidate   ○ Neither of these

61   How often do you use email?

○ At least once a day   ○ At least once a week   ○ Less often than once a week   ○ Never

62   How often do you go online to the Internet for news and information?

○ At least once a day   ○ At least once a week   ○ Less often than once a week   ○ Never

In politics people sometimes talk of 'Left' and 'Right'. Using the following scale, where 1 means Left and 10 means Right, where would you place:

63		1 - Left	2	3	4	5	6	7	8	9	10 - Right
A	Yourself	❏	❏	❏	❏	❏	❏	❏	❏	❏	❏
B	Conservative Party	❏	❏	❏	❏	❏	❏	❏	❏	❏	❏
C	Labour Party	❏	❏	❏	❏	❏	❏	❏	❏	❏	❏
D	Liberal Democrats	❏	❏	❏	❏	❏	❏	❏	❏	❏	❏
E	Scottish National Party	❏	❏	❏	❏	❏	❏	❏	❏	❏	❏
F	Plaid Cymru	❏	❏	❏	❏	❏	❏	❏	❏	❏	❏
G	UK Independence Party (UKIP)	❏	❏	❏	❏	❏	❏	❏	❏	❏	❏
H	Green Party	❏	❏	❏	❏	❏	❏	❏	❏	❏	❏
I	British National Party	❏	❏	❏	❏	❏	❏	❏	❏	❏	❏

From the following list, what for YOU are the TWO most pressing concerns facing Britain today? And what do you think the GENERAL PUBLIC considers being the TWO most pressing concerns?

64		Economy & taxation	Welfare, NHS, education, & other public services	Environment	Europe	Law & order	International relations, defence, & terrorism	Civil liberties
A	YOU - choice 1	❏	❏	❏	❏	❏	❏	❏
B	YOU - choice 2	❏	❏	❏	❏	❏	❏	❏
C	PUBLIC - choice 1	❏	❏	❏	❏	❏	❏	❏
D	PUBLIC - choice 2	❏	❏	❏	❏	❏	❏	❏

Addtional Questions for Local Councillors in England

65 Your age in whole years is... _____

66 Your sex is...
   O Female   O Male

67 Your ethnic group is...
   O White   O Non-White

68 Your marital status is...
   O Married   O Living with partner   O Widowed/divorced/separated   O Single

69 Do you think of yourself as belonging to any particular social class?
   O Upper class   O Middle class   O Working class   O No

70 When you were young, would you say that your family belonged to any particular social class?
   O Upper class   O Middle class   O Working class   O No

71 What is your highest educational qualification?
   O Primary school   O Secondary school or equivalent   O University/polytechnic or professional equivalent

72 Did you attend a fee-paying secondary school?
   O Yes   O No

73 Even if you do not consider yourself personally religious, what is your religious/confessional background?
   O Church of England/Anglican/Episcopal   O Other Protestant/Non-conformist
   O Roman Catholic   O Other Christian
   O Jewish   O Other non-Christian   O None at all

74 In what year did you first join the Conservative Party?   _____

75 In what year were you first elected as a Conservative local councillor?   _____

Please go to the final page of questions on the back cover

Before you joined the Conservative Party, had either your mother or father been a member?

76		Yes	No	Don't know	Not applicable
A	Mother	❑	❑	❑	❑
B	Father	❑	❑	❑	❑

77   Which one of the following best describes the residential make-up of the majority of your ward?

O Rural villages or farms   O Town   O Suburb or outskirts of a major city   O City or metropolitan

78   In your main accommodation, do you or your household...

O Own the property outright   O Own the property with a mortgage

O Rent from a private landlord   O Rent from your local authority or housing association

79   Excluding your work as a councillor, what sector of the economy do you work in? If you no longer work, which best describes your most recent occupation?

O Private   O Public   O Voluntary   O Other

80   Excluding your work as a councillor, are you employed or self-employed? If you no longer work, which best describes your most recent occupation?

O Employed   O Self-employed

81   Excluding your work as a councillor, please indicate your main area of occupation from the following list of broad categories. If you no longer work, which best describes your most recent occupation? Please tick one box only.

O Manufacturing or agriculture

O Service sector management or professions

O Armed services

O Retail

O Skilled artisan

O Other manual

O Other non-manual

O Other

This is the end of the questionnaire. Thank you for taking the time and trouble to complete it. Your contribution is greatly appreciated. Please return it in the SAE supplied.

INDEX

Alliance Party of Northern
Ireland, 138, 139, 141, 143, 144,
149, 150
Ancram, Michael, 83, 84, 220, 221,
225, 227, 228
Blair, Tony, 9, 16, 19, 185, 221, 237
Booker, Christopher, 242
British National Party, 93, 138,
139, 140, 142, 144, 145, 146,
147, 148, 151, 210, 252, 263,
282
Cameron, David, 107, 221, 274,
284, 289
Campbell, Menzies, 221
Clarke, Ken, 26, 220, 221, 222, 223,
224, 225, 226, 227, 228, 230,
231, 232, 233, 234, 235, 236,
237, 238, 239, 241, 243
Clegg, Nick, 284
Conservative Party, 5, 8, 9, 10, 11,
13, 14, 15, 16, 17, 18, 19, 20, 21,
22, 23, 24, 25, 27, 29, 30, 31, 32,
33, 34, 35, 38, 69, 70, 73, 74, 75,
77, 78, 79, 80, 82, 83, 84, 85, 86,
87, 88, 89, 90, 92, 93, 94, 95, 96,
97, 98, 99, 100, 101, 102, 106,
107, 109, 113, 114, 117, 118,
119, 120, 121, 122, 123, 124,
125, 126, 127, 130, 132, 133,
134, 137, 138, 142, 143, 146,
148, 149, 151, 153, 154, 156,
157, 158, 159, 161, 162, 165,
166, 169, 170, 171, 172, 173,
175, 176, 177, 180, 181, 184,
185, 186, 187, 190, 191, 192,
193, 196, 197, 198, 199, 202,
204, 209, 210, 211, 212, 213,
214, 219, 220, 221, 222, 223,
224, 226, 228, 229, 230, 233,
234, 235, 236, 237, 238, 240,
241, 242, 243, 245, 250, 251,
252, 253, 254, 255, 257, 258,
259, 260, 261, 262, 263, 264,
265, 266, 267, 268, 269, 270,
271, 272, 273, 274, 276, 277,
279, 280, 282, 283, 284, 285,
288, 289, 290, 337, 340, 341,
342
Davis, David, 220, 221, 225, 227,
228
Democratic Unionist Party, 138,
139, 141, 143, 144, 149, 150
Disraeli, Benjamin, 223
Dowds, Lizanne, 174
Duncan Smith, Ian, 11, 22, 26, 27,
117, 126, 127, 130, 131, 134,
135, 148, 181, 187, 191, 213,
219, 220, 221, 223, 224, 225,
226, 227, 228, 230, 231, 232,
233, 234, 236, 237, 239, 241,
242, 243, 253, 282, 283, 284
Duncan, Alan, 84
Evans, Tim, 132
Flew, Antony, 11
Forth, Eric, 8, 10, 11, 44, 46, 109,
337
Fortuyn, Pim, 58
Fox, Liam, 181
Gamble, Andrew, 240
Green Party, 82, 93, 138, 139, 140,
141, 142, 144, 145, 146, 148,
149, 151, 210, 212, 252, 282
Greenleaf, W.H., 75

Hague, William, 16, 22, 30, 90, 117, 126, 129, 131, 134, 204, 219, 220, 221, 223, 227, 236
Hayes, John, 79
Heath, Athony, 62, 128, 130, 131, 135
Heath, Edward, 24, 117, 126, 127, 128, 130, 131, 134, 240
Hitler, Adolph, 59, 68, 70
Howard, Michael, 191, 219, 243, 284
Hunt, John, 8
Hussein, Saddam, 127
Inglehart, Ronald, 246
Jong-il, Kim, 127
Kennedy, Charles, 221
Labour Party, 9, 14, 16, 19, 23, 25, 27, 82, 92, 93, 96, 99, 108, 118, 122, 124, 133, 137, 138, 139, 140, 141, 142, 144, 145, 151, 156, 176, 177, 191, 197, 199, 206, 210, 211, 214, 215, 221, 224, 228, 240, 241, 245, 251, 252, 253, 254, 255, 256, 257, 258, 259, 260, 262, 263, 264, 276, 280, 282, 283, 284
Liberal Democrats, 14, 19, 25, 27, 82, 93, 96, 122, 133, 137, 138, 139, 140, 141, 142, 144, 145, 151, 156, 177, 199, 210, 221, 224, 229, 241, 245, 251, 252, 253, 255, 256, 257, 258, 259, 260, 262, 264, 265, 280, 282, 284, 289
Maclean, David, 11
Macmillan, Harold, 240
Major, John, 19, 117, 126, 129, 131, 134, 138, 219, 224, 228, 240
Mandelson, Peter, 9
Mannheim, Karl, 14
Marquand, David, 14
May, Theresa, 20, 212
McKenzie, Robert, 14, 283

Mises, Ludwig von, 59
Oakeshott, Michael, 9
Plaid Cymru, 19, 82, 138, 139, 140, 141, 142, 144, 149, 252
Podoksik, Efraim, 9
Portillo, Michael, 219, 220, 221, 222, 223, 225, 226, 227, 228, 229, 231, 232, 236, 238, 239
Redwood, John, 220
Richardson, Jeremy, 30, 187
Royden, Maude, 186
Scottish National Party, 19, 125, 138, 139, 140, 141, 142, 144, 149, 252
Seyd, Patrick, 30, 187
Silver, Allen, 14
Sims, Roger, 8
Sinn Fein, 138, 139, 141, 142, 143, 144, 149, 150
Social Democratic and Labour Party, 138, 139, 141, 143, 144, 149, 150
Socialist Alliance/Scottish Socialist Party, 138, 139, 140, 141, 144, 149
Spencer, Herbert, 17
Stalin, Joseph, 59, 68, 70
Stuart, Gisela, 176
Tebbit, Norman, 132, 186
Thatcher, Margaret, 19, 24, 80, 101, 107, 117, 126, 127, 128, 129, 130, 131, 134, 135, 171, 186, 191, 223, 236, 240, 241, 274, 282, 284, 285
Tönnies, Ferdinand, 9
Topf, Richard, 62
UK Independence Party, 123, 138, 139, 140, 141, 144, 145, 146, 148, 151, 210, 212, 263, 282
Ulster Unionist Party, 138, 139, 141, 143, 144, 149, 150, 282
Whiteley, Paul, 30, 187
Young, Ken, 174